Teacher Edition 5

with Teacher Resources

Sue Clarke

Macmillan Education Limited
4 Crinan Street
London N1 9XW

Companies and representatives throughout the world

Story Central Plus Level 5 Teacher Edition ISBN 978-1-380-06126-3
Story Central Plus Level 5 Teacher Edition with Student eBook, Reader eBook, CLIL eBook, Digital Activity Book, Teacher Resource Center, and Test Generator ISBN 978-1-380-06124-9

Written by Sue Clarke

This edition published 2021
First edition entitled "Story Central" published 2015 by Macmillan Education Limited

Teacher Edition credits:
Designed by Red Phoenix Design
Page make-up by Mo Choy Design Ltd and Composure
Illustrated by Steven Wood (Advocate Art)
Cover design by Wild Apple Design Ltd

Designed by Liz Adcock and Pronk Media, Inc.
Illustrated by Aardvart pp. 93, 120b; Ilias Arahovitis (Beehive Illustration) p. 106; Valentina Belloni (MB Artists) pp. 122 -123, 125; Robin Boyden (Pickled Ink) pp. 94 -95, 96, 97; Paco Cavero (Sylvie Poggio Artist Agency) pp. 17, 31t, 59, 73, 87, 101t, 101, 129; Inna Chernyak (Plum Pudding) pp. 38 -39, 40, 41t; Marcus Cutler (Sylvie Poggio Artist Agency) pp. 108 -109, 110, 111; Anna Hancock (Beehive Illustration) pp. 11rm, 13b, 23, 25r, 27b, 29b, 37, 39r, 42b, 44m, 51t, 53r, 55b, 65, 67r, 69b, 79, 81r, 83b, 95r, 97b, 109r, 122, 123r, 125b; Beth Hughes (The Bright Agency) pp 18, 19, 20, 21, 46, 47, 48, 49, 74, 75, 76, 102, 103, 104, 105, 130, 131, 132, 133; Ellie Jenkins (Advocate Art) pp. 80 -81, 82, 83; Ayesha Lopez (Advocate Art) pp. 52 -53, 54, 55; Louise Redshaw (Plum Pudding) pp. 24 -25, 26, 27; Laszlo Veres (Beehive Illustration) pp. 8, 50, 64, 92; Dan Widdowson (The Bright Agency) pp 32, 33, 34, 35, 60, 61, 62, 63, 88, 89, 90, 91, 117, 118; Steven Wood (Advocate Art) pp 4-129 (border design and main character artwork) 4 -5, 6 -7, 10, 14, 24l, 28, 31m, 38l, 42, 52l, 56, 66l, 70, 80l, 84, 94l, 98, 108l, 112, 122l, 126; Patricia Yuste (Advocate Art) pp10, 11, 12, 13.
Cover design by Wild Apple Design Ltd. and Roberto Martinez
Cover illustration Steven Wood (Advocate Art)
Picture research by Composure

The authors and publishers would like to thank the following for permission to reproduce their photographs:
Alamy Stock Photo/Andrew Twort (ccr)p. 106, Alamy Stock Photo/Arco Images GmbH (tc)p. 43, Alamy Stock Photo/blickwinkel (br)p. 36, Alamy Stock Photo/Canva Pty Ltd (cr)p. 107, Alamy Stock Photo/Christopher Bradshaw (a)p. 22, Alamy Stock Photo/David Hoare (cr)p. 113, Alamy Stock Photo/Edwin Remsberg (cr)p. 127, Alamy Stock Photo/Emily Lai (cr)p. 15, Alamy Stock Photo/Eureka (bl)p. 36, Alamy Stock Photo/Golden Pixels LLC (cl)p. 120, Alamy Stock Photo/Iain Stuart MacGregor (tcl)p. 106, Alamy Stock Photo/Image Professionals GmbH (ccl)p. 106, (ccr)p. 119, Alamy Stock Photo/imageBROKER (tl)p. 120, Alamy Stock Photo/Juniors Bildarchiv GmbH (tl)p. 12, (tr)p. 85, Alamy Stock Photo/Leon Swart (2) p. 36, Alamy Stock Photo/Life on white (bc)p. 36, (bcr)p. 36, (tcr)p. 36, Alamy Stock Photo/Matthew Rex (4)p. 45, Alamy Stock Photo/neal and molly jansen (ccl)p. 113, Alamy Stock Photo/Oscar Calero (6)p. 36, Alamy Stock Photo/Paul Bradforth (tcr)p. 106, Alamy Stock Photo/Simon Reddy (3)p. 71, Alamy Stock Photo/Stocktrek Images, Inc. (cc)p. 99, Alamy Stock Photo/Tim Gainey (tr)p. 15, Alamy Stock Photo/toy Alan King (d)p. 22, Alamy Stock Photo/vanillaechoes (bcr)p. 106, Alamy Stock Photo/VeterinaryImages (tl)p. 85, Alamy Stock Photo/Viktor Fischer (tl)p. 106, Alamy Stock Photo/wacpan (tcl)p. 15; Getty Images/Chris Upton (cr)p. 43, Getty Images/Isu (tr)p. 12,Getty Images/jangeltun (cc)p. 119, Getty Images/Jose Luis Pelaez Inc (cc)p. 107, Getty Images/Jules Frazier (bl)p. 113, Getty Images/Londolozi Images/Mint Images (tr)p. 43, Getty Images/Manoj Shah (tl)p. 45, Getty Images/Massimo Mei (tcr)p. 43, Getty Images/Peter Dazeley (tl)p. 29, Getty Images/photoman73 (cc)p. 120, Getty Images/roevin (1)p. 71, Getty Images/spfoto (cl)p. 107, Getty Images/Stefan Auth (tc)p. 12, Getty Images/Stephen Frink (2)p. 45, Getty Images/Stockbyte (cl)p. 15, Getty Images/stockstudioX (3)p. 45, Getty Images/tacar (background) p. 113, Getty Images/Tomas Rodriguez (cc)p. 36, Getty Images/Travelpix Ltd (cc)p. 15, Getty Images/Winfried Wisniewski (3)p. 36, Getty Images/Zocha_K (1)p. 36; Macmillan Education Limited/59122 (tr) p. 106, Macmillan Education Limited/BRAND X (bcl)p. 113, Macmillan Education Limited/David Lee/Alamy Stock Photo (ccr)p. 113, Macmillan Education Limited/DIGITAL VISION (tcl)p. 29, Macmillan Education Limited/GeoffBlack,Geoff Black (c)p. 22, Macmillan Education Limited/GETTY (tc)p. 15, (tr)p. 36, (bl)p. 106, Macmillan Education Limited/ImageSource (br)p. 106, Macmillan Education Limited/Lisa Payne (bcl)p. 106, Macmillan Education Limited/MACMILLAN AUSTRALIA (tcr)p. 29, Macmillan Education Limited/NordicImages/Alamy Stock Photo (e)p. 22, Macmillan Education Limited/Paul Bricknell (b) p. 22, (f)p. 22, Macmillan Education Limited/PhotoDisc/Getty Images (cl)p. 113, Macmillan Education Limited/Stockbyte Royalty Free Photos (tr)p. 29; Shutterstock/fizkes (tr)p. 78, Shutterstock/Manny DaCunha (tc)p. 120, Shutterstock/Samuel Micut (tr)p. 120, Shutterstock/sduraku (cl)p. 127; Superstock/(cc)p. 78, Superstock/Blend Images/Blend Images (cr)p. 120, Superstock/Design Pics/Design Pics (cr) p. 57, Superstock/Jon Bower (tr)p. 57, Superstock/Otto Stadler/imageBROKER/imageBROKER (2)p. 71, Superstock/Salva Garrigues/ age fotostock (cc)p. 127.
Commissioned photography by MMStudios pp. 9, 16, 23, 30, 44, 51, 58, 72, 85, 86, 100, 114, 128.

Reader credits:

Written by Viv Lambert ELT Limited and Mo Choy Design Limited

Page design, layout and art editing by Wild Apple Design Ltd
Chen's Magic Pen illustrated by Patricia Yuste (Advocate Art); The Princess and the Teddy Bear illustrated by Louise Redshaw (Plum Pudding Illustration); The Hungry Giraffe illustrated by Inna Chernyak (Plum Pudding Illustration); The Mystery House illustrated by Ayesha Lopez (Advocate Art); Captain Navigate illustrated by Stephen Reed (The July Group); The Giant Turnip illustrated by Ellie Jenkins (Advocate Art); Good Friends illustrated by Robin Boyden (Pickled Ink); I Like Cake! illustrated by Marcus Cutler (Sylvie Poggio Artist Agency); The Magic Violin illustrated by Valentina Belloni (MB Artists).
Cover design by Wild Apple Design Ltd
Cover artwork: front cover, Patricia Yuste (Advocate Art), Inna Chernyak (Plum Pudding Illustration), and Stephen Reed (The July Group); back cover, Valentina Belloni (MB Artists) and Marcus Cutler (Sylvie Poggio Artist Agency)..

Activity Book credits:

Written by Viv Lambert ELT Limited
Additional material written by Tracy Traynor

Designed by Liz Adcock
Illustrated by Valentina Belloni (MB Artists) pp. 72 -73; Robin Boyden (Pickled Ink) p. 56; Inna Chernyak (Plum Pudding) p. 24; Marcus Cutler (Sylvie Poggio Artist Agency) p. 64; Sarah Horne (Advocate Art) pp. 10, 15, 22, 25, 26, 28, 31, 34, 42, 44, 47, 50, 52, 54, 55, 58, 59, 66, 73, 74; Ellie Jenkins (Advocate Art) pp. 48 -49; Andy Keylock (Beehive Illustration) pp. 6, 7, 10, 12 -14, 18, 20, 26, 30, 34, 37, 39, 42, 50, 51, 55, 62, 70, 74, 75, 77, 78, 81, 82, 83, 85, 88, 90, 92, 95, 98, 101; Ayesha Lopez (Advocate Art) pp. 32 -33; Louise Redshaw (Plum Pudding) pp16 -17; Stephen Reed (The July Group) pp. 12, 14, 23, 27, 29, 39, 35, 38, 40, 41, 43, 46, 49, 58, 63, 65, 67, 69, 71, 76, 70, 79, 83, 84, 86, 87, 89, 91 -94, 96; Steven Wood (Advocate Art) pp. 3 -77; Patricia Yuste (Advocate Art) pp. 8 -9.
Cover design by Wild Apple Design Ltd. and Roberto Martinez
Cover illustration Steven Wood (Advocate Art)
Picture research by Composure

Printed and bound in Singapore

2021
80

Contents

Contents

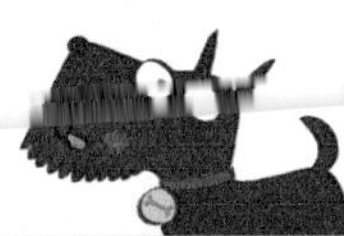

Competencies

me	act	think	learn	communicate
Activities that encourage children to accept responsibility and reflect on the consequences of lifestyle choices.	Activities that develop societal understanding and identification of children's own circumstances in a wider context.	Activities that develop critical thinking skills to reflect upon, manipulate, process, and interpret information.	Activities that foster learner autonomy, and allow children to demonstrate and put into practice learning strategies.	Activities that promote interpersonal and collaborative skills, develop teamwork, and allow children to express opinions and ideas.

Philosophy and Methodology

Philosophy

1 Language is power.

Story Central Plus empowers children to communicate effectively and develop their knowledge of the world around them through stories. The course enables children to become critical and active readers, writers, and storytellers through its strong focus on literacy development.

2 An empowered teacher empowers children and changes lives.

Story Central Plus provides teachers with all the support they need to deliver effective and inspiring lessons. Children will respond to the meaningful texts and activities, ensuring that both teachers and children feel a real sense of achievement. Children will develop the skills they need to participate fully in their lives both inside and outside the classroom.

3 The child is not a blank slate.

Children bring their culture, beliefs, and a rich inner world to the classroom. Our materials respect this and recognize that it is key to engaging and interesting children in learning English.

4 Nurturing critical and creative thinking helps children become well-rounded and innovative adults.

Story Central Plus actively encourages creative, divergent, and playful thinking, and consistently supports the acquisition of academic knowledge.

Methodology

Literacy

Reading and writing skills are developed throughout the course. Each chapter is based around a story. An extract from the story is introduced in Student Book Lesson 3, allowing opportunities to develop reading skills and encouraging children to think creatively as they analyze the language in a meaningful context, and predict story developments. The full story is given in the beautifully illustrated Reader. Use of the Reader is fully integrated and the story links together the chapter theme and target language, providing language-rich input and enabling holistic learning. Activities engage children's interest and imagination as they are encouraged to read for pleasure. After children have read the story, their writing skills are developed through personal responses and creative writing. A love of literature is further fostered by the Oral Storytelling Videos.

Critical Literacy

Story Central Plus takes children beyond understanding texts. The material and activities help them analyze and respond, as they develop the skills of questioning and interpreting the information they encounter. Children are encouraged to discuss the story's meaning and how the values expressed relate to their lives and the world around them. Children are supported in expressing their opinions through presentations, role play, and extended writing. These essential skills will empower them to use language effectively later in life.

Critical and Creative Thinking

Critical and creative thinking are actively encouraged. Children are given every opportunity to figure things out for themselves and share their ideas. Vocabulary is presented in context, requiring them to use textual and visual clues to process and deduce meaning. Prediction, reflection, and drawing conclusions all play an important part in developing an imaginative and reflective response.

A Cool Place to Hang Out With Friends!

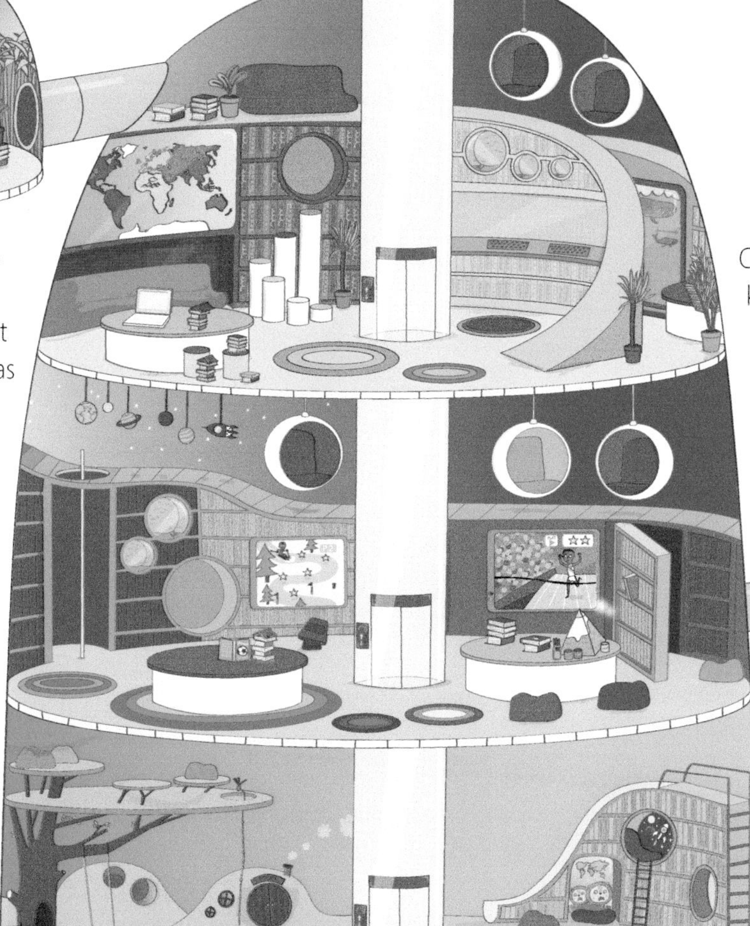

Story Central is a cool club where kids hang out with their friends and read great books. They also share ideas and stories, plan events, do homework, and drink milkshakes! In Story Central you can explore, discover, learn, research, and interact. It's the sort of place where kids really want to be!

Children will love getting to know the fun characters who hang out in Story Central. They appear in Lesson 3 and Lesson 5 in every chapter.

Level 5 Characters

Scarlett is an art student who runs Story Central with her twin brother, Rufus. She enjoys painting, poetry, and other creative activities.

Rufus studies IT. He shows everyone how to use the technology at Story Central—and fixes things when they break!

Hamish is Scarlett and Rufus's clever dog. He thinks a lot …

Yasmin is 14 years old. She is fascinated by science and nature and loves finding out about them at Story Central.

Angelo is 14 too. He loves literature, acting, and singing —and he has his own film blog!

Component Overview

For the Student

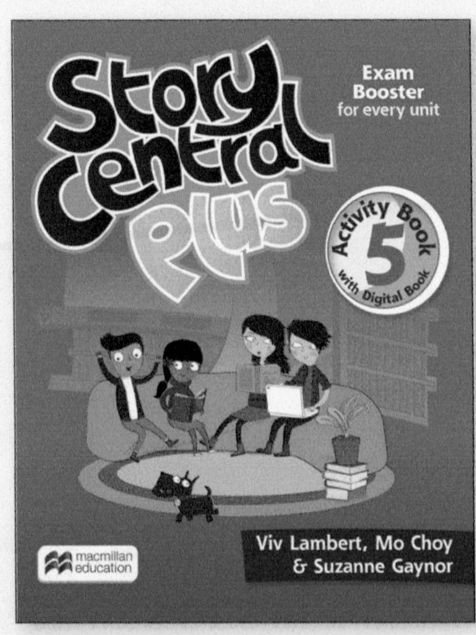

Student Book

Consists of 9 thematic chapters, featuring a story extract, literacy development, competency coverage, CLIL content, and project work. Focuses on developing critical thinking, creativity, communication, and collaboration. NEW! Grammar Booster section per chapter presents and provides further grammar practice of the target grammar.

Reader

Consists of 9 stories of different genres and styles. Focuses on promoting critical literacy and reading skills through developing a love of reading.

Activity Book

Consists of follow-on lessons for every Student Book lesson. Focuses on consolidating key language and skills, and developing creative use of language in writing. NEW! Exam Booster section per chapter provides Cambridge YLE practice activities.

eBooks

The Student Book has an access code which provides access to eBooks for the Student Book, Reader, and CLIL Book. The eBooks have embedded audio, video, and a set of tools to interact with the pages to provide flexibility for remote learning and give students more ways to read and learn.

The Inks Vocabulary Practice App

The Inks Apps provide a fun way for students to practice the vocabulary words they've learned for better retention. They're free and available to download from the App Store and Google Play.

Digital Activity Book

These books provide students an interactive way to practice. Students' answers are sent automatically to the gradebook so teachers and caregivers can monitor progress.

For the Teacher

Teacher Edition

Consists of teaching notes for each lesson of the Student Book, Reader, and Activity Book, and suggestions on when and how to use digital components. Focuses on providing clear and concise support for lesson planning and teaching.

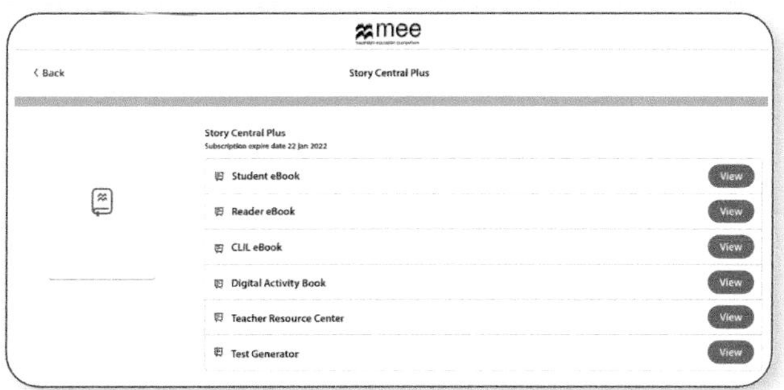

Teacher Resource Center

Consists of the class audio, and additional resources and ideas to extend lessons and learning, and give further practice of key language. Focuses on giving teachers flexibility and the means to deliver dynamic and varied lessons.

Test Generator

Pre-written tests for each chapter, mid-year, and end-of-year are available to download from the Teacher Resource Center. In addition, the Test Generator allows teachers to customize and create new tests from a bank of activities.

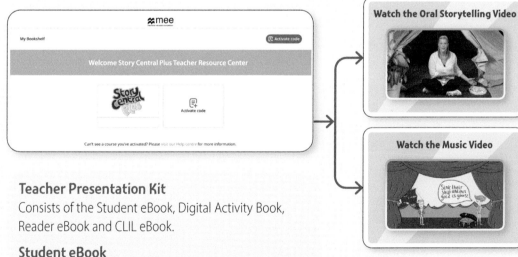

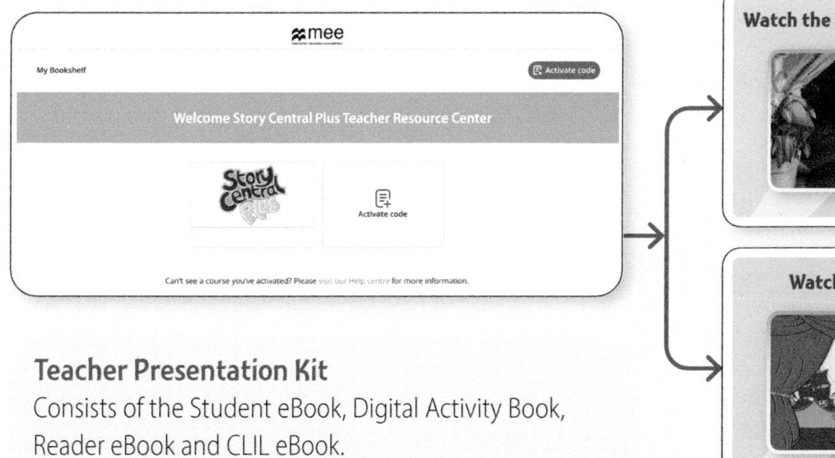

Watch the Oral Storytelling Video

Oral Storytelling Videos feature additional stories with mesmerizing narration set in *Story Central Plus*. These are related to Chapters 1, 3, 5, 7, and 9.

Watch the Music Video

Music Videos will get children singing! They can follow the lyrics on screen for the songs from Chapters 2, 4, 6, and 8.

Teacher Presentation Kit

Consists of the Student eBook, Digital Activity Book, Reader eBook and CLIL eBook.

Student eBook

This eBook provides a digital version of the Student Book with integrated audio, video and answer keys.

Digital Activity Book

This eBook provides an interactive version of the Activity Book that is linked to a gradebook.

Reader eBook

This eBook provides a digital version of the Reader with embedded audio and Storytelling Videos.

CLIL eBook

This eBook provides a digital version of the CLIL Book with embedded audio.

Teaching with Story Central Plus

Lesson 1 Vocabulary

High-impact openers introduce the chapter theme to create interest and engage children.

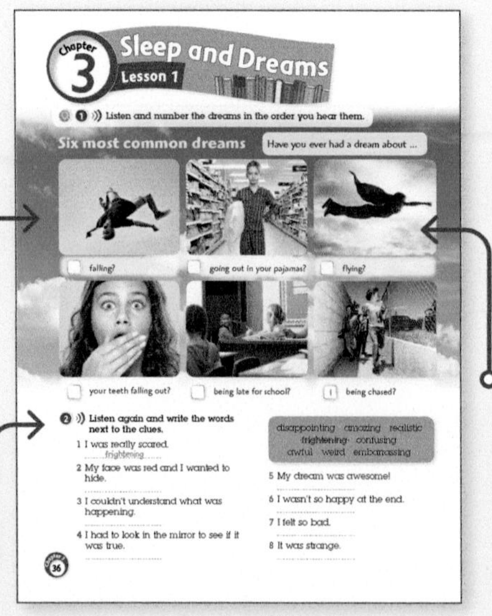

Chapter 3 Sleep and Dreams
Lesson 1

1 Listen and number the dreams in the order you hear them.

Six most common dreams

Have you ever had a dream about ...

falling?
going out in your pajamas?
flying?
your teeth falling out?
being late for school?
1 being chased?

2 Listen again and write the words next to the clues.

disappointing amazing realistic frightening confusing awful weird embarrassing

1 I was really scared. frightening
2 My face was red and I wanted to hide.
3 I couldn't understand what was happening.
4 I had to look in the mirror to see if it was true.
5 My dream was awesome!
6 I wasn't so happy at the end.
7 I felt so bad.
8 It was strange.

36

Vocabulary is introduced through visual and audio clues to develop **critical thinking skills**, encouraging children to deduce meaning.

Children use the **clues** to deduce meaning of the vocabulary.

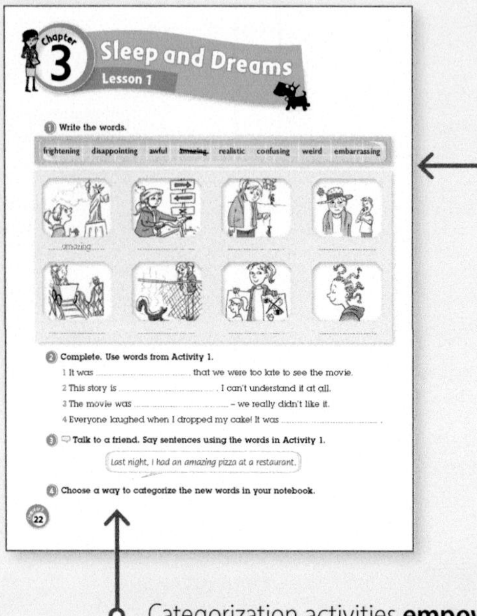

Chapter 3 Sleep and Dreams
Lesson 1

1 Write the words.

frightening disappointing awful ~~amazing~~ realistic confusing weird embarrassing

amazing

2 Complete. Use words from Activity 1.

1 It was ______ that we were too late to see the movie.
2 This story is ______. I can't understand it at all.
3 The movie was ______ – we really didn't like it.
4 Everyone laughed when I dropped my cake! It was ______.

3 Talk to a friend. Say sentences using the words in Activity 1.

Last night, I had an *amazing* pizza at a restaurant.

4 Choose a way to categorize the new words in your notebook.

22

Fun activities **consolidate new language** and provide opportunities for extra practice.

Categorization activities **empower children** by giving them **choices** about how they learn.

Lesson 2 Grammar

Grammar is presented clearly and accessibly, recycling Lesson 1 vocabulary.

Further grammar practice in the Activity Book consolidates language.

Lesson 2

1 Read. What's the name of the author?

Movie Review: Alice in Wonderland

Send us your comments.

The movie isn't as good as the book. (Jake, 12, USA)

I think the movie is better than the book, but the movie is more frightening. (Eleanor, 10, England)

Alice's dream is more amazing in the movie. (Helena, 11, Spain)

I thought the movie was disappointing. (Tom, 11, France)

I think the movie is just as good as the book. (Lily, 13, USA)

The plot was awful. The movie wasn't as exciting as the book. (Pablo, 14, Mexico)

The characters in the book aren't as realistic as the characters in the movie. (Sam, 11, Canada)

About the Movie

The movie tells a story about a young girl's amazing dream. Alice's dream takes place in an imaginary world called Wonderland. She meets the same weird and wonderful characters that she meets in the book and she has the same awesome adventures. The movie isn't as confusing as the book by Lewis Carroll because the plot is easier to follow.

2 Read again. Find the phrases in the text that mean the same.

1 The book is better than the movie. *The movie isn't as good as the book.*
2 The book isn't as good as the movie.
3 The book isn't as frightening as the movie.
4 The book was more exciting than the movie.
5 The book is just as good as the movie.

3 Talk to a friend. Compare a movie and a book.

more interesting than, not as exciting as, better than, just as good as

A: Do you like movies or books?
B: I like books. They're more interesting than movies.
A: I like movies. They aren't as confusing as books.

Grammar Central

Comparisons: *not as (adjective) as / just as (adjective) as*

The movie *isn't as good as* the book.
= The book is .... than the movie.
The book wasn't as .... as the movie.
= The movie was scarier .... the book.

Grammar Booster on page 46

37

Lesson 2

1 Circle to make the second sentence mean the same as the first.

1 The movie is worse than the book.
The movie **isn't as good as / is just as good as** the book.
2 The photo is better than the painting.
The painting **is just as good as / isn't as good as** the photo.
3 Your story is more realistic than my story.
My story **is just as realistic as / isn't as realistic as** your story.
4 Will's dream wasn't as frightening as Emma's dream.
Emma's dream **was more frightening than / was just as frightening as** Will's dream.

2 Complete the sentences for you. Tell a friend. Do you agree?

1 Adventure stories .... horror stories.
2 Baking cookies .... photography.
3 A carousel .... a roller coaster.
4 Learning Japanese .... learning English.
5 My hair .... your hair.

3 Choose two books. Write a review for the book review website and color the stars. Remember to add your name, age, and country.

My Review of .... and ....
I think that .... is ....
The plot in .... is ....
the plot in ....
The .... in .... isn't ....
the ending in ....

Why would you read a book review?

23

Grammar Central encourages children to complete the grammar structures themselves and provides a useful reference for activities.

Speaking activities give children the opportunity to use the new grammar in a meaningful context.

Writing activities provide well-supported and progressive development of writing skills.

NEW! Grammar Booster sections in the Student Book at the end of each chapter provide four pages of extra support. They include detailed grammar boxes and scaffolded practice for lessons 2 and 6, a review page that combines the grammar points in both lessons and a challenge page. These pages offer support for different language proficiency levels in the classroom. They can be assigned to individual children or the entire class.

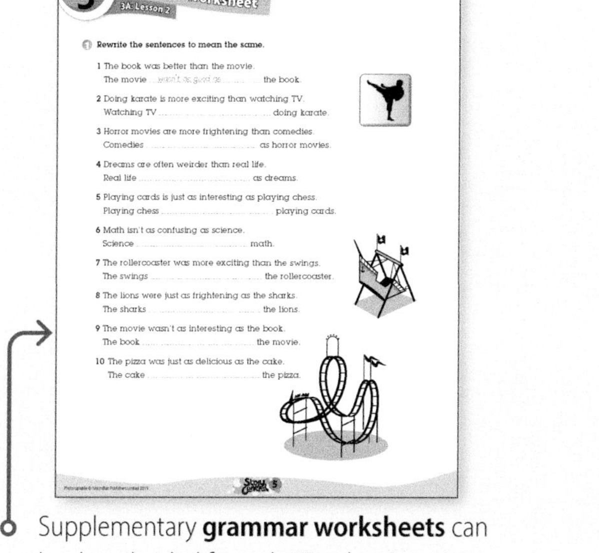

Chapter 3 Grammar Worksheet
3A: Lesson 2

1 Rewrite the sentences to mean the same.

1 The book was better than the movie.
The movie *isn't as good as* the book.
2 Doing karate is more exciting than watching TV.
Watching TV .... doing karate.
3 Horror movies are more frightening than comedies.
Comedies .... as horror movies.
4 Dreams are often weirder than real life.
Real life .... as dreams.
5 Playing cards is just as interesting as playing chess.
Playing chess .... playing cards.
6 Math isn't as confusing as science.
Science .... math.
7 The rollercoaster was more exciting than the swings.
The swings .... the rollercoaster.
8 The lions were just as frightening as the sharks.
The sharks .... the lions.
9 The movie wasn't as interesting as the book.
The book .... the movie.
10 The pizza was just as delicious as the cake.
The cake .... the pizza.

Supplementary **grammar worksheets** can be downloaded from the Teacher Resource Center to further consolidate learning in class or as homework.

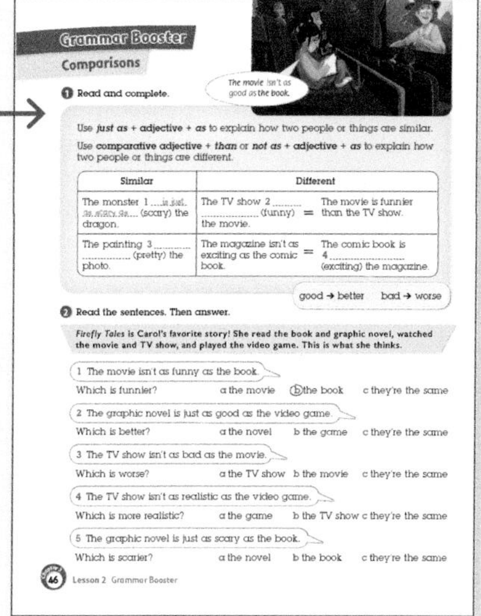

Grammar Booster
Comparisons

1 Read and complete.

The movie isn't as good as the book.

Use ***just as* + adjective + *as*** to explain how two people or things are similar.
Use **comparative adjective + *than*** or ***not as* + adjective + *as*** to explain how two people or things are different.

Similar	Different	
The monster 1 *is just as scary as* (scary) the dragon.	The TV show 2 .... (funny) the movie.	= The movie is funnier than the TV show.
The painting 3 .... (pretty) the photo.	The magazine isn't as exciting as the comic book.	= The comic book is 4 .... (exciting) the magazine.

good → better bad → worse

2 Read the sentences. Then answer.

Firefly Tales is Carol's favorite story! She read the book and graphic novel, watched the movie and TV show, and played the video game. This is what she thinks.

1 The movie isn't as funny as the book.
Which is funnier? a the movie (b) the book c they're the same
2 The graphic novel is just as good as the video game.
Which is better? a the novel b the game c they're the same
3 The TV show isn't as bad as the movie.
Which is worse? a the TV show b the movie c they're the same
4 The TV show isn't as realistic as the video game.
Which is more realistic? a the game b the TV show c they're the same
5 The graphic novel is just as scary as the book.
Which is scarier? a the novel b the book c they're the same

46 Lesson 2 Grammar Booster

Lesson 3 Reading: Story Extract

Children predict what the story is about before reading, to develop **visual literacy**.

A **functional dialogue** featuring the Story Central characters introduces and gives practice in useful everyday language.

Comprehension questions about the story extract check understanding.

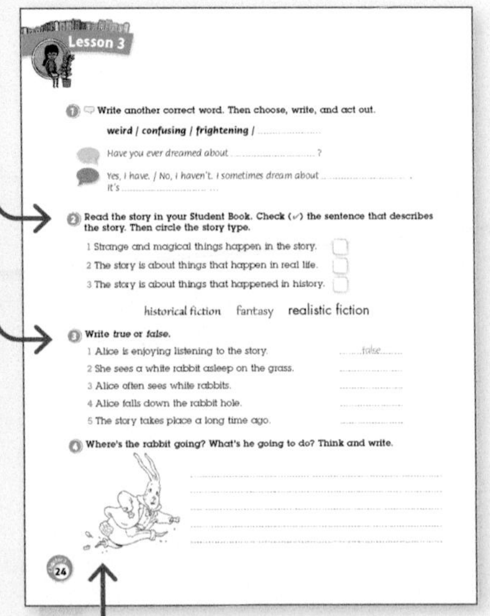

Comprehension and prediction questions develop reading skills and strategies.

The **story extract** (beginning, middle, or end) engages children but leaves plenty to the imagination.

A **prediction activity** asks children to use their **imagination** to figure out what will happen in the story.

Reader

Children read the whole story in their Reader.

A wide variety of story genres and narrative styles gives a **rich literary experience**.

Beautiful illustrations motivate children to **read for pleasure** and develop **a lifelong love of reading**.

Extensive language input allows **holistic language learning**, with the focus on overall understanding.

Lesson 4 Reading Comprehension and Critical Literacy

After reading the story in the Reader, children answer comprehension questions which help develop **reading strategies**.

The **Writing Tools** feature helps children identify and apply techniques to improve their writing.

Graphic organizer activities develop **study skills**.

Lesson 4 Time to Think

1 Read the story in your Reader on pages 8–10 again. What happens when Alice drinks from the bottle?

2 Comprehension
1 Why couldn't Alice go through the door?
2 Do you think Alice cried for a long time?
3 Why did the rabbit run away from her?
4 Do you think the rabbit was real?

3 Critical Literacy
1 Do you think Alice liked being in Wonderland?
2 Would you like to go to Wonderland?

Writing Workshop Linking parts of a story.

4 Find examples of sentence openers in the story. Continue Alice's account of her dream to her sister.
To my surprise, I saw ...
Suddenly I fell.

Writing Tools
Use sentence openers to start new sentences:
Soon, ...
To my surprise, ...
Fortunately, ...
Finally, ...

5 Text Connections
Do you know any other stories or movies about people who get bigger or smaller?

40

Children practice the Student Book **Writing Tools** techniques.

Lesson 4 Time to Think

1 Read and draw an arrow to the correct person for each thought.
This is a weird place.
Where's my fan?
Who's she?
How frightening: a giant!
This is so disappointing.
What big ears!

2 Complete. Then circle the time expressions.
~~To my surprise~~ Soon Fortunately Finally Unfortunately
1 To my surprise, a giant rabbit jumped out of a hole.
2 .... I found the key and could open the door.
3 .... I was bigger than the door and couldn't go into the garden.
4 .... it's going to get dark.
5 .... I went to bed and fell asleep.

3 Imagine that you went to Wonderland. Write about your adventure in your notebook. Use the Story Creator.

Story Creator
One night, I went to Wonderland.
To my surprise, there was a/were a lot of ...
Fortunately, I met/spoke to ...
He/She was very ...
Unfortunately, I ate/drank a ...
When I saw ..., I was very frightened/excited.
It was amazing/disappointing ...

4 Connect to Me
Have you ever had a bad dream that you thought was very realistic?
I dreamed ....

25

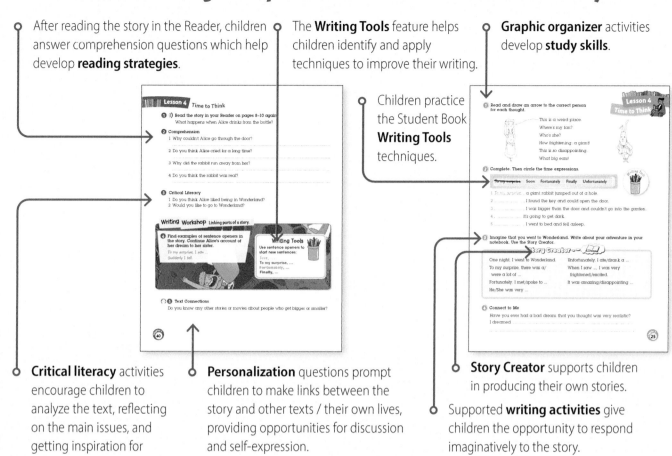

Critical literacy activities encourage children to analyze the text, reflecting on the main issues, and getting inspiration for their own writing.

Personalization questions prompt children to make links between the story and other texts / their own lives, providing opportunities for discussion and self-expression.

Story Creator supports children in producing their own stories.

Supported **writing activities** give children the opportunity to respond imaginatively to the story.

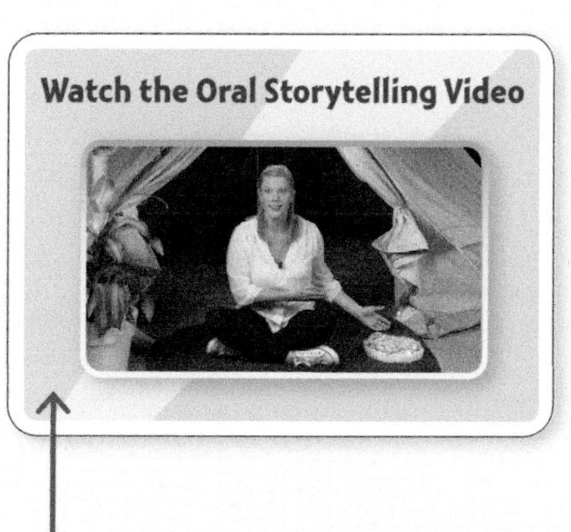

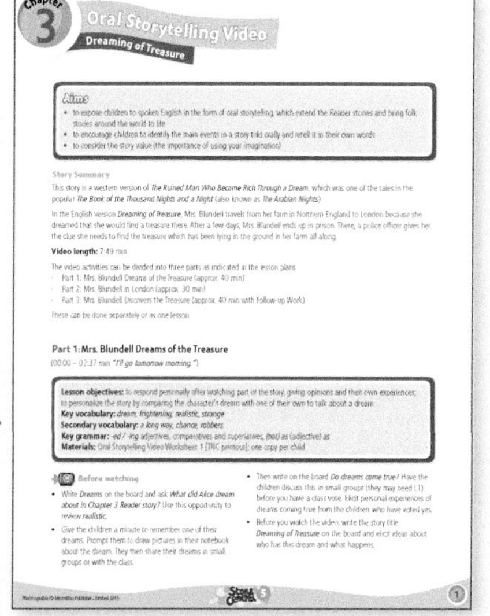
Chapter 3
Oral Storytelling Video
Dreaming of Treasure
Aims
Part 1: Mrs. Blundell Dreams of the Treasure

In the **Oral Storytelling Videos** professional storytellers act out and bring to life a different story on a related theme for Chapters 1, 3, 5, 7, and 9 (available in the Student eBook and the Reader eBook).

Teaching notes and worksheets for the Oral Storytelling Videos provide activity ideas to support comprehension and enhance enjoyment (downloadable from the Teacher Resource Center). A **Literacy Handbook** gives support and ideas for developing literacy skills with young learners.

Lesson 5 Grammar and Reading

In the Book Club the Story Central characters present new **grammar** in a lively, meaningful context which recycles the vocabulary from the chapter.

Lesson 5

Book Club

1 Listen and read. What did Angelo dream about?

Yasmin: Last night, I dreamed I could fly. It was an awesome dream. I was so disappointed when I woke up.
Scarlett: Yes, it's disappointing when you wake up from a good dream.
Angelo: I dreamed about a monster.
Yasmin: Oh, this dream is so boring! I've heard it already.
Scarlett: Sh! Yasmin. I'm not bored. I'm interested. Were you frightened, Angelo?
Angelo: Oh, yes! The monster looked really scary – big and ugly. It was frightening.
Scarlett: Well, that's an interesting dream.
Angelo: When I woke up I was shouting, "Mommy, Mommy, help!"
Scarlett: Ha, ha! Did your mom hear you?
Angelo: No, she didn't, but Yasmin heard me. I was so embarrassed!
Scarlett: Yes, that's really embarrassing.

2 Circle the correct word.

1 Yasmin was disappointed / disappointing when she woke up.
2 Yasmin is bored / boring because she has heard the dream before.
3 The monster in Angelo's dream was frightened / frightening.
4 Angelo's dream was interesting / interested.
5 Angelo was embarrassing / embarrassed because Yasmin heard him.

3 Talk to a friend. Use the adjectives in Activity 2.

A: I was disappointed when I failed my music exam.
B: I was embarrassed when I fell over in P.E.

Grammar Central

-ed / -ing adjectives
The book is boring. I feel bored.
I'm disappointed. The movie was ...

Grammar Booster on page 47

41

Grammar Central encourages children to complete the grammar structures themselves and provides a useful reference.

Speaking activities give children the opportunity to use the new grammar in a meaningful context.

Children are given the opportunity for controlled **written practice** of the new structures.

Grammar practice activities give staggered support.

Lesson 5

1 Circle.

I just read an 1 interested / interesting article about animals and sleeping. Do you know that cats can sleep for about 12 hours every day? When they're 2 boring / bored, they just fall asleep. Giraffes are completely different. They only sleep for a few minutes and they sleep with their eyes open. I think that's 3 frightening / frightened, don't you? When we're on the school bus, Angelo always sleeps with his mouth open. I'm always very 4 embarrassed / embarrassing when I'm sitting next to him.

2 Complete with ing or ed.

1 I'm frighten*ed* if I have to sleep in the dark.
2 It's disappoint .... when a friend forgets your birthday.
3 It's embarrass .... when I can't pronounce a word.
4 I'm interest .... when the teacher tells us funny stories.
5 It's bor .... when there aren't any good shows on TV.

3 Write about how you feel. Then talk to a friend.

1 If I have nothing to do, I ....
2 It's embarrassing when ....
3 It's .... when my friends don't call me.
4 Watching a horror movie before bed ....
5 When ....

If I have nothing to do, I'm bored.

26

A **guided writing** activity consolidates grammar and progressively develops writing skills.

NEW! Grammar Booster sections in the Student Book at the end of each chapter provide four pages of extra support. They include detailed grammar boxes and scaffolded practice for lessons 2 and 6, a review page that combines the grammar points in both lessons and a challenge page. These pages offer support for different language proficiency levels in the classroom. They can be assigned to individual children or the entire class.

Chapter 3 Grammar Worksheet

3A Lesson 2

1 Rewrite the sentences to mean the same.

1 The book was better than the movie.
The movie *wasn't as good as* the book.
2 Doing karate is more exciting than watching TV.
Watching TV .... doing karate.
3 Horror movies are more frightening than comedies.
Comedies .... as horror movies.
4 Dreams are often weirder than real life.
Real life .... as dreams.
5 Playing cards is just as interesting as playing chess.
Playing chess .... playing cards.
6 Math isn't as confusing as science.
Science .... math.
7 The rollercoaster was more exciting than the swings.
The swings .... the rollercoaster.
8 The lions were just as frightening as the sharks.
The sharks .... the lions.
9 The movie wasn't as interesting as the book.
The book .... the movie.
10 The pizza was just as delicious as the cake.
The cake .... the pizza.

Supplementary **grammar worksheets** can be downloaded from the Teacher Resource Center to further consolidate learning in class or as homework.

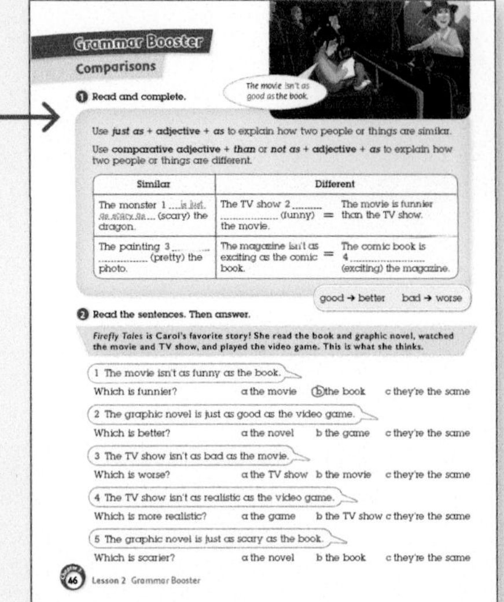
Grammar Booster

Comparisons

1 Read and complete.

Use *just as* + adjective + *as* to explain how two people or things are similar.
Use comparative adjective + *than* or *not as* + adjective + *as* to explain how two people or things are different.

Similar	Different		
The monster 1 *is just as scary as* (scary) the dragon.	The TV show 2 .... (funny)	=	The movie is funnier than the TV show.
The painting 3 .... (pretty) the photo.	The magazine isn't as exciting as the comic book.	=	The comic book is 4 .... (exciting) the magazine.

good → better bad → worse

2 Read the sentences. Then answer.

Firefly Tales is Carol's favorite story! She read the book and graphic novel, watched the movie and TV show, and played the video game. This is what she thinks.

1 The movie isn't as funny as the book.
Which is funnier? a the movie b the book c they're the same
2 The graphic novel is just as good as the video game.
Which is better? a the novel b the game c they're the same
3 The TV show isn't as bad as the movie.
Which is worse? a the TV show b the movie c they're the same
4 The TV show isn't as realistic as the video game.
Which is more realistic? a the game b the TV show c they're the same
5 The graphic novel is just as scary as the book.
Which is scarier? a the novel b the book c they're the same

46 Lesson 2 Grammar Booster

Lesson 6 Vocabulary, Listening or Song, and Spelling

A variety of interesting listening activities and catchy **songs** present new vocabulary in a fun, memorable, and motivating context.

Vocabulary is introduced through textual and visual clues to develop **critical thinking skills** (deduction of meaning).

Word work activities consolidate vocabulary and help develop strategies for memorizing vocabulary.

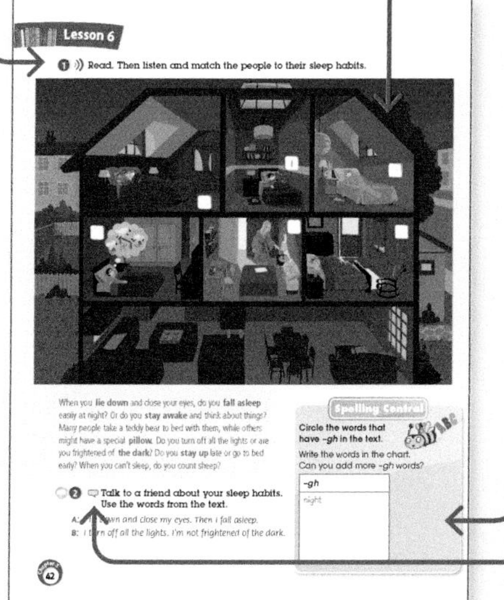

Lesson 6

1 Read. Then listen and match the people to their sleep habits.

When you **lie down** and close your eyes, do you **fall asleep** easily at night? Or do you **stay awake** and think about things? Many people take a teddy bear to bed with them, while others might have a special **pillow**. Do you turn off all the lights or are you frightened of **the dark**? Do you **stay up** late or go to bed early? When you can't sleep, do you count sheep?

2 Talk to a friend about your sleep habits. Use the words from the text.

A: [illegible]wn and close my eyes. Then I fall asleep.
B: I t[illegible]rn off all the lights. I'm not frightened of the dark.

Spelling Central

Circle the words that have *-gh* in the text.
Write the words in the chart.
Can you add more *-gh* words?

-gh
night

42

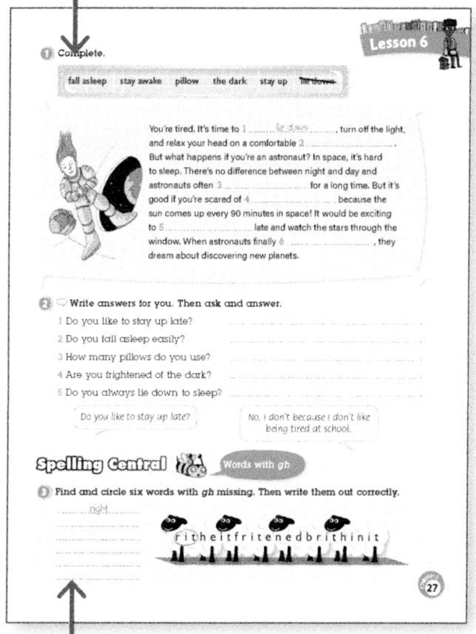

Lesson 6

1 Complete.

fall asleep · stay awake · pillow · the dark · stay up · ~~lie down~~

You're tired. It's time to 1 ...lie down..., turn off the light, and relax your head on a comfortable 2 .... But what happens if you're an astronaut? In space, it's hard to sleep. There's no difference between night and day and astronauts often 3 .... for a long time. But it's good if you're scared of 4 .... because the sun comes up every 90 minutes in space! It would be exciting to 5 .... late and watch the stars through the window. When astronauts finally 6 ...., they dream about discovering new planets.

2 Write answers for you. Then ask and answer.

1 Do you like to stay up late?
2 Do you fall asleep easily?
3 How many pillows do you use?
4 Are you frightened of the dark?
5 Do you always lie down to sleep?

Do you like to stay up late?

No, I don't because I don't like being tired at school.

Spelling Central — Words with *gh*

3 Find and circle six words with *gh* missing. Then write them out correctly.

night

ritheitfritenedbrithinit

27

Spelling tips are covered and practiced in **Spelling Central**.

Speaking activities give practice in a meaningful context to develop fluency.

Children identify and practice the spellings from the Student Book **Spelling Central** feature.

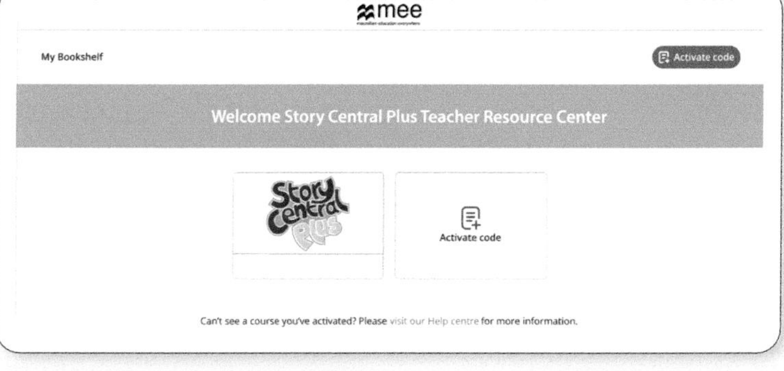

Supplementary **phonics worksheets** can be downloaded from the Teacher Resource Center to further consolidate learning in class or as homework.

Music Videos for Chapters 2, 4, 6, and 8 encourage children to sing along to the music, consolidating the learning of the target vocabulary (available in the Student eBook).

The lively clan of The Inks on the **Student's App** provide children with motivating and challenging games to practice the chapter vocabulary from Lesson 1 and Lesson 6 outside the classroom. *The Inks* Apps are free and available on the App Store and Google Play.

Lesson 7 CLIL

The **CLIL** focus gives the opportunity to find out about other curricular areas (such as science, math, social science) through English.

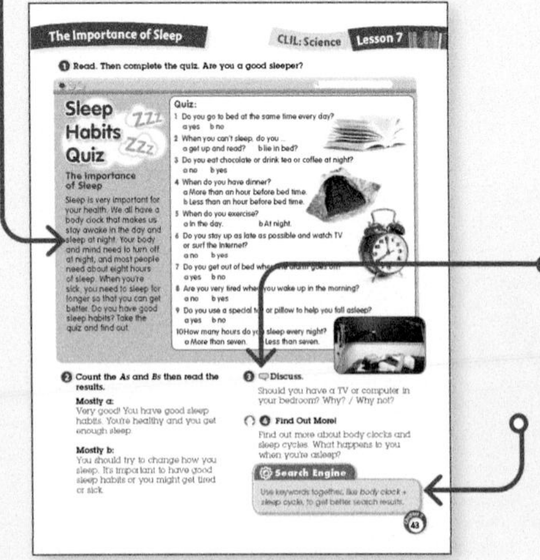
The Importance of Sleep

CLIL: Science Lesson 7

1 Read. Then complete the quiz. Are you a good sleeper?

Sleep Habits Quiz

The Importance of Sleep

Sleep is very important for your health. We all have a body clock that makes us stay awake in the day and sleep at night. Your body and mind need to turn off at night, and most people need about eight hours of sleep. When you're sick, you need to sleep for longer so that you can get better. Do you have good sleep habits? Take the quiz and find out.

Quiz:

1 Do you go to bed at the same time every day? a yes b no
2 When you can't sleep, do you ... a get up and read? b lie in bed?
3 Do you eat chocolate or drink tea or coffee at night? a no b yes
4 When do you have dinner? a More than an hour before bed time. b Less than an hour before bed time.
5 When do you exercise? a In the day. b At night.
6 Do you stay up as late as possible and watch TV or surf the Internet? a no b yes
7 Do you get out of bed wh[illegible] a yes b no
8 Are you very tired whe[illegible] you wake up in the morning? a no b yes
9 Do you use a special t[illegible] or pillow to help you fall asleep? a yes b no
10 How many hours do y[illegible] sleep every night? a More than seven. [illegible] Less than seven.

2 Count the *As* and *Bs* then read the results.

Mostly a:
Very good! You have good sleep habits. You're healthy and you get enough sleep.

Mostly b:
You should try to change how you sleep. It's important to have good sleep habits or you might get tired or sick.

3 Discuss.
Should you have a TV or computer in your bedroom? Why? / Why not?

4 Find Out More!
Find out more about body clocks and sleep cycles. What happens to you when you're asleep?

Search Engine
Use keywords together, like *body clock* + *sleep cycle*, to get better search results.

43

Children are encouraged to express their own opinions in a class discussion.

Search Engine gives tips to help children search for information online, developing their information literacy.

Children use their **Find Out More!** research to make an Info Card and complete a mini-project extending the CLIL topic.

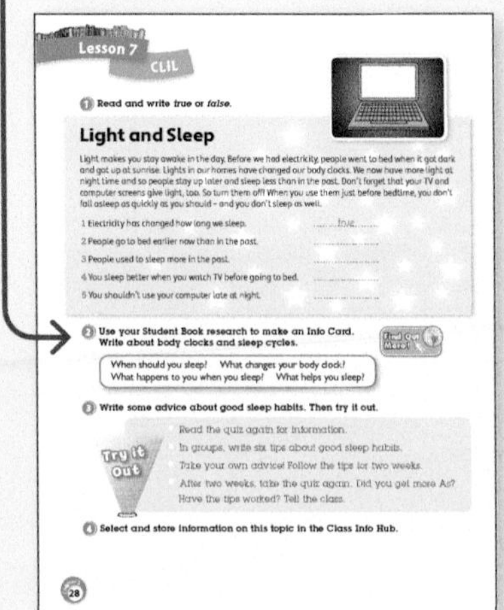
Lesson 7 CLIL

1 Read and write *true* or *false*.

Light and Sleep

Light makes you stay awake in the day. Before we had electricity, people went to bed when it got dark and got up at sunrise. Lights in our homes have changed our body clocks. We now have more light at night time and so people stay up later and sleep less than in the past. Don't forget that your TV and computer screens give light, too. So turn them off! When you use them just before bedtime, you don't fall asleep as quickly as you should – and you don't sleep as well.

1 Electricity has changed how long we sleep. ......true......
2 People go to bed earlier now than in the past. ....
3 People used to sleep more in the past. ....
4 You sleep better when you watch TV before going to bed. ....
5 You shouldn't use your computer late at night. ....

2 Use your Student Book research to make an Info Card. Write about body clocks and sleep cycles.

Find Out More!

When should you sleep? What changes your body clock? What happens to you when you sleep? What helps you sleep?

3 Write some advice about good sleep habits. Then try it out.

Try it Out

Read the quiz again for information.
In groups, write six tips about good sleep habits.
Take your own advice! Follow the tips for two weeks.
After two weeks, take the quiz again. Did you get more As? Have the tips worked? Tell the class.

4 Select and store information on this topic in the Class Info Hub.

28

Lesson 8 Project

Children do a **writing project** that relates to the chapter theme.

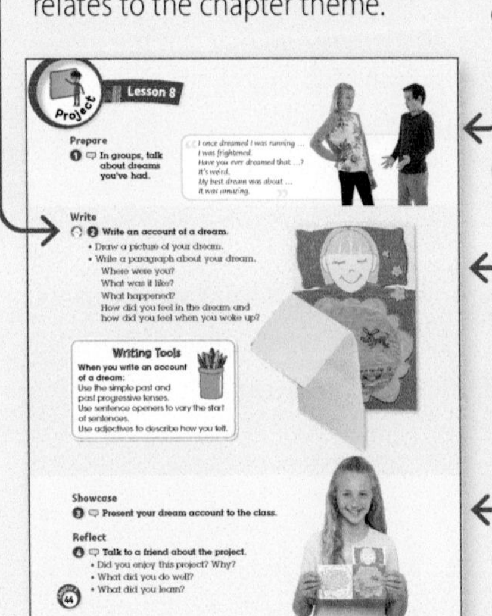
Project Lesson 8

Prepare

1 In groups, talk about dreams you've had.

I once dreamed I was running ...
I was frightened.
Have you ever dreamed that ...?
It's weird.
My best dream was about ...
It was amazing.

Write

2 Write an account of a dream.
- Draw a picture of your dream.
- Write a paragraph about your dream.
  Where were you?
  What was it like?
  What happened?
  How did you feel in the dream and how did you feel when you woke up?

Writing Tools
When you write an account of a dream:
Use the simple past and past progressive tenses.
Use sentence openers to vary the start of sentences.
Use adjectives to describe how you felt.

Showcase

3 Present your dream account to the class.

Reflect

4 Talk to a friend about the project.
- Did you enjoy this project? Why?
- What did you do well?
- What did you learn?

44

A **group discussion** helps children prepare.

A clear **structure** is given to support writing.

The children then **present** their project to the class.

An ongoing **quiz** for children to complete in pairs reviews language, gives speaking practice, and rounds off the chapter.

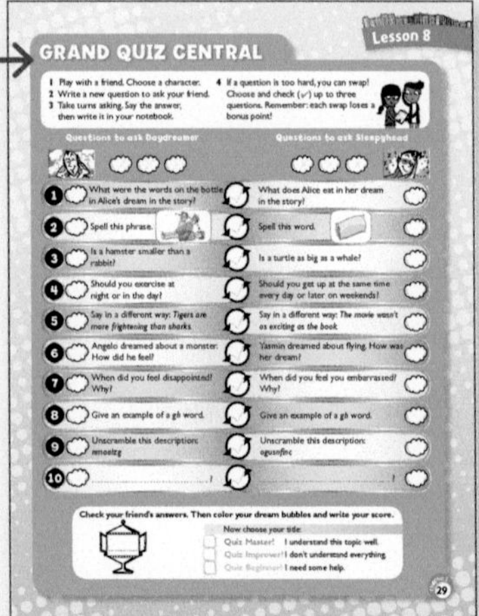
Lesson 8

GRAND QUIZ CENTRAL

1 Play with a friend. Choose a character.
2 Write a new question to ask your friend.
3 Take turns asking. Say the answer, then write it in your notebook.
4 If a question is too hard, you can swap! Choose and check (✓) up to three questions. Remember: each swap loses a bonus point!

	Questions to ask Daydreamer	Questions to ask Sleepyhead
1	What were the words on the bottle in Alice's dream in the story?	What does Alice eat in her dream in the story?
2	Spell this phrase.	Spell this word.
3	Is a hamster smaller than a rabbit?	Is a turtle as big as a whale?
4	Should you exercise at night or in the day?	Should you get up at the same time every day or later on weekends?
5	Say in a different way: *Tigers are more frightening than sharks.*	Say in a different way: *The movie wasn't as exciting as the book.*
6	Angelo dreamed about a monster. How did he feel?	Yasmin dreamed about flying. How was her dream?
7	When did you feel disappointed? Why?	When did you feel you embarrassed? Why?
8	Give an example of a *gh* word.	Give an example of a *gh* word.
9	Unscramble this description: *mnoelzg*	Unscramble this description: *ogusnfinc*
10	..............................?	..............................?

Check your friend's answers. Then color your dream bubbles and write your score.

Now choose your title:
Quiz Master! I understand this topic well.
Quiz Improver! I don't understand everything.
Quiz Beginner! I need some help.

29

The **CLIL eBook** expands the CLIL topics from the Student Book with **additional real-world content and practice activities.**

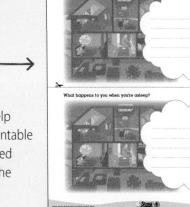

Chapter 3 Graphic Organizers

What happens to you when you're asleep?

What happens to you when you're asleep?

Each CLIL lesson has an optional **graphic organizer** template to help children organize their findings. Printable **writing templates** are also supplied for Lesson 8 (downloadable from the Teacher Resource Center).

Review

The Review lesson provides **further practice and consolidation** of language from the chapter.

Children reflect on their own progress and color in Hamish's bones to record their progress (**self-evaluation**).

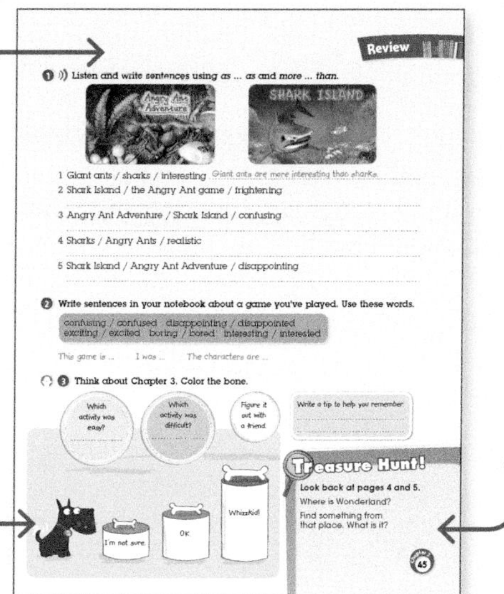

Review

1 Listen and write sentences using *as* ... *as* and *more* ... *than*.

1 Giant ants / sharks / interesting Giant ants are more interesting than sharks.

2 Shark Island / the Angry Ant game / frightening

3 Angry Ant Adventure / Shark Island / confusing

4 Sharks / Angry Ants / realistic

5 Shark Island / Angry Ant Adventure / disappointing

2 Write sentences in your notebook about a game you've played. Use these words.

confusing / confused disappointing / disappointed exciting / excited boring / bored interesting / interested

This game is ... I was ... The characters are ...

3 Think about Chapter 3. Color the bone.

Which activity was easy?

Which activity was difficult?

Figure it out with a friend.

Write a tip to help you remember

I'm not sure. OK WhizzKid!

Treasure Hunt!

Look back at pages 4 and 5.

Where is Wonderland?

Find something from that place. What is it?

45

A fun **Treasure Hunt!** activity takes children back to the Welcome section (pp. 4–5) to find an item from the chapter.

New! Exam Booster sections in the Activity Book (pp. 78–104) provides **Cambridge English Young Learners Exams**-style activities practicing the language from each chapter. These help prepare for the Reading and Writing, Listening and Speaking papers of the Cambridge English Flyers Exam.

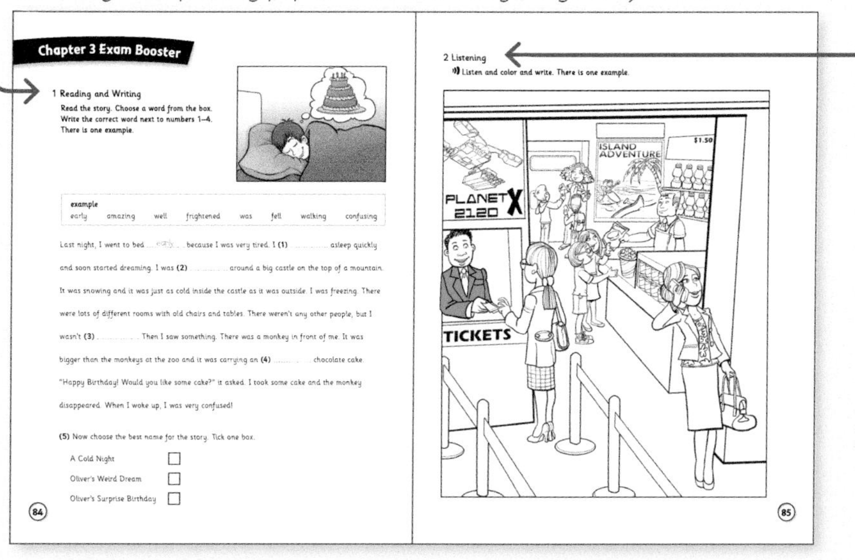

Chapter 3 Exam Booster

1 Reading and Writing

Read the story. Choose a word from the box. Write the correct word next to numbers 1–4. There is one example.

example

early amazing well frightened was fell walking confusing

Last night, I went to bed ...early... because I was very tired. I **(1)** .... asleep quickly and soon started dreaming. I was **(2)** .... around a big castle on the top of a mountain. It was snowing and it was just as cold inside the castle as it was outside. I was freezing. There were lots of different rooms with old chairs and tables. There weren't any other people, but I wasn't **(3)** .... Then I saw something. There was a monkey in front of me. It was bigger than the monkeys at the zoo and it was carrying an **(4)** .... chocolate cake. "Happy Birthday! Would you like some cake?" it asked. I took some cake and the monkey disappeared. When I woke up, I was very confused!

(5) Now choose the best name for the story. Tick one box.

A Cold Night ☐

Oliver's Weird Dream ☐

Oliver's Surprise Birthday ☐

84

2 Listening

Listen and color and write. There is one example.

85

Class audio for the listening activities are in the Teacher Resource Center.

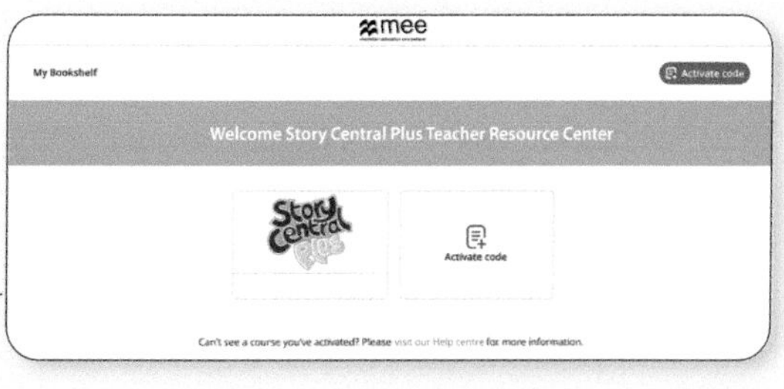

The Teacher Resource Center provides a wealth of assessment support including pre-written chapter, mid-year, and end-of-year tests. **CEYLT** (**Cambridge YLE**)-style speaking prompts and tips are also available.

Festivals worksheets and teaching notes to be used during the year bring the world outside into the classroom and help to foster an understanding of different cultures.

Teacher Edition Overview

Chapter Overview

An **Overview** at the start of every chapter provides a quick reference point to show what is covered. The **Competency Focus** shows where competencies are developed throughout the chapter.
The **Digital Overview** shows the variety of digital resources available for the chapter.

Student Book and Activity Book Lessons

Each lesson opens with the lesson objectives, key language, and any materials required.

A **Warmer** activity introduces children to the lesson topic, activating prior knowledge, and getting the children energized!

Reduced pages for the **Student Book** and the **Activity Book** give easy reference to the components being used.

Optional activities allow you to extend lessons and offer opportunities for further practice and personalization.

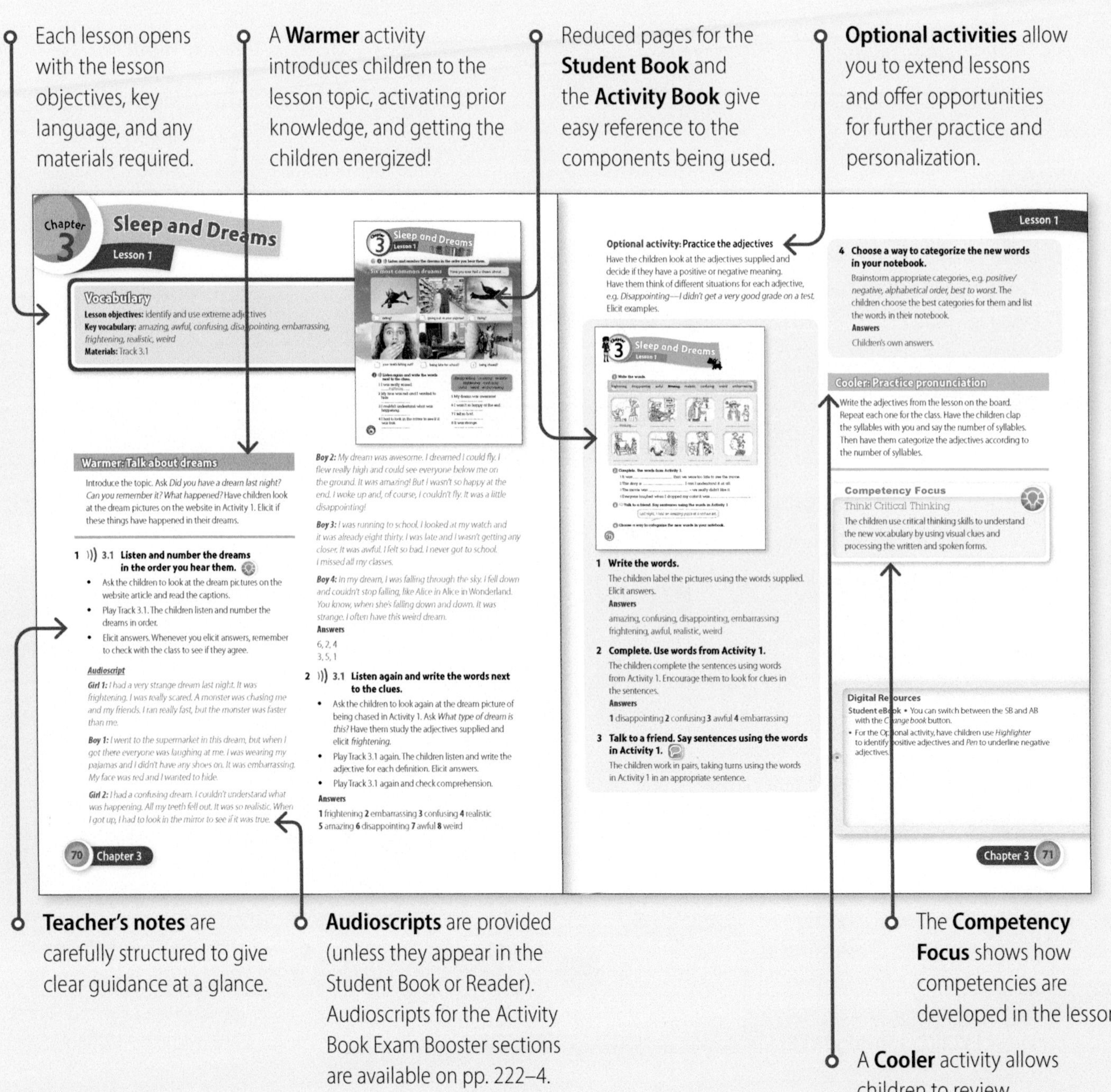

Chapter 3 Sleep and Dreams

Lesson 1

Vocabulary

Lesson objectives: identify and use extreme adjectives
Key vocabulary: *amazing, awful, confusing, disappointing, embarrassing, frightening, realistic, weird*
Materials: Track 3.1

Warmer: Talk about dreams

Introduce the topic. Ask *Did you have a dream last night? Can you remember it? What happened?* Have children look at the dream pictures on the website in Activity 1. Elicit if these things have happened in their dreams.

1 3.1 Listen and number the dreams in the order you hear them.

- Ask the children to look at the dream pictures on the website article and read the captions.
- Play Track 3.1. The children listen and number the dreams in order.
- Elicit answers. Whenever you elicit answers, remember to check with the class to see if they agree.

Audioscript

Girl 1: *I had a very strange dream last night. It was frightening. I was really scared. A monster was chasing me and my friends. I ran really fast, but the monster was faster than me.*

Boy 1: *I went to the supermarket in this dream, but when I got there everyone was laughing at me. I was wearing my pajamas and I didn't have any shoes on. It was embarrassing. My face was red and I wanted to hide.*

Girl 2: *I had a confusing dream. I couldn't understand what was happening. All my teeth fell out. It was so realistic. When I got up, I had to look in the mirror to see if it was true.*

Boy 2: *My dream was awesome. I dreamed I could fly. I flew really high and could see everyone below me on the ground. It was amazing! But I wasn't so happy at the end. I woke up and, of course, I couldn't fly. It was a little disappointing!*

Boy 3: *I was running to school. I looked at my watch and it was already eight thirty. I was late and I wasn't getting any closer. It was awful. I felt so bad. I never got to school. I missed all my classes.*

Boy 4: *In my dream, I was falling through the sky. I fell down and couldn't stop falling, like Alice in Alice in Wonderland. You know, when she's falling down and down. It was strange. I often have this weird dream.*

Answers
6, 2, 4
3, 5, 1

2 3.1 Listen again and write the words next to the clues.

- Ask the children to look again at the dream picture of being chased in Activity 1. Ask *What type of dream is this?* Have them study the adjectives supplied and elicit *frightening*.
- Play Track 3.1 again. The children listen and write the adjective for each definition. Elicit answers.
- Play Track 3.1 again and check comprehension.

Answers
1 frightening **2** embarrassing **3** confusing **4** realistic
5 amazing **6** disappointing **7** awful **8** weird

70 Chapter 3

Optional activity: Practice the adjectives

Have the children look at the adjectives supplied and decide if they have a positive or negative meaning. Have them think of different situations for each adjective, e.g. *Disappointing—I didn't get a very good grade on a test.* Elicit examples.

1 Write the words.
The children label the pictures using the words supplied. Elicit answers.
Answers
amazing, confusing, disappointing, embarrassing
frightening, awful, realistic, weird

2 Complete. Use words from Activity 1.
The children complete the sentences using words from Activity 1. Encourage them to look for clues in the sentences.
Answers
1 disappointing **2** confusing **3** awful **4** embarrassing

3 Talk to a friend. Say sentences using the words in Activity 1.
The children work in pairs, taking turns using the words in Activity 1 in an appropriate sentence.

Lesson 1

4 Choose a way to categorize the new words in your notebook.
Brainstorm appropriate categories, e.g. *positive/negative, alphabetical order, best to worst.* The children choose the best categories for them and list the words in their notebook.
Answers
Children's own answers.

Cooler: Practice pronunciation

Write the adjectives from the lesson on the board. Repeat each one for the class. Have the children clap the syllables with you and say the number of syllables. Then have them categorize the adjectives according to the number of syllables.

Competency Focus
Think! Critical Thinking
The children use critical thinking skills to understand the new vocabulary by using visual clues and processing the written and spoken forms.

Digital Resources
Student eBook • You can switch between the SB and AB with the *Change book* button.
• For the Optional activity, have children use *Highlighter* to identify positive adjectives and *Pen* to underline negative adjectives.

Chapter 3 71

Teacher's notes are carefully structured to give clear guidance at a glance.

Audioscripts are provided (unless they appear in the Student Book or Reader). Audioscripts for the Activity Book Exam Booster sections are available on pp. 222–4.

The **Competency Focus** shows how competencies are developed in the lesson.

A **Cooler** activity allows children to review language learned in a fun context.

Reader

The **Reader** lesson contains a range of additional activities that you can use as you please. You can get children to read the Reader story at home or in class.

Reading Strategy helps you develop children's literacy, with further explanation and activities in the **Literacy Handbook** on the Teacher Resource Center.

Story Time helps you get the most out of the Reader, helping you become a more effective storyteller in the classroom.

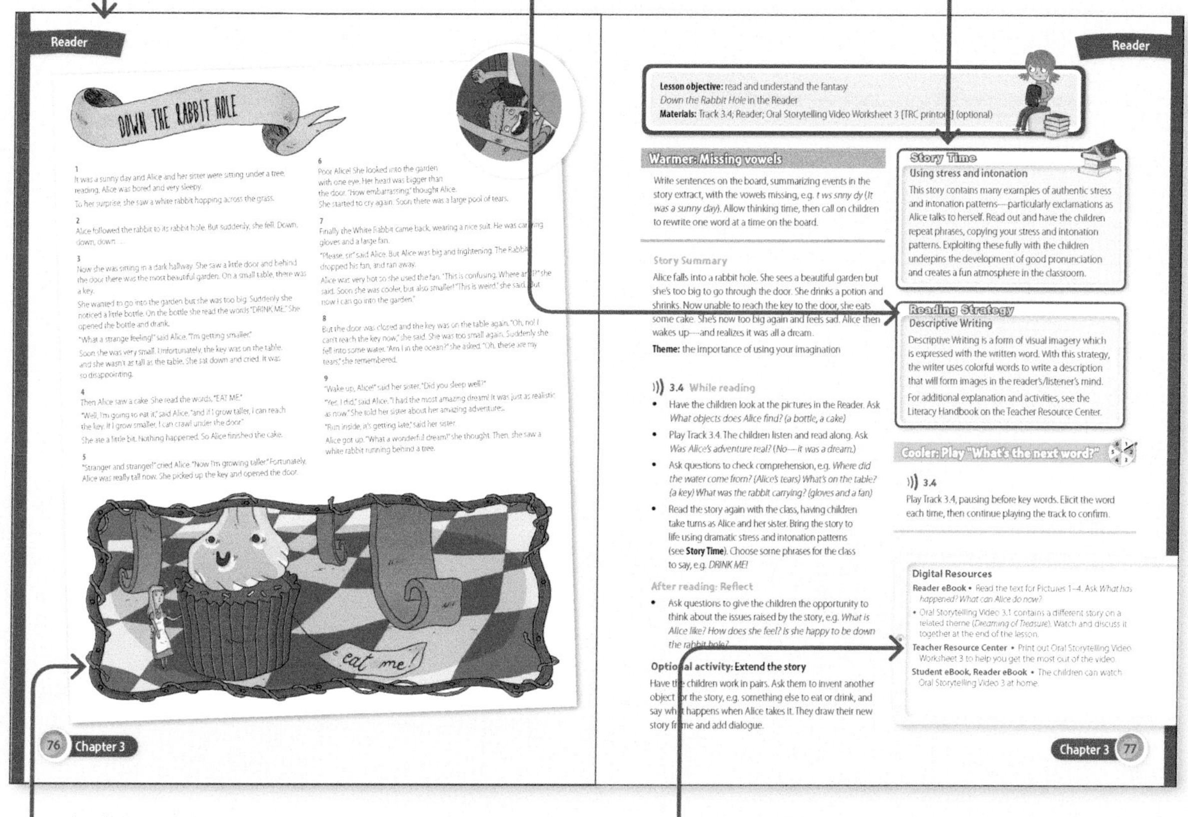

Reader

DOWN THE RABBIT HOLE

1
It was a sunny day and Alice and her sister were sitting under a tree, reading. Alice was bored and very sleepy.
To her surprise, she saw a white rabbit hopping across the grass.

2
Alice followed the rabbit to its rabbit hole. But suddenly, she fell. Down, down, down ...

3
Now she was sitting in a dark hallway. She saw a little door and behind the door there was the most beautiful garden. On a small table, there was a key.
She wanted to go into the garden but she was too big. Suddenly she noticed a little bottle. On the bottle she read the words "DRINK ME." She opened the bottle and drank.
"What a strange feeling!" said Alice. "I'm getting smaller."
Soon she was very small. Unfortunately, the key was on the table, and she wasn't as tall as the table. She sat down and cried. It was so disappointing.

4
Then Alice saw a cake. She read the words, "EAT ME."
"Well, I'm going to eat it," said Alice, "and if I grow taller, I can reach the key. If I grow smaller, I can crawl under the door."
She ate a little bit. Nothing happened. So Alice finished the cake.

5
"Stranger and stranger!" cried Alice. "Now I'm growing taller." Fortunately, Alice was really tall now. She picked up the key and opened the door.

6
Poor Alice! She looked into the garden with one eye. Her head was bigger than the door. "How embarrassing," thought Alice.
She started to cry again. Soon there was a large pool of tears.

7
Finally the White Rabbit came back, wearing a nice suit. He was carrying gloves and a large fan.
"Please, sir," said Alice. But Alice was big and frightening. The Rabbit dropped his fan, and ran away.
Alice was very hot so she used the fan. "This is confusing. Where am I?" she said. Soon she was cooler, but also smaller! "This is weird," she said. "But now I can go into the garden."

8
But the door was closed and the key was on the table again. "Oh, no! I can't reach the key now," she said. She was too small again. Suddenly she fell into some water. "Am I in the ocean?" she asked. "Oh, these are my tears," she remembered.

9
"Wake up, Alice!" said her sister. "Did you sleep well?"
"Yes, I did," said Alice. "I had the most amazing dream! It was just as realistic as now." She told her sister about her amazing adventures.
"Run inside, it's getting late," said her sister.
Alice got up. "What a wonderful dream!" she thought. Then, she saw a white rabbit running behind a tree.

76 Chapter 3

Reader

Lesson objective: read and understand the fantasy *Down the Rabbit Hole* in the Reader
Materials: Track 3.4; Reader; Oral Storytelling Video Worksheet 3 [TRC printout] (optional)

Warmer: Missing vowels

Write sentences on the board, summarizing events in the story extract, with the vowels missing, e.g. *t ws snny dy* (*It was a sunny day*). Allow thinking time, then call on children to rewrite one word at a time on the board.

Story Summary

Alice falls into a rabbit hole. She sees a beautiful garden but she's too big to go through the door. She drinks a potion and shrinks. Now unable to reach the key to the door, she eats some cake. She's now too big again and feels sad. Alice then wakes up—and realizes it was all a dream.

Theme: the importance of using your imagination

3.4 While reading

- Have the children look at the pictures in the Reader. Ask *What objects does Alice find? (a bottle, a cake)*
- Play Track 3.4. The children listen and read along. Ask *Was Alice's adventure real? (No—it was a dream.)*
- Ask questions to check comprehension, e.g. *Where did the water come from? (Alice's tears) What's on the table? (a key) What was the rabbit carrying? (gloves and a fan)*
- Read the story again with the class, having children take turns as Alice and her sister. Bring the story to life using dramatic stress and intonation patterns (see **Story Time**). Choose some phrases for the class to say, e.g. *DRINK ME!*

After reading: Reflect

- Ask questions to give the children the opportunity to think about the issues raised by the story, e.g. *What is Alice like? How does she feel? Is she happy to be down the rabbit hole?*

Optional activity: Extend the story

Have the children work in pairs. Ask them to invent another object for the story, e.g. something else to eat or drink, and say what happens when Alice takes it. They draw their new story frame and add dialogue.

Story Time
Using stress and intonation
This story contains many examples of authentic stress and intonation patterns—particularly exclamations as Alice talks to herself. Read out and have the children repeat phrases, copying your stress and intonation patterns. Exploiting these fully with the children underpins the development of good pronunciation and creates a fun atmosphere in the classroom.

Reading Strategy
Descriptive Writing
Descriptive Writing is a form of visual imagery which is expressed with the written word. With this strategy, the writer uses colorful words to write a description that will form images in the reader's/listener's mind.
For additional explanation and activities, see the Literacy Handbook on the Teacher Resource Center.

Cooler: Play "What's the next word?"

3.4
Play Track 3.4, pausing before key words. Elicit the word each time, then continue playing the track to confirm.

Digital Resources
Reader eBook • Read the text for Pictures 1–4. Ask *What has happened? What can Alice do now?*
• Oral Storytelling Video 3.1 contains a different story on a related theme (*Dreaming of Treasure*). Watch and discuss it together at the end of the lesson.
Teacher Resource Center • Print out Oral Storytelling Video Worksheet 3 to help you get the most out of the video.
Student eBook, Reader eBook • The children can watch Oral Storytelling Video 3 at home.

Chapter 3 77

The full text of the Reader story is provided, giving easy reference to the component being used.

Teaching notes suggest how and when to use the **digital components and resources**.

Games Bank

Here are details of popular and easy-to-use games that can be played in different lessons to engage, stimulate and, motivate children.

Bingo

Draw a grid with nine squares on the board and have the children copy it into their notebooks. The children add a vocabulary item to each square. Call out items. The children cross them off if they have them. When all are crossed off, they shout *Bingo!*

I Spy

Divide the children into two teams. Have a child from the first team look around the class and secretly choose one object. They say I spy with my little eye something beginning with (C)! The other team guesses the object. Teams take turns.

Ready, Set, Draw!

Divide the children into teams. Secretly give a child from each team a word to draw. The first team to identify the word correctly wins a point.

Simon Says

Have the children stand. Say actions for them to mime. They can only mime when you say Simon says (swim). If you say just Swim, they stand still. If a child does the wrong mime, they sit down. The last child standing is the winner.

Spelling Bee

Divide the class into two teams. Say a word. The children from each team take turns writing it on the board. Each correctly spelled word wins a point.

The Chain Game

Have the class stand. Start off a chain, e.g. I went to the store and I bought apples. Each child repeats the chain so far and adds an item, e.g. I went to the store and I bought apples and oranges. If a child makes a mistake or can't think of an item, they sit down. The last child standing wins.

The Shark Game

Draw on the board six steps leading down to water. On the top step, draw a stick person. In the water, draw a shark. Think of a word and draw a line to represent each letter. The children take turns calling out a letter. If it's correct, write the letter on the corresponding line. If it's wrong, erase the stick person and move him down one step, closer to the shark. If the children guess the word correctly, the class wins a point.

Story Central

Lesson objectives: introduce new Story Central characters; sing a song
Materials: Track 0.2; storybooks (Warmer)

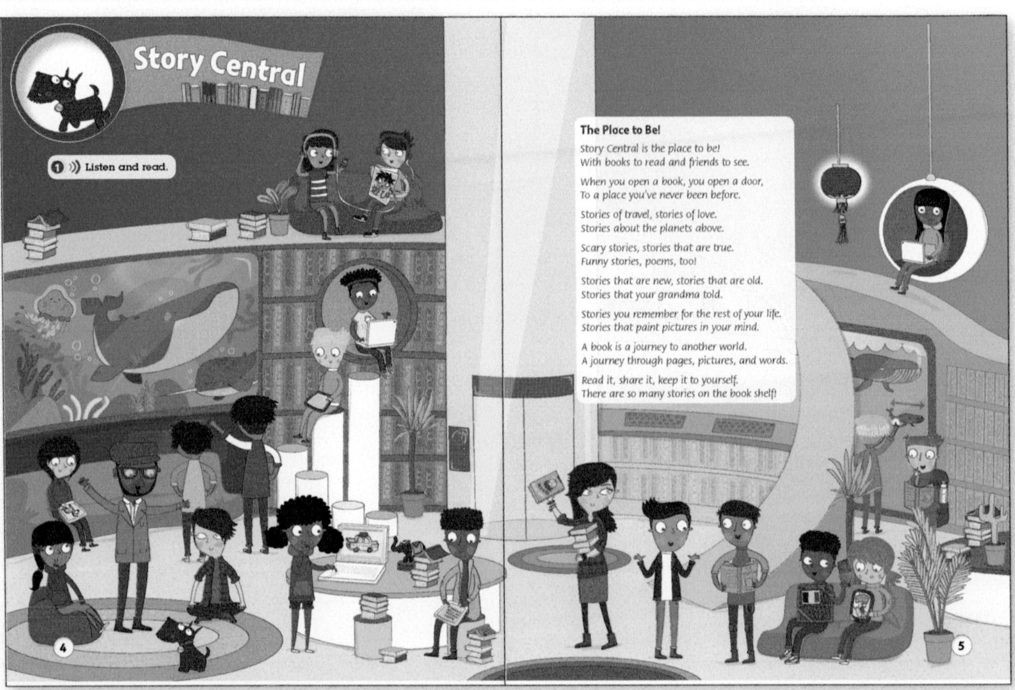

Story Central
1 Listen and read.
The Place to Be!
Story Central is the place to be!
With books to read and friends to see.
When you open a book, you open a door,
To a place you've never been before.
Stories of travel, stories of love.
Stories about the planets above.
Scary stories, stories that are true.
Funny stories, poems, too!
Stories that are new, stories that are old.
Stories that your grandma told.
Stories you remember for the rest of your life.
Stories that paint pictures in your mind.
A book is a journey to another world.
A journey through pages, pictures, and words.
Read it, share it, keep it to yourself.
There are so many stories on the book shelf!
4
5

Warmer: Our favorite stories

Turn the classroom into Story Central! Put storybooks around the classroom. Have the children walk around and discuss the books. Ask *What's your favorite kind of story? Why?*

1 0.2 Listen and read.

- Play Track 0.2. The children listen for the different kinds of stories.
- Agree on mimes for each kind of story in the song, e.g. story of travel—mime a plane, story of love—touch your heart, etc.
- Play Track 0.2 again for the children to sing along and mime.

Optional activity: Memory challenge

To practice the vocabulary of the lesson connected with reading, challenge the children to remember as many ways as possible of reading a story or poem in Story Central, e.g. reading a book, listening on headphones, reading an e-book on a computer/tablet, listening to the poet reciting/a Story Central helper reading.

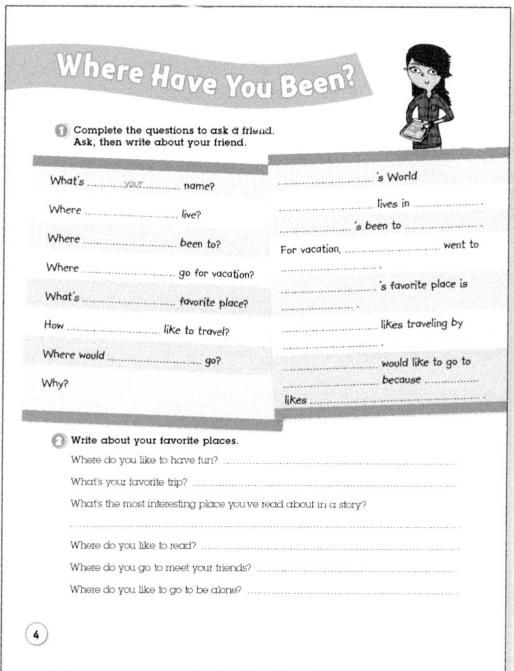

Where Have You Been?

1 Complete the questions to ask a friend. Ask, then write about your friend.

What's ....your.......... name?
Where .... live?
Where .... been to?
Where .... go for vacation?
What's .... favorite place?
How .... like to travel?
Where would .... go?
Why?

..........................'s World
.... lives in ....
..........................'s been to ....
For vacation, ... went to ....
..........................'s favorite place is ....
.... likes traveling by ....
.... would like to go to .... because ....
likes ....

2 Write about your favorite places.

Where do you like to have fun? ....
What's your favorite trip? ....
What's the most interesting place you've read about in a story? ....
Where do you like to read? ....
Where do you go to meet your friends? ....
Where do you like to go to be alone? ....

4

1 Complete the questions to ask a friend. Ask, then write about your friend.

The children complete the questions to ask a friend. Elicit answers. The children then take turns asking and answering the questions in pairs, and complete the form with their friend's information.

Answers

your, do you, have you, are you going to, your, do you, you like to

Children's own answers.

2 Write about your favorite places.

Elicit favorite places, writing suggestions on the board. The children write their answers. Elicit ideas.

Answers

Children's own answers.

Cooler: I'm in Story Central!

Tell the children they are going to spend an afternoon in Story Central and they can choose three activities. Elicit choices using *I'm going to … / then … / after that …*

Digital Resources

Student eBook, Digital Activity Book • All SB and AB pages can be shown on the board. Use them for "heads-up" teaching and reference throughout the lesson. For "heads-up" teaching activities, ask the children to close their book so that you have their full attention.

- You can access the tools in the tool bar along the top of the screen, e.g. *Timer*, *Highlighter*. The audio, answer keys and videos can be accessed by buttons next to the corresponding activities.

Where Have You Been?

Lesson objectives: review vocabulary and grammar from *Story Central Plus 4*
Key language: *Where did you go? What did you do? Did you . . .?*
Materials: Tracks 0.3 and 0.4

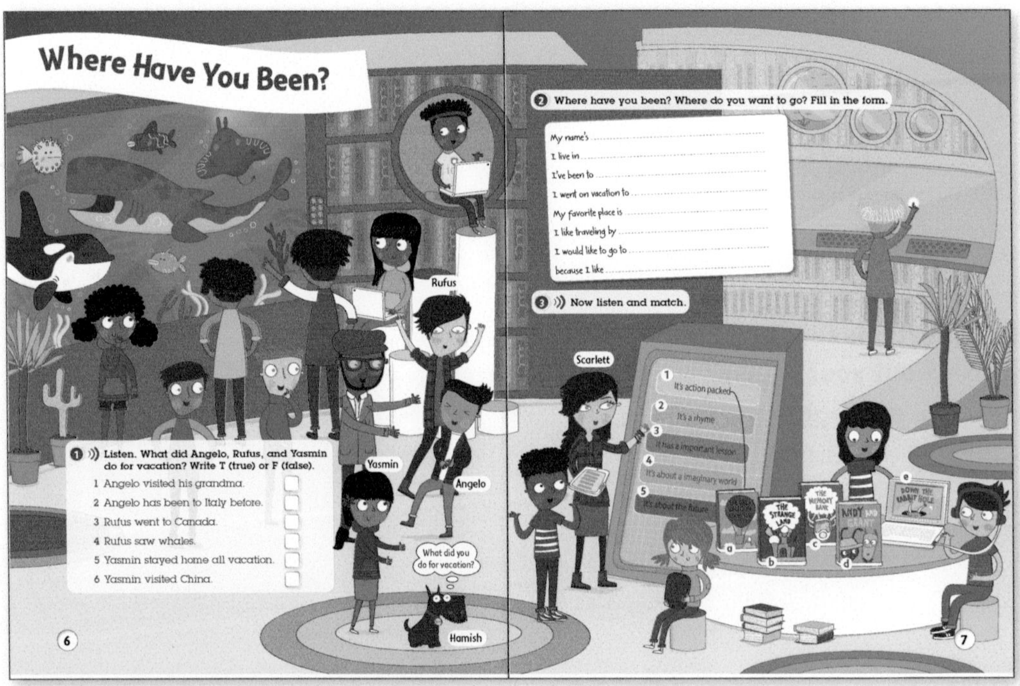

Warmer: What did you do for vacation?

Ask *Where did you go on vacation? What kind of vacation did you have? What did you do? Did you swim in the ocean?*

1 0.3 Listen. What did Angelo, Rufus, and Yasmin do for vacation? Write T (true) or F (false).

- Then introduce the characters for Level 5: Scarlett, Rufus, Yasmin, Angelo, Hamish the dog. Ask what each character is doing in the picture.
- Play Track 0.3. The children listen and write T (true) or F (false) for each sentence. Elicit answers, including the correct version of false sentences.

Audioscript

Poet: *So guys, have you all been thinking about something you did or where you went for vacation? Let's hear what ideas you have. Angelo!*
Angelo: *I flew to Europe, and I went to Italy.*
I met my grandma in Puglia. It's a place I've never been.
Um ...
Poet: *Good, Angelo! Rufus?*
Rufus: *We stayed in Canada for 14 days.*
I was sailing on a boat with my family.
We were looking for whales out at sea
But we didn't see a whale, only waves!
Poet: *That's great, Rufus! Yasmin, you next.*
Yasmin: *I read a lot of books. I love being alone!*
But Mom and Dad said you can't just stay home.
We traveled everywhere, all around the world.
I went to India and China—what a lucky girl!
Poet: *Excellent! Who's next? Jude? . . .*

Answers

1 T **2** F **3** T **4** F **5** F **6** T

2 Where have you been? Where do you want to go? Fill in the form.

- Ask *Which countries have you visited? Where would you like to visit?*
- Have the children complete the form with their own details.

Answers

Children's own answers.

3))) 0.4 Now listen and match.

- Play Track 0.4. The children listen to Scarlett explaining the stories, then match the titles. Elicit answers.

Audioscript

Scarlett: *OK, everyone, put your name on the list if you want to join Book Club. I need to know how many books to order.*
Yasmin: *What are the books this semester?*
Scarlett: *Um,* The Memory Bank, *that's about technology in the future.* Andy and Grant, *that's a story with an important lesson. Um,* Down the Rabbit Hole, *that's about a girl's imaginary world.* The Great Balloon Adventure, *an action-packed story about people traveling in a balloon!* This Strange Land. *That's a rhyme. There are so many good books this semester ... Take a look. This is the list.*

Answers

1 a **2** b **3** d **4** e **5** c

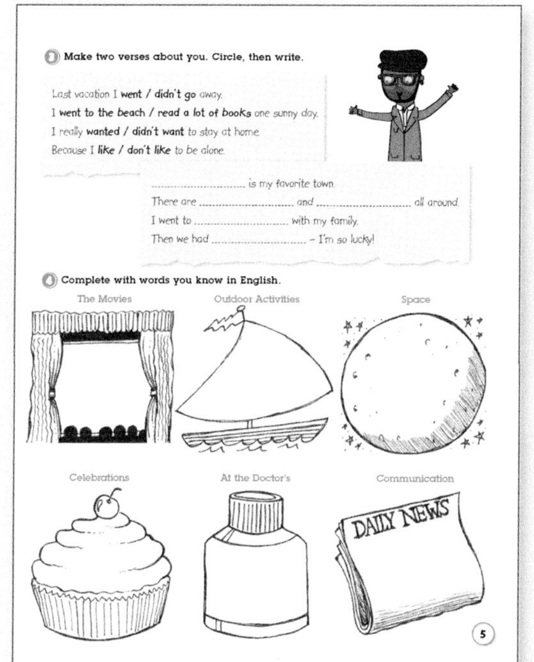

Make two verses about you. Circle, then write.

Last vacation I **went / didn't go** away.
I **went to the beach / read a lot of books** one sunny day.
I really **wanted / didn't want** to stay at home
Because I **like / don't like** to be alone.

.... is my favorite town.
There are .... and .... all around.
I went to .... with my family.
Then we had .... – I'm so lucky!

Complete with words you know in English.

The Movies | Outdoor Activities | Space | Celebrations | At the Doctor's | Communication

5

3 Make two verses about you. Circle, then write.

The children complete the first verse by circling the options that are correct for them. They then complete the second verse with their own details. Invite children to read out one of their verses.

Answers

Children's own answers.

4 Complete with words you know in English.

Elicit examples for each category. Then give the children two minutes to write words in all categories. Elicit answers.

Answers

Children's own answers.

Optional activity: Play "The Chain Game"

Make a chain around the class with vacation activities. Start it off: *On vacation I went swimming.* The next person repeats the chain so far and adds an activity. If the chain breaks down, start a new one.

Cooler: Story Central characters

Ask *What do you think Angelo is like?* (e.g. *funny, helpful*) Repeat with the other Story Central characters, including Hamish!

Digital Resources

Student eBook • Encourage the children to imagine a new friend and think up details about them using the SB Activity 3 prompts. Have children use *Pen* to write in a detail each.

Chapter 1

Then and Now

Overview

The children will:

- use critical thinking skills to identify past and present school items.
- talk about school in the past using the simple past and *used to*.
- read and understand a story about time travel.
- talk about technology and communication.
- find out about time capsules.
- write their own time travel story.

Reading Skills

Story: *A Boy Named Edward*
Genre: time travel story

Literacy Development

- use reading skills to understand and predict content
- relate story theme to personal experience
- use past/present time expressions

Key Vocabulary

School items, then and now: bell, chalk, chalkboard, dictionary, encyclopedia, hula-hoop, ink pen, interactive whiteboard, laptop
Technology and communication: chat online, download, earphones, emails, records, text, type, video call

Functional Language

- Do you remember … ?
- Yes, I do. I remember …

Spelling

Silent letters

Key Grammar

Simple past

- They studied reading, writing, and math.
- Did the girls wear dresses?
- Yes, they did. / No, they didn't.
- What did they write with?
- They wrote with ink pens.

used to + verb

- In 1950, the boys used to wear shorts.
- They didn't use to have computers.
- Did you use to have lunch at school when you were young?
- Yes, we did. / No, we didn't.

CLIL: History—Past, present, future

The children find out about time capsules.

Competency Focus

The children will:

use critical thinking skills to deduce the meaning of new vocabulary. (Lesson 1) predict the content of a story. (Lesson 3)	activate new vocabulary and apply new grammar knowledge. (Lesson 2) apply new grammar rules in a familiar context. (Lesson 5)	work in pairs to act out a dialogue. (Lesson 3) work in pairs to compare and contrast communication now and in the past. (Lesson 6)	relate the story theme to their personal experience. (Lesson 4) invent and write their own story. (Lesson 8) evaluate their own progress in the chapter. (Review)	develop their understanding of time capsules and the past by carrying out research. (Lesson 7)

Digital Overview

Teacher Presentation

Student eBook and Digital Activity Book

- Oral Storytelling Video 1.1: *George Washington and the Cherry Tree*
- Interactive versions of AB activities
- Integrated audio and answer key for all activities

Teacher resources for planning, lesson delivery, and homework

Teacher Resource Center

- Class Planner Chapter 1
- Worksheets to print out (including notes and answers):
  - Grammar Worksheet 1A: Simple past
  - Grammar Worksheet 1B: *used to* + verb
  - Phonics Worksheet 1
  - Oral Storytelling Video Worksheet 1: *George Washington and the Cherry Tree*
  - CLIL Graphic Organizer 1
  - Writing Template 1
  - Test Chapter 1
- Test Generator
- Literacy Handbook

Watch the Oral Storytelling Video

Children's resources for consolidation and practice at home

Story eBook and Reader eBook

- Oral Storytelling Video 1.1: *George Washington and the Cherry Tree*

The Inks Student's App

Vocabulary games: School items (then and now) and Technology/communication

Chapter 1

Then and Now

Lesson 1

Chapter 1 Then and Now Lesson 1

1 Listen and check (✓) the things Grandma had.

hula-hoops ✓ dictionaries ☐ computers ☐ an ink pen ☐ a car ☐ desks ☐

2 Listen again and write the words next to the clues.

laptop ~~chalk~~ encyclopedia interactive whiteboard ink pen chalkboard hula-hoops bell dictionary

1 She wrote with ....chalk........ on a ....
2 She brings her computer. It's a ....
3 We look at the .... on the wall.
4 We wrote in our notebooks with an ....
5 We use a .... to check spelling.
6 We use an .... to check facts.
7 She rang a big loud .... for recess.
8 The girls played with ....

8

Vocabulary

Lesson objective: identify and use vocabulary for school items in the past and now

Key vocabulary: *bell, chalk, chalkboard, dictionary, encyclopedia, hula-hoop, ink pen, interactive whiteboard, laptop*

Materials: Track 1.1

Warmer: Play "Vocabulary Review"

Divide the class into teams. Give them two minutes to write down as many things they can see in the classroom as they can. Elicit answers. Each correct word wins a point—two points if no other team has it. The team with the most points wins.

1 1.1 Listen and check (✓) the things Grandma had. 

- Throughout the Student Book and Activity Book, an example is generally given at the start of an activity. As in earlier levels, you can use this to talk through how the activity is done. Alternatively, you can encourage the children to use the examples as a guide themselves, to help promote more independent learning.
- Play Track 1.1. The children listen and check the items. Elicit answers. Whenever you elicit answers, remember to check with the class to see if they agree.

Audioscript

Girl: *Grandma, look at this!*
Grandma: *Ooh. This looks like my old school.*
Girl: *Where did you go to school, Grandma?*
Grandma: *I went to school here in the town. I walked to school. We didn't have a car.*
Girl: *What was your classroom like?*
Grandma: *Well, it was like this black and white picture. The teacher wrote with chalk on a chalkboard.*
Girl: *Our teacher brings her computer to class. It's a laptop. We sit in groups and look at the interactive whiteboard on the wall.*
Grandma: *We NEVER sat in groups! We sat at small desks like these and we wrote in our notebooks with an ink pen. There were a lot of books—big books! We had dictionaries to check spelling and encyclopedias to check facts. We didn't have computers or the Internet to find things out.*
Girl: *I use a dictionary on my computer.*
Grandma: *The teacher rang a big loud bell for recess and then we all ran outside. The girls played with hula-hoops and the boys played soccer. We didn't play together.*
Girl: *We all play soccer together at my school.*
Grandma: *Yes, things have changed.*

Answers

✓ *next to:* hula-hoops, dictionaries, an ink pen, desks

2 1.1 Listen again and write the words next to the clues.

- Look at the first clue together. Identify *wrote* as the key word in finding the answer. (*chalk*) Repeat with question 4, encouraging the children to use what they know and the context. (*ink pen*)
- The children discuss and complete the sentences in pairs, using the words supplied.
- Play Track 1.1 again for them to check. Elicit answers.

Answers

1 chalk, chalkboard **2** laptop **3** interactive whiteboard **4** ink pen **5** dictionary **6** encyclopedia **7** bell **8** hula-hoops

Optional activity: Then and now

Have the children draw two pictures in their notebook of a classroom then and now. Ask them to label items in their pictures and write two or three sentences about each.

Chapter 1 **Then and Now**
Lesson 1

1 **Unscramble and write the words. Then find, count, and write the number.**

a tolpap ......laptop...... 4
b hlack ....
c peolicycedna ....
d kin nep ....
e bocharlkda ....
f luah-hopo ....
g lebl ....
h nirodicaty ....
i trainceveti borwehitad ....

2 **Now circle in the picture the objects in your classroom. Talk to a friend.**

There's a laptop. *We don't have any ink pens.*

3 **Complete with words from Activity 1.**

1 If you want to know what a word means, use a ......dictionary...... .
2 When you hear the ...., you can go outside.
3 Don't write in the book with your .... Always use a pencil!
4 You can find the important facts in an ....
5 We watched a DVD of the school trip on the teacher's ....

4 **Choose a way to categorize the new words in your notebook.**

6

1 Unscramble and write the words. Then find, count, and write the number.

The children figure out the school items and write the words. They then count and write the number of each item pictured.

Answers

a laptop 4, **b** chalk 9, **c** encyclopedia 1, **d** ink pen 12, **e** chalkboard 3, **f** hula-hoop 5, **g** bell 3, **h** dictionary 3, **i** interactive whiteboard 3

2 Now circle in the picture the objects in your classroom. Talk to a friend.

The children circle the items which are in their classroom. They then describe their classroom in pairs.

3 Complete with words from Activity 1.

The children complete the sentences using words from Activity 1. Elicit answers.

Answers

1 dictionary **2** bell **3** ink pen **4** encyclopedia **5** laptop

4 Choose a way to categorize the new words in your notebook.

Brainstorm appropriate categories, e.g. *in my class/not in my class, modern/old, easy to spell/difficult to spell.* The children choose the best categories for them and list the words in their notebook. Remind them that organizing vocabulary makes it easier to memorize.

Answers

Children's own answers.

Cooler: Play "Spelling Bee"

Play the game with words from the lesson (see Games Bank p. 19).

Competency Focus

Think! Critical Thinking

The children use critical thinking skills to understand the new vocabulary by using visual clues and processing the written and spoken forms.

Digital Resources

Student eBook, Digital Activity Book • All SB and AB pages can be shown on the board. Use them for "heads-up" teaching and reference throughout the lesson.

• TIP All audio is accessible within the SB/AB pages: choose the audio buttons next to the corresponding activities.

Grammar

Lesson objective: talk about schools in the past
Key grammar: simple past—statements, questions, short answers
Secondary language: *dress up, separately, misbehaved, corner, factories*
Materials: Grammar Worksheet 1A [TRC printout] (optional)

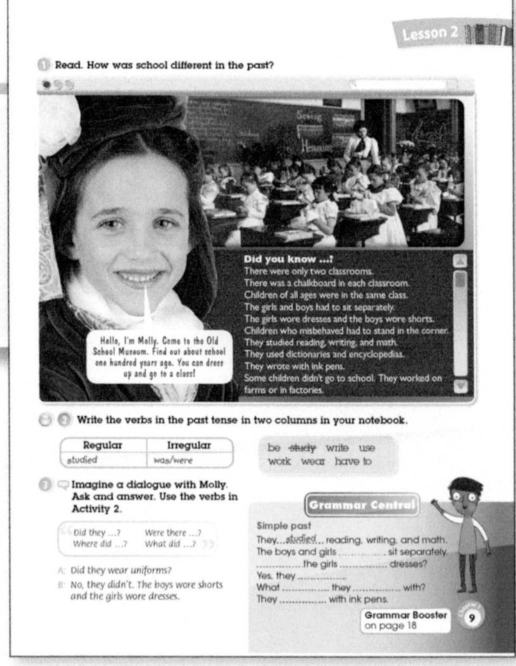

Lesson 2

1 Read. How was school different in the past?

Hello, I'm Molly. Come to the Old School Museum. Find out about school one hundred years ago. You can dress up and go to a class!

Did you know ...?
There were only two classrooms.
There was a chalkboard in each classroom.
Children of all ages were in the same class.
The girls and boys had to sit separately.
The girls wore dresses and the boys wore shorts.
Children who misbehaved had to stand in the corner.
They studied reading, writing, and math.
They used dictionaries and encyclopedias.
They wrote with ink pens.
Some children didn't go to school. They worked on farms or in factories.

2 Write the verbs in the past tense in two columns in your notebook.

Regular	Irregular
studied	*was/were*

be ~~study~~ write use work wear have to

3 Imagine a dialogue with Molly. Ask and answer. Use the verbs in Activity 2.

Did they ...? Were there ...? Where did ...? What did ...?

A: *Did they wear uniforms?*
B: *No, they didn't. The boys wore shorts and the girls wore dresses.*

Grammar Central

Simple past
They ...*studied*... reading, writing, and math.
The boys and girls .... sit separately.
.... the girls .... dresses?
Yes, they ....
What .... they .... with?
They .... with ink pens.

Grammar Booster on page 18

9

Warmer: Our grandparents' school

To review vocabulary from Lesson 1, give prompts for the children to respond with the correct time, e.g. *laptop* (*now*), *ink pen* (*then*), *dictionary* (*both*). Ask the children to think about their grandparents' school. Ask *What was/wasn't in the classroom? What did they wear?*

1 Read. How was school different in the past?

- Ask the children to look at the picture and compare it with their ideas from the Warmer.
- They then read the text. Ask *Which fact did you think was the most interesting?* Check comprehension by asking *What did they study? What things did they use in the classroom?*
- Elicit what kind of text it is. (*a website giving factual information*)

Answers

Children's own answers.

2 Write the verbs in the past tense in two columns in your notebook.

- Have the children categorize the verbs in two lists in their notebook (regular and irregular). Invite children to write the answers on the board. Remind them of the spelling change *–y becomes –ied*, e.g. *study—studied.*

Answers

Regular: studied, used, worked
Irregular: was/were, wrote, wore, had to

Grammar Central

Simple past

Have the children complete the grammar examples. Elicit answers. Elicit the rules for simple past questions, highlighting the use of *did*. Ask *Did they use pencils?* (*Yes, they did.*) *What did they wear?* (*Girls wore dresses.*) The children write further examples about school in the past in their notebook. For extra practice, try the **Grammar Booster** section in the Student Book (p. 18).

Answers p. 18

Activity 1: **1** rode **2** walked **3** left **4** brought **5** didn't eat **6** have to stay

Activity 2: **1** had **2** write **3** wore **4** had to stay **5** didn't have to **6** studied **7** had to use **8** went

3 Imagine a dialogue with Molly. Ask and answer. Use the verbs in Activity 2.

- Choose two children to read the example dialogue.
- Divide the class into pairs to practice the dialogue using the verbs in Activity 2. Have pairs perform for the class.

Optional activity: School history

Have the children make up a questionnaire about school to ask their parents/grandparents. Write prompts on the board, e.g. *drive/bike ride/walk to school; use a computer/dictionary.* The children write five questions, e.g. *Did you walk to school?* to ask a family member for homework.

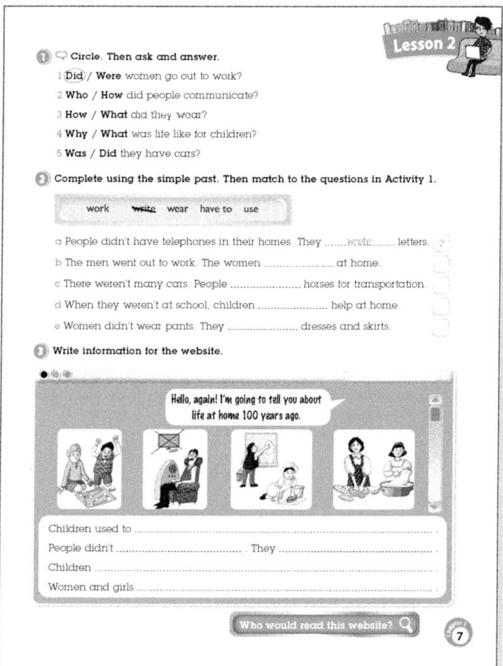
Lesson 2

1 Circle. Then ask and answer.

1 Did / Were women go out to work?
2 Who / How did people communicate?
3 How / What did they wear?
4 Why / What was life like for children?
5 Was / Did they have cars?

2 Complete using the simple past. Then match to the questions in Activity 1.

work ~~write~~ wear have to use

a People didn't have telephones in their homes. They ....wrote.... letters. 2
b The men went out to work. The women .... at home.
c There weren't many cars. People .... horses for transportation.
d When they weren't at school, children .... help at home.
e Women didn't wear pants. They .... dresses and skirts.

3 Write information for the website.

Children used to ....
People didn't .... They ....
Children ....
Women and girls ....

Who would read this website?

7

1 Circle. Then ask and answer. 

The children circle the correct word to complete the questions in the simple past. Elicit answers.

Answers

1 Did **2** How **3** What **4** What **5** Did

2 Complete using the simple past. Then match to the questions in Activity 1.

The children complete the sentences with the simple past form of the present tense verbs supplied. They then match the sentences to the questions in Activity 1. Elicit answers.

Answers

a wrote 2, **b** worked 1, **c** used 5, **d** had to 4, **e** wore 3

3 Write information for the website.

Ask *How was life different for people 100 years ago?* Elicit ideas. The children then write their website page. They compare with a friend. Ask *Who would read this website?* (*someone doing a history project/planning a school trip/ planning a day out*)

Answers

Children's own answers.

Cooler: Play "Word Ping-Pong"

Divide the class into two teams. You "serve" the first verb in the present tense, e.g. *watch*. The first team gives the simple past form, e.g. *watched*. The teams continue taking turns with different verbs. Each correct answer gets a point. The team with the most points wins.

Competency Focus

Learn

By reading the text and identifying the verbs in the simple past, the children demonstrate their understanding of the new grammatical structures.

Digital Resources

Student eBook • Use *Highlighter* to select *They used dictionaries and encyclopedias* in the SB Activity 1 text. Elicit what happens today. (*We use the Internet.*) Repeat with other prompts.

Digital Activity Book • Children use *Pen* to write AB Activity 3 answers. The class raises their hand if they have the same answers.

Teacher Resource Center • Print out Grammar Worksheet 1A for extra practice after SB Activity 2.

Reading: Story Extract

Lesson objectives: talk about the past using *remember*, use the title and pictures to predict story content; read the extract from the time travel story *A Boy Named Edward* (start)
Functional language: *Do you remember … ? Yes, I do. I remember …*
Secondary language: *the Aztecs, inside, crawled*
Materials: Tracks 1.2 and 1.3; first grade photo of yourself (optional)

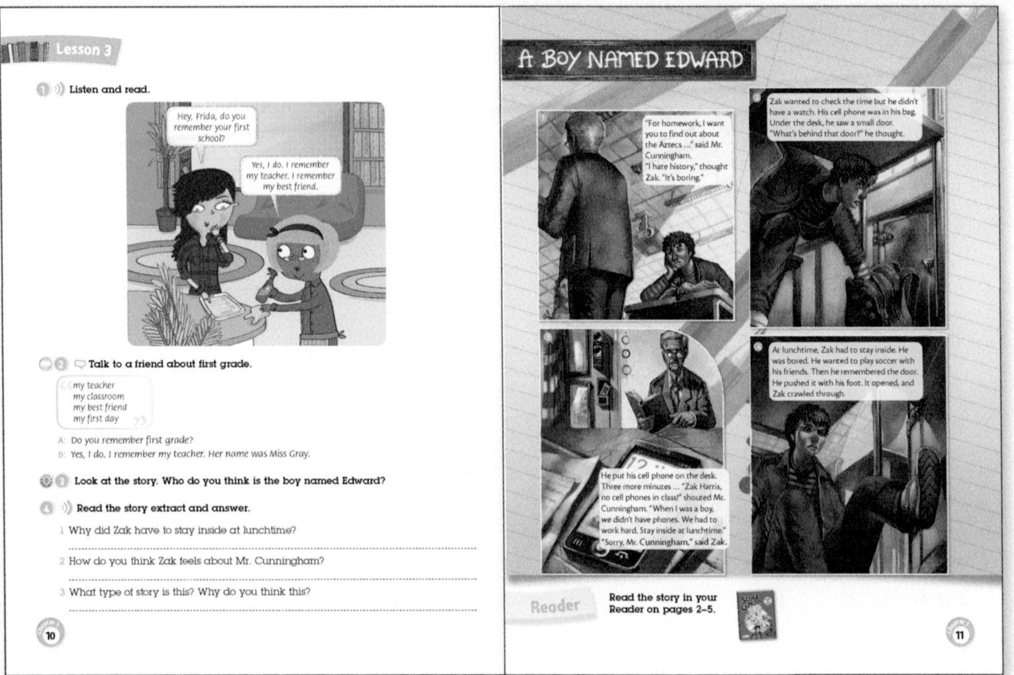

Lesson 3

1 Listen and read.

2 Talk to a friend about first grade.

my teacher
my classroom
my best friend
my first day

A: Do you remember first grade?
B: Yes, I do. I remember my teacher. Her name was Miss Gray.

3 Look at the story. Who do you think is the boy named Edward?

4 Read the story extract and answer.

1 Why did Zak have to stay inside at lunchtime?

2 How do you think Zak feels about Mr. Cunningham?

3 What type of story is this? Why do you think this?

10

Reader Read the story in your Reader on pages 2–5.

11

Warmer: Remember, remember!

Ask the children about their first day at school. Ask *Do you remember your teacher? Who was your best friend?* Ask them to guess when you started school. Tell them about your first grade teacher and your classroom. You could show a photo!

Functional language

1 1.2 Listen and read.

- Play Track 1.2. The children listen and read along. Play Track 1.2 again for them to repeat.
- Divide the class into pairs to practice the dialogue.

2 Talk to a friend about first grade.  

- Choose two children to read the example dialogue.
- The children practice in pairs using the prompts supplied and adding details. Have pairs do a dialogue for the class.

Before reading

3 Look at the story. Who do you think is the boy named Edward?

- Have the children study the pictures and identify the characters. (*Zak and Mr. Cunningham*)
- Elicit answers, but do not confirm predictions: explain that they will have to read the story to find out.

4 1.3 Read the story extract and answer.

- Play Track 1.3. The children listen and read along. Have them answer questions 1 and 2.
- Play Track 1.3 again so they can write their ideas for question 3. Encourage them to use the reading skills they have practiced in earlier levels, e.g. using the title, pictures, and context.

Answers

1 He had a cell phone in class. **2** Children's own answers. **3** Children's own answers/fantasy/time travel.

Lesson 3

1 Cross out the incorrect phrase. Then choose, write, and act out.

your 10th birthday / your first pet / next weekend / your last vacation

Do you remember ....?

Yes, I do. I remember ....

2 Read the story in your Student Book. Check (✓) the most important thing in Picture 2.

1 Zak's bag ☐ 2 the door ☐ 3 the cell phone ☐

3 Circle.

1 Mr. Cunningham talks about things **in the past / now**.
2 Zak wants to know the time, so he looks **in his bag / at the wall**.
3 Zak **likes / doesn't like** history.
4 At lunchtime, Zak has to **go outside / sit at his desk**.
5 Zak is usually **home / on the playground** at lunchtime.

4 What's behind the door? Think and write.

Behind the door, ...

8

1 Cross out the incorrect phrase. Then choose, write, and act out.

The children identify which phrase is incorrect. (*next weekend*) They then choose one of the others and act out the dialogue with a friend. In this level, encourage the children to use what they know to adapt and extend the dialogue. Have pairs act out their dialogue for the class.

2 Read the story in your Student Book. Check (✓) the most important thing in Picture 2.

The children read the Student Book story extract again, then look at Picture 2 and check the most important thing shown there. Elicit the answer with reasons. (*the door*)

3 Circle.

The children complete each sentence by circling the correct option from the two supplied. Elicit answers.

Answers

1 in the past **2** in his bag **3** doesn't like **4** sit at his desk **5** on the playground

4 What's behind the door? Think and write.

Ask *What's behind the door?* The children write their own ideas, then compare with a friend. Elicit ideas.

Answers

Children's own answers.

Cooler: What did you remember?

Write on the board *toy, friend, game, food.* Have the children close their eyes for one minute and think about when they were five years old, using these topics. Then have them open their eyes. Ask *What was your favorite toy? Who was your best friend?*, etc. The children work in pairs and say what they remembered.

Competency Focus

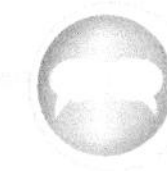

Collaborate and Communicate

The children work together, putting into practice new functional language by acting out a realistic dialogue.

Think! Critical Thinking

By analyzing visual clues and deducing from the context, the children use prediction skills to help them engage with the story.

Digital Resources

Student eBook, Digital Activity Book • Hover over each icon in the tool bar to reveal the function of each button.

• TIP Select answer key to show the answers all at once or one by one.

A BOY NAMED EDWARD

1
"For homework, I want you to find out about the Aztecs …" said Mr. Cunningham.

"I hate history," thought Zak. "It's boring."

2
Zak wanted to check the time but he didn't have a watch. His cell phone was in his bag. Under the desk, he saw a small door. "What's behind that door?" he thought.

3
He put his cell phone on the desk. Three more minutes … "Zak Harris, no cell phones in class!" shouted Mr. Cunningham. "When I was a boy, we didn't have phones. We had to work hard. Stay inside at lunchtime."

"Sorry, Mr. Cunningham," said Zak.

4
At lunchtime, Zak had to stay inside. He was bored. He wanted to play soccer with his friends. Then he remembered the door. He pushed it with his foot. It opened, and Zak crawled through.

5
He was in his classroom, but it was different. There wasn't a laptop or whiteboard, there was a chalkboard and chalk. The children used ink pens and big dictionaries. No one saw Zak.

6
Then a boy said, "Come and sit here." Zak sat down next to the boy. "I'm Edward," said the boy.

7
"We have to write about the Aztecs," said Edward. "I love history."

"Really?" asked Zak.

"Yes," said Edward. He opened his encyclopedia. "Look! Look at the amazing temples the Aztecs built …"

"Oh, that is kind of interesting. I guess I've never thought about that before," said Zak.

At twelve forty-five, the bell rang. "It's lunchtime!" said Edward. "Let's go outside. Do you have a cap? It's cold."

8
Edward ran onto the playground. Zak watched. This was his school. Some boys were playing tag. Some girls were playing with hula-hoops. "Come and play," said Edward.

9
"Who are you talking to, Edward?" laughed another boy. "Your imaginary friend?"

The boys chased Edward. He ran away. His cap fell off. Zak wanted to help Edward. He was picking up Edward's cap when the boys ran past and knocked him over.

10
Suddenly, the bell rang. It was the end of lunchtime. Zak was in his own classroom. His head hurt. He had Edward's cap in his hand.

Mr. Cunningham walked in. "So, Zachary Harris," he said. "DON'T use your phone in class again."

11
Then, he saw the cap. "I used to wear a cap like that at school," he said. "EHC: Edward Howard Cunningham! That's me!" said Mr. Cunningham. "I remember this cap. I lost it on this playground almost 60 years ago. Thank you!"

12
Mr. Cunningham started to walk away. "When I was your age, I had a very good friend. He was named Zak, too."

"Mr. Cunningham," said Zak. "I'm sorry I misbehaved in class. This lunchtime, I learned something about the past. You're right. History *is* interesting."

Lesson objective: read and understand the time travel story *A Boy Named Edward* in the Reader
Materials: Track 1.4; Reader, cap (Warmer), props (e.g. large book, hula-hoop); Oral Storytelling Video Worksheet 1 [TRC printout] (optional)

Warmer: Look at the cap

Show the children the cap and have them try it on. Tell them that a character in the story has to wear a cap as part of his school uniform. Ask the children in pairs to predict the rest of his uniform. They check in the Reader.

Story Summary

Zak is bored at school. When his history teacher, Mr. Cunningham, makes him stay in at recess, Zak crawls through a small door into a classroom from the past. He makes friends with a schoolboy, Edward. When Zak returns to the present, he realizes that Mr. Cunningham is Edward! After that, he finds history interesting.

Theme: learning about the past is interesting and relevant

1.4 While reading

- Have the children look at the pictures in the Reader. Ask *Who are the main characters?*
- Play Track 1.4. The children listen and read along. Ask *Who did Zak meet?* (*a boy named Edward*)
- Ask questions to check comprehension, e.g. *How did Zak help Edward?* (*He picked up his cap.*) *What was in Zak's hand when the bell rang?* (*Edward's cap*)
- Have the class read the story aloud. Allocate roles (narrator, Zak, Edward, and Mr. Cunningham). Bring the story to life using props (see **Story Time**).

After reading: Reflect

- Ask questions to give the children the opportunity to think about the issues raised by the story, e.g. *What kind of character was Edward in the past? What is he like now? How does Zak feel at the end of the story?*

Optional activity: Role-play

Have the children imagine Edward is visiting! They need to tell him about their school and ask him questions, e.g. *Did you have a uniform?*, etc. Divide the class into pairs to role-play the meeting. Have pairs act out for the class.

Story Time

Using props

Use props (or pictures) to bring the story to life and emphasize the time changes, e.g. a cap, a hula-hoop. Acting out or reading the story with props is motivating and fun as well as supporting comprehension.

Reading Strategy

Making Inferences

Making Inferences is essential in understanding the plot and what role each character plays. It is particularly useful when trying to solve a mystery. It requires readers to use their own knowledge and apply critical and visual reading skills.

For additional explanation and activities, see the Literacy Handbook on the Teacher Resource Center.

Cooler: Play "The A-Z Game"

Play the game using vocabulary connected with school (see Games Bank p. 19).

Digital Resources

Reader eBook • Display the Reader story. Review the story extract. Elicit story predictions before the children read the rest of it.

• Oral Storytelling Video 1.1 contains a different story on a related theme (*George Washington and the Cherry Tree*). Watch and discuss it at the end of the lesson.

Teacher Resource Center • Print out Oral Storytelling Video Worksheet 1 to help you get the most out of the video.

Student eBook, Reader eBook • The children can watch Oral Storytelling Video 1.1 at home.

Reading Comprehension and Critical Literacy

Lesson objectives: understand and evaluate the story; relate story theme to personal experience; write about the difference between the past and the present

Materials: Track 1.4; Reader; Oral Storytelling Video Worksheet 1 [TRC printout] (optional)

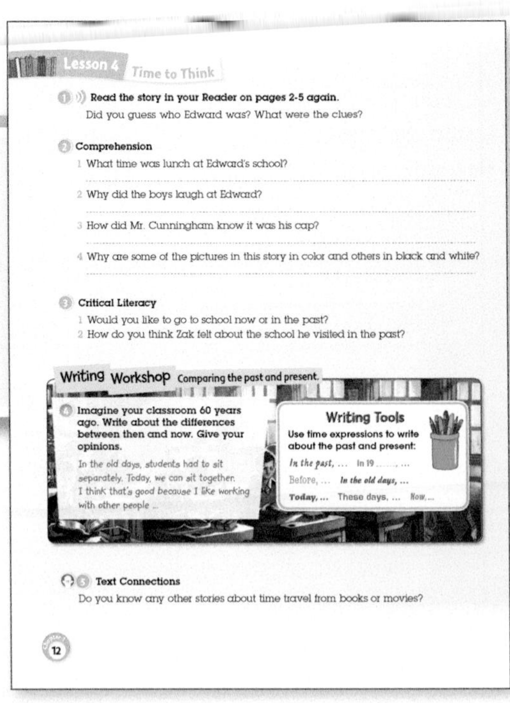

Lesson 4 Time to Think

1 Read the story in your Reader on pages 2-5 again.
Did you guess who Edward was? What were the clues?

2 Comprehension
1 What time was lunch at Edward's school?
2 Why did the boys laugh at Edward?
3 How did Mr. Cunningham know it was his cap?
4 Why are some of the pictures in this story in color and others in black and white?

3 Critical Literacy
1 Would you like to go to school now or in the past?
2 How do you think Zak felt about the school he visited in the past?

Writing Workshop Comparing the past and present.

4 Imagine your classroom 60 years ago. Write about the differences between then and now. Give your opinions.

In the old days, students had to sit separately. Today, we can sit together. I think that's good because I like working with other people ...

Writing Tools
Use time expressions to write about the past and present:
In the past, ... In 19 ..., ... Before, ... *In the old days, ...* **Today, ...** These days, ... Now, ...

5 Text Connections
Do you know any other stories about time travel from books or movies?

12

Note: Please ensure that your class has read the Reader story before you do this lesson.

Warmer: True or false?

Review the story extract by making statements to elicit *true* or *false*, e.g. *Zak's cell phone was in his pocket.* (*false*) Elicit the correct versions of the false statements, e.g. *His cell phone wasn't in his pocket. It was in his bag.* Invite children to make up their own statements.

1 1.4 Read the story in your Reader.

- Have the children read the story. (Alternatively, play Track 1.4 and have them read along.) Elicit whether they were correct in their predictions in Lesson 3 Activity 4.
- Ask the children if their idea about Edward was correct. Ask *What clues did you use?* (*he loves history, the letters on his cap, he's wearing the same glasses*)

2 Comprehension

- Ask the children to look at the first three questions in the activity. Have them look at the story and find their answers. Elicit answers. Then discuss question 4. Make it clear that the shift back in time is shown by the black and white pictures, like an old movie.

Answers

1 Twelve forty-five./12:45. **2** He had an imaginary friend. **3** His initials were inside the cap. **4** The black and white pictures show the past.

3 Critical Literacy

- In pairs, the children compare school in the past to their own experience. As they analyze and evaluate details, encourage them to justify their reasons.
- Ask *How does Zak feel?* Write adjectives they suggest on the board. Empathizing with characters helps the children interpret and engage with the text on a personal level.
- In class discussions it is important that the children learn to respect everyone's right to be heard. You could use a prop, like a ruler: only the person holding it speaks. Phase this out in time so that the children learn the correct way to behave without the prompt.

Writing Workshop

Comparing the past and present

4 Imagine your classroom 60 years ago. Write about the difference between then and now. Give your opinions.

Have a child read the example. Elicit other differences, using phrases from the **Writing Tools** box. Prompt as necessary, e.g. *walk to school, carry heavy bags*, etc. The children write about differences and give their opinion in their notebook, then compare with a friend.

Answers

Children's own answers.

5 Text Connections 

- Write *Books and Movies* on the board. Elicit time travel stories the children have read or seen. List them on the board. Elicit comparisons with the Reader story.

Optional activity: The time traveler

Ask the children to each prepare two questions to ask to identify a year you have chosen, e.g. *What did people use at school?* Invite three children to the front and show them the year (e.g. 1980). They answer the class's questions. The child who guesses the closest year wins.

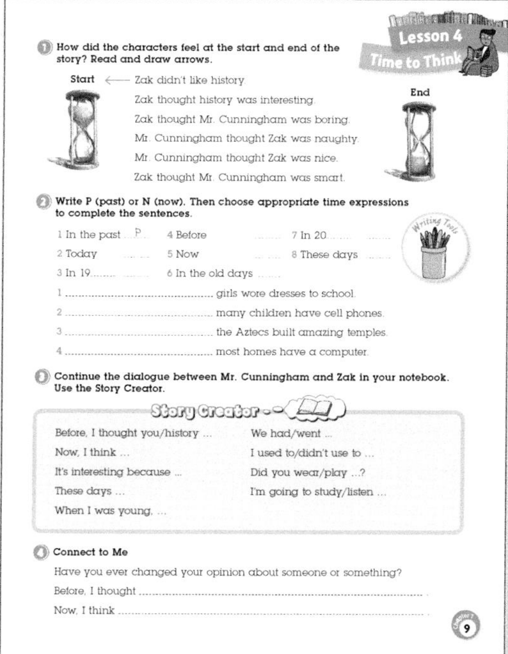

Lesson 4
Time to Think

1 How did the characters feel at the start and end of the story? Read and draw arrows.

Start ← Zak didn't like history.
Zak thought history was interesting.
Zak thought Mr. Cunningham was boring.
Mr. Cunningham thought Zak was naughty.
Mr. Cunningham thought Zak was nice.
Zak thought Mr. Cunningham was smart.
End

2 Write P (past) or N (now). Then choose appropriate time expressions to complete the sentences.

Writing Tools

1 In the past ..P.. 4 Before .... 7 In 20........ ....
2 Today .... 5 Now .... 8 These days ....
3 In 19........ .... 6 In the old days ....

1 .... girls wore dresses to school.
2 .... many children have cell phones.
3 .... the Aztecs built amazing temples.
4 .... most homes have a computer.

3 Continue the dialogue between Mr. Cunningham and Zak in your notebook. Use the Story Creator.

Story Creator

Before, I thought you/history ... We had/went ...
Now, I think ... I used to/didn't use to ...
It's interesting because ... Did you wear/play ...?
These days ... I'm going to study/listen ...
When I was young, ...

4 Connect to Me

Have you ever changed your opinion about someone or something?
Before, I thought ....
Now, I think ....

Chapter 1 9

1 How did the characters feel at the start and end of the story? Read and draw arrows.

The children decide if each sentence refers to the start or end of the story, drawing an arrow pointing to the appropriate egg timer. Elicit answers.

Answers

start, end, start, start, end, end

2 Write P (past) or N (now). Then choose appropriate time expressions to complete the sentences.

The children decide if the phrases describe the past or now and write the appropriate letter. Elicit answers. They then complete the sentences with an appropriate time expression.

Answers

1 P **2** N **3** P **4** P **5** N **6** P **7** P+N **8** N

1 *one of:* 1, 3, 4, 6 **2** *one of:* 2, 5, 7 (if this year), 8

3 *one of:* 1, 4, 6 **4** *one of:* 2, 5, 7 (if this year), 8

3 Continue the dialogue between Mr. Cunningham and Zak in your notebook. Use the Story Creator.

Use the **Story Creator** prompts to elicit ideas. The children write a dialogue in their notebook, then compare with a friend.

4 Connect to Me

Elicit examples of a change of opinion (e.g. *feelings towards a friend once they got to know them better*). The children write their own response, then compare with a friend.

Cooler: Play "The Spelling Game"

Spell out a word from the chapter slowly. Have children raise their hands when they know the answer. Have the children play in groups and take turns spelling out words.

Competency Focus

Me: Critical Literacy

The children use critical literacy skills to reflect on the story and relate it to their own experiences.

Digital Resources

Student eBook • Have children use *Pen* to write the answers for SB Activity 2.

Student eBook, Reader eBook • If you haven't already, watch Oral Storytelling Video 1.1, which contains a different story on a related theme.

Teacher Resource Center • If you haven't already, print out Oral Storytelling Video Worksheet 1 for support activities on the new story.

Grammar and Reading

Lesson objectives: talk about what life used to be like in the past
Key grammar: *used to*—statements, questions, short answers
Secondary language: *back in time, imaginary, stay in*
Materials: Track 1.5 ; Grammar Worksheet 1B [TRC printout] (optional)

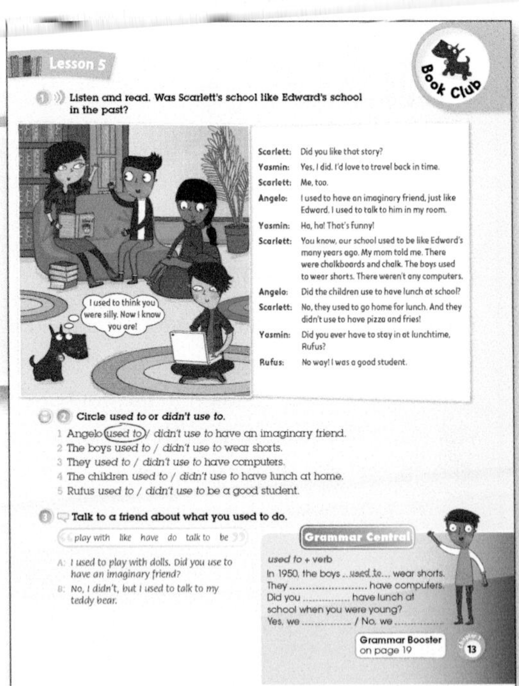
Lesson 5

Book Club

1 Listen and read. Was Scarlett's school like Edward's school in the past?

Scarlett: Did you like that story?
Yasmin: Yes, I did. I'd love to travel back in time.
Scarlett: Me, too.
Angelo: I used to have an imaginary friend, just like Edward. I used to talk to him in my room.
Yasmin: Ha, ha! That's funny!
Scarlett: You know, our school used to be like Edward's many years ago. My mom told me. There were chalkboards and chalk. The boys used to wear shorts. There weren't any computers.
Angelo: Did the children use to have lunch at school?
Scarlett: No, they used to go home for lunch. And they didn't use to have pizza and fries!
Yasmin: Did you ever have to stay in at lunchtime, Rufus?
Rufus: No way! I was a good student.

2 Circle *used to* or *didn't use to*.

1 Angelo *used to* / *didn't use to* have an imaginary friend.
2 The boys *used to* / *didn't use to* wear shorts.
3 They *used to* / *didn't use to* have computers.
4 The children *used to* / *didn't use to* have lunch at home.
5 Rufus *used to* / *didn't use to* be a good student.

3 Talk to a friend about what you used to do.

play with like have do talk to be

A: *I used to play with dolls. Did you use to have an imaginary friend?*
B: *No, I didn't, but I used to talk to my teddy bear.*

Grammar Central

used to + verb
In 1950, the boys ...used to... wear shorts.
They .... have computers.
Did you .... have lunch at school when you were young?
Yes, we .... / No, we ....

Grammar Booster on page 19

13

Warmer: Toy survey

Brainstorm the children's favorite toys from when they were younger. Write their suggestions on the board. As you call out the toys, have the class vote on their favorite by holding up their hand. Ask a child to count the hands each time and write the number on the board. At the end, elicit the class's favorite toy.

1 1.5 Listen and read. Was Scarlett's school like Edward's school in the past?

- Play Track 1.5. The children listen and read along. Ask *Was Scarlett's school like Edward's? (yes)*
- Play and here Track 1.5 again and ask the children to underline differences between schools now and Scarlett's school in the past.
- Elicit which verb is used to talk about the past. (*used to*)

2 Circle *used to* or *didn't use to.* 

- Ask the children to read the sentences and circle the correct answer. Elicit answers.
- Have the class identify the spelling difference between the positive and negative forms of *used to.*

Answers

1 used to **2** used to **3** didn't use to **4** used to **5** used to

Grammar Central

used to + verb

Have the children complete the grammar examples. Elicit answers and the rules for the positive, negative, and question forms. Ask further questions to elicit and practice short answers. For extra practice, try the **Grammar Booster** section in the Student Book (pp. 19–21).

Answers p. 19

Activity 1: **1** used to play **2** played **3** did, use to **4** used to read **5** Did, use to have **6** didn't

Activity 2: **1** She didn't use to listen to music. **2** She didn't use to watch videos. **3** She didn't use to read books. **4** She didn't use to take pictures. **5** She used to make phone calls. **6** She used to send text messages.

p. 20

Activity 1: **1** use to draw **2** did **3** drew **4** use to do **5** used to play **6** used to listen **7** used to have to wash **8** bought

Activity 2: **1** d **2** c **3** a **4** e **5** b

p. 21

Activity 1: **1** there were **2** used to **3** were **4** was **5** had to **6** When **7** talked **8** built **9** who **10** were **11** bought **12** paid **13** had **14** had to **15** used to

Activity 2: Children's own answers.

3 Talk to a friend about what you used to do. 

- Choose two children to read the example dialogue.
- Divide the class into pairs to practice the dialogue using the verbs supplied and their own ideas. Have pairs perform for the class.

Optional activity: Practice pronunciation

Write on the board *I used to have a dog. I didn't use to have a computer.* Have the children repeat the sentences, practicing the weak form of *to* in *used to.* Elicit other examples with *used to* and *didn't use to* in pairs.

Lesson 5

① Complete Yasmin's text.

When I was young, I 1 ✗ ......didn't use to...... have an imaginary friend. I 2 ✓ .... have a pet spider. His name was Arthur. I liked spiders. I liked birds, too. My mom 3 ✓ .... take me to the park to watch the birds. We 4 ✓ .... take my favorite peanut butter sandwiches. I 5 ✗ .... like any other food! I 6 ✓ .... read a lot of books about animals. I 7 ✗ .... like sports or watching TV or playing with dolls.

② Write the questions. Then ask and answer with a friend.

1 use / you / an imaginary friend / Did / to have / ?
Did you use to have an imaginary friend?
2 Did / to jump / use / on your bed / you / ?
....
3 to eat / you / broccoli / use / Did / ?
....
4 trees / to climb / you / Did / use / ?
....
5 use / to do / you / gymnastics / Did / ?
....

Did you use to have an imaginary friend?
No, I didn't.

③ Write about what you *used to* / *didn't use to* do when you were young.

When I was young, I ....
I didn't ....
I ....
I ....

Chapter 1 10

1 Complete Yasmin's text.

Make sure the children understand ✗ = negative verb form and ✓= positive verb form. The children use the prompts to complete the verbs. Elicit answers.

Answers

1 didn't use to **2** used to **3** used to **4** used to **5** didn't use to **6** used to **7** didn't use to

2 Write the questions. Then ask and answer with a friend.

The children unscramble and write the questions. They then ask and answer the questions in pairs.

Answers

1 Did you use to have an imaginary friend?
2 Did you use to jump on your bed?
3 Did you use to eat broccoli?
4 Did you use to climb trees?
5 Did you use to do gymnastics?

3 Write about what you *used to / didn't use to* do when you were young.

Elicit examples of things which were different when the children were aged four, e.g. food they liked/didn't like. They write their own responses, then compare with a friend. Elicit examples.

Answers

Children's own answers.

Cooler: Guess about the teacher

Write five sentences about you with *used to / didn't use to* on the board, e.g. *I used to have blond hair. I didn't use to like pizza.* Have the children work in pairs to decide whether sentences are true or false.

Competency Focus

Learn

The children demonstrate their understanding of the new language by reading the text and completing the activity.

Digital Resources

Student eBook • Use *Timer* to give the children working in pairs two minutes to recall as many things as possible that Scarlett says about schools in the past in SB Activity 1. Children use *Highlighter* to identify the answers in the text.

Teacher Resource Center • For extra grammar practice, print out Grammar Worksheet 1B.

Vocabulary, Song, and Spelling

Lesson objectives: identify and talk about technology and types of communication; practice spelling words with silent letters

Key vocabulary: *chat online, download, earphones, emails, records, text, type, video call*

Secondary language: *facts, miles away, I miss you*

Materials: Track 1.6; pictures for Key vocabulary (Warmer); Phonics Worksheet 1 [TRC printout] (optional)

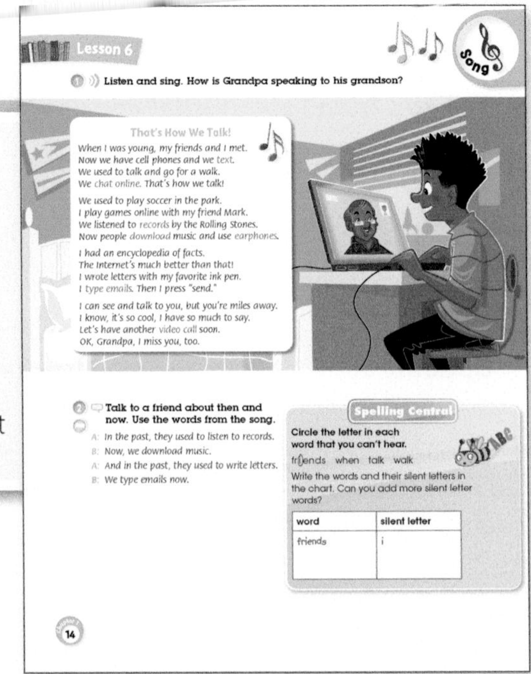

Lesson 6

Song

1 Listen and sing. How is Grandpa speaking to his grandson?

That's How We Talk!

When I was young, my friends and I met.
Now we have cell phones and we text.
We used to talk and go for a walk.
We chat online. That's how we talk!

We used to play soccer in the park.
I play games online with my friend Mark.
We listened to records by the Rolling Stones.
Now people download music and use earphones.

I had an encyclopedia of facts.
The Internet's much better than that!
I wrote letters with my favorite ink pen.
I type emails. Then I press "send."

I can see and talk to you, but you're miles away.
I know, it's so cool, I have so much to say.
Let's have another video call soon.
OK, Grandpa, I miss you, too.

2 Talk to a friend about then and now. Use the words from the song.

A: In the past, they used to listen to records.
B: Now, we download music.
A: And in the past, they used to write letters.
B: We type emails now.

Spelling Central

Circle the letter in each word that you can't hear.

friends when talk walk

Write the words and their silent letters in the chart. Can you add more silent letter words?

word	silent letter
friends	i

14

Warmer: Pre-teach vocabulary

Pre-teach the vocabulary by showing pictures, or draw icons on the board. Tell the class to stand. Ask questions using each of the words, e.g. *Do you chat online?* The class raise their hands for *yes* or sit down for *no*.

1 1.6 Listen and sing. How is Grandpa speaking to his grandson?

- Play Track 1.6. The children listen for the different ways of communicating. Ask *How is Grandpa speaking to his grandson?* (*They're having a video call.*)
- Play Track 1.6 again for the children to sing along.
- Ask them to underline the activities in the song that they do, then compare with a friend.

2 Talk to a friend about then and now. Use the words from the song.

- Divide the class into pairs. Read the example with the class. Then have them talk about ways of communicating in the past (then) and now.

Spelling Central

Silent letters

Write *Where?* on the board and elicit the silent letter. (*h*) Read the first verse of the song aloud. Have the children say the four words in **Spelling Central** and identify the silent letters. The children list more words in their notebook. Elicit suggestions. Have children write words on the board and circle the silent letter. Elicit other examples. (e.g. *listened, wrote,* etc.)

Answers

friends—i, when—h, talk—l, walk—l

Optional activity: Do a class survey

Write on the board *text, email, chat online, video call.* Divide the class into groups. Have them ask each other *Which do you use the most?* and keep a tally of responses. Elicit findings. They could create a bar graph with the information.

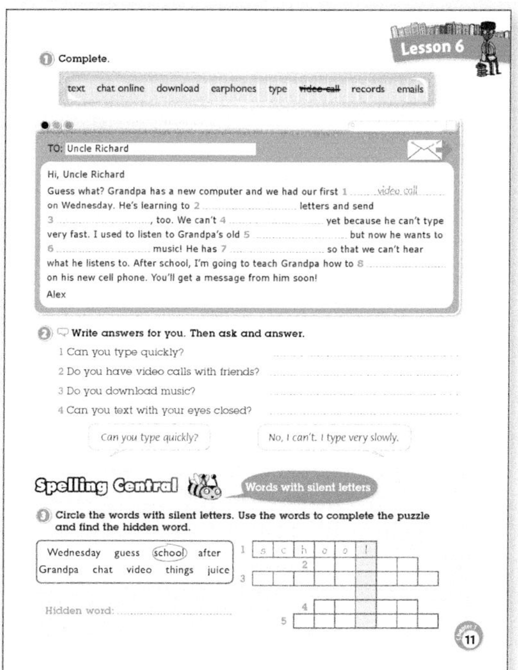

Lesson 6

1 Complete.

text chat online download earphones type ~~video call~~ records emails

TO: Uncle Richard

Hi, Uncle Richard

Guess what? Grandpa has a new computer and we had our first 1 ......video call...... on Wednesday. He's learning to 2 .... letters and send 3 ...., too. We can't 4 .... yet because he can't type very fast. I used to listen to Grandpa's old 5 .... but now he wants to 6 .... music! He has 7 .... so that we can't hear what he listens to. After school, I'm going to teach Grandpa how to 8 .... on his new cell phone. You'll get a message from him soon!

Alex

2 Write answers for you. Then ask and answer.

1 Can you type quickly? ....

2 Do you have video calls with friends? ....

3 Do you download music? ....

4 Can you text with your eyes closed? ....

Can you type quickly?

No, I can't. I type very slowly.

Spelling Central — Words with silent letters

3 Circle the words with silent letters. Use the words to complete the puzzle and find the hidden word.

Wednesday guess (school) after Grandpa chat video things juice

1 s c h o o l

Hidden word: ....

11

Cooler: Play "Silent Letters"

Divide the class into teams. Ask them to write down six words beginning with *w* + *silent h* (e.g. *where, why*). The first team to finish (with correct spelling) is the winner.

Competency Focus

Collaborate and communicate

The children work together and use their interpersonal skills to share their ideas on the topic, incorporating the new vocabulary.

1 Complete.

The children complete the text using the words supplied. Elicit answers.

Answers

1 video call **2** type **3** emails **4** chat online **5** records **6** download **7** earphones **8** text

2 Write answers for you. Then ask and answer.

Elicit an example answer for each question. The children write answers for themselves, then ask and answer in pairs. Invite pairs to ask and answer for the class.

Answers

Children's own answers.

3 Circle the words with silent letters. Use the words to complete the puzzle and find the hidden word.

To practice the **Spelling Central** feature, the children circle the words with silent letters, then use these words to complete the puzzle. They write the hidden word (using the letters in shaded boxes and adding the silent letter). Elicit answers.

Answers

1 school **2** juice **3** Wednesday **4** guess **5** Grandpa

Hidden word: lis(t)en

Digital Resources

Student eBook • TIP Children use *Highlighter* to identify the words which illustrate the spelling feature on the page (here, words with silent letters).

Teacher Resource Center • For phonics practice, print out Phonics Worksheet 1.

CLIL: History—Past, present, future

Lesson objective: find out about time capsules
Materials: CLIL Graphic Organizer 1 [TRC printout] (optional); box of small items for a "time capsule" (Cooler)

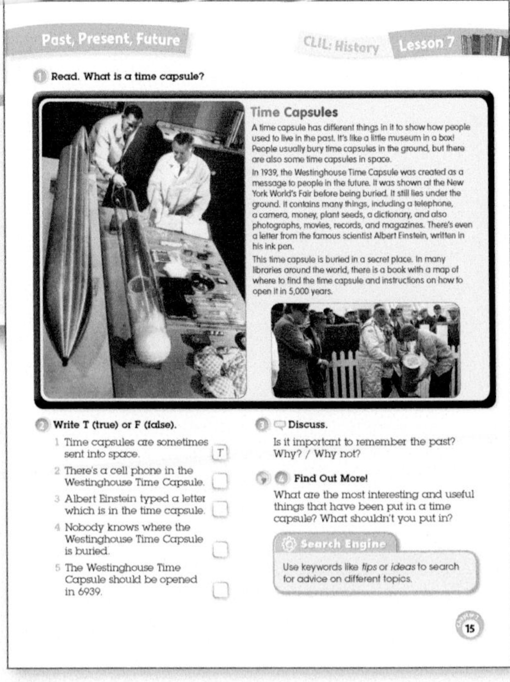

Past, Present, Future — CLIL: History — Lesson 7

1 Read. What is a time capsule?

Time Capsules

A time capsule has different things in it to show how people used to live in the past. It's like a little museum in a box! People usually bury time capsules in the ground, but there are also some time capsules in space.

In 1939, the Westinghouse Time Capsule was created as a message to people in the future. It was shown at the New York World's Fair before being buried. It still lies under the ground. It contains many things, including a telephone, a camera, money, plant seeds, a dictionary, and also photographs, movies, records, and magazines. There's even a letter from the famous scientist Albert Einstein, written in his ink pen.

This time capsule is buried in a secret place. In many libraries around the world, there is a book with a map of where to find the time capsule and instructions on how to open it in 5,000 years.

2 Write T (true) or F (false).

1 Time capsules are sometimes sent into space. T
2 There's a cell phone in the Westinghouse Time Capsule.
3 Albert Einstein typed a letter which is in the time capsule.
4 Nobody knows where the Westinghouse Time Capsule is buried.
5 The Westinghouse Time Capsule should be opened in 6939.

3 Discuss.

Is it important to remember the past? Why? / Why not?

4 Find Out More!

What are the most interesting and useful things that have been put in a time capsule? What shouldn't you put in?

Search Engine

Use keywords like *tips* or *ideas* to search for advice on different topics.

15

Warmer: Play "Ready, Set, Draw"

Play the game to review school objects (see Games Bank p. 19).

1 Read. What is a time capsule?

- Ask the children to focus on the first picture. Ask *Which items are on the table?*
- The children read the text. Ask *What is a time capsule? (a box with different things in it to show how people used to live)*
- Ask *Are all capsules in the ground? (No—some are in space.) How can you find the Westinghouse Time Capsule? (In many libraries around the world there is a book with a map of where to find it.) When will it be opened? (6939)*

2 Write T (true) or F (false).

- The children read the text again and decide whether each sentence is true or false. Elicit answers, including the correct version of the false sentences.

Answers

1 T **2** F **3** F **4** F **5** T

3 Discuss.

- Ask *Where can you learn about the past? (museums, websites, history books, parents, grandparents,* etc.)
- Divide the class into groups of three and ask them to discuss reasons why it is/is not important to learn about the past. Monitor and help as necessary.
- Elicit answers and list the reasons on the board, e.g. *We can learn from past mistakes. We can understand which decisions were good and bad.*, etc.

4 Find Out More!

- The children research the most interesting and useful things to put in a time capsule, and items that should not be included. The **Search Engine** feature gives support on where to look. The children will need to complete this research before doing the follow-up activity in the Activity Book. (It could be set as homework.)

Optional activity: Design a time capsule!

Divide the class into pairs and have them write a list of ten items they would want to put in their own time capsule. They compare their lists with another pair and decide on ten items between them.

Lesson 7 CLIL

1 Read and complete.

Dear Friend,

Hello from the past! Congratulations! You found our time capsule.

We are from 1 ......Park Side...... School in the 2 .... We buried this capsule in 3 19....... .

We like listening to 4 ....

We like reading 5 ....

Our favorite food is 6 ....

Our favorite sport is 7 ....

We hope you enjoyed our letter.

Have a great future!

2 Use your Student Book research to make an Info Card. Write about what to put in a time capsule. Find Out More!

clothes food money movies
TV music places news

3 Make a time capsule.

Try it Out

Fill a big plastic box with things to show how you live.
Write a letter to the person who will find your time capsule.
Find a place and bury the time capsule.
Leave it for someone to find, or you can open it in ten years!

4 Select and store information on this topic in the Class Info Hub.

12

1 Read and complete.

The children read the letter. They identify the time capsule objects pictured. They then complete the text. Elicit answers.

Answers

1 Park Side **2** USA **3** 1969 **4** records **5** comic books **6** pizza **7** soccer

2 Use your Student Book research to make an Info Card. Write about what to put in a time capsule.

Divide the class into groups. Have the children pool the information learned from their research in the Student Book and the Activity Book. The children write about and illustrate their ideas individually. Have the groups present their Info Cards to the class.

3 Make a time capsule.

In their groups, the children follow the **Try It Out** instructions to make a time capsule. Then they present it to the class.

4 Select and store information on this topic in the Class Info Hub.

Create an Info Hub to file the five best Info Cards and the best example of any larger project work in each topic. This will motivate the children to work creatively and also help them develop critical assessment skills. You can use the Info Hub as a resource for fast finishers or as an extension activity at the end of a lesson. Archive a time capsule and the five best Info Cards (by class vote) in a folder called **Chapter 1 Time Travel**.

Cooler: Play "What's in the Box?"

Prepare your "time capsule" box before the lesson. Use any small box and place objects inside, e.g. a dictionary, a pen, a coin. Have the children guess what is in your time capsule. Provide clues if necessary, e.g. *I can find out words with it.*

Competency Focus

Act

The children carry out research to find out more about time capsules. This helps them expand their learning and relate it to their world, both inside and outside the classroom.

Digital Resources

Student eBook • Display the SB page on the board to do Activity 1 for an alternative "heads-up" introduction to the topic. This helps the children engage.

• TIP Research and store links to pictures from the past in *Add personal note* in preparation for the next lesson.

Teacher Resource Center • Print out CLIL Graphic Organizer 1 for the children to use in collating their Find Out More! research.

CLIL eBook • The children can use the CLIL eBook to expand their knowledge of the lesson topic.

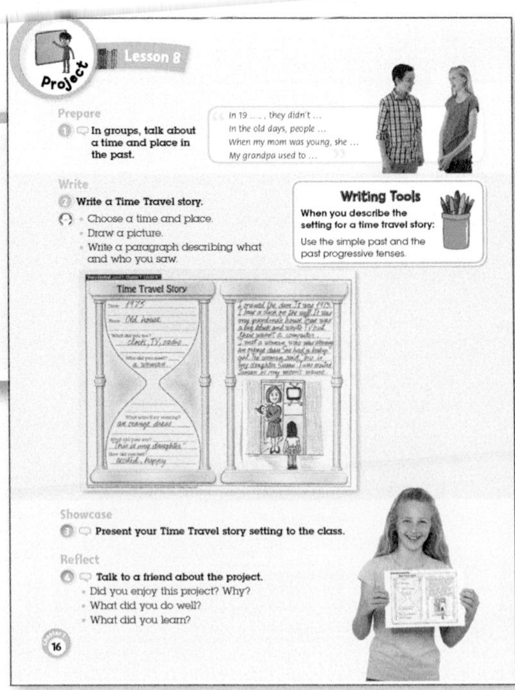

Project Lesson 8

Prepare

1 In groups, talk about a time and place in the past.

In 19 ... , they didn't ...
In the old days, people ...
When my mom was young, she ...
My grandpa used to ...

Write

2 Write a Time Travel story.

- Choose a time and place.
- Draw a picture.
- Write a paragraph describing what and who you saw.

Writing Tools

When you describe the setting for a time travel story:
Use the simple past and the past progressive tenses.

Time Travel Story

Showcase

3 Present your Time Travel story setting to the class.

Reflect

4 Talk to a friend about the project.

- Did you enjoy this project? Why?
- What did you do well?
- What did you learn?

16

Writing Project

Lesson objectives: review language from Chapter 1; write a time travel story and present it to the class

Materials: a few historical pictures (Warmer); Writing Template 1 [TRC printout] (optional)

Warmer: Historical photos

Show the class two or three photos of the past. They could be real or from a magazine/the Internet. Have the children guess what year they were taken. Ask them to describe life at the time of the photos, e.g. *People didn't have … They used to …*

Prepare

1 In groups, talk about a time and place in the past.

- In groups, the children choose and discuss a time and place in the past, using the prompts supplied.
- Groups report back to the class.

Write

2 Write a Time Travel story.

- Have the children read the story as a model for their own writing.
- Read the **Writing Tools** box together. Elicit examples in the model of simple past and past progressive verbs.
- The children prepare a story outline, using the instructions and the model story. They write and illustrate their story, then compare with a friend. Give support as necessary.

Showcase

3 Present your Time Travel story setting to the class.

- Choose children to read their stories to the class. Ask the class to listen for the place and time.

Reflect

4 Vote for the best Time Travel story and talk to the class.

- Have children say which story they liked best and why. You could have a class vote to elicit their favorite.

Optional activity: Act out a story

Choose one of the children's stories to act out, allocating roles.

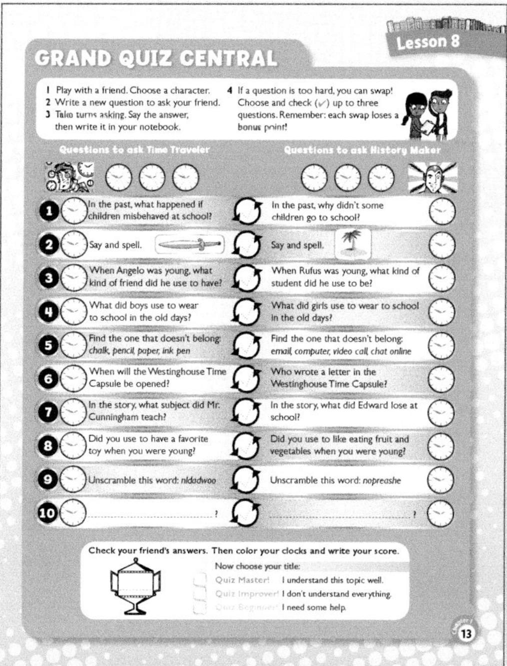

Lesson 8

GRAND QUIZ CENTRAL

1 Play with a friend. Choose a character.
2 Write a new question to ask your friend.
3 Take turns asking. Say the answer, then write it in your notebook.
4 If a question is too hard, you can swap! Choose and check (✓) up to three questions. Remember: each swap loses a bonus point!

	Questions to ask Time Traveler	Questions to ask History Maker
1	In the past, what happened if children misbehaved at school?	In the past, why didn't some children go to school?
2	Say and spell.	Say and spell.
3	When Angelo was young, what kind of friend did he use to have?	When Rufus was young, what kind of student did he use to be?
4	What did boys use to wear to school in the old days?	What did girls use to wear to school in the old days?
5	Find the one that doesn't belong: *chalk, pencil, paper, ink pen*	Find the one that doesn't belong: *email, computer, video call, chat online*
6	When will the Westinghouse Time Capsule be opened?	Who wrote a letter in the Westinghouse Time Capsule?
7	In the story, what subject did Mr. Cunningham teach?	In the story, what did Edward lose at school?
8	Did you use to have a favorite toy when you were young?	Did you use to like eating fruit and vegetables when you were young?
9	Unscramble this word: *nldadwoo*	Unscramble this word: *nopreashe*
10	..................................?	..................................?

Check your friend's answers. Then color your clocks and write your score.

Now choose your title:
Quiz Master! I understand this topic well.
Quiz Improver! I don't understand everything.
Quiz Beginner! I need some help.

13

Competency Focus

Me

The children invent and write their own Time Travel story, exploring their imagination and creativity.

Grand Quiz Central

Explain the game. The children play in pairs. They choose a character and answer questions from that character's section. They take turns asking questions. They give answers orally and in writing in their notebook. They can choose up to three questions to swap if their own question is too difficult. (They will get a bonus point for each of the three they do not swap.) They write question 10 using language from the chapter.

They color in a symbol for each correct answer. They tally and write their score (adding in any swap symbols they did not use), then evaluate and check their Quiz title.

Answers

1 They had to stand in the corner. / They had to work (on farms or in factories). **2** sword / island **3** an imaginary friend / a good student **4** shorts / dresses **5** paper / computer **6** 6939 / Albert Einstein **7** history / his cap **8** Yes, I used to ... (or) No, I didn't use to ... **9** download / earphones **10** Children's own answers.

Cooler: Play "Time Traveling"

Divide the class into groups and write a year on the board, e.g. 1925. Ask the first group to say the year. Award one point for a correct answer. Continue writing years for the other groups. Make the dates increasingly difficult, e.g. *1899, 1642, 1204*. The team with the most points wins.

Digital Resources

Student eBook • Have children use *Highlighter* to identify examples in the model text of the key features of the writing task: time, place, what and who the writer saw.

• TIP Use *Add personal note* for easy access to links to the pictures for the Warmer activity.

Teacher Resource Center • Print out Writing Template 1 to use for the SB writing activity.

Language Review

Lesson objective: review language from Chapter 1
Materials: Tracks 1.7 and AB 1.1

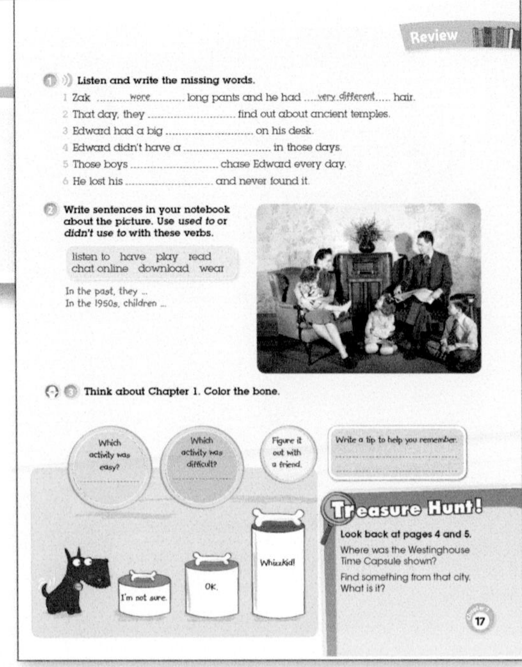

Warmer: Recap the story

Write *Zak and Edward/Mr. Cunningham* on the board. Ask the children to write down two or three key words from the story connected with each character. Elicit words and children's reasons for choosing them.

1 1.7 Listen and write the missing words.

- Play Track 1.7. The children listen and complete the text. Elicit answers.

Audioscript

I'm Edward. I had an imaginary friend when I was young. His name was Zak. He wore long pants. And he had very different hair!

I met him in history class. We used to have history every Thursday afternoon. That day, we had to find out about ancient temples. He was surprised when I opened the big encyclopedia on my desk. Now, I have a laptop for looking up facts, but we didn't have computers in those days.

I remember that my friends chased me in the school yard that day. Those boys used to chase me every day. I ran away but I lost my cap and my ink pen. I have my cap now, but I never found my ink pen. I don't remember my imaginary friend very well because the next day he wasn't there.

Answers

1 wore, different hair **2** had to **3** encyclopedia **4** laptop/computer **5** used to **6** ink pen

2 Write sentences in your notebook about the picture. Use *used to* or *didn't use to* with these verbs.

- Write *1950* on the board and ask *How did people live then?*
- Have the children look at the picture and words supplied, then write sentences about life in 1950 in their notebook. Have them compare with a friend.

Answers

Children's own answers.

3 Think about Chapter 1. Color the bone. 

- Have the children look back at Chapter 1 and color the bone to evaluate their progress (self-evaluation). Discuss ideas for remembering vocabulary, e.g. spend five minutes every day reading new word lists. The children choose and write a tip in their Student Book.

Treasure Hunt!

Ask *In which country and city was the Westinghouse Time Capsule shown?* (*the USA, New York*) Have the children find something from that city. (*a taxi*)

Cooler: Play "Back to the Board"

Play the game using vocabulary from the chapter (see Games Bank p. 19).

Chapter 1 Exam Booster

1 Reading and Writing
Look at the three pictures. Write about this story. Write 20 or more words.

78

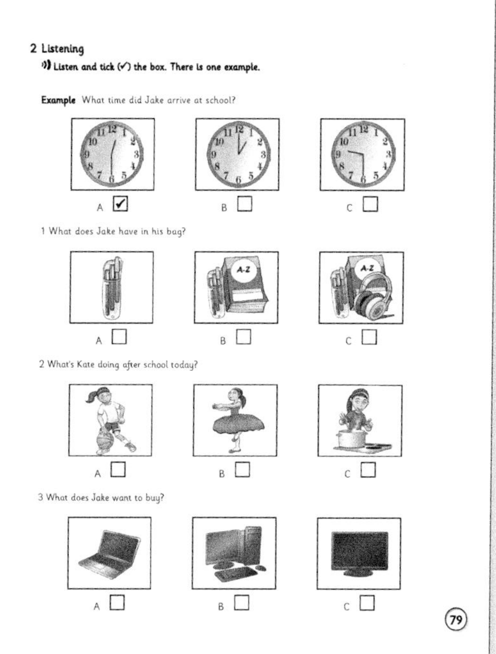
2 Listening
Listen and tick (✓) the box. There is one example.

Example What time did Jake arrive at school?

A ☑ B ☐ C ☐

1 What does Jake have in his bag?

A ☐ B ☐ C ☐

2 What's Kate doing after school today?

A ☐ B ☐ C ☐

3 What does Jake want to buy?

A ☐ B ☐ C ☐

79

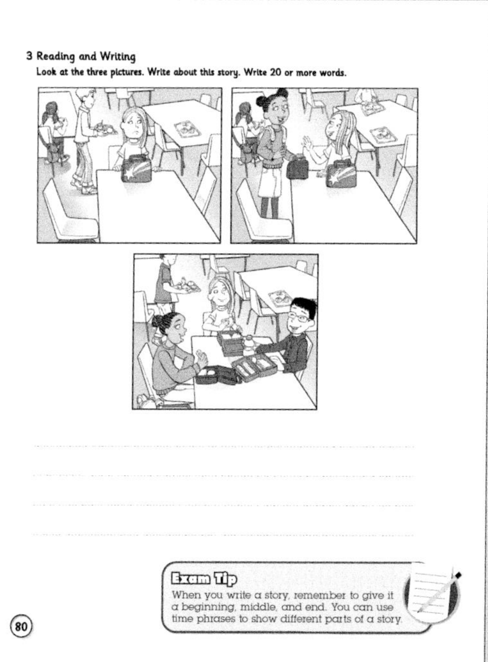
3 Reading and Writing
Look at the three pictures. Write about this story. Write 20 or more words.

Exam Tip
When you write a story, remember to give it a beginning, middle, and end. You can use time phrases to show different parts of a story.

80

1 Reading and Writing. Look at the three pictures. Write about this story. Write 20 or more words.

The children use the pictures to write a story about what the woman is doing. Check answers.

Answers

Children's own answers

2 AB 1.1 Listening. Listen and tick (✓) the box. There is one example.

The children read the questions. Play AB Track 1.1 twice. They listen and tick the correct box for each question. Check answers.

Answers (Audioscript on p. 222)

1 b **2** b **3** a

3 Reading and Writing. Look at the three pictures. Write about this story. Write 20 or more words.

The children use the pictures to write a story about what is happening. Check answers.

Answers

Children's own answers

Competency Focus

Me: Self-evaluation

The children reflect on the chapter and express their opinions about their own progress. This encourages them to evaluate and make decisions about how they learn and what they need to revisit.

Digital Resources

Teacher Resource Center • Print out Test Chapter 1 to use at the end of this lesson. The Test Generator also allows you to create customized tests.

Student's App • Encourage the children to play the games on their smartphone/tablet as a fun way to review the chapter vocabulary. (*The Inks* Apps are free and available on the App Store and Google Play.)

Chapter 2

Work Hard, Play Hard!

Overview

The children will:

- use critical thinking skills to identify challenging hobbies.
- talk about what they have done and for how long using *for* and *since*.
- read and understand a story with a message.
- talk about definite plans and possible actions using *going to* and *might*.
- talk about past achievements and future challenges.
- find out about charity expeditions.
- make their own personal achievements and goals vision board.

Key Vocabulary

Challenging hobbies: baking, chess, Japanese, karate, photography, poetry
Future aspirations: certificates, challenges, college, competitions, fail, grades, pass, succeed, taking part, tests, trophies

Key Grammar

Present perfect: *for* and *since*

- I've lived here for 35 years.
- He's lived there for three years.
- How long have you lived in Japan?
- I've lived here since I was five.

going to and *might*

- I'm going to go to music school.
- She isn't going to go to college.
- He might be a singer.
- Are you going to be a vet?

Reading Skills

Story: *Andy and Grant*
Genre: modern fable

Literacy Development

- use reading skills to understand and predict content
- relate story theme to personal experience
- use time expressions with *for/since*

Functional Language

- I haven't seen you for ages!
- I've been at … I've stayed … since …

Spelling

Double consonant *ll*

CLIL: Social sciences—Volunteer projects

The children find out about charity expeditions.

Competency Focus

The children will:

use critical thinking skills to deduce the meaning of new vocabulary. (Lesson 1) predict the content of a story. (Lesson 3)	activate new vocabulary and apply new grammar knowledge. (Lesson 2) apply new grammar rules in a familiar context. (Lesson 5)	work in pairs to act out a dialogue. (Lesson 3) work in pairs to talk about past achievements and future challenges. (Lesson 6)	relate the story theme to their personal experience. (Lesson 4) invent and write their own vision board. (Lesson 8) evaluate their own progress in the chapter. (Review)	develop their understanding of the needs of their local community and identify solutions. (Lesson 7)

Digital Overview

Teacher Presentation

Student eBook and Digital Activity Book

- Music Video 2.1: *Life is Full of Challenges*
- Interactive versions of AB activities
- Integrated audio and answer key for all activities

Teacher resources for planning, lesson delivery, and homework

Teacher Resource Center

- Class Planner Chapter 2
- Worksheets to print out (including notes and answers):
  - Grammar Worksheet 2A: Present perfect: *for* and *since*
  - Grammar Worksheet 2B: *going to* and *might*
  - Phonics Worksheet 2
  - CLIL Graphic Organizer 2
  - Writing Template 2
  - Festival Worksheet: Halloween
  - Test Chapter 2
- Test Generator
- Literacy Handbook

Children's resources for consolidation and practice at home

Student eBook

- Music Video 2.1: *Life is Full of Challenges*

The Inks Student's App

Vocabulary games: Challenging hobbies and Future aspirations

Work Hard, Play Hard!

Lesson 1

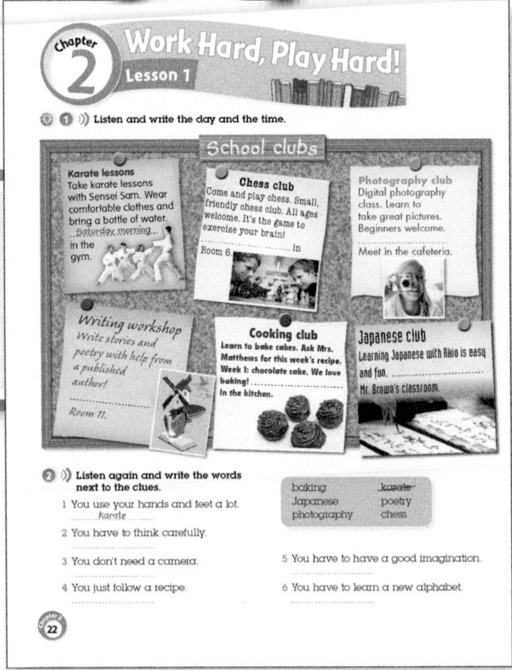

Chapter 2 Work Hard, Play Hard! Lesson 1

1 Listen and write the day and the time.

School clubs

Karate lessons
Take karate lessons with Sensei Sam. Wear comfortable clothes and bring a bottle of water. Saturday morning in the gym.

Chess club
Come and play chess. Small, friendly chess club. All ages welcome. It's the game to exercise your brain! .... in Room 6.

Photography club
Digital photography class. Learn to take great pictures. Beginners welcome. .... Meet in the cafeteria.

Writing workshop
Write stories and poetry with help from a published author! .... Room 11.

Cooking club
Learn to bake cakes. Ask Mrs. Matthews for this week's recipe. Week 1: chocolate cake. We love baking! .... In the kitchen.

Japanese club
Learning Japanese with Akio is easy and fun. .... Mr. Brown's classroom.

2 Listen again and write the words next to the clues.

baking, ~~karate~~, Japanese, poetry, photography, chess

1 You use your hands and feet a lot. Karate
2 You have to think carefully. ....
3 You don't need a camera. ....
4 You just follow a recipe. ....
5 You have to have a good imagination. ....
6 You have to learn a new alphabet. ....

Chapter 2 22

Vocabulary

Lesson objectives: identify and use vocabulary for challenging hobbies
Key vocabulary: *baking, chess, Japanese, karate, photography, poetry*
Materials: Track 2.1

Warmer: Brainstorm vocabulary

Brainstorm hobbies vocabulary on the board with the class. Ask the children to work in pairs and put the hobbies in order of difficulty. Feedback as a class on the easiest and most difficult hobbies. Then elicit more challenging hobbies and write them on the board.

1 2.1 Listen and write the day and the time.

- Play Track 2.1. The children listen and write the day and the time for each club. Elicit answers. Whenever you elicit answers, remember to check with the class to see if they agree.

Audioscript

Karate lessons are on Saturday morning at ten o'clock. I've done karate for three years. You use your hands and feet a lot, and you have to be very strong.

Chess club is on Wednesday at lunchtime. Chess is a great game. You have to think carefully and guess what the other player is going to do.

Photography club is on Monday after school. You don't need a camera—you can borrow one. You do need a good eye, though.

Writing workshop is on Tuesday at lunchtime. We write short stories and poetry. You have to have a good imagination and you should enjoy reading.

Cooking club is on Thursday after school. We're learning about baking. The teacher shows us how to bake cakes. It isn't difficult. You just follow a recipe. This week, it's chocolate cake!

Japanese club is on Friday after school. Akio is a fantastic teacher. Speaking Japanese isn't so difficult, but you have to learn a new alphabet.

Answers

Karate lessons—Saturday morning
Chess club—Wednesday lunchtime
Photography club—Monday after school
Writing workshop—Tuesday lunchtime
Cooking club—Thursday after school
Japanese club—Friday after school

2 2.1 Listen again and write the words next to the clues.

- In the first clue, point out the word *feet*, which helps the children find the answer. Ask them to study familiar words in the other clues.
- Play Track 2.1. The children listen and choose the correct answers from the words supplied. Elicit answers.

Answers

1 karate **2** chess **3** photography **4** baking **5** poetry
6 Japanese

Optional activity: Our school clubs

Ask *Which clubs are there in your school? When do they happen?* Ask the children to invent a new club for their school with a challenging hobby. Have them write a notice for the board using Activity 1 as an example.

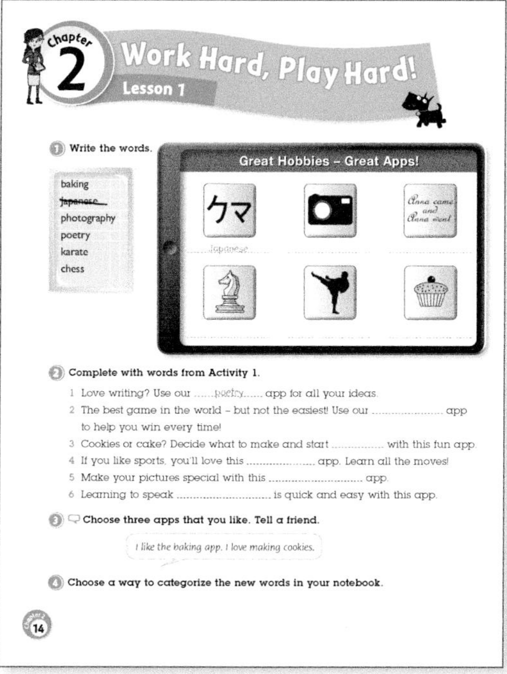

Chapter 2 Work Hard, Play Hard!
Lesson 1

1 Write the words.

baking
~~Japanese~~
photography
poetry
karate
chess

Great Hobbies – Great Apps!

クマ ... Japanese ...

Anna came and Anna went

2 Complete with words from Activity 1.

1 Love writing? Use our ......poetry...... app for all your ideas.
2 The best game in the world – but not the easiest! Use our .... app to help you win every time!
3 Cookies or cake? Decide what to make and start .... with this fun app.
4 If you like sports, you'll love this .... app. Learn all the moves!
5 Make your pictures special with this .... app.
6 Learning to speak .... is quick and easy with this app.

3 Choose three apps that you like. Tell a friend.

I like the baking app. I love making cookies.

4 Choose a way to categorize the new words in your notebook.

14

1 Write the words.

The children label the apps using the words supplied. Elicit answers.

Answers

Japanese, photography, poetry
chess, karate, baking

2 Complete with words from Activity 1.

The children complete the descriptions using words from Activity 1. Elicit answers.

Answers

1 poetry **2** chess **3** baking **4** karate **5** photography
6 Japanese

3 Choose three apps that you like. Tell a friend.

Elicit apps the children like. Encourage them to say why they like them. They then discuss their likes in pairs.

4 Choose a way to categorize the new words in your notebook.

Brainstorm appropriate categories, e.g. *creative/not creative, physical/mental, easy to do/difficult to do.* The children choose the best categories for them and list the words in their notebook.

Answers

Children's own answers.

Cooler: Play "Tic Tac Toe"

Play the game using *gym, recipe, brain, camera, play, photography, kitchen, poetry, learning* (see Games Bank p. 19). The children say a sentence with the word to win the box.

Competency Focus

Think! Critical Thinking

The children use critical thinking skills to understand the new vocabulary by using visual clues and processing the written and spoken forms.

Digital Resources

Digital Activity Book • Say *I want to start a new hobby. I like learning languages.* Children use *Pen* to circle the correct symbol in AB Activity 1. Repeat with other *I like …* sentences.

Grammar

Lesson objective: talk about how long they have done things
Key grammar: present perfect—statements, questions
Secondary language: *black belt, worked hard*
Materials: Grammar Worksheet 2A [TRC printout] (optional)

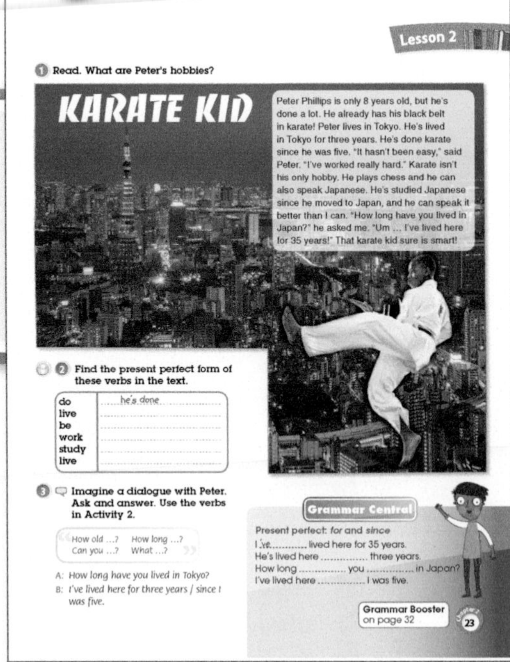

Lesson 2

1 Read. What are Peter's hobbies?

KARATE KID

Peter Phillips is only 8 years old, but he's done a lot. He already has his black belt in karate! Peter lives in Tokyo. He's lived in Tokyo for three years. He's done karate since he was five. "It hasn't been easy," said Peter. "I've worked really hard." Karate isn't his only hobby. He plays chess and he can also speak Japanese. He's studied Japanese since he moved to Japan, and he can speak it better than I can. "How long have you lived in Japan?" he asked me. "Um ... I've lived here for 35 years!" That karate kid sure is smart!

2 Find the present perfect form of these verbs in the text.

do	he's done
live	
be	
work	
study	
live	

3 Imagine a dialogue with Peter. Ask and answer. Use the verbs in Activity 2.

How old ...? How long ...?
Can you ...? What ...?

A: *How long have you lived in Tokyo?*
B: *I've lived here for three years / since I was five.*

Grammar Central

Present perfect: *for* and *since*
I 've .... lived here for 35 years.
He's lived here .... three years.
How long .... you .... in Japan?
I've lived here .... I was five.

Grammar Booster on page 32

Chapter 2 23

Warmer: Talk about karate

Elicit what the children know about karate. Ask *What color/order are the belts? Which is the most challenging?* Have them work in pairs to try to decide on the order from beginner level. (*white, yellow, orange, green, brown, black*)

1 Read. What are Peter's hobbies?

- Have the children look at the magazine article—a biography. Ask *What color is Peter's karate belt?* (*black*) *Is he good at karate? How old do you think he is?*
- The children read the text. Elicit Peter's hobbies. (*karate, chess, learning Japanese*)
- Ask *What type of person is Peter?* to elicit *smart, interesting, hard-working,* etc.

2 Find the present perfect form of these verbs in the text.

- Have the children read the text again and underline the example *he's done*. Remind them that present perfect is composed of *has/have* + past participle.
- They complete the grid. Elicit answers.

Answers

do—he's done, live—he's lived, be—it hasn't been, work—I've worked, learn—he's learned, live—have you lived?/I've lived

Grammar Central

Present perfect: *for* and *since*

Have the children complete the grammar examples. Elicit answers. Then elicit the rules for using *for* and *since* (*for* with a period of time and *since* with a point in time). The children write an example with each in their notebook. For extra practice, try the **Grammar Booster** section in the Student Book (p. 32).

Answers p. 32

Activity 1: **1** have, lived **2** have lived **3** since **4** has, done **5** for **6** has done

Activity 2: **1** I've played tennis since I was eight. **2** My brother studied English for four years. **3** He has done ballet since he was ten. **4** My aunt has lived in Brazil since last summer. **5** We have stayed at home for two weeks. **6** How long have you worked at the library?

3 Imagine a dialogue with Peter. Ask and answer. Use the verbs in Activity 2.

- Choose two children to read the example dialogue.
- Divide the class into pairs to practice the dialogue using the verbs in Activity 2.
- Have pairs perform for the class.

Optional activity: Chess Charlie and friends

Tell the class that Peter has friends named Chess Charlie, Photography Phil, and Cooking Cathy. Ask them to prepare questions in their notebook for them, e.g. *How long have you done photography?* Ask children to be Peter's friends and have the class ask them questions.

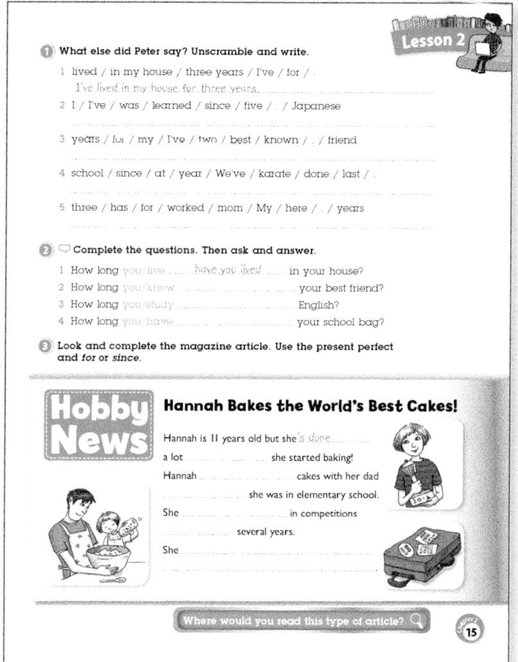
Lesson 2

1 What else did Peter say? Unscramble and write.

1 lived / in my house / three years / I've / for / .
I've lived in my house for three years.
2 I / I've / was / learned / since / five / . / Japanese
3 years / for / my / I've / two / best / known / . / friend
4 school / since / at / year / We've / karate / done / last / .
5 three / has / for / worked / mom / My / here / . / years

2 Complete the questions. Then ask and answer.

1 How long you/live have you lived in your house?
2 How long you/know .... your best friend?
3 How long you/study .... English?
4 How long you/have .... your school bag?

3 Look and complete the magazine article. Use the present perfect and *for* or *since*.

Hobby News

Hannah Bakes the World's Best Cakes!

Hannah is 11 years old but she's done .... a lot .... she started baking! Hannah .... cakes with her dad .... she was in elementary school. She .... in competitions .... several years. She ....

Where would you read this type of article?

15

1 What else did Peter say? Unscramble and write.

The children unscramble and write the questions. Elicit answers.

Answers

1 I've lived in my house for three years.
2 I've learned Japanese since I was five.
3 I've known my best friend for two years.
4 We've done karate at school since last year.
5 My mom has worked here for three years.

2 Complete the questions. Then ask and answer. 

The children complete the questions with the present perfect form of the verb prompts. Elicit the questions and sample answers. The children then ask and answer in pairs.

Answers

1 have you lived **2** have you known **3** have you studied **4** have you had

3 Look and complete the magazine article. Use the present perfect and *for* or *since*.

The children look at the pictures and say what Hannah has done. They complete the article text using the present perfect and *for/since*, then compare with a friend. Elicit answers in the form of sentences.

Ask *Where would you read this type of article?* Encourage the children to think about where we read about people's lives. (e.g. *in a magazine / a school newspaper*)

Answers (suggested)

's done, since, has made/baked, since, 's been, for, 's
Children's own answers.

Cooler: My personal hobbies

Ask the children to write three active hobbies they have done for a while. Have them mingle to find out who has the same hobby and how long they have done it, e.g. *How long have you played tennis? I've played tennis for three years / since I was eight.* Elicit examples from pairs.

Competency Focus

Learn

By reading the text and identifying the verbs in the present perfect, the children demonstrate their understanding of the new grammatical structures.

Digital Resources

Student eBook • Show the SB Grammar Central box. Use *Highlighter* to focus on key grammar structures.

Teacher Resource Center • For extra grammar practice, print out Grammar Worksheet 2A.

Reading: Story Extract

Lesson objectives: talk about what you've done; use the title and pictures to predict story content; read the extract from the modern fable *Andy and Grant* (middle)

Functional language: *I haven't seen you for ages! I've been at … I've stayed … since …*

Secondary language: *picked up, hole, ground, wasted time*

Materials: Tracks 2.2 and 2.3

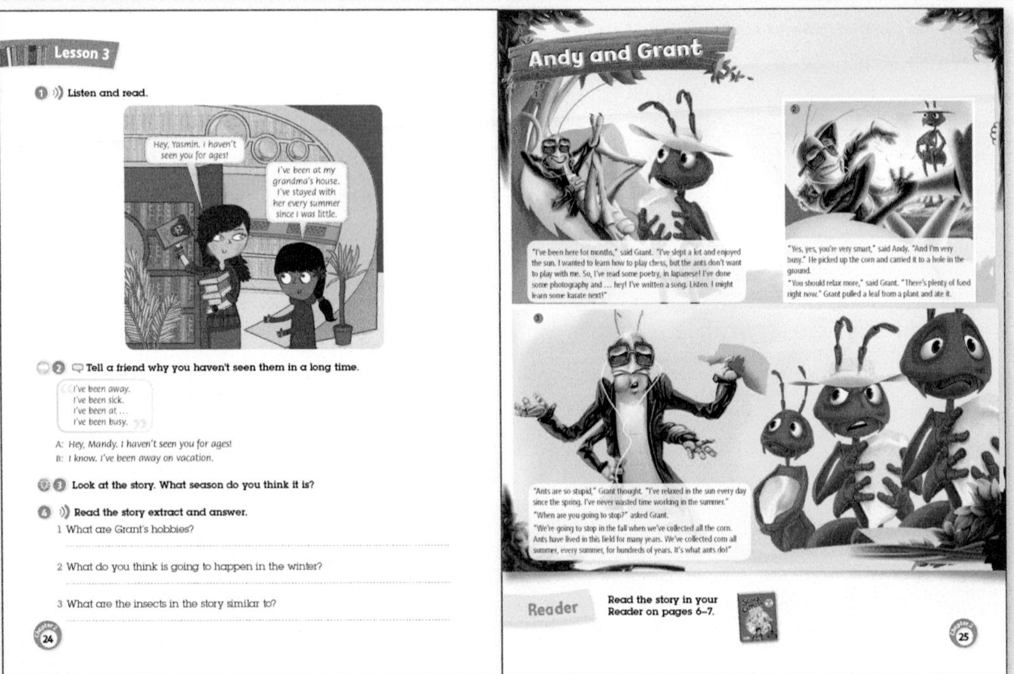

Lesson 3

1 Listen and read.

Hey, Yasmin. I haven't seen you for ages!

I've been at my grandma's house. I've stayed with her every summer since I was little.

2 Tell a friend why you haven't seen them in a long time.

I've been away.
I've been sick.
I've been at …
I've been busy.

A: Hey, Mandy. I haven't seen you for ages!
B: I know. I've been away on vacation.

3 Look at the story. What season do you think it is?

4 Read the story extract and answer.

1 What are Grant's hobbies?

2 What do you think is going to happen in the winter?

3 What are the insects in the story similar to?

24

Andy and Grant

"I've been here for months," said Grant. "I've slept a lot and enjoyed the sun. I wanted to learn how to play chess, but the ants don't want to play with me. So, I've read some poetry, in Japanese! I've done some photography and … hey! I've written a song. Listen. I might learn some karate next!"

"Yes, yes, you're very smart," said Andy. "And I'm very busy." He picked up the corn and carried it to a hole in the ground.

"You should relax more," said Grant. "There's plenty of food right now." Grant pulled a leaf from a plant and ate it.

"Ants are so stupid," Grant thought. "I've relaxed in the sun every day since the spring. I've never wasted time working in the summer."

"When are you going to stop?" asked Grant.

"We're going to stop in the fall when we've collected all the corn. Ants have lived in this field for many years. We've collected corn all summer, every summer, for hundreds of years. It's what ants do!"

Reader — Read the story in your Reader on pages 6–7.

25

Warmer: Review *for* and *since*

Call out time expressions with *for* or *since*, e.g. *since yesterday/March, for two days/a year.* Have the children stamp their feet when they hear a *for* expression and clap their hands for a *since* expression.

Functional language

1 2.2 Listen and read.

- Play Track 2.2. The children listen and read along.
- Play Track 2.2 again for them to repeat.
- Divide the class into pairs to practice the dialogue.

2 Tell a friend why you haven't seen them in a long time.

- Choose two children to read the example dialogue.
- The children practice in pairs, using the prompts supplied and adding details. Have pairs do a dialogue for the class.

Before reading

3 Look at the story. What season do you think it is?

- Have the children study the pictures, identify the characters, and describe the background. Ask *Can you describe the trees?*
- They read the story and underline words connected with nature, e.g. *sun, leaf.* Have them find the seasons in picture three—*spring, summer, fall. Which season is it?* (*summer*) *What are Andy and Grant doing in the summer?* (*Andy is working. Grant is relaxing.*) Check comprehension of *corn* and *collect.*

4 2.3 Read the story extract and answer.

- Have the children read the extract and answer question 1. Then play Track 2.3. They listen and complete their ideas for questions 2 and 3. Remind them to use reading skills (looking at the title, pictures, context, using their general knowledge, etc.).

- Elicit answers, but do not confirm predictions: explain that they will have to read the story to find out.

Answers

1 reading Japanese poetry, photography, writing songs
2 Children's own answers. **3** Children's own answers/people.

Lesson 3

1 Cross out the incorrect phrase. Then choose, write, and act out.

tomorrow / for a week / for ages / since this morning

I haven't seen you .... !

I've been .... I've .... since ....

2 Read the story in your Student Book. Circle the words that describe Andy. Then check (✓) the sentence that describes the story.

busy hard-working stupid smart relaxed

1 It has clues and puzzles.
2 It uses animal characters to teach us about life.
3 It's about a dark and scary place.

3 Write answers.

1 Is Grant happy with his life? Yes, he is.
2 Does Andy think Grant is smart?
3 Why doesn't Grant collect food for the winter?
4 Where does Andy put the food?
5 When is Andy going to relax?

4 Imagine Andy at home in the winter. Check (✓) the correct descriptions.

At home in the winter, Andy ...

is warm	is cold	
is alone	is hungry	is with his family
relaxes	works	has a lot to eat

16

1 Cross out the incorrect phrase. Then choose, write, and act out.

The children identify which phrase is incorrect. (*tomorrow*) They then choose one of the others and act out the dialogue with a friend. Encourage them to adapt and extend the dialogue. Have pairs act out for the class.

2 Read the story in your Student Book. Circle the words that describe Andy. Then check (✓) the sentence that describes the story.

The children read the extract again, and circle the appropriate adjectives for Andy. They then choose the sentence that best describes the story.

Answers

Circled: busy, hard-working, smart; ✓ *by* 2

3 Write answers.

The children write answers to the comprehension questions. Elicit answers.

Answers

1 Yes, he is. **2** No, he doesn't. **3** There is plenty of food now./He's doing other things. **4** In a hole in the ground. **5** In the fall/winter.

4 Imagine Andy at home in the winter. Check (✓) the correct descriptions.

Elicit ideas on the consequences of Andy's hard work and planning. The children then check the appropriate words. Elicit answers.

Answers

✓ *by:* is warm, relaxes, is with his family, has a lot to eat

Cooler: Play "The Chain Game"

Have the class stand. Say *I went to the forest and saw … an ant.* Have a child repeat the sentence and add an appropriate item, e.g. … *and saw an ant and a leaf.* Continue around the class. If a child makes a mistake or cannot continue, they are out and have to sit down. The last child standing wins.

Competency Focus

Collaborate and Communicate

The children work together, putting into practice new functional language by acting out a realistic dialogue.

Think! Critical Thinking

By analyzing visual clues and deducing from the context, the children use prediction skills to help them engage with the story.

Digital Resources

Student eBook • Have the children identify the words connected with nature in the story extract in SB Activity 3. Have them use *Pen* to circle the words for the seasons.

- TIP Choose the audio button on the SB page to access recordings for listening activities.

Andy and Grant

1
Grant was sunbathing and listening to music when he saw his friend Andy carrying some corn.

"Hey, Andy!" said Grant. "I haven't seen you for ages. Where have you been?"

"We've been in the field," answered Andy.

"What are you doing?" asked Grant. "Why are you working so hard? It's a beautiful day."

"We're collecting corn for the winter. We haven't finished yet," said Andy. "How long have you been there?"

"I've been here for months," said Grant. "I've slept a lot and enjoyed the sun. I wanted to learn how to play chess, but the ants don't want to play with me. So, I've read some poetry, in Japanese! I've done some photography and … hey! I've written a song. Listen. I might learn some karate next!"

2
"Yes, yes, you're very smart," said Andy. "And I'm very busy." He picked up the corn and carried it to a hole in the ground.

"You should relax more," said Grant. "There's plenty of food right now." Grant pulled a leaf from a plant and ate it.

3
"Ants are so stupid," Grant thought. "I've relaxed in the sun every day since the spring. I've never wasted time working in the summer."

"When are you going to stop?" asked Grant.

"We're going to stop in the fall when we've collected all the corn. Ants have lived in this field for many years. We've collected corn all summer, every summer, for hundreds of years. It's what ants do!"

"Haven't you heard? It's going to be a very cold winter," said Andy. But Grant wasn't listening. He was listening to his music and singing his song.

"Goodbye," said Andy. "I'm going to collect some more corn. I might see you later."

4
Summer turned to fall and fall turned to winter. The days were short and gray. The nights were long and dark. Grant was cold and hungry. There was no food. Then, he remembered the ants.

"I haven't seen them for a long time," he thought. "I'm going to find them. They might give me some food."

5
He went to Andy's house. Andy was baking a corn cake. "Hey, Andy! That cake smells good. I'm hungry," he said.

Andy said, "Sorry! I worked hard all summer while you were relaxing and listening to music. You've enjoyed yourself but you haven't been very smart. I can't help you. I need this corn for my family."

And he shut the door in Grant's face.

6
"What have I done? I've been so stupid," said Grant. "I didn't use my time well … and I've lost a friend."

Lesson objectives: read and understand the modern fable *Andy and Grant* in the Reader
Materials: Track 2.4; Reader

Warmer: Who did it?

Recap the story extract by describing an action from the story and have the children say if Andy or Grant did it, e.g. *He wrote a song.* (*Grant!*)

Story Summary

Andy, an ant, works hard all summer collecting corn for his family to eat during the winter. Grant, a grasshopper, relaxes and does not use his time well. Grant becomes hungry during the winter because he has not saved any food. Andy refuses to help him because he has his own family to feed.

Theme: the importance of working hard and saving for the future

2.4 While reading

- Have the children look at the pictures in the Reader. Ask *How does the landscape change each season?*
- Play Track 2.4. The children listen and read along. Ask *Did Andy help Grant?* (*no*)
- Ask questions to check comprehension, e.g. *What important information does Grant not listen to? (It's going to be a very cold winter.) Why does Grant want to find the ants? (because he's hungry) Why can't Andy help Grant? (He needs the corn for his family.)*
- Have the class read the story again, with children taking turns as Andy and Grant and using different voices for each character (see **Story Time**).

After reading: Reflect

- Ask questions to give the children the opportunity to think about the issues raised by the story, e.g. *How does Grant feel? How does Andy feel? Is Grant happy he enjoyed the summer?*

Optional activity: Think of a different character

Have the children look at the story again. In pairs, have them write another character's part using a different insect/animal. Ask pairs to present their ideas to the class.

Story Time

Using different voices

You can use different voices to emphasize the differences in the main characters. Read out part of the story, exaggerating the voices of each character—Grant has a laid-back accent while Andy's voice is quick and busy. Have children practice reading and copying the voices.

Reading Strategy

Drawing Conclusions

The ability to draw conclusions is very important when reading a story, as the underlying message might not always be obvious. A good reader draws conclusions based on facts extracted from the text as well as on their personal experiences and knowledge.

For additional explanation and activities, see the Literacy Handbook on the Teacher Resource Center.

Cooler: Disappearing text

Write sentences from Grant's part on the board and have the children read them using Grant's voice and accent. Erase a word from the first sentence and have the children say the whole sentence, remembering the erased word. Continue until they can say the whole sentence/text without any prompts.

Digital Resources

Reader eBook • Have the children recall their predictions for what is going to happen in the winter. Ask *How does Grant feel now?* The children raise their hand to answer as soon as they know.

- Look at Pictures 5 and 6. Elicit what is happening in both. Ask *What happens? How does Grant feel? How does Andy feel? Who do you agree with?* to elicit the children's opinion of what happens.

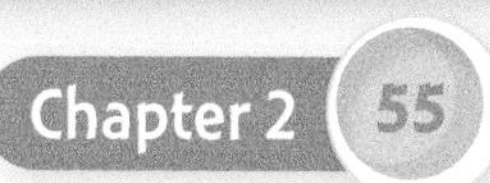

Reading Comprehension and Critical Literacy

Lesson objectives: understand and evaluate the story; relate story theme to personal experience; write about what hobbies you have done

Materials: Track 2.4; Reader

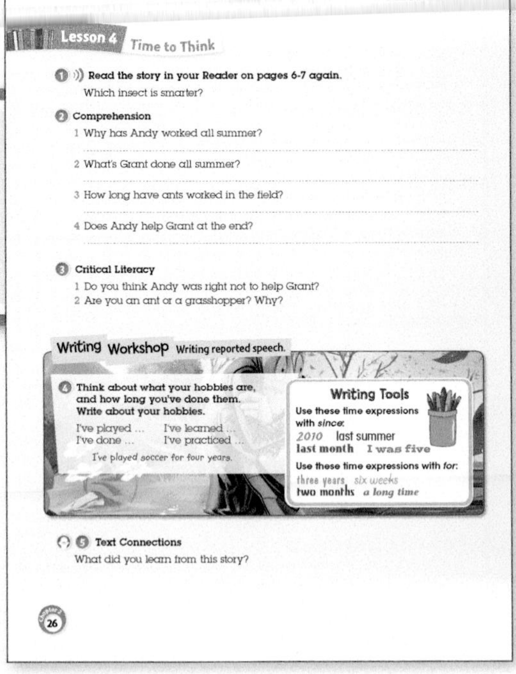

Lesson 4 Time to Think

1 Read the story in your Reader on pages 6-7 again.
Which insect is smarter?

2 Comprehension
1 Why has Andy worked all summer?
2 What's Grant done all summer?
3 How long have ants worked in the field?
4 Does Andy help Grant at the end?

3 Critical Literacy
1 Do you think Andy was right not to help Grant?
2 Are you an ant or a grasshopper? Why?

Writing Workshop Writing reported speech.

4 Think about what your hobbies are, and how long you've done them. Write about your hobbies.
I've played ... I've learned ...
I've done ... I've practiced ...
I've played soccer for four years.

Writing Tools
Use these time expressions with *since*:
2010 last summer
last month I was five
Use these time expressions with *for*:
three years six weeks
two months a long time

5 Text Connections
What did you learn from this story?

26

Note: Please ensure that your class has read the Reader story before you do this lesson.

Warmer: Play "Ready, Set, Draw"

Play the game using vocabulary from the story extract (see Games Bank p. 19). Then ask the children to work in pairs to retell what happened in the story extract.

1 2.4 Read the story in your Reader.

- Have the children read the story. (Alternatively, play Track 2.4 and have them read along.) Elicit whether they were correct in their predictions in Lesson 3 Activity 4.
- Ask *Who is smarter—the grasshopper or the ant?* Elicit ideas with reasons.

2 Comprehension

- Have the children answer the questions. Elicit answers. Discuss question 4 in more detail and ask *Why do you think Andy doesn't help Grant?*

Answers

1 Andy has worked all summer to collect corn/food for the winter. **2** Grant has relaxed and played all summer. **3** Ants have worked in the field for hundreds of years. **4** No, he doesn't.

3 Critical Literacy

- Ask *Was Andy right not to help Grant?* Encourage the children to relate the story to their own experience when giving their opinion.
- Have the children compare their own behavior with the characters and give examples of when they had to work hard, e.g. *an exam, a sports game*, etc.

Writing Workshop

Writing about what you've done

4 Think about what your hobbies are, and how long you've done them. Write about your hobbies.

Have a child read the example. Ask children to say what their hobbies are and how long they have done them, using time phrases with *since/for* from the **Writing Tools** box. The children write about four hobbies in their notebook, then compare with a friend.

5 Text Connections

- Write *Andy* and *Grant* on the board. Elicit two adjectives for each, e.g. *Andy—busy, hard-working; Grant—lazy, relaxed.*
- Ask *What kind of story is this? What can we learn?*
- Elicit the moral of the story. (*We should prepare for difficult times ahead.*)

Optional activity: Design a cover

Have the children design a book cover for this story, showing the main characters. Ask them to try to convey the message of the story in their drawing and the sentences for the blurb on the back of the book.

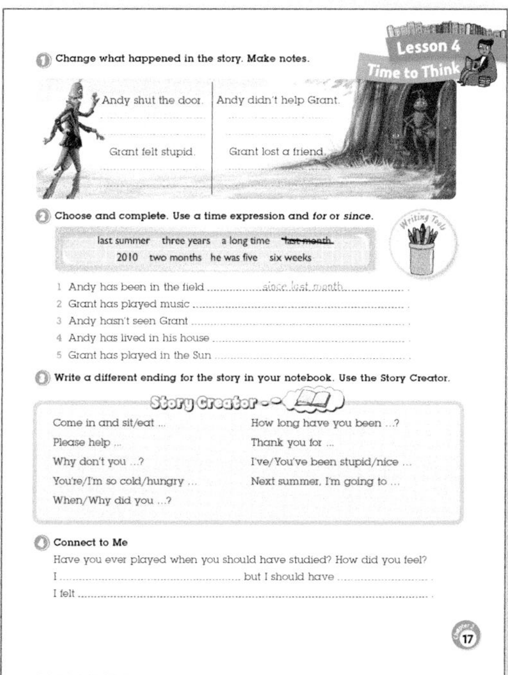

Lesson 4
Time to Think

1 Change what happened in the story. Make notes.

Andy shut the door.	Andy didn't help Grant.
Grant felt stupid.	Grant lost a friend.

2 Choose and complete. Use a time expression and *for* or *since*.

last summer three years a long time ~~last month~~ 2010 two months he was five six weeks

1 Andy has been in the field since last month.
2 Grant has played music ....
3 Andy hasn't seen Grant ....
4 Andy has lived in his house ....
5 Grant has played in the Sun ....

3 Write a different ending for the story in your notebook. Use the Story Creator.

Story Creator

Come in and sit/eat ...	How long have you been ...?
Please help ...	Thank you for ...
Why don't you ...?	I've/You've been stupid/nice ...
You're/I'm so cold/hungry ...	Next summer, I'm going to ...
When/Why did you ...?	

4 Connect to Me

Have you ever played when you should have studied? How did you feel?

I .... but I should have ....

I felt ....

17

1 Change what happened in the story. Make notes.

The children discuss a different ending to the story in pairs. They then make notes individually. Elicit ideas.

Answers

Children's own answers.

2 Choose and complete. Use a time expression and *for* or *since*.

The children complete the sentences appropriately, using the time expressions supplied and *for* or *since*. Elicit answers.

Answers (suggested)

since + last summer/last month/2010/he was five
for + three years/a long time/two months/six weeks

3 Write a different ending for the story in your notebook. Use the Story Creator.

Use the **Story Creator** prompts to elicit ideas. The children write a different ending to the story in their notebook, then compare with a friend. Invite children to read their ending for the class.

4 Connect to Me

Elicit examples of things the children have done instead of studying (e.g. *playing soccer*) and the consequences. The children write their own response, then compare with a friend.

Cooler: Play "Odd One Out"

Play the game with the vocabulary from the chapter so far (see Games Bank p. 19).

Competency Focus

Me: Critical Literacy

The children use critical literacy skills to reflect on the story and think about what they have learned from it.

Digital Resources

Student eBook, Digital Activity Book • TIP Use the forward and backward arrows to go to previous or later lessons.

Student eBook • Write *last month* on *Add personal note* and say *Last month—"for" or "since"?* Have a child write the answer on *Add personal note*. (*since*) Repeat with other *for/since* time expressions and different children.

Grammar and Reading

Lesson objective: talk about future plans and intentions
Key grammar: future—statements, questions with *going to/might*
Secondary language: *get into, famous, band*
Materials: Track 2.5; Grammar Worksheet 2B [TRC printout] (optional); children's cell phones or organizers (optional)

Lesson 5

Book Club

1 Listen and read. What jobs are Angelo and Yasmin going to do?

I might go and find something more interesting to listen to.

Angelo: I loved Grant's music. I'm going to go to music school.
Yasmin: You might not get into music school.
Angelo: I'm going to work really hard. Who knows? I might be a famous pop star one day!
Yasmin: Ha, ha! Oh, yeah? You aren't going to be famous!
Angelo: Don't laugh. It might take a long time, but you might see me on TV.
Scarlett: What are you going to do, Yasmin? Are you going to be a doctor?
Yasmin: Hm, I don't know. I'm not going to go to college right after school. I might travel for a year first. Then I might study to be a vet. Or I might be a singer and join your band, Angelo.
Angelo: Oh, no!

2 Write about the characters' future plans.

Definite plans	Possible actions
Angelo is going to go to music school. He's going to work really hard.	He might be famous.

3 Talk to a friend about your weekend plans.

I'm going to … I'm not going to …
I might … I might not …

A: What are you going to do this weekend?
B: I'm going to play soccer on Saturday. What about you?
A: Oh! I don't know, I might come and watch.

Grammar Central

going to and *might*
I'm ..going to... go to music school.
She isn't .... go to college.
He .... be a singer.
Are you .... be a vet?

Grammar Booster on page 33

27

Warmer: Jobs for famous people

Write *famous* and *normal* on the board. Ask the children to suggest what jobs famous people do, e.g. *pop star, soccer player.* In pairs, have them write down five famous jobs and five normal jobs. Write their suggestions on the board. Give an extra point to pairs who can name famous people for each job.

1 2.5 Listen and read. What jobs are Angelo and Yasmin going to do?

- Play Track 2.5 and ask children to listen for possible jobs.
- Play Track 2.5 again. Elicit the possible future jobs for Angelo and Yasmin. (*Angelo might be a pop star. Yasmin might be a vet.*)

2 Write about the characters' future plans. 

- Have children identify the verbs used for definite plans (*going to*) and possible actions (*might*).
- Ask the children to find and note down examples of each category in their notebook. Elicit responses.

Answers

Definite plans: Angelo is going to go to music school. He's going to work really hard. Yasmin isn't going to go to college right after school.
Possible actions: He might be famous. It might take a long time. They might see him on TV. She might travel. She might study to be a vet. She might join Angelo's band.

Grammar Central

going to and *might*

Have the children complete the grammar examples. Elicit answers. Elicit the structure for plans and intentions (*going to*) and the structure for possible actions (*might*). Elicit personalized examples. For extra practice, try the **Grammar Booster** section in the Student Book (p. 98) and Activity Book (pp. 33–35).

Answers p. 33

Activity 1: **1** Is, going to **2** 's/is going to **3** isn't going to **4** might **5** might not

Activity 2: **1** going to join **2** 'm (am) not going to take **3** might go **4** going to do **5** might not win **6** 'm (am) going to try

p. 34

Activity 1: **1** for **2** I've been **3** We've stayed **4** we're going to move **5** for **6** I'm going to join **7** might try **8** since

Activity 2: Ben has been really busy since he returned from China. **2**. He has stayed with his grandma for three months. **3** He's going to move next month to a new house. **4** He's been at his new school for six weeks. **5** He isn't going to try Tae Kwon Do.

p. 35

Activity 1: **1** for **2** since **3** since **4** were **5** for **6** invented **7** had to practice **8** has uploaded **9** have helped **10** used to take **11** going to **12** might **13** going to

Activity 2: Children's own answers.

3 Talk to a friend about your weekend plans. 

- Choose two children to read the example dialogue.
- Divide the class into pairs to practice the dialogue using the prompts supplied and their own ideas. Have pairs perform for the class.

Optional activity: Make plans—use an organizer!

Have the children take out their organizer (calendar/cell phone, if you allow phones in class). Ask them to make a definite plan for this weekend and add a note to their schedule. Elicit plans, e.g. *On Sunday, I'm going to play soccer in the morning.*

Lesson 5

(1) Complete Scarlett's old diary entry.

might study
's going to bring
'm not going to take
~~is going to talk~~
might stay
's going to show

Tomorrow, a famous artist 1 ...is going to talk... to us. He 2 .... his paintings into the class so that we can see them. After lunch, he 3 .... us how to draw animals because they're very difficult. I haven't decided yet, but I 4 .... art at college after school. Rufus doesn't know if he wants to go to the talk or not. He says he 5 .... home because he doesn't like art very much. We have to take a picture to show the artist, but I 6 .... this picture of Hamish – it's awful!

(2) Now circle the definite plans and underline the possible actions in the diary.

(3) Write the questions. Then ask and answer with a friend.

1 What / you / do / this evening? ..What are you going to do this evening?..
2 you / watch / a movie? ..Are you going to watch a movie?..
3 you / go / to the park? ....
4 you / chat online / with your friends? ....
5 What / you / get / for your birthday? ....

What are you going to do this evening?
I might go to my friend's house. What about you?
I'm going to bake a cake.

(4) Write about what you're going to do and might do this evening.

After school, I'm going to ....
I might not ....
After that, I ....

18

1 Complete Scarlett's old diary entry.

The children complete the text using the verb forms supplied. Elicit answers.

Answers

1 is going to talk **2** 's going to bring **3** 's going to show **4** might study **5** might stay **6** 'm not going to take

2 Now circle the definite plans and underline the possible actions in the diary.

The children circle the definite plans (*going to*) and underline the possible actions (*might*) in the text. Elicit answers.

Answers

Circled (definite plans): is going to talk, he's going to bring, he's going to show, not going to take
Underlined (possible actions): might study, might stay

3 Write the questions. Then ask and answer with a friend.

The children write questions with *going to*. Elicit answers. They then ask and answer in pairs.

Answers

1 What are you going to do this evening? **2** Are you going to watch a movie? **3** Are you going to go to the park? **4** Are you going to chat online with your friends? **5** What are you going to get for your birthday?

4 Write about what you're going to do and might do this evening.

Elicit ideas, supplying any necessary vocabulary for local activities. Have the children write their answers, then compare with a friend. Elicit answers.

Answers

Children's own answers.

Cooler: Play "20 Questions"

Tell the children to imagine a job for the class to guess. The class ask questions with *going to* to elicit *Yes, I am. / No, I'm not.* or *I might.* answers. Tally the number of questions. Whoever keeps the class guessing the longest wins!

Competency Focus

Learn

The children demonstrate their understanding of the new language by reading the text and completing the activity.

Digital Resources

Digital Activity Book • Have children use *Pen* to write AB Activity 4 answers. The class raises their hand if they have the same response.

Teacher Resource Center • For extra grammar practice, print out Grammar Worksheet 2B.

Lesson 6

1 Listen and sing. What is the most important thing?

Life is Full of Challenges

Life is full of challenges.
Competitions, tests.
You might win or lose; you might pass or fail.
Just try your very best.

If you're going to go to college,
You have to get the grades.
If at first you don't succeed,
Try again; you've got it made!

Trophies look good.
And certificates on the wall.
But remember taking part,
Is most important of all!

2 Talk to a friend about your past and future. Use the words from the song.

Have you ever ...? I've ... I haven't ...
I might ... I want to ...
Are you going to ...?

A: Have you ever won a competition?
B: No, I haven't. I'm going to take part in a dance competition. I might win!

Spelling Central

Circle the words with double consonants *ll*.

Write the words in the chart. Can you add more *ll* words?

ll at the end	*ll* in the middle
full	

28

Vocabulary, Song, and Spelling

Lesson objectives: identify and talk about past achievements and future challenges; practice spelling words with double consonant *ll*
Key vocabulary: *certificates, challenges, college, competitions, fail, grades, pass, succeed, taking part, tests, trophies*
Secondary language: *win, lose, got it made*
Materials: Track 2.6; Phonics Worksheet 2 [TRC printout] (optional)

Warmer: Pre-teach vocabulary

Pre-teach the vocabulary by giving definitions or sentences showing the words in context, e.g. *A certificate is a piece of paper you get when you are good at something. The work was very hard but Ben liked a challenge.* Repeat the definitions/sentences, pausing to elicit the key word.

1 2.6 Listen and sing. What is the most important thing?

- Play Track 2.6. Ask the children to focus on words connected with tests and challenges. Ask *What is the most important thing?* (*taking part*)
- Play Track 2.6 again for the children to sing along.
- Elicit what types of activities the children get trophies and certificates for.

2 Talk to a friend about your past and future. Use the words from the song.  

- Choose two children to read the example dialogue. Ask the class to form further questions about different activities with *Have you ever …?*
- The children ask and answer in pairs using the prompts supplied. Invite pairs to perform their dialogue for the class.

Spelling Central

Double consonant *ll*

Write *full* on the board and circle the double consonant *ll*. Ask the children to circle words with *ll* in the song. Write them on the board and have the children repeat. Have the children list more words with double *ll* in their notebook. (e.g. *doll, ball, call, gorilla, dollar, umbrella*) Provide clues as necessary, e.g. *It's a very big monkey.* Children write more suggestions on the board.

Answers

Circled: full, challenges, college, wall, all
ll at the end: full, wall, all
ll in the middle: challenges, college

Optional activity: My challenges

Have the children think about things they have already achieved and things they are going to do. Ask them to make a "report card" with their best achievements, e.g. *I've got a good grade in English this year.* Ask them to add two sentences about next year and illustrate it.

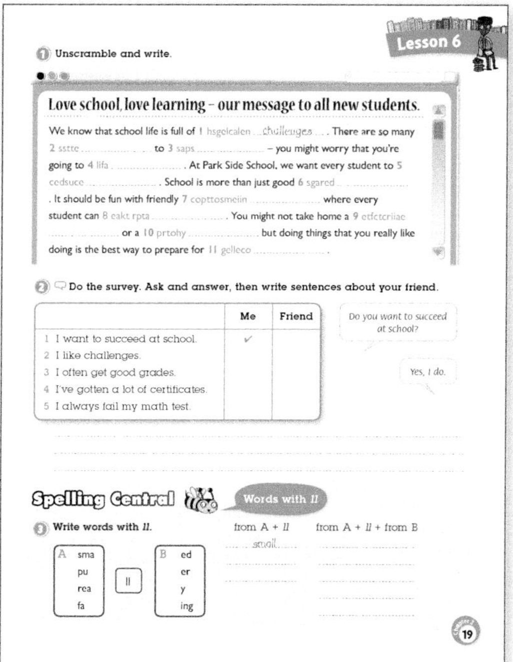

Lesson 6

1 Unscramble and write.

Love school, love learning – our message to all new students.

We know that school life is full of 1 hsgelcalen *challenges*. There are so many 2 sstte ………… to 3 saps ………… – you might worry that you're going to 4 lifa …………. At Park Side School, we want every student to 5 cedsuce …………. School is more than just good 6 sgared …………. It should be fun with friendly 7 copttosmeiin ………… where every student can 8 eakt rpta …………. You might not take home a 9 etfctcriiae ………… or a 10 prtohy ………… but doing things that you really like doing is the best way to prepare for 11 gelleco ………….

2 Do the survey. Ask and answer, then write sentences about your friend.

	Me	Friend
1 I want to succeed at school.	✓	
2 I like challenges.		
3 I often get good grades.		
4 I've gotten a lot of certificates.		
5 I always fail my math test.		

Spelling Central — Words with *ll*

3 Write words with *ll*.

A: sma, pu, rea, fa — ll — B: ed, er, y, ing

from A + *ll*: *small*

from A + *ll* + from B

19

Cooler: Mime time

Have the children choose one of the words with double *ll* to mime for the class to guess and spell, e.g. *gorilla, umbrella, college.*

Competency Focus

Collaborate and communicate

The children work together and use their interpersonal skills to share their ideas on the topic, incorporating the new vocabulary.

1 Unscramble and write.

The children unscramble the words, using clues in the text to work them out. They then check in pairs. Elicit answers.

Answers

1 challenges **2** tests **3** pass **4** fail **5** succeed **6** grades **7** competitions **8** take part **9** certificate **10** trophy **11** college

2 Do the survey. Ask and answer, then write sentences about your friend.

Elicit the survey questions first. The children then work in pairs to ask and answer. They use the survey information to write sentences about their friend. Elicit responses.

Answers

Children's own answers.

3 Write words with *ll*.

To practice the **Spelling Central** feature, write *sma–* on the board and ask the children to make words with *ll*, e.g. *small, smaller.* They use the prompts to write down as many words as they can. They then compare their words in pairs. Choose children to write their words on the board.

Answers

ll at the end: small, pull, fall

ll in the middle: smaller, pulled, pulling, really, falling

Digital Resources

Student eBook • After SB Activity 2, play Music Video 2.1 and encourage the children to sing along, using the graphic lyrics on screen. Associating movements with words makes them more memorable. Pause the video for the children to continue singing.

Teacher Resource Center • For phonics practice, print out Phonics Worksheet 2.

Student eBook • Encourage the children to share Music Video 2.1 at home with their family.

CLIL: Social sciences—Volunteer projects

Lesson objective: find out about charity expeditions
Materials: CLIL Graphic Organizer 2 [TRC printout] (optional); world map in an atlas or on the Internet (optional)

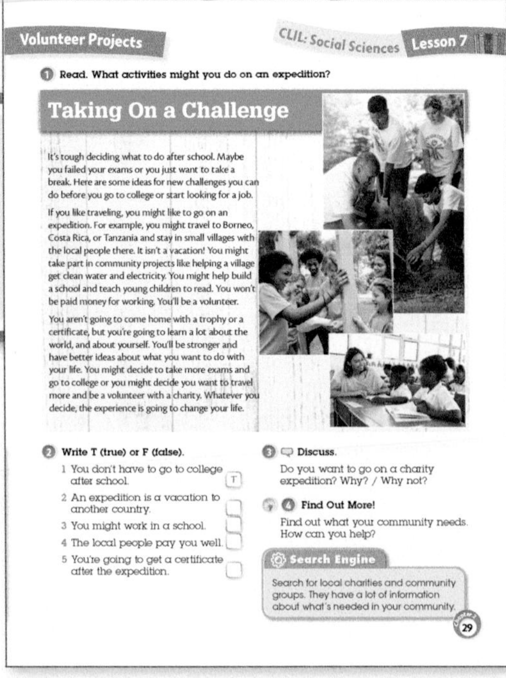

Volunteer Projects — CLIL: Social Sciences — Lesson 7

1 Read. What activities might you do on an expedition?

Taking On a Challenge

It's tough deciding what to do after school. Maybe you failed your exams or you just want to take a break. Here are some ideas for new challenges you can do before you go to college or start looking for a job.

If you like traveling, you might like to go on an expedition. For example, you might travel to Borneo, Costa Rica, or Tanzania and stay in small villages with the local people there. It isn't a vacation! You might take part in community projects like helping a village get clean water and electricity. You might help build a school and teach young children to read. You won't be paid money for working. You'll be a volunteer.

You aren't going to come home with a trophy or a certificate, but you're going to learn a lot about the world, and about yourself. You'll be stronger and have better ideas about what you want to do with your life. You might decide to take more exams and go to college or you might decide you want to travel more and be a volunteer with a charity. Whatever you decide, the experience is going to change your life.

2 Write T (true) or F (false).

1 You don't have to go to college after school. T
2 An expedition is a vacation to another country.
3 You might work in a school.
4 The local people pay you well.
5 You're going to get a certificate after the expedition.

3 Discuss.

Do you want to go on a charity expedition? Why? / Why not?

4 Find Out More!

Find out what your community needs. How can you help?

Search Engine

Search for local charities and community groups. They have a lot of information about what's needed in your community.

29

Warmer: Play "The A-Z Game"

Play the game using vocabulary that the children can connect to the pictures on the page (see Games Bank p. 19).

1 Read. What activities might you do on an expedition?

- Ask the children to study the pictures again. Ask *Where do you think they are?* to elicit countries.
- The children read the text. Ask *What activities might you do as a volunteer on an expedition?* (*help a village get clean water and electricity, build a school, teach*)

2 Write T (true) or F (false).

- Elicit why the first sentence is true. (*You might have failed your exams or you might want to take a break before going to college.*)
- The children read the text again and decide for the other sentences. Elicit answers, including the correct version of the false sentences.

Answers

1 T **2** F **3** T **4** F **5** F

3 Discuss.

- Ask *Would you like to go on a charity expedition?* Have the children raise their hands for *yes.* Ask *What activity would you do?* Encourage them to suggest new ideas.
- Now ask them to raise their hands for *no.* Ask them what difficulties and problems they might face.

4 Find Out More!

- The children research what their community needs and how they can help achieve this. The **Search Engine** feature gives support on where to look. The children will need to complete this research before doing the follow-up activity in the Activity Book. (It could be set as homework.)

Optional activity: Find the places on a map!

Ask the children to identify the three expedition places in the text. (*Borneo, Costa Rica, Tanzania*) Ask *Which continents are these countries in?* Use an atlas or Internet map to show the children the location of each place. They can choose and say which place they want to go to.

Lesson 7 CLIL

~~succeed~~ might
website take part
certificate going to

1 Read and complete.

Pick Up Trash Day

We've helped a village in Nicaragua get clean water. It's changed their lives. Now we need money for more projects like this – and we need YOUR help to 1 ....succeed.... . 2 .... in Pick Up Trash Day on July 15th. For every street we clean, we make $5 for Nicaragua. It 3 .... be hard work, but it's 4 .... be fun, too! Everyone who takes part gets a 5 ....

Go to our 6 .... for more information or to give money.

2 Use your Student Book research to make an Info Card. Write about what your community needs.

Find Out More!

children schools trees food sports water

3 Do a project to help your community.

Try it Out

Choose a project or decide on a challenge to make money.
Make posters and ask friends and family to take part.
Do the challenge. Make it fun for everyone.
After, thank everyone who helped you and tell them what you succeeded in doing. Give them certificates!

4 Select and store information on this topic in the Class Info Hub.

20

1 Read and complete.

The children read the text. Ask *Who does the project help?* (*people in Nicaragua who need clean water; people in their own community*) They read the text again and complete it using the words supplied. Elicit answers.

Answers

1 succeed **2** Take part **3** might **4** going to **5** certificate **6** website

2 Use your Student Book research to make an Info Card. Write about what your community needs.

Divide the class into groups. Have the children pool the information learned from their research in the Student Book and the Activity Book. The children write about and illustrate their ideas individually. Have the groups present their Info Cards to the class.

Answers

Children's own answers.

3 Do a project to help your community.

Brainstorm ideas for projects to help the community, e.g. *plant trees, recycling, collect food, clothes and toys, read to people*, etc. Read the **Try It Out** instructions aloud. Discuss with the class how they can set up the project and write a step-by-step plan on the board. Divide the children into groups to carry out their project. Give support as necessary. The groups present their ideas to the class.

4 Select and store information on this topic in the Class Info Hub.

Have the children vote for the five most interesting Info Cards. Archive these in your Class Hub (see p. 41) in a folder called **Chapter 2 Our Community**.

Cooler: Remember the word

Have the children close their books. Read out a sentence from the text, replacing a word with the nonsense word *zonk*. Elicit the missing word. Repeat with a different sentence. The children continue in pairs.

Ask the children to bring in for the next lesson some photos or draw pictures of some of their recent achievements they are proud of (photos could be on cell phones).

Competency Focus

Act

The children carry out research to find out more about the needs of their local community and identify solutions to local problems. They learn more about welfare in society and the contribution they can make.

Digital Resources

Digital Activity Book • As support for less confident children, you could elicit findings orally before the children do AB Activity 2.

Student eBook, Digital Activity Book • Use *Add personal note* to remind you to ask the children to bring in pictures of their recent achievements for the next lesson.

Teacher Resource Center • Print out CLIL Graphic Organizer 2 for the children to use in collating their Find Out More! research.

CLIL eBook • The children can use the CLIL eBook to expand their knowledge of the lesson topic.

Writing Project

Lesson objectives: review language from Chapter 2; make a "My Life" vision board and present it to the class
Materials: the children's own photos of their achievements (Warmer); Writing Template 2 [TRC printout] (optional)

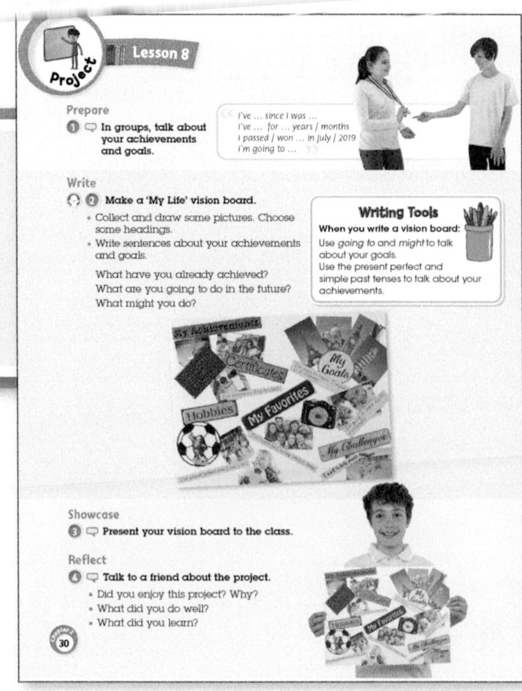
Project
Lesson 8

Prepare

1 In groups, talk about your achievements and goals.

I've … since I was …
I've … for … years / months
I passed / won … in July / 2019
I'm going to …

Write

2 Make a 'My Life' vision board.

- Collect and draw some pictures. Choose some headings.
- Write sentences about your achievements and goals.

What have you already achieved?
What are you going to do in the future?
What might you do?

Writing Tools
When you write a vision board:
Use *going to* and *might* to talk about your goals.
Use the present perfect and simple past tenses to talk about your achievements.

Showcase

3 Present your vision board to the class.

Reflect

4 Talk to a friend about the project.

- Did you enjoy this project? Why?
- What did you do well?
- What did you learn?

Chapter 2
30

Warmer: Look at my photos

Have the children show photos of their achievements to the class. Photos could be on their cell phones. Have them work in groups, show their photos, and say what they have done, e.g. *I've won a game with my soccer team.*

Prepare

1 In groups, talk about your achievements and goals.

- Have the children look at the prompts in Activity 1. Ask them to give examples of achievements with the present perfect and goals using *going to/might,* e.g. *I've won a swimming competition. I'm going to take part in a quiz.*
- The children talk about their achievements and goals in groups. Groups report back to the class.

Write

2 Make a "My Life" vision board.

- Have the children look at the vision board headings as a model for their own writing.
- Read the **Writing Tools** box together. Elicit examples of the present perfect for their achievements and *going to/might* for goals.
- The children prepare an outline, using the instructions and the headings. They write and illustrate their vision board, then compare with a friend. Give support as necessary.

Showcase

3 Present your vision board to the class. 

- Choose children to present their vision boards to the class. Ask the class to listen and choose the most interesting activity on each board.

Reflect

4 Vote for the best vision boards. 

- Choose three or four really good vision boards. Have these children stand at the front of the class, holding up their vision boards for the class to compare. Then, have a class vote for the best one.

Optional activity: Vocabulary extension

Elicit hobbies the children might try in the future, e.g. *sailing, surfing.* Write them on the board and ask them each to choose one secretly. The children mingle and ask *Are you going to …?* to find someone else with the same hobby.

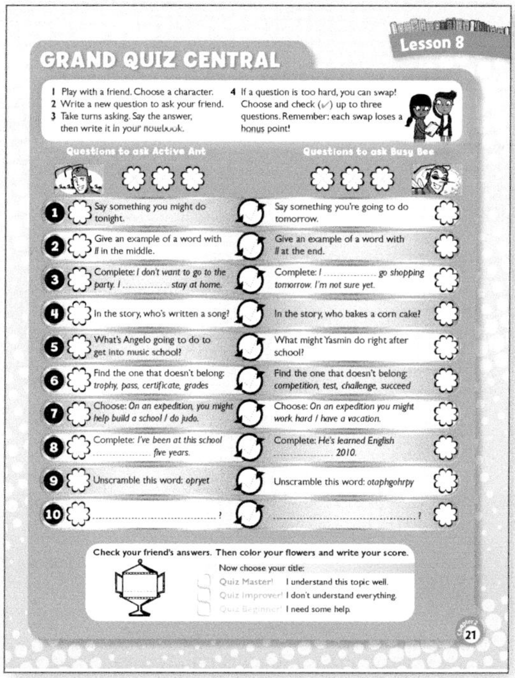

Lesson 8

GRAND QUIZ CENTRAL

1 Play with a friend. Choose a character.
2 Write a new question to ask your friend.
3 Take turns asking. Say the answer, then write it in your notebook.
4 If a question is too hard, you can swap! Choose and check (✓) up to three questions. Remember: each swap loses a bonus point!

	Questions to ask Active Ant	Questions to ask Busy Bee
1	Say something you might do tonight.	Say something you're going to do tomorrow.
2	Give an example of a word with *ll* in the middle.	Give an example of a word with *ll* at the end.
3	Complete: *I don't want to go to the party. I .... stay at home.*	Complete: *I .... go shopping tomorrow. I'm not sure yet.*
4	In the story, who's written a song?	In the story, who bakes a corn cake?
5	What's Angelo going to do to get into music school?	What might Yasmin do right after school?
6	Find the one that doesn't belong: *trophy, pass, certificate, grades*	Find the one that doesn't belong: *competition, test, challenge, succeed*
7	Choose: *On an expedition, you might help build a school / do judo.*	Choose: *On an expedition you might work hard / have a vacation.*
8	Complete: *I've been at this school .... five years.*	Complete: *He's learned English .... 2010.*
9	Unscramble this word: *opryet*	Unscramble this word: *otaphgohrpy*
10	...............................?	...............................?

Check your friend's answers. Then color your flowers and write your score.

Now choose your title:

Quiz Master! I understand this topic well.
Quiz Improver! I don't understand everything.
Quiz Beginner! I need some help.

Chapter 2 21

Grand Quiz Central

See p. 43 for details of how to take the quiz.

Answers

1 I might ... / I'm going to ... **2** *Any two of:* called, pulling, hello, filled, etc. / small, ball, ill, full, etc.
3 'm going to / might **4** Grant / Andy **5** He's going to work really hard. / She might travel for a year. **6** pass / succeed **7** build a school / work hard **8** for / since **9** poetry / photography **10** Children's own answers.

Cooler: Play "True or False"

Tell the children you are going to say a sentence describing your own achievements and that they have to decide if it is true or false, e.g. *I have climbed Mount Everest.* (*false*) *I have visited a different country.* (*true*) Have children make true/false sentences for the class.

Competency Focus

Me

The children invent and write their own vision board, developing their sense of achievement and setting goals for the future.

Digital Resources

Teacher Resource Center • Print out Writing Template 2 to use for the SB writing activity.

Language Review

Lesson objective: review language from Chapter 2
Materials: Tracks 2.7, AB 2.1 and AB 2.2

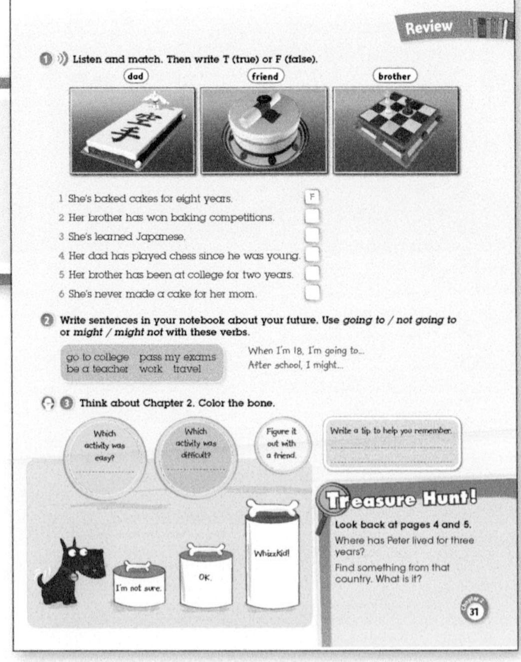
Review

1 Listen and match. Then write T (true) or F (false).

dad friend brother

1 She's baked cakes for eight years. F
2 Her brother has won baking competitions.
3 She's learned Japanese.
4 Her dad has played chess since he was young.
5 Her brother has been at college for two years.
6 She's never made a cake for her mom.

2 Write sentences in your notebook about your future. Use *going to / not going to* or *might / might not* with these verbs.

go to college pass my exams be a teacher work travel

When I'm 18, I'm going to...
After school, I might...

3 Think about Chapter 2. Color the bone.

Which activity was easy? Which activity was difficult? Figure it out with a friend. Write a tip to help you remember.

I'm not sure. OK. Whizz Kid!

Treasure Hunt!
Look back at pages 4 and 5.
Where has Peter lived for three years?
Find something from that country. What is it?

31

Warmer: Brainstorm vocabulary

Draw an oval for a mind map on the board and write *Hobbies* inside it. Add categories: *Sports, Games, Other.* The children copy the mind map and add their own vocabulary.

1 2.7 Listen and match. Then write T (true) or F (false).

- Play Track 2.7. The children listen and match.
- Play Track 2.7. Children write T (true) or F (false).

Audioscript

I like baking and I've baked cakes since I was eight years old. I'm twelve now. Here are some of the cakes I've baked. My brother took most of the pictures. He likes photography. He's won a lot of photography competitions.

This cake was for my friend who likes karate. She has a lot of trophies. It was a big challenge! It has Japanese writing on it and I haven't learned Japanese!

I made this cake for my dad last year because he's really good at chess. He's played since he was young.

And look at this cake. It has a certificate! I made it for my brother because he passed his exams. He's been away at college for three years. I've never made a cake for my mom. She's a chef!

Answers

dad—chess cake, friend—Japanese cake, brother—certificate cake
1 F **2** F **3** F **4** T **5** F **6** T

2 Write sentences in your notebook about your future. Use *going to / not going to* or *might / might not* with these verbs.

- The children write a few sentences in their notebook.

Answers

Children's own answers.

3 Think about Chapter 2. Color the bone. 

- Have the children look back at Chapter 2 and color the bone to evaluate their progress (self-evaluation). Discuss ideas for using examples. The children write a tip.

Treasure Hunt!

Ask *Where has Peter lived for three years?* (*Tokyo*) *Which country is it in?* (*Japan*) Have the children look at pp. 4–5 to find something from that country. (*comic book*)

Cooler: Play "Running Board Race"

Play the game using vocabulary from the chapter (see Games Bank p. 19).

Competency Focus

Me: Self-evaluation

The children reflect on the chapter and express their opinions about their own progress.

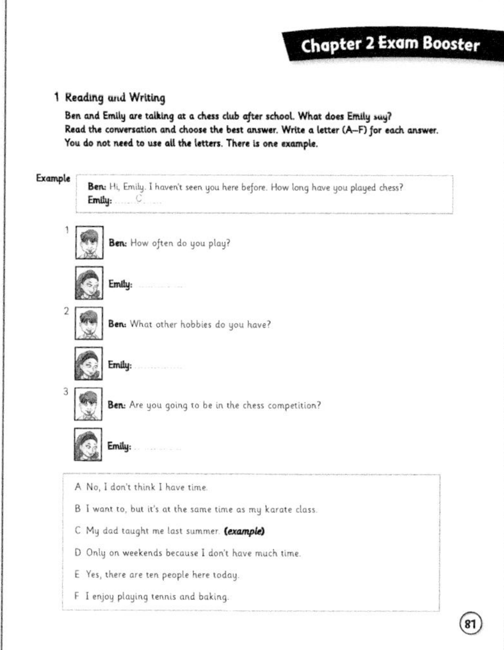

Chapter 2 Exam Booster

1 Reading and Writing

Ben and Emily are talking at a chess club after school. What does Emily say?
Read the conversation and choose the best answer. Write a letter (A–F) for each answer.
You do not need to use all the letters. There is one example.

Example
Ben: Hi, Emily. I haven't seen you here before. How long have you played chess?
Emily: ...C...

1 Ben: How often do you play?
Emily: ....

2 Ben: What other hobbies do you have?
Emily: ....

3 Ben: Are you going to be in the chess competition?
Emily: ....

A No, I don't think I have time.
B I want to, but it's at the same time as my karate class.
C My dad taught me last summer. (example)
D Only on weekends because I don't have much time.
E Yes, there are ten people here today.
F I enjoy playing tennis and baking.

81

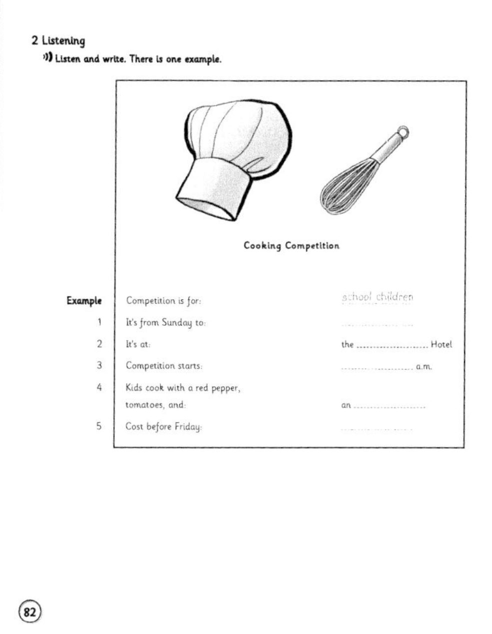

2 Listening

Listen and write. There is one example.

Cooking Competition

Example	Competition is for:	school children
1	It's from Sunday to:	....
2	It's at:	the .... Hotel
3	Competition starts:	.... a.m.
4	Kids cook with a red pepper, tomatoes, and:	an ....
5	Cost before Friday:	....

82

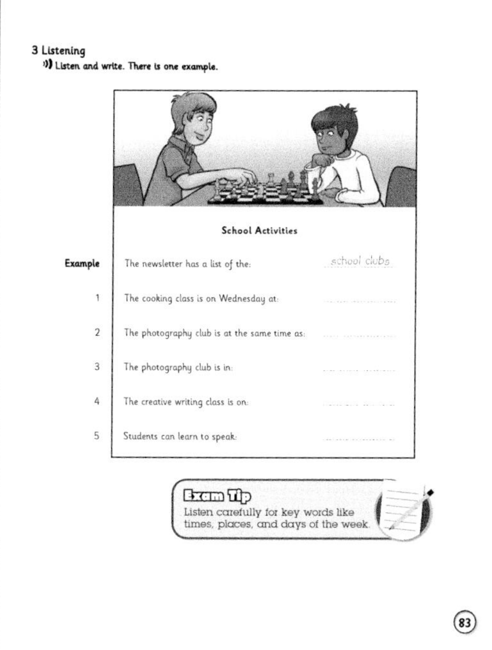

3 Listening

Listen and write. There is one example.

School Activities

Example	The newsletter has a list of the:	school clubs
1	The cooking class is on Wednesday at:	....
2	The photography club is at the same time as:	....
3	The photography club is in:	....
4	The creative writing class is on:	....
5	Students can learn to speak:	....

Exam Tip
Listen carefully for key words like times, places, and days of the week.

83

1 Reading and Writing. Ben and Emily are talking at a chess club after school. What does Emily say? Read the conversation and choose the best answer. Write a letter (A–F) for each answer. You do not need to use all the letters. There is one example.

The children read the questions and write the letter for the appropriate response each time. Elicit answers.

Answers

1 d **2** f **3** a

2 AB 2.1 Listening. Listen and write. There is one example.

The children read the notice. Play AB Track 2.1 twice. They listen and write the answer for each prompt. Elicit answers.

Answers (Audioscript on p. 222)

1 Tuesday **2** Dalmeny **3** 9 **4** an onion **5** $30

3 AB 2.2 Listening. Listen and write. There is one example.

Play AB Track 2.2. Children listen and write the answer for each prompt. Elicit answers.

Answers (Audioscript on p. 222)

1 3pm **2** the cooking class **3** Room 7 **4** Thursday **5** Japanese

Digital Resources

Teacher Resource Center • Print out Test Chapter 2 to use at the end of this lesson. The Test Generator also allows you to create customized tests.

- Print out Festival Worksheet: Halloween to expand the children's knowledge of celebrations throughout the world.

Chapter 3

Sleep and Dreams

Overview

Key Grammar

than / (*not*) *as* [adjective] *as* / *just as* [adjective] *as*

- The movie isn't as good as the book.
- The book is better than the movie.
- The book wasn't as scary as the movie.
- The movie was scarier than the book.

–ed/–ing adjectives

- The book is boring. I feel bored.
- I'm disappointed. The movie was disappointing.

Reading Skills

Story: *Down the Rabbit Hole*
Genre: fantasy

Literacy Development

- use reading skills to understand and predict content
- relate story theme to personal experience
- use sentence openers

The children will:

- use critical thinking skills to identify extreme adjectives.
- compare movies and books.
- read and understand a story about a dream world.
- give opinions.
- talk about sleep habits.
- find out about sleeping habits and cycles.
- write their own account of a dream.

Functional Language

- Did you sleep well?
- Yes, I did, but I had a strange dream about … Have you ever dreamed about … ?
- Yes, I have.

Spelling

Silent *gh*

Key Vocabulary

Adjectives for common dreams: amazing, awful, confusing, disappointing, embarrassing, frightening, realistic, weird
Sleep habits: fall asleep, lie down, pillow, stay awake, stay up, the dark

CLIL: Science—The importance of sleep

The children find out about sleeping habits and cycles.

Competency Focus

The children will:

use critical thinking skills to deduce the meaning of new vocabulary. (Lesson 1)	activate new vocabulary and apply new grammar knowledge. (Lesson 2)	work in pairs to act out a dialogue. (Lesson 3)	relate the story theme to their personal experience. (Lesson 4)	write an account of their own dream story. (Lesson 8)
predict the content of a story. (Lesson 3)	apply new grammar rules in a familiar context. (Lesson 5)	work in pairs to talk about their own sleep habits. (Lesson 6)	develop their understanding of their own sleep cycle. (Lesson 7)	evaluate their own progress in the chapter. (Review)

Digital Overview

Teacher Presentation

Student eBook and Digital Activity Book

- Oral Storytelling Video 3.1: *Dreaming of Treasure*
- Interactive versions of AB activities
- Integrated audio and answer key for all activities

Teacher resources for planning, lesson delivery, and homework

Teacher Resource Center

- Class Planner Chapter 3
- Worksheets to print out (including notes and answers):
  - Grammar Worksheet 3A: *than / (not) as* (adjective) *as*
  - Grammar Worksheet 3B: *–ed/–ing* adjectives
  - Oral Storytelling Video Worksheet 3: *Dreaming of Treasure*
  - CLIL Graphic Organizer 3
  - Phonics Worksheet 3
  - Writing Template 3
  - Festival Worksheet: New Year's Eve
  - Test Chapter 3
- Test Generator
- Speaking Assessment: Cambridge English Young Learners Exams

Watch the Oral Storytelling Video

- Literacy Handbook

Children's resources for consolidation and practice at home

Student eBook and Reader eBook

- Oral Storytelling Video 3.1: *Dreaming of Treasure*

The Inks Student's App

Vocabulary games: Adjectives for common dreams and Sleep habits

Chapter 3 Sleep and Dreams

Lesson 1

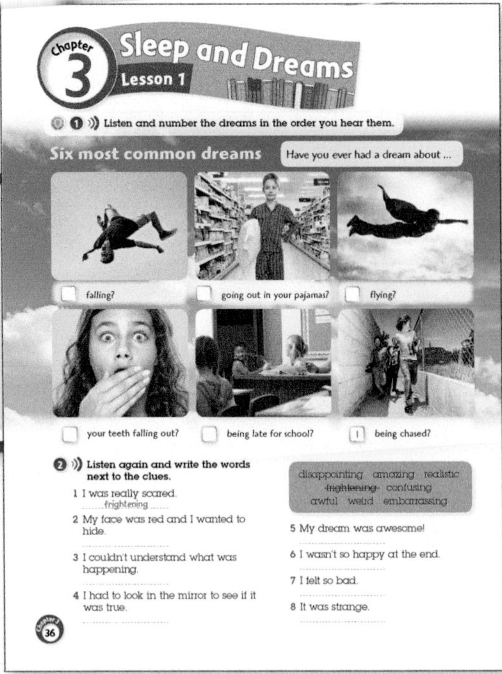
Chapter 3 Sleep and Dreams

Lesson 1

1 Listen and number the dreams in the order you hear them.

Six most common dreams

Have you ever had a dream about ...

falling?

going out in your pajamas?

flying?

your teeth falling out?

being late for school?

1 being chased?

2 Listen again and write the words next to the clues.

disappointing amazing realistic ~~frightening~~ confusing awful weird embarrassing

1 I was really scared. frightening

2 My face was red and I wanted to hide.

3 I couldn't understand what was happening.

4 I had to look in the mirror to see if it was true.

5 My dream was awesome!

6 I wasn't so happy at the end.

7 I felt so bad.

8 It was strange.

Chapter 3 36

Vocabulary

Lesson objectives: identify and use extreme adjectives

Key vocabulary: *amazing, awful, confusing, disappointing, embarrassing, frightening, realistic, weird*

Materials: Track 3.1

Warmer: Talk about dreams

Introduce the topic. Ask *Did you have a dream last night? Can you remember it? What happened?* Have children look at the dream pictures on the website in Activity 1. Elicit if these things have happened in their dreams.

1 3.1 Listen and number the dreams in the order you hear them.

- Ask the children to look at the dream pictures on the website article and read the captions.
- Play Track 3.1. The children listen and number the dreams in order.
- Elicit answers. Whenever you elicit answers, remember to check with the class to see if they agree.

Audioscript

Girl 1: *I had a very strange dream last night. It was frightening. I was really scared. A monster was chasing me and my friends. I ran really fast, but the monster was faster than me.*

Boy 1: *I went to the supermarket in this dream, but when I got there everyone was laughing at me. I was wearing my pajamas and I didn't have any shoes on. It was embarrassing. My face was red and I wanted to hide.*

Girl 2: *I had a confusing dream. I couldn't understand what was happening. All my teeth fell out. It was so realistic. When I got up, I had to look in the mirror to see if it was true.*

Boy 2: *My dream was awesome. I dreamed I could fly. I flew really high and could see everyone below me on the ground. It was amazing! But I wasn't so happy at the end. I woke up and, of course, I couldn't fly. It was a little disappointing!*

Boy 3: *I was running to school. I looked at my watch and it was already eight thirty. I was late and I wasn't getting any closer. It was awful. I felt so bad. I never got to school. I missed all my classes.*

Boy 4: *In my dream, I was falling through the sky. I fell down and couldn't stop falling, like Alice in* Alice in Wonderland. *You know, when she's falling down and down. It was strange. I often have this weird dream.*

Answers

6, 2, 4
3, 5, 1

2 3.1 Listen again and write the words next to the clues.

- Ask the children to look again at the dream picture of being chased in Activity 1. Ask *What type of dream is this?* Have them study the adjectives supplied and elicit *frightening.*
- Play Track 3.1 again. The children listen and write the adjective for each definition. Elicit answers.
- Play Track 3.1 again and check comprehension.

Answers

1 frightening **2** embarrassing **3** confusing **4** realistic **5** amazing **6** disappointing **7** awful **8** weird

Optional activity: Practice the adjectives

Have the children look at the adjectives supplied and decide if they have a positive or negative meaning. Have them think of different situations for each adjective, e.g. *Disappointing—I didn't get a very good grade on a test.* Elicit examples.

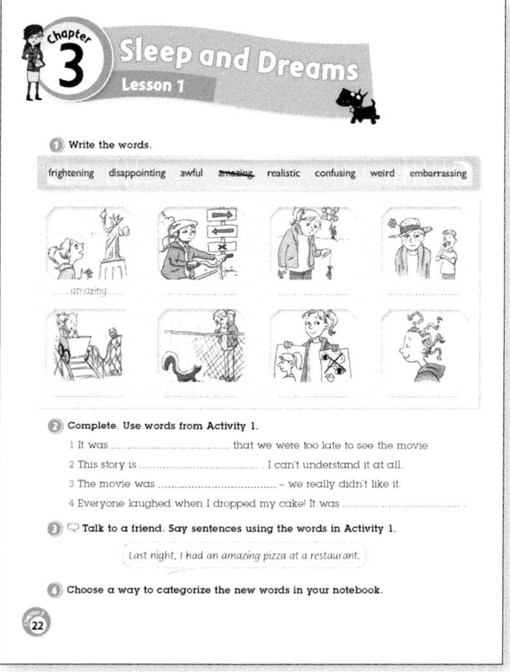

Chapter 3 Sleep and Dreams
Lesson 1

1 Write the words.

frightening disappointing awful ~~amazing~~ realistic confusing weird embarrassing

amazing

2 Complete. Use words from Activity 1.

1 It was .... that we were too late to see the movie.
2 This story is .... I can't understand it at all.
3 The movie was .... – we really didn't like it.
4 Everyone laughed when I dropped my cake! It was ....

3 Talk to a friend. Say sentences using the words in Activity 1.

Last night, I had an amazing pizza at a restaurant.

4 Choose a way to categorize the new words in your notebook.

22

1 Write the words.

The children label the pictures using the words supplied. Elicit answers.

Answers

amazing, confusing, disappointing, embarrassing frightening, awful, realistic, weird

2 Complete. Use words from Activity 1.

The children complete the sentences using words from Activity 1. Encourage them to look for clues in the sentences.

Answers

1 disappointing **2** confusing **3** awful **4** embarrassing

3 Talk to a friend. Say sentences using the words in Activity 1.

The children work in pairs, taking turns using the words in Activity 1 in an appropriate sentence.

4 Choose a way to categorize the new words in your notebook.

Brainstorm appropriate categories, e.g. *positive/negative, alphabetical order, best to worst.* The children choose the best categories for them and list the words in their notebook.

Answers

Children's own answers.

Cooler: Practice pronunciation

Write the adjectives from the lesson on the board. Repeat each one for the class. Have the children clap the syllables with you and say the number of syllables. Then have them categorize the adjectives according to the number of syllables.

Competency Focus

Think! Critical Thinking

The children use critical thinking skills to understand the new vocabulary by using visual clues and processing the written and spoken forms.

Digital Resources

Student eBook • For the Optional activity, have children use *Highlighter* to identify positive adjectives and *Pen* to underline negative adjectives.

Grammar

Lesson objective: compare books and movies
Key grammar: comparatives
Secondary language: *adventures, comments, plot*
Materials: Grammar Worksheet 3A [TRC printout] (optional); any book which has been made into a movie (Warmer)

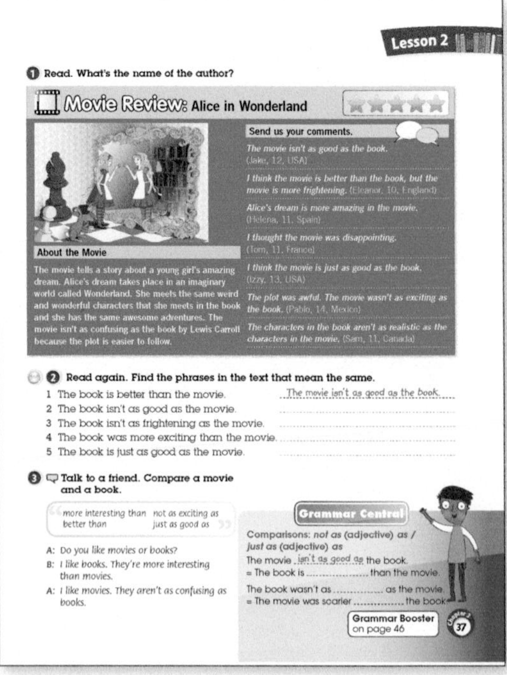

Lesson 2

1 Read. What's the name of the author?

Movie Review: Alice in Wonderland

Send us your comments.

The movie isn't as good as the book. (Jake, 12, USA)

I think the movie is better than the book, but the movie is more frightening. (Eleanor, 10, England)

Alice's dream is more amazing in the movie. (Helena, 11, Spain)

I thought the movie was disappointing. (Tom, 11, France)

I think the movie is just as good as the book. (Izzy, 13, USA)

The plot was awful. The movie wasn't as exciting as the book. (Pablo, 14, Mexico)

The characters in the book aren't as realistic as the characters in the movie. (Sam, 11, Canada)

About the Movie

The movie tells a story about a young girl's amazing dream. Alice's dream takes place in an imaginary world called Wonderland. She meets the same weird and wonderful characters that she meets in the book and she has the same awesome adventures. The movie isn't as confusing as the book by Lewis Carroll because the plot is easier to follow.

2 Read again. Find the phrases in the text that mean the same.

1 The book is better than the movie. The movie isn't as good as the book.
2 The book isn't as good as the movie. ....
3 The book isn't as frightening as the movie. ....
4 The book was more exciting than the movie. ....
5 The book is just as good as the movie. ....

3 Talk to a friend. Compare a movie and a book.

more interesting than / better than / not as exciting as / just as good as

A: *Do you like movies or books?*
B: *I like books. They're more interesting than movies.*
A: *I like movies. They aren't as confusing as books.*

Grammar Central

Comparisons: *not as* (adjective) *as* / *just as* (adjective) *as*

The movie isn't as good as the book.
= The book is .... than the movie.
The book wasn't as .... as the movie.
= The movie was scarier .... the book.

Grammar Booster on page 46

37

Warmer: Books or movies?

Ask *Do you prefer books or movies?* Show them a story book they are familiar with that has been made into a movie, e.g. *Harry Potter*. Ask them if they prefer the book or the movie and encourage them to give reasons. Review the comparative structure *It's better than …*

1 Read. What's the name of the author?

- The children look at the picture on the website and say if they recognize the story. Ask *What's the name of the author?* (*Lewis Carroll*) Have a show of hands for who has read the book / has seen the movie.
- Have the children read the movie review webpage. Discuss it, asking *Do the reviewers prefer the movie or the book?*

2 Read again. Find the phrases in the text that mean the same.

- Ask the children to look at the example. Point out that they need to use a different subject each time and think about how to reword the comparison appropriately.
- The children read the text again and find sentences to complete the activity. Elicit answers.

Answers

1 The movie isn't as good as the book. **2** The movie is better than the book. **3** The movie's more frightening than the book. **4** The movie wasn't as exciting as the book. **5** The movie is just as good as the book.

Grammar Central

than* / (*not*) *as* [adjective] *as* / *just as* [adjective] *as

Have the children complete the grammar examples. Elicit answers. Elicit the two different ways of making comparisons (*–er than, as … as*). For extra practice, try the **Grammar Booster** section in the Student Book (p. 46).

Answers p. 46

Activity 1: **1** just as scary as **2** isn't as funny as **3** is just as pretty as **4** more exciting than

Activity 2: **1** b **2** c **3** b **4** a **5** c

3 Talk to a friend. Compare a movie and a book.

- Choose two children to read the example dialogue. Elicit other books which have been made into a movie.
- Divide the class into pairs to practice the dialogue using the prompts supplied. Once they feel confident, encourage them to adapt it using different adjectives.
- Have pairs perform their dialogue for the class.

Optional activity: More comparisons

Elicit the names of two TV shows, two computer games, and two websites, and write them on the board. Elicit comparisons between the pairs of objects, using the new adjectives from Lesson 1. They could write answers in pairs.

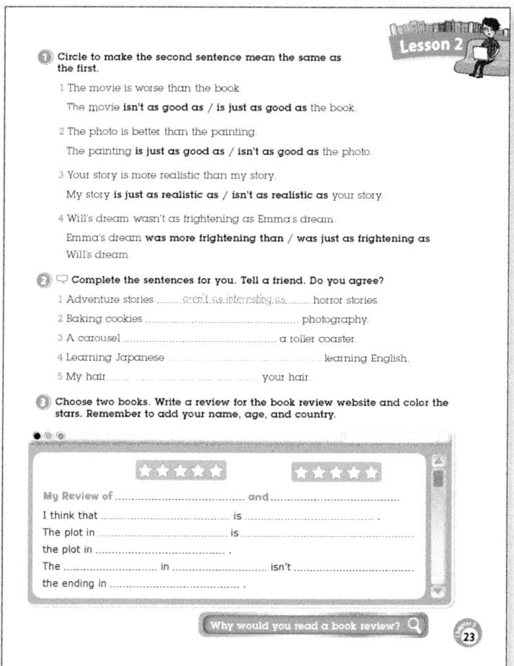

Lesson 2

1 Circle to make the second sentence mean the same as the first.

1 The movie is worse than the book.
The movie **isn't as good as / is just as good as** the book.

2 The photo is better than the painting.
The painting **is just as good as / isn't as good as** the photo.

3 Your story is more realistic than my story.
My story **is just as realistic as / isn't as realistic as** your story.

4 Will's dream wasn't as frightening as Emma's dream.
Emma's dream **was more frightening than / was just as frightening as** Will's dream.

2 Complete the sentences for you. Tell a friend. Do you agree?

1 Adventure stories ....aren't as interesting as........ horror stories.
2 Baking cookies .... photography.
3 A carousel .... a roller coaster.
4 Learning Japanese .... learning English.
5 My hair .... your hair.

3 Choose two books. Write a review for the book review website and color the stars. Remember to add your name, age, and country.

My Review of .... and ....
I think that .... is ....
The plot in .... is ....
the plot in ....
The .... in .... isn't ....
the ending in ....

Why would you read a book review?

23

1 Circle to make the second sentence mean the same as the first.

Read the example. Explain that the sentences have the same meaning although they use different structures. The children circle the phrase which makes the second sentence mean the same as the first. Elicit answers.

Answers

1 isn't as good as **2** isn't as good as
3 isn't as realistic as **4** was more frightening than

2 Complete the sentences for you. Tell a friend. Do you agree?

The children write their opinions. They compare in pairs and see if their friend agrees. Elicit responses.

Answers

Children's own answers.

3 Choose two books. Write a review for the book review website and color the stars. Remember to add your name, age, and country.

Elicit books in English that the children have read or recognize and write them on the board. Ask the children to choose two. They complete their book review, awarding and coloring stars appropriately. They then compare with a friend. Ask *Why would you read a book review? (to discover new books, if a book is good or bad, what the book is about, what other people think)*

Answers

Children's own answers.

Cooler: Have a class vote

Write four pairs of movie titles on the board, e.g. *Batman* vs. *Superman*, etc. Ask the children to discuss them in pairs, e.g. *X isn't as good/funny/scary/exciting as Y.* Have a class vote on each pair and ask the class for reasons.

Competency Focus

Learn

By reading the movie review and identifying phrases with the same meanings, the children demonstrate their understanding of the new grammatical structures.

Digital Resources

Student eBook, Digital Activity Book • TIP You can move the answer key pop-up window around the screen to have the activity and the answers side by side.

Teacher Resource Center • For extra grammar practice, print out Grammar Worksheet 3A.

Reading: Story Extract

Lesson objectives: talk about their dreams; use the title and pictures to predict story content; read the extract from the fantasy *Down the Rabbit Hole* (start)

Functional language: *Did you sleep well? Yes, I did, but I had a strange dream about … Have you ever dreamed about …? Yes, I have.*

Secondary language: *surprise, hopping, suddenly*

Materials: Tracks 3.2 and 3.3

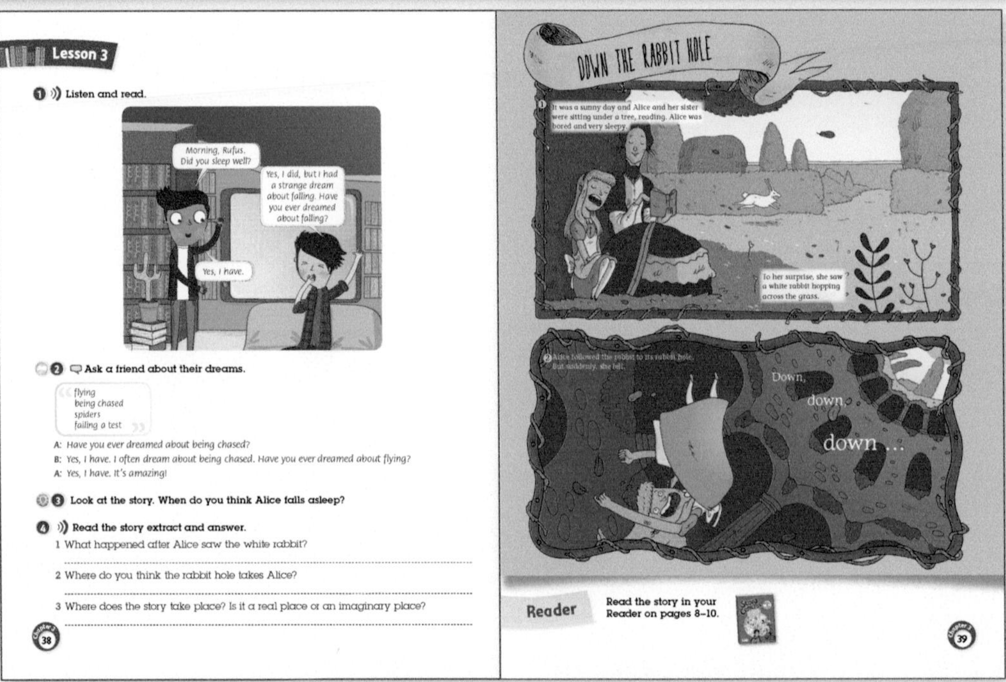

Lesson 3

1 Listen and read.

2 Ask a friend about their dreams.

flying
being chased
spiders
failing a test

A: Have you ever dreamed about being chased?
B: Yes, I have. I often dream about being chased. Have you ever dreamed about flying?
A: Yes, I have. It's amazing!

3 Look at the story. When do you think Alice falls asleep?

4 Read the story extract and answer.

1 What happened after Alice saw the white rabbit?

2 Where do you think the rabbit hole takes Alice?

3 Where does the story take place? Is it a real place or an imaginary place?

38

DOWN THE RABBIT HOLE
It was a sunny day and Alice and her sister were sitting under a tree, reading. Alice was bored and very sleepy.
To her surprise, she saw a white rabbit hopping across the grass.
Down,
down,
down …

Reader Read the story in your Reader on pages 8–10.

39

Warmer: Unscramble the words

Write scrambled versions of dream vocabulary on the board, e.g. *dream, falling, amazing, confusing, realistic, weird.* Have the children unscramble the words in pairs. Then call on children to write the answers on the board.

Functional language

1 3.2 Listen and read

- Play Track 3.2. The children listen and read along.
- Play Track 3.2 again for them to repeat.
- Divide the class into pairs to practice the dialogue.

2 Ask a friend about their dreams.  

- Choose two children to read the example dialogue.
- The children practice in pairs using the prompts supplied and adding details. Have pairs do a dialogue for the class.

Before reading

3 Look at the story. When do you think Alice falls asleep?

- Have the children study the pictures. Ask *When do you think Alice falls asleep?* to elicit ideas.
- Ask *Was Alice interested in the book?* Elicit answers.

4 3.3 Read the story extract and answer.

- Have the children read the extract and answer question 1.
- Play Track 3.3. The children listen and write ideas for questions 2 and 3 using reading skills (looking at the pictures and context, applying general knowledge, etc.).
- Elicit answers, but do not confirm predictions: explain that they will have to read the story to find out.

Answers

1 She followed it and fell down the hole. **2** Children's own answers. **3** Children's own answers/an imaginary place.

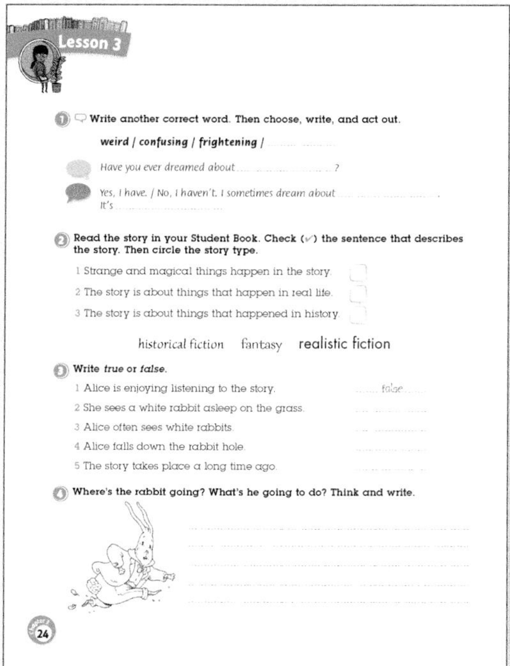

Lesson 3

1 Write another correct word. Then choose, write, and act out.

weird / confusing / frightening / ....

Have you ever dreamed about .... ?

Yes, I have. / No, I haven't. I sometimes dream about ....
It's ....

2 Read the story in your Student Book. Check (✓) the sentence that describes the story. Then circle the story type.

1 Strange and magical things happen in the story.
2 The story is about things that happen in real life.
3 The story is about things that happened in history.

historical fiction fantasy realistic fiction

3 Write *true* or *false*.

1 Alice is enjoying listening to the story. false
2 She sees a white rabbit asleep on the grass.
3 Alice often sees white rabbits.
4 Alice falls down the rabbit hole.
5 The story takes place a long time ago.

4 Where's the rabbit going? What's he going to do? Think and write.

24

1 Write another correct word. Then choose, write, and act out.

Elicit other negative adjectives about dreams. The children choose a topic and complete the dialogue, then act it out in pairs. Encourage the children to adapt and extend the dialogue. Have pairs act out for the class.

Answers (suggested)

awful, embarrassing, etc.

2 Read the story in your Student Book. Check (✓) the sentence that describes the story. Then circle the story type.

The children read the story extract again, then choose the best sentence to describe what the story is about. They then identify and circle the type of story.

Answer

✓ *by* 1; *circled:* fantasy

3 Write *true* or *false*.

The children write true or false for each sentence. Elicit answers, including the correct version of the false sentences.

Answers

1 false **2** false **3** false **4** true **5** true

4 Where's the rabbit going? What's he going to do? Think and write.

Elicit suggestions on where the rabbit is going and what he's going to do. The children write their own ideas, then compare with a friend. Elicit ideas.

Answers

Children's own answers.

Cooler: Play "Running Board Race"

Play the game using words from the story extract (see Games Bank p. 19).

Competency Focus

Collaborate and Communicate

The children work together, putting into practice new functional language by acting out a realistic dialogue.

Think

By analyzing visual clues and deducing from the context, the children make inferences about the underlying events of the story.

Digital Resources

Student eBook, Digital Activity Book, Reader eBook, CLIL eBook • Do not be afraid to turn off the screen! Children benefit from variety and sometimes you will want to work just with books or without prompts. Work the digital materials into your teaching in the way that suits you best.

Student eBook • Use *Pen* for the Warmer activity.

Down the Rabbit Hole

1
It was a sunny day and Alice and her sister were sitting under a tree, reading. Alice was bored and very sleepy.

To her surprise, she saw a white rabbit hopping across the grass.

2
Alice followed the rabbit to its rabbit hole. But suddenly, she fell. Down, down, down …

3
Now she was sitting in a dark hallway. She saw a little door and behind the door there was the most beautiful garden. On a small table, there was a key.

She wanted to go into the garden but she was too big. Suddenly she noticed a little bottle. On the bottle she read the words "DRINK ME." She opened the bottle and drank.

"What a strange feeling!" said Alice. "I'm getting smaller."

Soon she was very small. Unfortunately, the key was on the table, and she wasn't as tall as the table. She sat down and cried. It was so disappointing.

4
Then Alice saw a cake. She read the words, "EAT ME."

"Well, I'm going to eat it," said Alice, "and if I grow taller, I can reach the key. If I grow smaller, I can crawl under the door."

She ate a little bit. Nothing happened. So Alice finished the cake.

5
"Stranger and stranger!" cried Alice. "Now I'm growing taller." Fortunately, Alice was really tall now. She picked up the key and opened the door.

6
Poor Alice! She looked into the garden with one eye. Her head was bigger than the door. "How embarrassing," thought Alice. She started to cry again. Soon there was a large pool of tears.

7
Finally the White Rabbit came back, wearing a nice suit. He was carrying gloves and a large fan.

"Please, sir," said Alice. But Alice was big and frightening. The Rabbit dropped his fan, and ran away.

Alice was very hot so she used the fan. "This is confusing. Where am I?" she said. Soon she was cooler, but also smaller! "This is weird," she said. "But now I can go into the garden."

8
But the door was closed and the key was on the table again. "Oh, no! I can't reach the key now," she said. She was too small again. Suddenly she fell into some water. "Am I in the ocean?" she asked. "Oh, these are my tears," she remembered.

9
"Wake up, Alice!" said her sister. "Did you sleep well?"

"Yes, I did," said Alice. "I had the most amazing dream! It was just as realistic as now." She told her sister about her amazing adventures.

"Run inside, it's getting late," said her sister.

Alice got up. "What a wonderful dream!" she thought. Then, she saw a white rabbit running behind a tree.

Lesson objective: read and understand the fantasy *Down the Rabbit Hole* in the Reader
Materials: Track 3.4; Reader; Oral Storytelling Video Worksheet 3 [TRC printout] (optional)

Warmer: Missing vowels

Write sentences on the board, summarizing events in the story extract, with the vowels missing, e.g. *t ws snny dy* (*It was a sunny day*). Allow thinking time, then call on children to rewrite one word at a time on the board.

Story Summary

Alice falls into a rabbit hole. She sees a beautiful garden but she's too big to go through the door. She drinks a potion and shrinks. Now unable to reach the key to the door, she eats some cake. She's now too big again and feels sad. Alice then wakes up—and realizes it was all a dream.

Theme: the importance of using your imagination

3.4 While reading

- Have the children look at the pictures in the Reader. Ask *What objects does Alice find? (a bottle, a cake)*
- Play Track 3.4. The children listen and read along. Ask *Was Alice's adventure real?* (*No—it was a dream.*)
- Ask questions to check comprehension, e.g. *Where did the water come from? (Alice's tears) What's on the table? (a key) What was the rabbit carrying? (gloves and a fan)*
- Read the story again with the class, having children take turns as Alice and her sister. Bring the story to life using dramatic stress and intonation patterns (see **Story Time**). Choose some phrases for the class to say, e.g. *DRINK ME!*

After reading: Reflect

- Ask questions to give the children the opportunity to think about the issues raised by the story, e.g. *What is Alice like? How does she feel? Is she happy to be down the rabbit hole?*

Optional activity: Extend the story

Have the children work in pairs. Ask them to invent another object for the story, e.g. something else to eat or drink, and say what happens when Alice takes it. They draw their new story frame and add dialogue.

Story Time

Using stress and intonation

This story contains many examples of authentic stress and intonation patterns—particularly exclamations as Alice talks to herself. Read out and have the children repeat phrases, copying your stress and intonation patterns. Exploiting these fully with the children underpins the development of good pronunciation and creates a fun atmosphere in the classroom.

Reading Strategy

Descriptive Writing

Descriptive Writing is a form of visual imagery which is expressed with the written word. With this strategy, the writer uses colorful words to write a description that will form images in the reader's/listener's mind.

For additional explanation and activities, see the Literacy Handbook on the Teacher Resource Center.

Cooler: Play "What's the next word?"

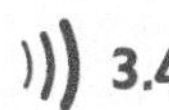

3.4

Play Track 3.4, pausing before key words. Elicit the word each time, then continue playing the track to confirm.

Digital Resources

Reader eBook • Read the text for Pictures 1–4. Ask *What has happened? What can Alice do now?*

• Oral Storytelling Video 3.1 contains a different story on a related theme (*Dreaming of Treasure*). Watch and discuss it together at the end of the lesson.

Teacher Resource Center • Print out Oral Storytelling Video Worksheet 3 to help you get the most out of the video.

Student eBook, Reader eBook • The children can watch Oral Storytelling Video 3.1 at home.

Reading Comprehension and Critical Literacy

Lesson objectives: understand and evaluate the story; relate story theme to personal experience; write an account of Alice's dream using sentence openers

Materials: Track 3.4; Reader; Oral Storytelling Video Worksheet 3 [TRC printout] (optional)

Lesson 4 *Time to Think*

1 Read the story in your Reader on pages 8–10 again.
What happens when Alice drinks from the bottle?

2 Comprehension
1 Why couldn't Alice go through the door?
2 Do you think Alice cried for a long time?
3 Why did the rabbit run away from her?
4 Do you think the rabbit was real?

3 Critical Literacy
1 Do you think Alice liked being in Wonderland?
2 Would you like to go to Wonderland?

Writing Workshop Linking parts of a story.

4 Find examples of sentence openers in the story. Continue Alice's account of her dream to her sister.
To my surprise, I saw ...
Suddenly I fell ...

Writing Tools
Use sentence openers to start new sentences:
Soon, ...
To my surprise, ...
Fortunately, ...
Finally, ...

5 Text Connections
Do you know any other stories or movies about people who get bigger or smaller?

40

Note: Please ensure that your class has read the Reader story before you do this lesson.

Warmer: Story recap

Write the key events from the story on the board in random order, e.g. *She found a bottle. She fell down a hole. She got bigger. Alice fell asleep.* Have the children reorder them, then retell and recap the story.

1 3.4 Read the story in your Reader.

- Have the children read the story. (Alternatively, play Track 3.4 and have them read along.) Elicit whether they were correct in their predictions in Lesson 3 Activity 4.
- Ask *What happens when Alice drinks from the bottle? (She gets very small.)*

2 Comprehension

- The children write answers to the first three questions. Elicit answers. Then discuss question 4. Ask the children to justify their answers.

Answers

1 She was too big. **2** Children's own answers. **3** She was big and frightening. **4** Children's own answers.

3 Critical Literacy

- Say *Imagine you are Alice. How do you feel?* Empathizing with the main character will help the children engage with the story.
- Ask *Would you like to go to Wonderland?* Help the children apply what they have read to their own experience. Ask *How would you react in a similar situation?*

Writing Workshop

Linking parts of a story

4 Find examples of sentence openers in the story. Continue Alice's account of her dream to her sister.

Have a child read the example sentence openers in the **Writing Tools** box. The children look back at the story and find sentences which open like this and in other ways, e.g. *Then, …* They continue the story of Alice's dream in their notebook, using appropriate sentence openers, then compare with a friend. Invite children to read out their accounts.

Answers

Children's own answers.

5 Text Connections 

- Ask *What type of stories have people getting smaller or bigger? (fairy tales, science fiction, fantasy, cartoons)*
- Ask the class if they know any specific examples of stories, e.g. *Thumbelina, Clifford the Dog, Monsters vs. Aliens.* Ask how they resemble this story.

Optional activity: Build a mini-story

Have children use the sentence openers in Activity 4 to build a mini-story about their own visit to Wonderland. Ask children to work in pairs to produce a story of about 50 words. Then choose pairs to read out their mini-story to the class.

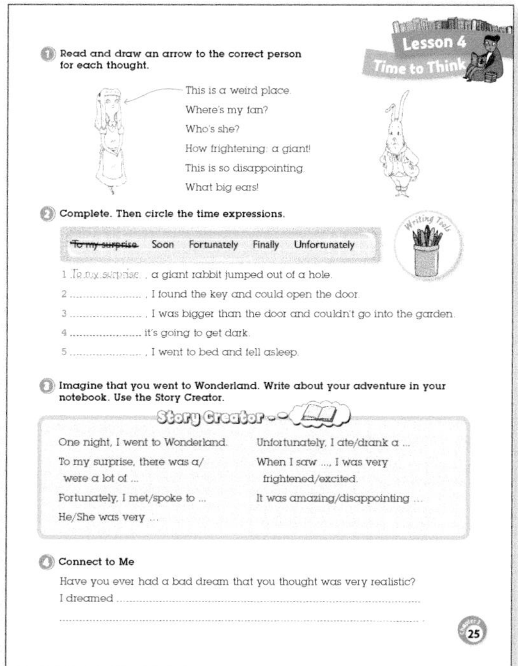

Lesson 4
Time to Think

1 Read and draw an arrow to the correct person for each thought.

This is a weird place.
Where's my fan?
Who's she?
How frightening: a giant!
This is so disappointing.
What big ears!

2 Complete. Then circle the time expressions.

~~To my surprise~~ Soon Fortunately Finally Unfortunately

1 To my surprise , a giant rabbit jumped out of a hole.
2 .... , I found the key and could open the door.
3 .... , I was bigger than the door and couldn't go into the garden.
4 .... it's going to get dark.
5 .... , I went to bed and fell asleep.

Writing Tools

3 Imagine that you went to Wonderland. Write about your adventure in your notebook. Use the Story Creator.

Story Creator

One night, I went to Wonderland.
To my surprise, there was a/ were a lot of ...
Fortunately, I met/spoke to ...
He/She was very ...
Unfortunately, I ate/drank a ...
When I saw ..., I was very frightened/excited.
It was amazing/disappointing ...

4 Connect to Me

Have you ever had a bad dream that you thought was very realistic?
I dreamed ....

25

1 Read and draw an arrow to the correct person for each thought.

The children identify the correct person for each thought, drawing an arrow pointing to Alice or the rabbit, as appropriate. Elicit answers, asking children to read them out in the voice of Alice or the rabbit each time.

Answers

Alice, Rabbit, Rabbit, Rabbit, Alice, Alice

2 Complete. Then circle the time expressions.

The children complete the sentences using the words supplied. They then identify and circle the words supplied which are time expressions. Elicit answers.

Answers

1 To my surprise **2** Fortunately **3** Unfortunately
4 Soon **5** Finally
Circled: Soon, Finally

3 Imagine that you went to Wonderland. Write about your adventure in your notebook. Use the Story Creator.

Use the **Story Creator** to elicit ideas. The children write a story in their notebook, then compare with a friend. Have children read out their story for the class.

4 Connect to Me

Elicit examples of a realistic dream which was scary. The children write their own response, then compare with a friend.

Cooler: Play "Change a Word"

Write on the board *Suddenly, I was smaller than the table.* Have children repeat the sentence, replacing one of the words to make a sentence which is still grammatically correct. The class confirms whether they are correct or not. Write correct sentences on the board. At the end, compare the final sentence with the first!

Competency Focus

Me: Critical Literacy

The children use critical literacy skills to reflect on the theme of the story and relate it to their own personal literary experience and prior knowledge.

Digital Resources

Digital Activity Book • Give feedback on AB activities using the answer keys or the built-in interactive activities.

Student eBook, Digital Activity Book, Reader eBook, CLIL eBook • TIP Give children the opportunity to be your assistant! Ask a child to be responsible for choosing the relevant buttons (e.g. to go to the next activity or answer key).

Student eBook, Reader eBook • If you haven't already, show Oral Storytelling Video 3.1.

Teacher Resource Center • If you haven't already, print out Oral Storytelling Video Worksheet 3 to do the support activities.

Grammar and Reading

Lesson objectives: describe things and feelings using adjectives correctly
Key grammar: statements using adjectives with *–ing/–ed* endings
Secondary language: *woke up, fail* (*an exam*), *fell over*
Materials: Track 3.5; Grammar Worksheet 3B [TRC printout] (optional); text with mistakes (optional)

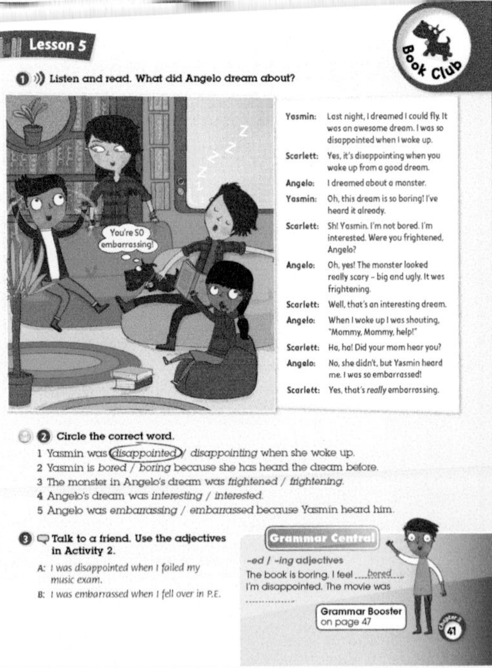
Lesson 5
Book Club
1 Listen and read. What did Angelo dream about?

Yasmin: Last night, I dreamed I could fly. It was an awesome dream. I was so disappointed when I woke up.
Scarlett: Yes, it's disappointing when you wake up from a good dream.
Angelo: I dreamed about a monster.
Yasmin: Oh, this dream is so boring! I've heard it already.
Scarlett: Sh! Yasmin. I'm not bored. I'm interested. Were you frightened, Angelo?
Angelo: Oh, yes! The monster looked really scary – big and ugly. It was frightening.
Scarlett: Well, that's an interesting dream.
Angelo: When I woke up I was shouting, "Mommy, Mommy, help!"
Scarlett: Ha, ha! Did your mom hear you?
Angelo: No, she didn't, but Yasmin heard me. I was so embarrassed!
Scarlett: Yes, that's *really* embarrassing.

2 Circle the correct word.
1 Yasmin was *disappointed* / *disappointing* when she woke up.
2 Yasmin is *bored* / *boring* because she has heard the dream before.
3 The monster in Angelo's dream was *frightened* / *frightening*.
4 Angelo's dream was *interesting* / *interested*.
5 Angelo was *embarrassing* / *embarrassed* because Yasmin heard him.

3 Talk to a friend. Use the adjectives in Activity 2.
A: *I was disappointed when I failed my music exam.*
B: *I was embarrassed when I fell over in P.E.*

Grammar Central
–ed / *–ing* adjectives
The book is boring. I feel ...*bored*...
I'm disappointed. The movie was ....
Grammar Booster on page 47

41

Warmer: Draw a face!

Draw an oval on the board to represent a face. Have the children copy the shape four times in their notebook. Say an adjective and have them draw the expression on a face. Do *happy* on the board as an example. Say *bored, frightened, embarrassed, disappointed*. Have the children compare the faces they have drawn in pairs.

1 3.5 Listen and read. What did Angelo dream about?

- Play Track 3.5. The children listen and read along. Ask *What did Angelo dream about?* (*a monster*)
- Play Track 3.5 again. Ask *How do the children feel?* Elicit the difference between the *–ed* and *–ing* ending, e.g. *frightened, frightening*. (*–ed for how the people feel; –ing for the dream*)

2 Circle the correct word. 

- Have the children look at the sentences and apply the rules for adjectives which they deduced in Activity 1. Ask them to circle the correct adjective.
- Elicit answers.

Answers

1 disappointed **2** bored **3** frightening **4** interesting **5** embarrassed

Grammar Central

–ed / –ing adjectives

Have the children complete the grammar examples. Elicit answers. The children then write other personalized examples with different adjectives in their notebook. For extra practice, try the **Grammar Booster** section in the Student Book (pp. 47–49)

Answers p. 47

Activity 1: **1** bored **2** boring **3** amazed **4** embarrassing

Activity 2: **1** boring **2** embarrassed **3** interesting **4** disappointed **5** frightening **6** confused

p. 48

Activity 1: **1** awful **2** frightened **3** bigger **4** as tall as **5** as talented as **6** confusing

Activity 2: **1** c **2** b **3** e **4** d **5** a

p. 49

Activity 1: **1** learned **2** as big as **3** confused **4** amazing **5** slept **6** frightened **7** relaxing **8** as comfortable as **9** excited **10** going to **11** might be / is going to be **12** as warm as **13** better

Activity 2: Children's own answers.

3 Talk to a friend. Use the adjectives in Activity 2.

- Choose two children to read the example dialogue.
- Divide the class into pairs to practice dialogues using the adjectives in Activity 2. Have pairs perform for the class.

Optional activity: Spot the mistake

Prepare a short text about yourself containing five grammatical mistakes, e.g. *I went to the movies last night. It was a horror movie and I was very frightening.* Read it out and have the children raise their hands when they hear a mistake.

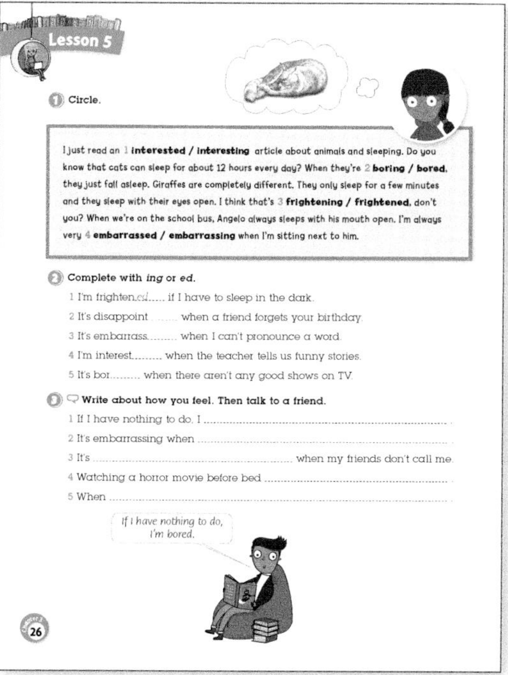

Lesson 5

1 Circle.

I just read an 1 **interested / interesting** article about animals and sleeping. Do you know that cats can sleep for about 12 hours every day? When they're 2 **boring / bored**, they just fall asleep. Giraffes are completely different. They only sleep for a few minutes and they sleep with their eyes open. I think that's 3 **frightening / frightened**, don't you? When we're on the school bus, Angelo always sleeps with his mouth open. I'm always very 4 **embarrassed / embarrassing** when I'm sitting next to him.

2 Complete with *ing* or *ed*.

1 I'm frighten*ed*...... if I have to sleep in the dark.
2 It's disappoint......... when a friend forgets your birthday.
3 It's embarrass......... when I can't pronounce a word.
4 I'm interest......... when the teacher tells us funny stories.
5 It's bor......... when there aren't any good shows on TV.

3 Write about how you feel. Then talk to a friend.

1 If I have nothing to do, I ....
2 It's embarrassing when ....
3 It's .... when my friends don't call me.
4 Watching a horror movie before bed ....
5 When ....

26

1 Circle.

The children complete the text by circling the correct option in each pair of adjectives. Elicit answers.

Answers

1 interesting **2** bored **3** frightening **4** embarrassed

2 Complete with *ing* or *ed*.

The children complete the adjectives using the *ing* or *ed* ending as appropriate. Elicit answers.

Answers

1 frightened **2** disappointing **3** embarrassing
4 interested **5** boring

3 Write about how you feel. Then talk to a friend.

The children write about how they feel in the situations outlined. They then share ideas in pairs.

Answers

Children's own answers.

Cooler: Mime time

First have the children secretly choose an *–ed* adjective. Invite children to mime their word for the class to guess. To practice the *–ing* adjectives, ask them to choose and mime a movie or a book title.

Competency Focus

Learn

The children demonstrate their understanding of the new language by reading the text and completing the activity.

Digital Resources

Student eBook • Have children use *Highlighter* to identify *–ing* and *–ed* adjectives in the SB Activity 1 text.

Teacher Resource Center • For extra grammar practice, print out Grammar Worksheet 3B.

Vocabulary, Listening, and Spelling

Lesson objectives: identify and talk about sleep habits; practice spelling words with silent *gh*
Key vocabulary: *fall asleep, lie down, pillow, stay awake, stay up, the dark*
Secondary language: *special, turn off, count sheep*
Materials: Track 3.6; Phonics Worksheet 3 [TRC printout] (optional)

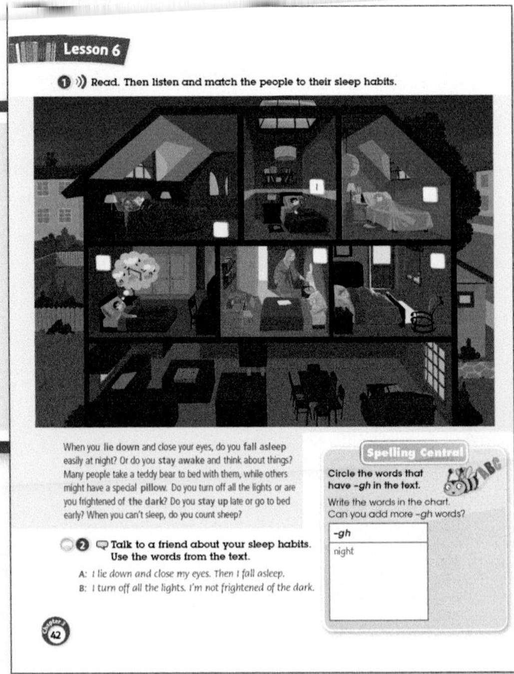

Lesson 6

1 Read. Then listen and match the people to their sleep habits.

When you **lie down** and close your eyes, do you **fall asleep** easily at night? Or do you **stay awake** and think about things? Many people take a teddy bear to bed with them, while others might have a special **pillow**. Do you turn off all the lights or are you frightened of **the dark**? Do you **stay up** late or go to bed early? When you can't sleep, do you count sheep?

Spelling Central

Circle the words that have -*gh* in the text.

Write the words in the chart.
Can you add more -*gh* words?

-*gh*
night

2 **Talk to a friend about your sleep habits. Use the words from the text.**

A: *I lie down and close my eyes. Then I fall asleep.*
B: *I turn off all the lights. I'm not frightened of the dark.*

42

Warmer: Pre-teach vocabulary

Pre-teach the vocabulary by miming the words. Then make statements to the class about your sleep habits, e.g. *I have a teddy bear in my bed. I go to bed at ten o'clock. I read a book in bed every night. I watch TV in bed at night. I drink hot chocolate before bed.* The children identify whether each one is true or false.

1 3.6 Read. Then listen and match the people to their sleep habits.

- Have the children look at the pictures, then read the text. Ask *How do you get to sleep?*
- Play Track 3.6. They listen and match each person with their sleep habit, writing the correct number. Encourage them to listen for familiar words to help them. Elicit answers.
- Ask them to look at the highlighted vocabulary and find four verbs about sleep habits which have two parts—*lie down, fall asleep, stay awake, stay up.* Check understanding.

Answers

4, 1, 5
6, 2, 3

Audioscript

1
Boy 1: *It's a little embarrassing, but I still need my teddy bear to fall asleep.*
2
Girl 1: *I take a book to bed. I lie down and read, but I just can't stay awake for more than ten pages, even if the book is very interesting. My mom has to turn off the light for me.*
3
Girl 2: *I turn off all the lights in the room, but I leave a small light on outside my bedroom. I'm frightened of the dark.*
4
Boy 2: *I have a special pillow. I even take it with me on vacation!*
5
Girl 3: *I can't sleep when I stay up late and watch a movie, so I go to bed before ten o'clock. I usually drink hot chocolate first.*
6
Boy 3: *When I can't sleep, I close my eyes and count sheep.*

2 Talk to a friend about your sleep habits. Use the words from the text.  

- Choose two children to read the example dialogue to the class.
- Divide the class into pairs. Have them talk to their friend about sleep habits using as many words as possible from Activity 1.

Spelling Central

***gh* words**

Write *light* on the board and circle *gh*. Ask the children to look at the text in Activity 1 again and find more words with *gh* and complete the chart. Give the children time to think of other words with *gh*. (e.g. *fight, right, height, sight, tight, bright*) Provide clues as necessary.

Answers

Circled: night, might, lights, frightened

Optional activity: Play "True or False"

Ask the children to make true/false sentences similar to those in the Warmer but about themselves. Have the children write four sentences in their notebook, then exchange books to decide if the statements are true or false for their friend.

Lesson 6

1 Complete.

fall asleep | stay awake | pillow | the dark | stay up | ~~lie down~~

You're tired. It's time to 1 ....lie down...., turn off the light, and relax your head on a comfortable 2 .... But what happens if you're an astronaut? In space, it's hard to sleep. There's no difference between night and day and astronauts often 3 .... for a long time. But it's good if you're scared of 4 .... because the sun comes up every 90 minutes in space! It would be exciting to 5 .... late and watch the stars through the window. When astronauts finally 6 ...., they dream about discovering new planets.

2 Write answers for you. Then ask and answer.

1 Do you like to stay up late? ....
2 Do you fall asleep easily? ....
3 How many pillows do you use? ....
4 Are you frightened of the dark? ....
5 Do you always lie down to sleep? ....

Do you like to stay up late?

No, I don't because I don't like being tired at school.

Spelling Central — Words with *gh*

3 Find and circle six words with *gh* missing. Then write them out correctly.

....right....

ritheitfritenedbrithinit

27

1 Complete.

The children complete the text using the words supplied. Elicit answers.

Answers

1 lie down **2** pillow **3** stay awake **4** the dark **5** stay up **6** fall asleep

2 Write answers for you. Then ask and answer.

Elicit an example answer for each question. The children write answers for themselves, then ask and answer in pairs. Invite pairs to ask and answer for the class.

Answers

Children's own answers.

3 Find and circle six words with *gh* missing. Then write them out correctly.

To practice the **Spelling Central** feature, the children circle the prompts and write the words with the missing *gh*. Elicit answers, asking children to spell the words.

Answers

right, height, frightened, bright, high, night

Cooler: Play "Spelling Bee"

Play the game with words from the lesson (see Games Bank p. 19).

Competency Focus

Collaborate and communicate

The children work together and use their interpersonal skills to activate the new vocabulary from the text to talk about their own sleep habits.

Digital Resources

Student eBook • Have children use *Pen* to highlight *gh* words in the SB Activity 1 text.

Teacher Resource Center • For phonics practice, print out Phonics Worksheet 3.

Student's App • Encourage the children to play the games on their smartphone/tablet. Ask them to record their scores to compare in the next lesson. (*The Inks* Apps are free and available on the App Store and Google Play.)

CLIL: Science—The importance of sleep

Lesson objective: find out about sleeping habits and cycles
Materials: CLIL Graphic Organizer 3 [TRC printout] (optional)

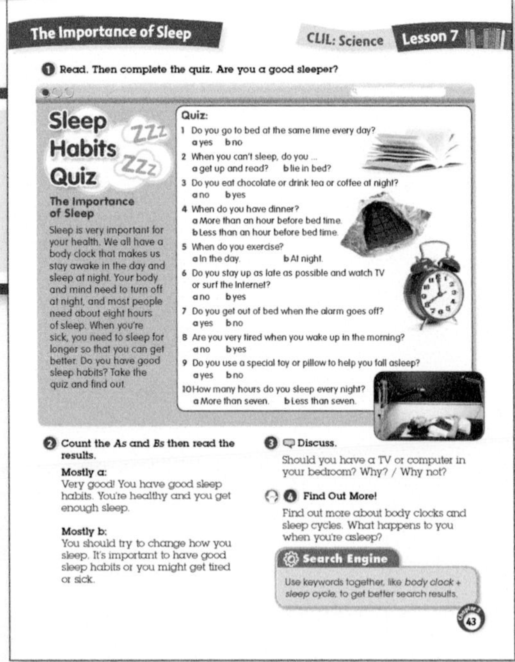
The Importance of Sleep — CLIL: Science — Lesson 7

1 Read. Then complete the quiz. Are you a good sleeper?

Sleep Habits Quiz

The Importance of Sleep

Sleep is very important for your health. We all have a body clock that makes us stay awake in the day and sleep at night. Your body and mind need to turn off at night, and most people need about eight hours of sleep. When you're sick, you need to sleep for longer so that you can get better. Do you have good sleep habits? Take the quiz and find out.

Quiz:
1 Do you go to bed at the same time every day? a yes b no
2 When you can't sleep, do you ... a get up and read? b lie in bed?
3 Do you eat chocolate or drink tea or coffee at night? a no b yes
4 When do you have dinner? a More than an hour before bed time. b Less than an hour before bed time.
5 When do you exercise? a In the day. b At night.
6 Do you stay up as late as possible and watch TV or surf the Internet? a no b yes
7 Do you get out of bed when the alarm goes off? a yes b no
8 Are you very tired when you wake up in the morning? a no b yes
9 Do you use a special toy or pillow to help you fall asleep? a yes b no
10 How many hours do you sleep every night? a More than seven. b Less than seven.

2 Count the As and Bs then read the results.
Mostly a: Very good! You have good sleep habits. You're healthy and you get enough sleep.
Mostly b: You should try to change how you sleep. It's important to have good sleep habits or you might get tired or sick.

3 Discuss. Should you have a TV or computer in your bedroom? Why? / Why not?

4 Find Out More! Find out more about body clocks and sleep cycles. What happens to you when you're asleep?

Search Engine: Use keywords together, like *body clock + sleep cycle*, to get better search results.

43

Warmer: Play "All About Sleep"

Divide the class into teams and give each team a piece of paper and a pen. Write *Sleep* on the board. Explain that they have two minutes to write as many words as they can think of related to sleep. At the end of the time, ask the team with the most answers to read them out. Then elicit any words not yet covered. A correct answer wins one point – two points if no other team has come up with it. The team with the most points wins.

1 Read. Then complete the quiz. Are you a good sleeper?

- Have the children look at the quiz. Ask *When do you need to sleep for longer?*
- They read the quiz questions and choose their own answers.

2 Count the *As* and *Bs* then read the results.

- Have the children total their As and Bs. Ask them to read their results and say if they agree.
- Elicit good sleeping habits, e.g. *don't stay up too late, don't have dinner too late.*

3 Discuss.

- Ask the children to raise their hand if they have a TV and/or a computer in their bedroom. Ask them if they think this is a good idea. Have them give reasons and justify their answers.

4 Find Out More!

- The children research body clocks and sleep cycles. The **Search Engine** feature gives support on where to look. The children will need to complete this research before doing the follow-up activity in the Activity Book. (It could be set as homework.)

Optional activity: Class survey

Ask *What time did you go to bed last night? What time did you get up this morning?* Elicit answers. Then divide the class into groups to do a survey, asking *How long do you sleep?* They tally their friends' sleeping hours and analyze the results. Ask groups to present their findings to the class and comment on their friends' sleeping habits.

Lesson 7
CLIL

1 Read and write *true* or *false*.

Light and Sleep

Light makes you stay awake in the day. Before we had electricity, people went to bed when it got dark and got up at sunrise. Lights in our homes have changed our body clocks. We now have more light at night time and so people stay up later and sleep less than in the past. Don't forget that your TV and computer screens give light, too. So turn them off! When you use them just before bedtime, you don't fall asleep as quickly as you should - and you don't sleep as well.

1 Electricity has changed how long we sleep. ....true..........
2 People go to bed earlier now than in the past. ....
3 People used to sleep more in the past. ....
4 You sleep better when you watch TV before going to bed. ....
5 You shouldn't use your computer late at night. ....

2 Use your Student Book research to make an Info Card. Write about body clocks and sleep cycles. Find Out More!

When should you sleep? What changes your body clock?
What happens to you when you sleep? What helps you sleep?

3 Write some advice about good sleep habits. Then try it out.

Try It Out
Read the quiz again for information.
In groups, write six tips about good sleep habits.
Take your own advice! Follow the tips for two weeks.
After two weeks, take the quiz again. Did you get more As? Have the tips worked? Tell the class.

4 Select and store information on this topic in the Class Info Hub.

28

1 Read and write *true* or *false*.

The children read the text. Elicit why the example answer is true. (*We used to go to sleep when it got dark.*) They read the text again and decide if the sentences are true or false. Elicit answers, including the correct version of the false sentences.

Answers

1 true **2** false **3** true **4** false **5** true

2 Use your Student Book research to make an Info Card. Write about body clocks and sleep cycles.

Divide the class into groups. Have the children pool the information learned from their research in the Student Book and the Activity Book. They write about and illustrate their ideas individually. Have the groups present their Info Cards to the class.

3 Write some advice about good sleep habits. Then try it out.

In their groups, the children follow the **Try It Out** instructions and write a list of six tips for sleeping well. Elicit ideas. The groups try out their tips at home. Make a note to have the children take the quiz in Student Book Activity 1 again in two weeks to see if the class gets more As.

Answers

Children's own answers.

4 Select and store information on this topic in the Class Info Hub.

Have the children vote for the most interesting Info cards. Archive these in your Class Hub (see p. 41) in a folder called **Chapter 3 The Importance of Sleep**.

Cooler: Play "Match It"

Write on the board in two columns the following words, one word in each column with the order of the second column jumbled: *lie down, stay awake, fall asleep, stay up, teddy bear, turn off, wake up, bed time*, etc. Have children draw lines to match pairs of words.

Competency Focus

Me

The children find out information about sleep cycles and relate it to their own experiences.

Digital Resources

Student eBook • TIP When using the board for "heads-up" teaching, give the children as much opportunity as possible to participate. Make sure you ask plenty of questions so they engage with the text.

• Have different children use *Pen* to circle their SB quiz answers. Elicit class agreement by a show of hands.

Teacher Resource Center • Print out CLIL Graphic Organizer 3 for the children to use in collating their Find Out More! research.

CLIL eBook • The children can use the CLIL eBook to expand their knowledge of the lesson topic.

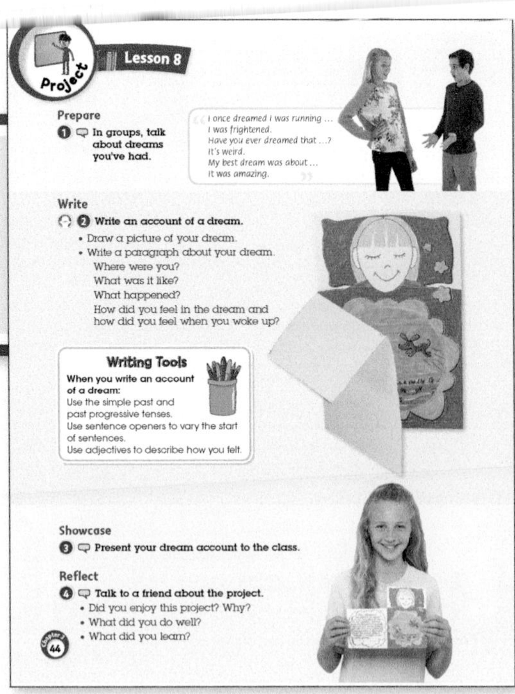
Lesson 8

Project

Prepare

1 In groups, talk about dreams you've had.

I once dreamed I was running ...
I was frightened.
Have you ever dreamed that ...?
It's weird.
My best dream was about ...
It was amazing.

Write

2 Write an account of a dream.

- Draw a picture of your dream.
- Write a paragraph about your dream.
  Where were you?
  What was it like?
  What happened?
  How did you feel in the dream and how did you feel when you woke up?

Writing Tools

When you write an account of a dream:
Use the simple past and past progressive tenses.
Use sentence openers to vary the start of sentences.
Use adjectives to describe how you felt.

Showcase

3 Present your dream account to the class.

Reflect

4 Talk to a friend about the project.

- Did you enjoy this project? Why?
- What did you do well?
- What did you learn?

44

Writing Project

Lesson objectives: review language from Chapter 3; write an account of a dream and present it to the class

Materials: Writing Template 3 [TRC printout] (optional)

Warmer: Brainstorm vocabulary

Brainstorm vocabulary connected to sleeping and dreams to review language from the chapter. Draw a mind map on the board and ask children to write in vocabulary items, e.g. *lie down*, *stay awake*, etc.

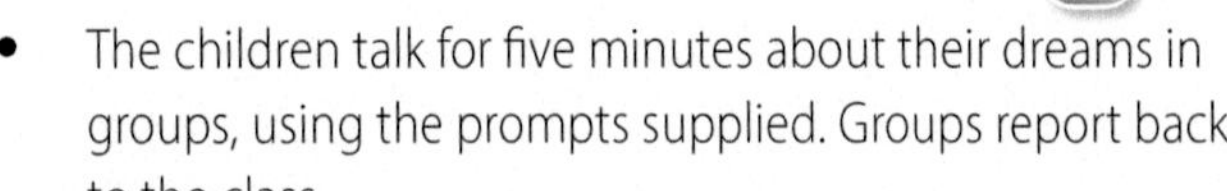

Prepare

1 In groups, talk about dreams you've had.

- The children talk for five minutes about their dreams in groups, using the prompts supplied. Groups report back to the class.

Write

2 Write an account of a dream.

- Have the children read the instructions.
- Read the **Writing Tools** box together. Elicit examples of simple past and past progressive verbs, sentence openers, and adjectives.
- The children prepare an outline, using the instructions and the questions. They write about and illustrate their dream, then compare with a friend. Give support as necessary.

Showcase

3 Present your dream account to the class. 

- Choose children to read their dream stories to the class. Ask the rest of the class to listen for the main events in the story and how the person felt.

Reflect

4 Vote for the best account of a dream and talk to the class.

- Ask the class to choose five good dream stories. Ask them to choose which one they like best and have a class vote.
- Have the children choose two of the stories to compare and justify their decision. Review the comparative structure (*not*) *as* + [adjective] + *as*.

Optional activity: Mime time

Have the children choose a dream from Activity 1. They plan their mime and action sequence in pairs. Call on pairs to act out their dreams. Have the class make sentences (oral or written) to describe what they think is happening in the dream.

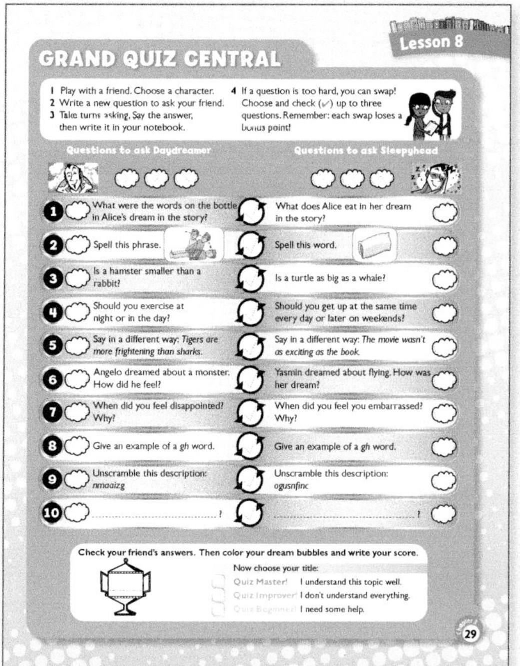

Lesson 8

GRAND QUIZ CENTRAL

1 Play with a friend. Choose a character.
2 Write a new question to ask your friend.
3 Take turns asking. Say the answer, then write it in your notebook.
4 If a question is too hard, you can swap! Choose and check (✓) up to three questions. Remember: each swap loses a bonus point!

	Questions to ask Daydreamer	Questions to ask Sleepyhead
1	What were the words on the bottle in Alice's dream in the story?	What does Alice eat in her dream in the story?
2	Spell this phrase.	Spell this word.
3	Is a hamster smaller than a rabbit?	Is a turtle as big as a whale?
4	Should you exercise at night or in the day?	Should you get up at the same time every day or later on weekends?
5	Say in a different way: *Tigers are more frightening than sharks.*	Say in a different way: *The movie wasn't as exciting as the book.*
6	Angelo dreamed about a monster. How did he feel?	Yasmin dreamed about flying. How was her dream?
7	When did you feel disappointed? Why?	When did you feel you embarrassed? Why?
8	Give an example of a *gh* word.	Give an example of a *gh* word.
9	Unscramble this description: *nmaaizg*	Unscramble this description: *ogusnfinc*
10	……………………………………?	……………………………………?

Check your friend's answers. Then color your dream bubbles and write your score.

Now choose your title:
Quiz Master! I understand this topic well.
Quiz Improver! I don't understand everything.
Quiz Beginner! I need some help.

29

Competency Focus

Me

The children write an account of their own dream story, exploring their imagination and creativity.

Grand Quiz Central

See p. 43 for details of how to take the quiz.

Answers

1 Drink me! / a cake **2** lie down / pillow **3** Yes, it is. / No, it isn't. **4** in the day / at the same time **5** Sharks aren't as frightening as tigers. / The book was more exciting than the movie. **6** He was frightened. / It was awesome. **7** I felt disappointed when … / I was embarrassed when ... **8** *any one of:* frightening/ frightened, light, might, night, fight, right, height, sight, tight, bright **9** amazing / confusing **10** Children's own answers.

Cooler: Play "Consequences"

Distribute pieces of paper to groups of four children. Say *My dream last night was very* … The children copy this then write a word to complete the sentence. They fold over the paper and pass it on. Repeat with *I dreamed about* …, *I was wearing* …, *I went to* … Then the groups unfold the paper and read the dream together. Ask groups to read their dreams out loud.

Digital Resources

Student eBook, Digital Activity Book • Review a vocabulary topic from previous chapters. Have the children raise their hand to vote to select a topic. Then use *Timer* and give the class one minute to recall all the words in the topic. Repeat with a different topic if you have time.

Teacher Resource Center • Print out Writing Template 3 to use for the SB writing activity.

Language Review

Lesson objective: review language from Chapter 3

Materials: Tracks 3.7, AB 3.1, AB 3.2 and AB 3.3

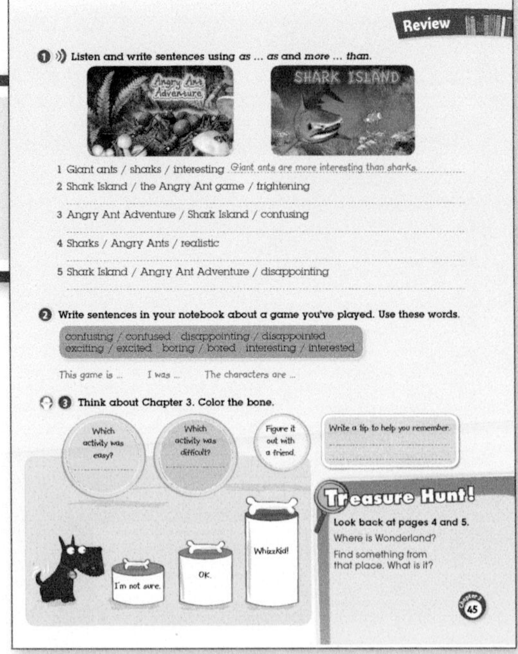

Review

1 Listen and write sentences using *as ... as* and *more ... than*.

1 Giant ants / sharks / interesting Giant ants are more interesting than sharks.
2 Shark Island / the Angry Ant game / frightening
3 Angry Ant Adventure / Shark Island / confusing
4 Sharks / Angry Ants / realistic
5 Shark Island / Angry Ant Adventure / disappointing

2 Write sentences in your notebook about a game you've played. Use these words.

confusing / confused disappointing / disappointed
exciting / excited boring / bored interesting / interested

This game is ... I was ... The characters are ...

3 Think about Chapter 3. Color the bone.

Treasure Hunt!

Look back at pages 4 and 5.
Where is Wonderland?
Find something from that place. What is it?

45

Warmer: Computer/video games

Ask the children which computer/video games they play. Write the names on the board. Have them compare the games and review comparatives.

1 3.7 Listen and write sentences using *as … as* and *more … than.*

- Play Track 3.7. The children listen, then write sentences using *as … as …* and *more … than.*

Audioscript

I like Angry Ant Adventure. *It's exciting being chased by giant ants. They're more interesting than sharks. But the shark game isn't as frightening as* Angry Ant Adventure. *I'm not scared of ants, but some levels have a lot of ants and they're really big. You can't find a way out and it's more confusing than* Shark Island. *You have to pay attention.*

The sharks are amazing but they aren't as realistic as the ants. I stayed up late playing Shark Island *but I was disappointed at the end. The final level was awful.* Shark Island *was more disappointing. I fell asleep before the end!*

Answers

1 Giant ants are more interesting than sharks.
2 Shark Island isn't as frightening as the Angry Ant game.
3 Angry Ant Adventure is more confusing than Shark Island.
4 The Sharks aren't as realistic as the Angry Ants.
5 Shark Island was more disappointing than Angry Ant Adventure.

2 Write sentences in your notebook about a game you've played. Use these words.

- Have children choose one of the games from the Warmer.
- The children write sentences in their notebook.

Answers

Children's own answers.

3 Think about Chapter 3. Color the bone. 

- Have the children look back at Chapter 3 and color the bone to evaluate their progress (self-evaluation). Discuss ideas for remembering spelling. The children write a tip.

Treasure Hunt!

Ask *Does Wonderland really exist?* (*no*). Have the children look at pp. 4–5 to find something from Alice's adventure in Wonderland. (*the DRINK ME bottle in the boy's backpack*)

Cooler: Play "The Shark Game"

Play the game using vocabulary from the chapter (see Games Bank p. 19).

Competency Focus

Me: Self-evaluation

The children reflect on the chapter and express their opinions about their own progress.

Chapter 3 Exam Booster

1 Reading and Writing

Read the story. Choose a word from the box. Write the correct word next to numbers 1–4. There is one example.

example							
early	amazing	well	frightened	was	fell	walking	confusing

Last night, I went to bed ....early.... because I was very tired. I **(1)** .... asleep quickly and soon started dreaming. I was **(2)** .... around a big castle on the top of a mountain. It was snowing and it was just as cold inside the castle as it was outside. I was freezing. There were lots of different rooms with old chairs and tables. There weren't any other people, but I wasn't **(3)** .... Then I saw something. There was a monkey in front of me. It was bigger than the monkeys at the zoo and it was carrying an **(4)** .... chocolate cake. "Happy Birthday! Would you like some cake?" it asked. I took some cake and the monkey disappeared. When I woke up, I was very confused!

(5) Now choose the best name for the story. Tick one box.

A Cold Night ☐

Oliver's Weird Dream ☐

Oliver's Surprise Birthday ☐

84

2 Listening

Listen and color and write. There is one example.

85

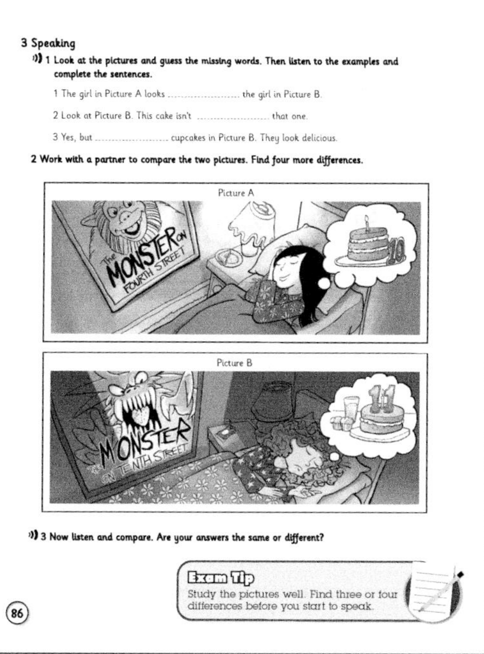

3 Speaking

1 Look at the pictures and guess the missing words. Then listen to the examples and complete the sentences.

1 The girl in Picture A looks .... the girl in Picture B.

2 Look at Picture B. This cake isn't .... that one.

3 Yes, but .... cupcakes in Picture B. They look delicious.

2 Work with a partner to compare the two pictures. Find four more differences.

Picture A

Picture B

3 Now listen and compare. Are your answers the same or different?

Exam Tip

Study the pictures well. Find three or four differences before you start to speak.

86

1 Reading and Writing. Read the story. Choose a word from the box. Write the correct word next to numbers 1–4. There is one example.

The children complete the text using the words supplied and choose the best title. Check answers.

Answers

1 fell **2** walking **3** frightened **4** amazing **5** b

2 AB 3.1 Listening. Listen and color, and write. There is one example.

Play AB Track 3.1 twice. The children listen and color, write, or draw. Check answers.

Answers (Audioscript on p. 222)

Boat on beach: colored red; Write New Movie on the post for the movie; Small boy's backpack: colored green; Woman on phone: skirt colored yellow; Sign with price: DRINKS written on it

3.1 AB 3.2 Speaking. Look at the pictures and guess the missing words. Then listen to the examples and complete the sentences.

Play AB Track 3.2 twice. Children complete the sentences.

Answers (Audioscript on p. 222)

1 happier than **2** as big as **3** there are

3.2 AB 3.3 Speaking. Work with a partner to compare the two pictures. Find four more differences.

Put the children in pairs find four differences.

(Audioscript on p.222)

Digital Resources

Teacher Resource Center • Print out Test Chapter 3 to use at the end of this lesson. The Test Generator also allows you to create customized tests.

- For the Cambridge English Young Learners Exams preparation activities, there are Speaking prompts available for this chapter.
- Print out Festival Worksheet: New Year's Eve to expand the children's knowledge of celebrations throughout the world.

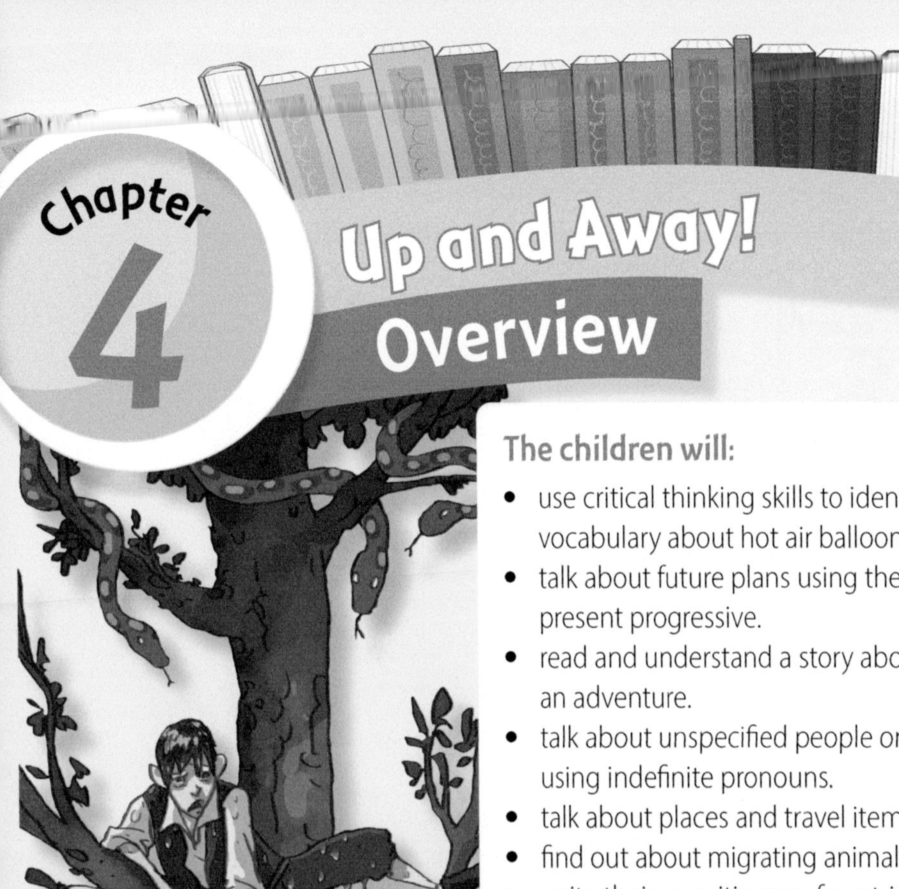

Up and Away!
Overview

The children will:
- use critical thinking skills to identify vocabulary about hot air balloons.
- talk about future plans using the present progressive.
- read and understand a story about an adventure.
- talk about unspecified people or objects using indefinite pronouns.
- talk about places and travel items.
- find out about migrating animals.
- write their own itinerary for a trip.

Literacy Development
- use reading skills to understand and predict content
- relate story theme to personal experience
- use time expressions to link and order events

Key Vocabulary
Hot air balloons: balloon, basket, flight, hot air, land, passengers, pilot, ropes, safe, takes off, view
Continents and world travel: Africa, Antarctica, Asia, Australia, Europe, North America, South America; airplane, backpack, passport, ship, train

Functional Language
- What are you doing for vacation next week?
- We're staying at home and … What about you?
- I'm flying to … to see … ! I can't wait!
- That sounds great.

Key Grammar
Present progressive for future
- We're flying to New York tomorrow.
- I'm not going to school.
- Are you eating at Joe's cafe on Tuesday?

Indefinite pronouns
- Someone gave me a book.
- I don't know anything about the Montgolfier brothers.
- Did anyone travel in it?

Spelling
Compound nouns

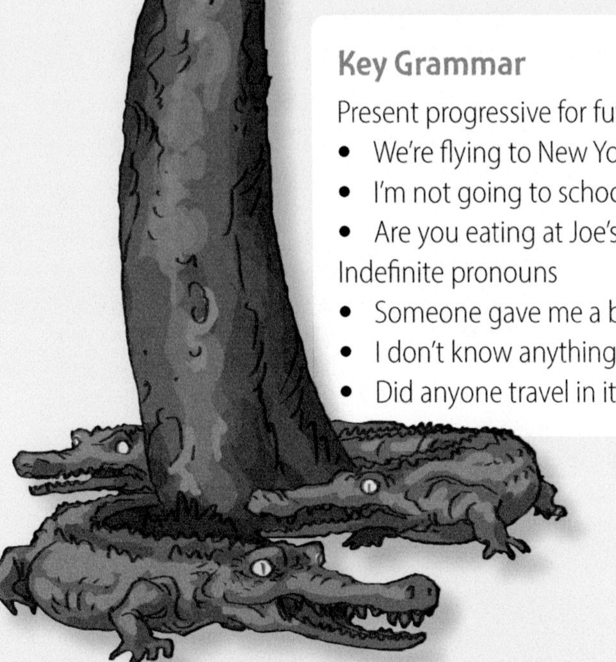

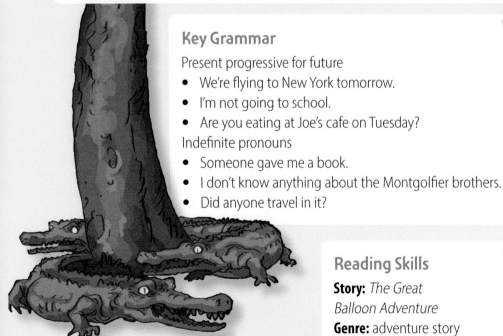

Reading Skills
Story: *The Great Balloon Adventure*
Genre: adventure story

CLIL: Geography—Turtle migration
The children find out about migrating animals.

Competency Focus

The children will:

use critical thinking skills to deduce the meaning of new vocabulary. (Lesson 1) predict the content of a story. (Lesson 3)	activate new vocabulary and apply new grammar knowledge. (Lesson 2) apply new grammar rules in a familiar context. (Lesson 5)	work in pairs to act out a dialogue. (Lesson 3) work in pairs to talk about their own imaginary trip. (Lesson 6)	relate the story theme to their personal experience. (Lesson 4) write their own itinerary for a trip. (Lesson 8) evaluate their own progress in the chapter. (Review)	find out more about migrating animals. (Lesson 7)

Digital Overview

Teacher Presentation

Student eBook and Digital Activity Book

- Music Video 4.1: *I'm Going Around the World*
- Interactive versions of AB activities
- Integrated audio and answer key for all activities

Teacher resources for planning, lesson delivery, and homework

Teacher Resource Center

- Class Planner Chapter 4
- Worksheets to print out (including notes and answers):
  - Grammar Worksheet 4A: Present progressive for future
  - Grammar Worksheet 4B: Indefinite pronouns
  - Phonics Worksheet 4
  - CLIL Graphic Organizer 4
  - Writing Template 4
  - Test Chapter 4
- Test Generator
- Literacy Handbook

Watch the Music Video

Children's resources for consolidation and practice at home

Student eBook

- Music Video 4.1: *I'm Going Around the World*

The Inks Student's App

Vocabulary games: Hot air balloons and Continents/world travel

Chapter 4

Up and Away!

Lesson 1

Vocabulary

Lesson objectives: identify and use vocabulary to describe a hot air balloon flight

Key vocabulary: *balloon, basket, flight, hot air, land, passengers, pilot, ropes, safe, takes off, view*

Materials: Track 4.1

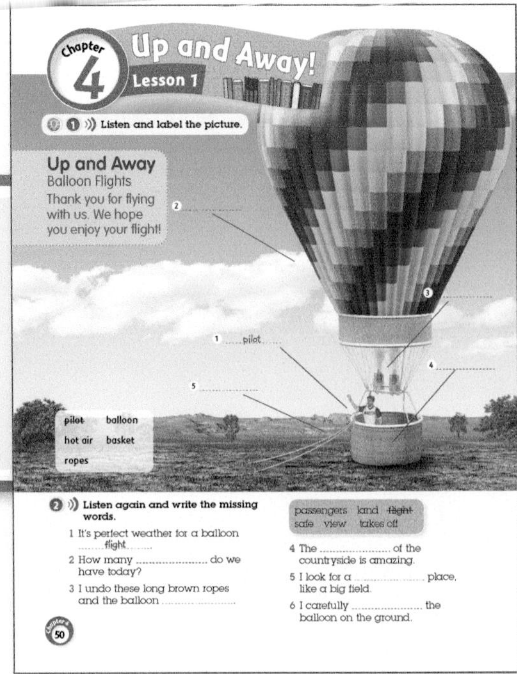
Chapter 4 Up and Away! Lesson 1

1 Listen and label the picture.

2 Listen again and write the missing words.

passengers land ~~flight~~ safe view takes off

1 It's perfect weather for a balloon ....flight........
2 How many .... do we have today?
3 I undo these long brown ropes and the balloon ....
4 The .... of the countryside is amazing.
5 I look for a .... place, like a big field.
6 I carefully .... the balloon on the ground.

50

Warmer: Introduce the hot air balloon

Start to draw a picture of a hot air balloon little by little, e.g. basket, ropes, pilot, balloon. Get the children to guess what the object is as you draw. Elicit any information the children already have about hot air balloons and how they fly. Write any vocabulary they know on the board, e.g. *pilot, basket.*

1 4.1 Listen and label the picture. 

- Play Track 4.1. The children listen and label the picture using the words supplied.
- Elicit answers. You could ask children to label the balloon picture you have on the board. Whenever you elicit answers, remember to check with the class to see if they agree.

Audioscript

Good morning! I'm Martin and I'm your pilot. I fly this beautiful hot air balloon. It's red, yellow, green, blue, orange: all the colors of the rainbow! Today, it's a clear, sunny day, with no clouds. Perfect weather for a balloon flight.

Have you ever flown in a hot air balloon? Well, it's a lot of fun.

First, I fill the balloon with hot air. The balloon is attached to the ground with strong ropes.

Then you can climb into the basket. How many passengers do we have today? … thirteen, fourteen, fifteen people. That's great!

Then, I undo these long brown ropes and the balloon takes off and we go up into the sky! Our flight lasts for one hour. You should take your camera. The view of the countryside is amazing.

After an hour, I look for a safe place, like a big field. Then I carefully land the balloon on the ground. The basket usually touches the ground on its side, so hold on tight!

Enjoy your flight!

Answers

1 pilot **2** balloon **3** hot air **4** basket **5** ropes

2 4.1 Listen again and write the missing words.

- Play Track 4.1 again. The children listen and complete the sentences with the words supplied.
- Play Track 4.1 again. They complete any missing answers and/or check.
- Elicit answers.

Answers

1 flight **2** passengers **3** takes off **4** view **5** safe **6** land

Optional activity: How to fly a balloon

Have the children work in pairs to write instructions for flying the balloon using the words supplied. Give an example, e.g. *Fill the balloon with hot air.* Have pairs come to the front of the class. One child mimes the actions as the other child reads the instructions.

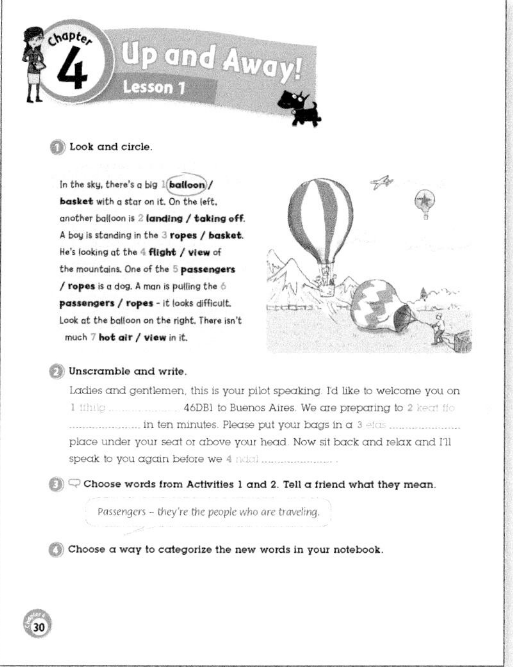

Chapter 4 **Up and Away!**
Lesson 1

1 Look and circle.

In the sky, there's a big 1 **balloon / basket** with a star on it. On the left, another balloon is 2 **landing / taking off**. A boy is standing in the 3 **ropes / basket**. He's looking at the 4 **flight / view** of the mountains. One of the 5 **passengers / ropes** is a dog. A man is pulling the 6 **passengers / ropes** - it looks difficult. Look at the balloon on the right. There isn't much 7 **hot air / view** in it.

2 Unscramble and write.

Ladies and gentlemen, this is your pilot speaking. I'd like to welcome you on 1 tfhilg .... 46DB1 to Buenos Aires. We are preparing to 2 keat ffo .... in ten minutes. Please put your bags in a 3 efas .... place under your seat or above your head. Now sit back and relax and I'll speak to you again before we 4 ndal ....

3 Choose words from Activities 1 and 2. Tell a friend what they mean.

Passengers – they're the people who are traveling.

4 Choose a way to categorize the new words in your notebook.

30

1 Look and circle.

The children complete the text by circling the correct option in each pair. Elicit answers.

Answers

1 balloon **2** taking off **3** basket **4** view **5** passengers **6** ropes **7** hot air

2 Unscramble and write.

The children unscramble and write the words, using the clues in the sentences to figure them out. Elicit answers.

Answers

1 flight **2** take off **3** safe **4** land

3 Choose words from Activities 1 and 2. Tell a friend what they mean.

Ask a child to read the example. Elicit a definition for *view*. (e.g. *It's what you can see from the balloon.*) Have children choose words and give definitions in pairs.

4 Choose a way to categorize the new words in your notebook.

Brainstorm appropriate categories, e.g. *verbs/nouns/adjectives, alphabetical order, one/two/three syllables.* The children choose the best categories for them and list the words in their notebook.

Answers

Children's own answers.

Cooler: Visualization

Have the children imagine they are in a balloon basket and are flying. Ask *Where are you? What can you see? Who are you with? How do you feel?* Invite children to describe their balloon journey. Have them use their hands to mime binoculars to show *I can see.*

Competency Focus

Think! Critical Thinking

The children use critical thinking skills to understand the new vocabulary by using visual clues and processing the written and spoken form.

Digital Resources

Student eBook, Digital Activity Book • TIP When using the board for "heads-up" teaching, give the children as much opportunity as possible to participate. Make sure you ask plenty of questions so they engage with the text.

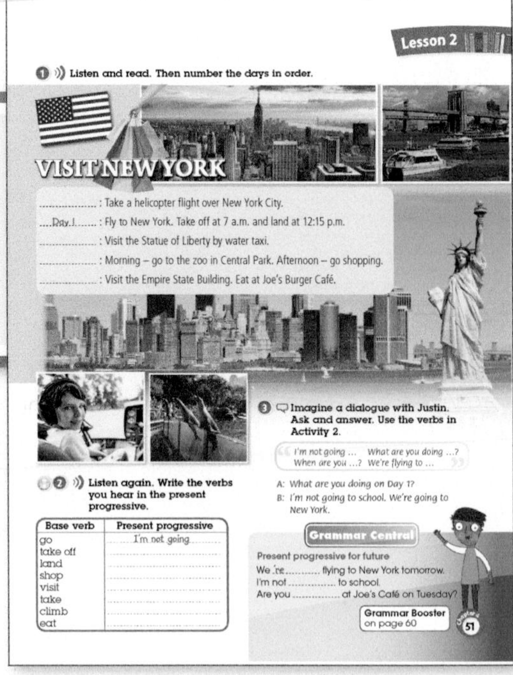
Lesson 2

1 Listen and read. Then number the days in order.

VISIT NEW YORK

.... : Take a helicopter flight over New York City.
....Day 1....... : Fly to New York. Take off at 7 a.m. and land at 12:15 p.m.
.... : Visit the Statue of Liberty by water taxi.
.... : Morning – go to the zoo in Central Park. Afternoon – go shopping.
.... : Visit the Empire State Building. Eat at Joe's Burger Café.

2 Listen again. Write the verbs you hear in the present progressive.

Base verb	Present progressive
go	I'm not going
take off	
land	
shop	
visit	
take	
climb	
eat	

3 Imagine a dialogue with Justin. Ask and answer. Use the verbs in Activity 2.

"I'm not going ... What are you doing ...? When are you ...? We're flying to ..."

A: What are you doing on Day 1?
B: I'm not going to school. We're going to New York.

Grammar Central

Present progressive for future
We 're........ flying to New York tomorrow.
I'm not .... to school.
Are you .... at Joe's Café on Tuesday?

Grammar Booster on page 60

51

Grammar

Lesson objective: talk about definite future plans
Key grammar: present progressive (for future)—statements, questions
Secondary language: *helicopter, water taxi*
Materials: Track 4.2; Grammar Worksheet 4A [TRC printout] (optional)

Warmer: Play "The Shark Game"

Play the game using key vocabulary from Lesson 1 (see Games Bank p. 19).

1 4.2 Listen and read. Then number the days in order.

- Have the children identify the places in New York. Explain *itinerary* (*a plan of things to do*).
- Play Track 4.2. They write the correct day for each activity. Elicit answers. Children say which day is the most exciting.

Audioscript

Hi, I'm Justin. I'm not going to school tomorrow. I'm so excited because we're going on a five-day trip to New York.

On Day 1, that's tomorrow, we're flying to New York. We're taking off at 7 a.m. and we're landing at 12:15 p.m. We're going straight to the hotel.

On Day 2, we're going to the zoo in Central Park. We're going to feed the sea lions! Don't worry, it's safe! In the afternoon, we're going shopping.

On Day 3, we're visiting the Statue of Liberty. We're taking a water taxi with a lot of other passengers. I'm taking my camera.

On Day 4, we're going to the top of the Empire State Building. It's really high. There are 86 floors. There's an amazing view of the city. Don't worry, we aren't climbing the stairs. We're taking the elevator. Then we're eating at Joe's Burger Café. The best burgers in New York City!

Day 5 is our last day. We're taking a helicopter flight over New York City. And then we're flying home that night.

Answers

Day 5, Day 1, Day 3, Day 2, Day 4

Grammar Central

Present progressive for future

Have the children complete the grammar examples. Elicit answers. Elicit how the present progressive is formed for future statements and question forms. The children write further examples in their notebook. For extra practice, try the **Grammar Booster** section in the Student Book (p. 60).

Answers p.60

Activity 1: **1** are, doing **2** 'm/am visiting **3** 'm/am not going **4** Are, having **5** are **6** aren't

Activity 2: **1** Everyone is going to Buckingham Palace today. **2** Mom and Jenny are visiting the British Museum tomorrow. **3** Dad and Liam are watching a soccer game in the afternoon. **4** Dad is riding the London Eye on Friday morning. **5** Mom, Jenny, and Liam are eating in Covent Garden on Saturday. **6** They're not going shopping on this trip.

2 4.2 Listen again. Write the verbs you hear in the present progressive.

- Play Track 4.2 again and have the children write the correct forms of the verbs they hear.

Answers

go—I'm not going/we're going, take off—we're taking off, land—we're landing, shop—we're going shopping, visit—we're visiting, take—I'm taking/we're taking, climb—we aren't climbing, eat—we're eating

3 Imagine a dialogue with Justin. Ask and answer. Use the verbs in Activity 2.

- Choose two children to read the example dialogue.
- Divide the class into pairs to practice the dialogue using the verbs in Activity 2 and their own ideas for activities. Have pairs perform for the class.

Optional activity: Plan a trip to the USA

Tell the children they are going on a five-day trip to the USA. Brainstorm any other cities/famous places they know in the USA on the board. Have them work in pairs and plan their itinerary. Then choose pairs to report their plans to the class.

2 Look at your itinerary. Write questions. Then ask and answer.

The children write questions. Elicit responses. The children then ask and answer in pairs. Have pairs read out questions and answers.

Answers

1 When are you going to the zoo? **2** Are you flying home on Friday? **3** What are you doing on Thursday? **4** Where are you eating on Tuesday? **5** Are you watching a baseball game?

3 Now complete the itinerary for Saturday and Sunday. Then write.

Brainstorm more ideas for the trip. The children complete the sentences and compare in pairs. Elicit responses. Ask *What type of information is in an itinerary?* (*times, places, activities*)

Answers

Children's own answers.

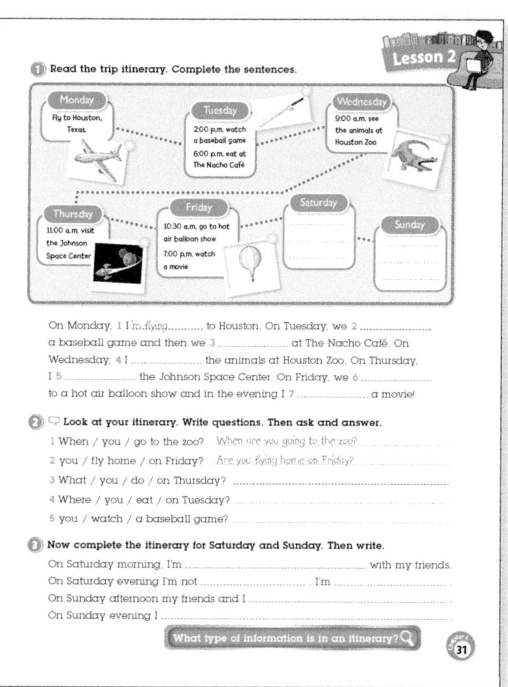

Lesson 2

1 Read the trip itinerary. Complete the sentences.

On Monday, 1 I 'm flying .... to Houston. On Tuesday, we 2 .... a baseball game and then we 3 .... at The Nacho Café. On Wednesday, 4 I .... the animals at Houston Zoo. On Thursday, I 5 .... the Johnson Space Center. On Friday, we 6 .... to a hot air balloon show and in the evening I 7 .... a movie!

2 Look at your itinerary. Write questions. Then ask and answer.

1 When / you / go to the zoo? When are you going to the zoo?
2 you / fly home / on Friday? Are you flying home on Friday?
3 What / you / do / on Thursday? ....
4 Where / you / eat / on Tuesday? ....
5 you / watch / a baseball game? ....

3 Now complete the itinerary for Saturday and Sunday. Then write.

On Saturday morning, I'm .... with my friends.
On Saturday evening I'm not .... I'm ....
On Sunday afternoon my friends and I ....
On Sunday evening I ....

What type of information is in an itinerary?

31

1 Read the trip itinerary. Complete the sentences.

Remind the children of how to skim read a text for key information and how useful the pictures can be. The children complete the sentences individually. Suggest verbs if they have difficulty. Elicit answers.

Answers

1 'm flying **2** 're watching **3** 're eating **4** 'm seeing **5** 'm visiting **6** 're going **7** 'm watching

Cooler: Play "Spelling Bee"

Play the game with *–ing* words from the lesson (see Games Bank p. 19).

Competency Focus

Learn

By listening to the itinerary and writing the verbs in the present progressive, the children demonstrate their understanding of the new grammatical structures.

Digital Resources

Digital Activity Book • Do the AB interactive digital activities as a class, or set them for homework.

Teacher Resource Center • For extra grammar practice, print out Grammar Worksheet 4A.

Reading: Story Extract

Lesson objectives: talk about their next vacation; use the title and pictures to predict story content; read the extract from the adventure story *The Great Balloon Adventure* (middle)

Functional language: *What are you doing for vacation next week? We're staying at home and … What about you? I'm flying to … to see … ! I can't wait! That sounds great.*

Secondary language: *throw out, attacking, splash*

Materials: Tracks 4.3 and 4.4

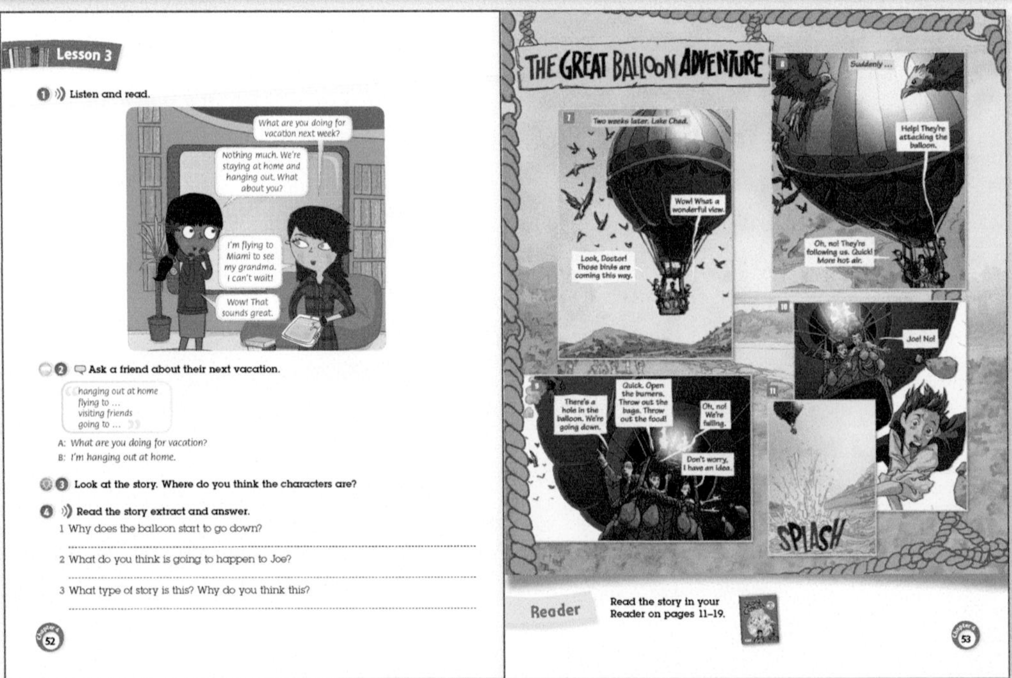

Lesson 3

1 Listen and read.

2 Ask a friend about their next vacation.

hanging out at home
flying to …
visiting friends
going to …

A: What are you doing for vacation?
B: I'm hanging out at home.

3 Look at the story. Where do you think the characters are?

4 Read the story extract and answer.

1 Why does the balloon start to go down?

2 What do you think is going to happen to Joe?

3 What type of story is this? Why do you think this?

52

THE GREAT BALLOON ADVENTURE

Reader Read the story in your Reader on pages 11–19.

53

Warmer: Play "The A-Z Game"

Play the game using vacation vocabulary. (see Games Bank p. 19).

Functional language

1 4.3 Listen and read.

- Play Track 4.3. The children listen and read along.
- Play Track 4.3 again for them to repeat.
- Divide the class into pairs to practice the dialogue.

2 Ask a friend about their next vacation.  

- Choose two children to read the example dialogue.
- The children practice in pairs using the prompts supplied and adding details. Have pairs do a dialogue for the class.

Before reading

3 Look at the story. Where do you think the characters are?

- Have the children identify the characters and describe the landscape in picture 1. Ask *Where are the characters?*

4 4.4 Read the story extract and answer.

- Have the children read the extract and answer question 1.
- Play Track 4.4. They listen and complete their ideas for questions 2 and 3.
- Elicit answers, but do not confirm predictions: explain that they will have to read the story to find out.

Answers

1 There's a hole in it/the balloon. **2** Children's own answers. **3** Children's own answers/Adventure story.

Lesson 3

1 Cross out the incorrect phrase. Then choose, write, and act out.

last Saturday / for your birthday / after school / tomorrow

What are you doing .... ?

I'm ....

2 Read the story in your Student Book. Check (✓) the sentence that describes the story. Then circle the story type.

1 The story is about how people used to live every day in the past.
2 Everything in the story is true.
3 Dangerous and exciting things happen.

factual/non-fiction   science fiction   adventure

3 Write *true* or *false*.

1 The doctor is flying the balloon. ......true......
2 The birds aren't dangerous. ....
3 Hot air should make the balloon go up. ....
4 The birds make a hole in the balloon. ....
5 The men throw out the food because they aren't hungry. ....

4 Where do Richard and the doctor fly to next? Think and write.

32

1 Cross out the incorrect phrase. Then choose, write, and act out.

The children identify which phrase is incorrect. (*last Saturday*) They then choose one of the others and act out the dialogue with a friend. Encourage the children to use what they know to adapt and extend the dialogue. Have pairs act out their dialogue for the class.

2 Read the story in your Student Book. Check (✓) the sentence that describes the story. Then circle the story type.

The children read the Student Book story extract again, then choose the best sentence to describe what the story is about. They then circle the type of story. Elicit answers.

Answers

✓ *by* 3; *circled:* adventure

3 Write *true* or *false*.

The children write true or false for each sentence. Elicit answers, including the correct version of the false sentences.

Answers

1 true **2** false **3** true **4** true **5** false

4 Where do Richard and the doctor fly to next? Think and write.

Elicit other adventurous destinations for Richard and the doctor to fly to. The children write their own ideas, then compare with a friend. Elicit ideas.

Answers

Children's own answers.

Cooler: Practice pronunciation

Write sentences from the story extract on the board, e.g. *Wow! What a wonderful view.* Read them aloud twice, emphasizing the stress pattern. Have children mark or underline the stressed words/syllables.

Competency Focus

Collaborate and Communicate

The children work together, putting into practice new functional language by acting out a realistic dialogue.

Think! Critical Thinking

By analyzing visual clues and deducing from the context, the children use prediction skills to help them engage with the story and understand the characters.

Digital Resources

Student eBook • For SB Activity 1, use *Highlighter* on the sentences starting *We're staying at home ...* and *I'm flying to Miami ...* and elicit different things you could say in this context.

1
Doctor Samuel Ferguson's study.

Dr.: What are you doing for vacation, Richard?

Richard: Oh, nothing much, Samuel. I'm hanging out at home.

Dr.: OK! You're coming with me! We're going on a trip.

2
Dr.: Here's the itinerary. We're leaving in the spring! We're taking off from the island of Zanzibar, close to the east coast of Africa. Joe! Have my bags packed and ready then.

3
Dr.: We're flying west over Lake Victoria.

Richard: Flying?

Dr.: Yes! In a hot air balloon. A balloon flight! Then we're flying to Lake Chad. After that, we're going to Timbuktu and then to the west coast.

4
Joe: Can I come too, Doctor?

Dr.: No, Joe, you're too young. We're looking for adventure! We're going to find the source of the Nile.

5
One month later. Spring time, Zanzibar.

6
Dr.: Joe! What are you doing here?

Joe: I'm sorry! I want to see Africa, too.

Richard: Well, I hope the balloon will carry all three passengers.

7
Two weeks later. Lake Chad.

Richard: Wow! What a wonderful view.

Joe: Look, Doctor! Those birds are coming this way.

8
Suddenly . . .

Richard: Oh, no! They're following us. Quick! More hot air.

Joe: Help! They're attacking the balloon.

9
Richard: There's a hole in the balloon. We're going down.

Dr.: Quick. Open the burners. Throw out the bags. Throw out the food!

Richard: Oh, no! We're falling.

Joe: Don't worry, I have an idea.

10
Dr.: Joe! No!

11
SPLASH!

12
Later, close to the lake ...

Dr.: Let's fix the balloon and sleep here tonight. But tomorrow, we're going back to find Joe.

Richard: Poor Joe. I hope he's safe.

13
Meanwhile . . .

Joe: *I know there are crocodiles in the water, but I have to swim to land.*

15
Joe: *I am so tired. I'm going to sleep in this tree.*

16
The next morning . . .

Dr.: The wind is blowing to the east. We're going back to the lake. He might see the balloon.

17
Joe: I can't believe it! It's the balloon. My friends are here.

18
Dr.: Look! There's Joe.

Richard: Smart Joe! He's running in the same direction as the wind. But we're going too fast.

19
Dr.: We can't land here, Joe! There are too many trees.

Joe: Come on, boy, we're going for a ride.

20
Dr.: Throw him the rope!

Richard: Catch it, Joe!

21
Richard: Jump in, Joe.

22
Richard: Joe, you are safe now.

Joe: Thank you.

Richard: More hot air, Doctor!

Dr.: We're going to go home now.

23
A year later ...

Dr.: What are you doing for vacation this year?

Richard: Nothing much, I'm staying home . . . I *am* staying home. I'm not going on any more of your adventures.

Lesson objective: read and understand the adventure story *The Great Balloon Adventure* in the Reader
Materials: Track 4.5; Reader; map of Africa

Warmer: Who said it?

Have the children remember the names of the characters. Read out a phrase from the story extract and ask the children to identify the speaker. Repeat with other phrases.

Story Summary

A doctor and his friend go on a hot air balloon trip in Africa. Joe, the doctor's young servant, hides in the basket. Birds attack the balloon and Joe ends up in the lake. The doctor and his friend finally rescue Joe, with the help of a camel.

Theme: the importance of friendship and helping others

4.5 While reading

- Have the children look at the pictures in the Reader. Ask them to identify the locations where the story takes place. Have them identify the places on a map.
- Play Track 4.5. The children listen and read along. Ask *Does Joe enjoy his adventure?*
- Ask questions to check comprehension, e.g. *What are they going to find? (the source of the Nile) What's in the water? (crocodiles) What happens when the balloon can't land? (Joe uses a rope to climb up to the basket.)*
- Have the children practice reading the story in groups (see **Story Time**). Choose three groups to read aloud the story for the class.

After reading: Reflect

- Ask questions to give the children the opportunity to think about the issues raised by the story, e.g. *Which three adjectives would you use to describe Joe? Do you think they all sleep well? Are they all enjoying the expedition?*

Optional activity: Add a scene

Have the children imagine that they are traveling over Lake Chad. Ask *What other dangers might you meet?* Have them work in pairs to draw and write captions for the new scene.

Story Time

Group reading

This is a long story to read or act out in class. Divide the class into groups of three and allocate different scenes for them to practice. The story naturally divides into three parts, so you could allocate the beginning, middle, or end to each group. This also underpins the narrative sequence and structure of the story.

Reading Strategy

Reader's Theater

In the Reader's Theater strategy, the children collaborate to read a story aloud. It is similar to a role-play, but offers more support because the children read from the page. They can work on their fluency and develop their confidence performing.

For additional explanation and activities, see the Literacy Handbook on the Teacher Resource Center.

Cooler: Focus on text style

Ask *Do you like reading comic books? Why/Why not?* Have the children think about how they differ from a normal narrative story. Ask them to look at the captions, e.g. *SPLASH!* Elicit other comic books they have read or comics they like reading.

Digital Resources

Student eBook • For the Warmer activity, have the children use *Pen* to circle the speaker in response to the prompt each time.

Reader eBook • Elicit what has happened to Joe and how he feels in each picture. Then have children mime being Joe in different parts of the story. The class guesses what has happened to Joe each time and how he feels.

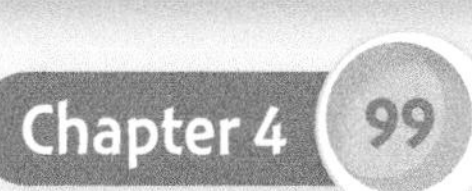

Reading Comprehension and Critical Literacy

Lesson objectives: understand and evaluate the story; relate story theme to personal experience; write a story summary in captions
Materials: Track 4.5; Reader, a balloon (optional)

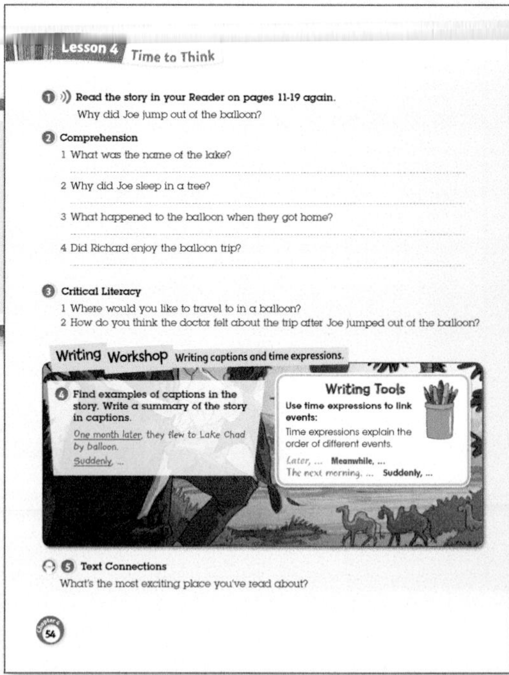
Lesson 4 Time to Think

1 Read the story in your Reader on pages 11-19 again.
Why did Joe jump out of the balloon?

2 Comprehension
1 What was the name of the lake?
2 Why did Joe sleep in a tree?
3 What happened to the balloon when they got home?
4 Did Richard enjoy the balloon trip?

3 Critical Literacy
1 Where would you like to travel to in a balloon?
2 How do you think the doctor felt about the trip after Joe jumped out of the balloon?

Writing Workshop Writing captions and time expressions.

4 Find examples of captions in the story. Write a summary of the story in captions.
One month later, they flew to Lake Chad by balloon.
Suddenly, ...

Writing Tools
Use time expressions to link events:
Time expressions explain the order of different events.
Later, ... Meanwhile, ...
The next morning, ... Suddenly, ...

5 Text Connections
What's the most exciting place you've read about?

54

Note: Please ensure that your class has read the Reader story before you do this lesson.

Warmer: Play "Back to the Board"

Play the game using scenes from the story, e.g. *Joe jumps.* (see Games Bank p. 19).

1 4.5 Read the story in your Reader.

- Have the children read the story. (Alternatively, play Track 4.5 and have them read along.) Elicit whether they were correct in their predictions in Lesson 3 Activity 4.
- Ask *Why did Joe jump out of the balloon?* (*to make the balloon lighter / to save the others*)

2 Comprehension

- Have the children answer the first three questions in the activity. Elicit answers. Then discuss question 4. Ask them to justify their answers.

Answers

1 Lake Chad **2** To get away from the crocodiles.
3 They made curtains from the balloon. **4** No, he didn't.

3 Critical Literacy

- Elicit suggestions on where the children would like to travel in a balloon.
- Ask *How did the Doctor and Richard feel when Joe jumped?* (e.g. *scared, terrible*) Empathizing with the characters and imagining themselves in their situations help children engage creatively with the story.

Writing Workshop

Writing captions and time expressions

4 Find examples of captions in the story. Write a summary of the story in captions.

Have a child read the time expressions in the **Writing Tools** box. The children look back at the story and find examples. They write a summary of the story in captions using time expressions in their notebook, then compare with a friend. Invite children to read out their stories.

Answers

Children's own answers.

5 Text Connections 

- Ask *Which exciting places have you read about in stories?* Make a list on the board.
- The children work in pairs to rank the places in order. Elicit answers.

Optional activity: Tap the balloon!

Hold a balloon up and say *I'm flying across the Sahara Desert tomorrow.* Tap the balloon onto a child and they say where and when they are going before passing the balloon on. If a child makes a mistake, start again. Count the taps made without making a mistake.

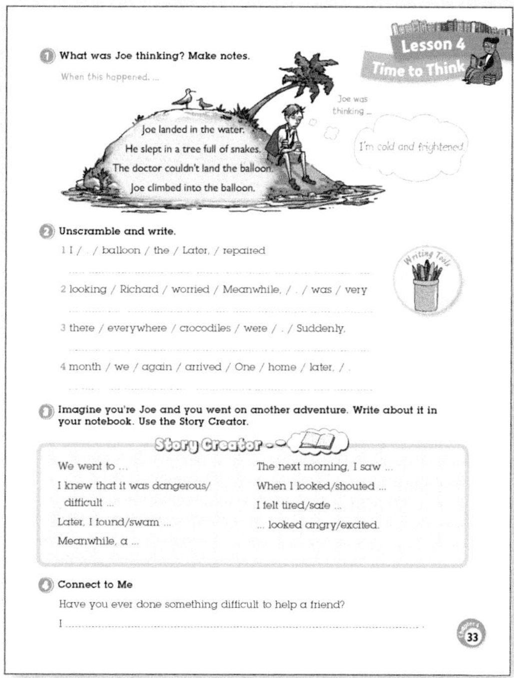
Lesson 4
Time to Think

1 What was Joe thinking? Make notes.

When this happened, ... Joe was thinking ...

Joe landed in the water.
He slept in a tree full of snakes.
The doctor couldn't land the balloon.
Joe climbed into the balloon.

I'm cold and frightened.

2 Unscramble and write.

1 I / . / balloon / the / Later, / repaired
2 looking / Richard / worried / Meanwhile, / . / was / very
3 there / everywhere / crocodiles / were / . / Suddenly,
4 month / we / again / arrived / One / home / later, / .

3 Imagine you're Joe and you went on another adventure. Write about it in your notebook. Use the Story Creator.

Story Creator

We went to ...
I knew that it was dangerous/difficult ...
Later, I found/swam ...
Meanwhile, a ...
The next morning, I saw ...
When I looked/shouted ...
I felt tired/safe ...
... looked angry/excited.

4 Connect to Me

Have you ever done something difficult to help a friend?
I ...

33

1 What was Joe thinking? Make notes.

The children consider what Joe was thinking when each event happened and write notes. Elicit answers.

Answers

Children's own answers.

2 Unscramble and write.

The children unscramble and write the sentences in the correct order. Elicit answers.

Answers

1 Later, I repaired the balloon.
2 Meanwhile, Richard was looking very worried.
3 Suddenly, there were crocodiles everywhere.
4 One month later, we arrived home again.

3 Imagine you're Joe and you went on another adventure. Write about it in your notebook. Use the Story Creator.

Use the **Story Creator** to elicit ideas. The children write a story in their notebook, then compare with a friend. Have children read out their story for the class.

4 Connect to Me

Elicit examples of difficult things the children have done to help their friends. The children write their own response, then compare with a friend.

Cooler: Interview Joe

Tell the children they are journalists. They are going to interview Joe about his amazing balloon adventure. Have the children prepare two or three questions, e.g. *Why did you jump out of the balloon? How did you escape from the crocodiles?* Then choose a child to come to the front of the class and act as Joe.

Competency Focus

Me: Critical Literacy

The children use critical literacy skills to reflect on the story and relate it to their personal experiences.

Digital Resources

Reader eBook • Display the Reader on the board. Show Picture 10. Elicit what happened before and after this. Repeat with Pictures 14 and 20.

- Have children identify captions in the story for the SB Writing Workshop activity.

Student eBook, Digital Activity Book • You can move the answer key pop-up window around the screen to have the activity and the answers side by side.

Grammar and Reading

Lesson objectives: make positive/negative statements and questions with indefinite pronouns
Key grammar: indefinite pronouns—statements, questions
Secondary language: *invented, inventors, hiding*
Materials: Track 4.6; Grammar Worksheet 4B [TRC printout] (optional)

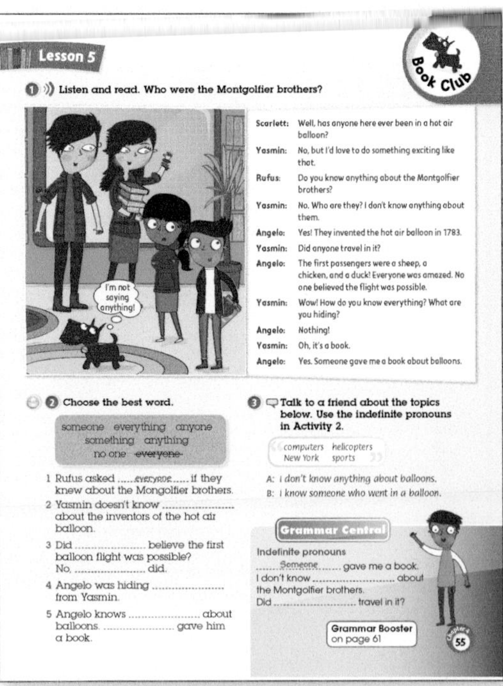

Lesson 5

Book Club

1 Listen and read. Who were the Montgolfier brothers?

Scarlett: Well, has anyone here ever been in a hot air balloon?
Yasmin: No, but I'd love to do something exciting like that.
Rufus: Do you know anything about the Montgolfier brothers?
Yasmin: No. Who are they? I don't know anything about them.
Angelo: Yes! They invented the hot air balloon in 1783.
Yasmin: Did anyone travel in it?
Angelo: The first passengers were a sheep, a chicken, and a duck! Everyone was amazed. No one believed the flight was possible.
Yasmin: Wow! How do you know everything? What are you hiding?
Angelo: Nothing!
Yasmin: Oh, it's a book.
Angelo: Yes. Someone gave me a book about balloons.

2 Choose the best word.

someone everything anyone something anything no one ~~everyone~~

1 Rufus asked ......*everyone*...... if they knew about the Mongolfier brothers.
2 Yasmin doesn't know .... about the inventors of the hot air balloon.
3 Did .... believe the first balloon flight was possible? No, ... did.
4 Angelo was hiding .... from Yasmin.
5 Angelo knows .... about balloons. .... gave him a book.

3 Talk to a friend about the topics below. Use the indefinite pronouns in Activity 2.

computers helicopters New York sports

A: *I don't know anything about balloons.*
B: *I know someone who went in a balloon.*

Grammar Central

Indefinite pronouns
......*Someone*...... gave me a book.
I don't know .... about the Montgolfier brothers.
Did .... travel in it?

Grammar Booster on page 61

55

Warmer: Make guesses and predict!

Write on the board in random order *bicycle, car, horse-drawn bus, helicopter, plane, hot air balloon.* Ask the class to number them in the order they were invented. (*1 hot air balloon 2 bicycle 3 horse-drawn bus 4 car 5 plane 6 helicopter*) Ask *What year was the hot air balloon invented?* Have them write down a year in their notebook.

1 4.6 Listen and read. Who were the Montgolfier brothers?

- Play Track 4.6. The children listen for the date the hot air balloon was invented. (*1783*)
- Play Track 4.6 again. Ask *Who were the Montgolfier brothers?* (*the inventors of the hot air balloon*)

2 Choose the best word. 

- The children complete the sentences with the indefinite pronouns supplied. Elicit answers.

Answers

1 everyone **2** anything **3** anyone, no one **4** something **5** everything, Someone

3 Talk to a friend about the topics below. Use the indefinite pronouns in Activity 2.

- Choose two children to read the example dialogue.
- Divide the class into pairs to practice dialogues on the topics supplied, using the indefinite pronouns in Activity 2. Have pairs perform for the class.

Grammar Central

Indefinite pronouns

Have the children complete the grammar examples. Elicit answers. Elicit *–one* words are used for people, *–thing* words for things, and *any–* words in questions and with negatives. For extra practice, try the **Grammar Booster** section in the Student Book (pp. 61–63).

Answers p. 61

Activity 1: **1** anyone **2** someone **3** anyone **4** no one **5** anything **6** something **7** nothing

Activity 2: **1** anything **2** someone **3** everyone **4** no one **5** anyone **6** something

p. 62

Activity 1: **1** anyone **2** 're/are leaving **3** 'are/are taking **4** something **5** 're/are eating **6** anything **7** everyone **8** 're/are climbing

Activity 2: **1** They're taking a train (from London to Paris). **2** They can buy something (at the store near the museum). **3** (They're eating dinner) at a restaurant downtown. **4** Everyone can (eat chocolate cake for dessert). **5** They're climbing the Eiffel Tower (on Sunday).

p. 63

Activity 1: are traveling **2** someone **3** are meeting **4** are flying **5** tired **6** are landing **7** anything **8** are taking **9** are bringing **10** anything **11** are taking **12** has studied **13** someone

Activity 2: Children's own answers.

Optional activity: Dozy Darren and Smart Sam

Draw and label two faces on the board, Dozy Darren and Smart Sam. Say *Darren is hopeless with computers and technology and Sam is a whizz kid.* Elicit positive and negative sentences, e.g. *Sam knows everything about smartphones. Darren doesn't know anything about computer games.*

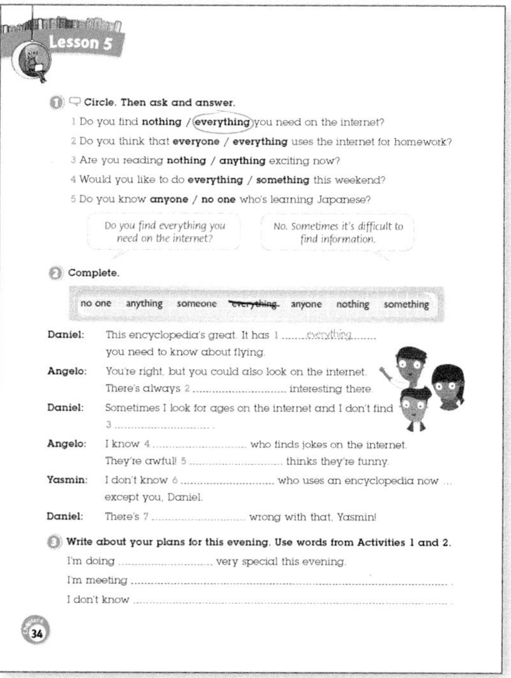

Lesson 5

1 Circle. Then ask and answer.

1 Do you find **nothing** / **everything** you need on the internet?
2 Do you think that **everyone** / **everything** uses the internet for homework?
3 Are you reading **nothing** / **anything** exciting now?
4 Would you like to do **everything** / **something** this weekend?
5 Do you know **anyone** / **no one** who's learning Japanese?

Do you find everything you need on the internet?
No. Sometimes it's difficult to find information.

2 Complete.

no one anything someone ~~everything~~ anyone nothing something

Daniel: This encyclopedia's great. It has 1 ......everything...... you need to know about flying.
Angelo: You're right, but you could also look on the internet. There's always 2 .... interesting there.
Daniel: Sometimes I look for ages on the internet and I don't find 3 ....
Angelo: I know 4 .... who finds jokes on the internet. They're awful! 5 .... thinks they're funny.
Yasmin: I don't know 6 .... who uses an encyclopedia now ... except you, Daniel.
Daniel: There's 7 .... wrong with that, Yasmin!

3 Write about your plans for this evening. Use words from Activities 1 and 2.

I'm doing .... very special this evening.
I'm meeting ....
I don't know ....

34

1 Circle. Then ask and answer. 

The children complete the sentences by circling the correct option in each pair. Elicit answers. Then the children ask and answer the questions in pairs.

Answers

1 everything **2** everyone **3** anything **4** something **5** anyone

2 Complete.

The children work in pairs to complete the dialogue using the words supplied. Elicit answers.

Answers

1 everything **2** something **3** anything **4** someone **5** No one **6** anyone **7** nothing

3 Write about your plans for this evening. Use words from Activities 1 and 2.

Ask *What plans do you have for this evening?* The children can talk about themselves or imagine a special evening. They complete the sentences individually, then compare with a friend.Elicit ideas.

Answers

Children's own answers.

Cooler: Play "Tic Tac Toe"

Play the game using indefinite pronouns (see Games Bank p. 19). Give children the pronoun and ask for correct sentences.

Competency Focus

Learn

The children demonstrate their understanding of the new language by reading the text and completing the activity.

Digital Resources

Student eBook • Display the SB page. Use *Highlighter* to show the indefinite pronouns in the story.

Digital Activity Book • Have children use *Pen* to write their answers to AB Activity 3. Elicit who has the same plans by a show of hands.

Teacher Resource Center • For extra grammar practice, print out Grammar Worksheet 4B.

Lesson 6

Song

1 Listen and sing. Which continents is he visiting?

I'm Going Around the World

I'm leaving tomorrow, I'm going on a trip.
I'm traveling by airplane, balloon, train, and ship.
Asia and Africa, Europe, Australia.
North and South America and Antarctica.

I'm going around the world with a compass and a map.
A tent and my passport in a heavy backpack.
I'm visiting every continent. North, south, east, and west.
Then I'm coming home because home is always best.

Everyone needs someone.
And somewhere to call their own.
For me that somewhere is here,
And this house is my home.

Spelling Central

Circle the compound nouns in the song. Compound nouns are made with two or more words.

Write the words in the chart. Can you add more compound nouns?

compound nouns	made with these words
airplane	air + plane

2 Talk to a friend about your trip. Use the words from the song.

A: *I'm traveling by airplane to Australia.*
B: *I'm taking my passport in my backpack.*

Chapter 4 56

Vocabulary, Song, and Spelling

Lesson objectives: identify and talk about places and travel items; practice spelling compound nouns

Key vocabulary: *Africa, Antarctica, Asia, Australia, Europe, North America, South America; airplane, backpack, passport, ship, train*

Secondary language: *trip, compass, tent*

Materials: Track 4.7; world map and pictures for Key vocabulary (Warmer); Phonics Worksheet 4 [TRC printout] (optional)

Warmer: Pre-teach vocabulary

Pre-teach the vocabulary using a map and by showing pictures or drawing icons on the board. Then point to the map/pictures and say the words, sometimes giving the wrong word. The children clap if the label is correct and correct you if it is wrong.

1 4.7 Listen and sing. Which continents is he visiting?

- Have the children look at the pictures.
- Play Track 4.7. The children listen. Ask *Which continents is he visiting?* (*Asia, Africa, Europe, Australia, North America, South America, Antarctica*)
- Play Track 4.7 again. Elicit which objects he is going to take. (*compass, map, tent, passport, backpack*)
- Check comprehension of the new vocabulary by asking children to mime using the objects, e.g. *map, backpack.*
- Play the song again for the children to sing along.

2 Talk to a friend about your trip. Use the words from the song.

- Choose two children to read the example dialogue to the class. Then tell them to imagine their own trip.
- Divide the class into pairs and have them talk about their trips.
- Ask pairs to tell the class about their trips.

Spelling Central

Compound nouns

Ask the children to look back at the song and find the word *airplane.* Write this on the board in two halves and explain that two words can be put together to make a compound noun: *air* + *plane* = *airplane.* They circle other examples and complete the chart. Ask children to write more compound nouns on the board. (e.g. *download, bedroom, swimming pool*)

Answers

Circled and in chart: airplane—air + plane, backpack—back + pack, everyone—every + one, someone—some + one, somewhere—some + where

Optional activity: Which continent?

Ask *Where is Spain?* (*in Europe*) *In which continent can you find kangaroos?* (*Australia*) Have the children work in pairs to write a continent quiz question (with answer). Then have pairs read their questions for the class to answer

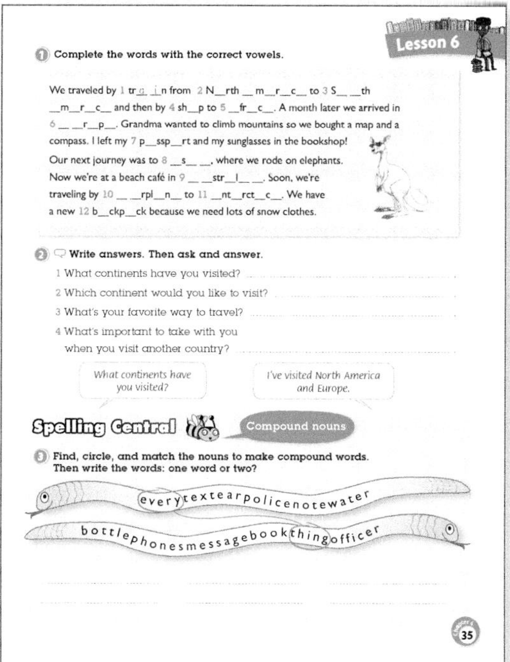

1 Complete the words with the correct vowels.

The children complete the words by writing in the missing vowels. Elicit answers, asking children to spell out the whole word each time.

Answers

1 train **2** North America **3** South America **4** ship **5** Africa **6** Europe **7** passport **8** Asia **9** Australia **10** airplane **11** Antarctica **12** backpack

2 Write answers. Then ask and answer. 

The children write their answers individually. They then ask and answer in pairs.

Answers

Children's own answers.

3 Find, circle, and match the nouns to make compound words. Then write the words: one word or two?

To practice the **Spelling Central** feature, the children circle the words in the puzzle and write them, deciding whether each answer is one word or two words. Elicit answers and ask *Is it one word or two?*

Answers

everything, text message, earphones, police officer, notebook, water bottle

Cooler: Play "20 Questions"

Choose a destination and have the children ask you questions to figure it out, e.g. *Is it in Asia? Are you going to see elephants?*, etc. Divide the class into groups to continue the game, with each child taking turns to choose a destination.

Competency Focus

Collaborate and communicate

The children work together and use their interpersonal skills to talk about their own trip, incorporating the new vocabulary.

Digital Resources

Student eBook • Use *Add personal note* to store links to key vocabulary pictures for the Warmer.

- For SB Activity 1, play Music Video 4.1 and encourage the children to sing along, using the graphic lyrics on screen. Pause the video for the children to continue singing.
- Remind the children to access Music Video 4.1 at home to practice the song.

Teacher Resource Center • For phonics practice, print out Phonics Worksheet 4.

CLIL: Geography—Turtle migration

Lesson objective: find out about migrating turtles and other migrating animals

Materials: CLIL Graphic Organizer 4 [TRC printout] (optional)

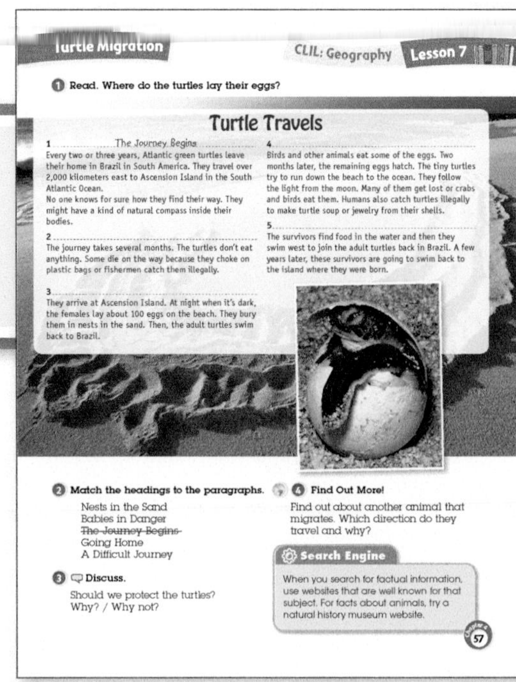

Turtle Migration | CLIL: Geography | Lesson 7

1 Read. Where do the turtles lay their eggs?

Turtle Travels

1 The Journey Begins
Every two or three years, Atlantic green turtles leave their home in Brazil in South America. They travel over 2,000 kilometers east to Ascension Island in the South Atlantic Ocean.
No one knows for sure how they find their way. They might have a kind of natural compass inside their bodies.

2 ....
The journey takes several months. The turtles don't eat anything. Some die on the way because they choke on plastic bags or fishermen catch them illegally.

3 ....
They arrive at Ascension Island. At night when it's dark, the females lay about 100 eggs on the beach. They bury them in nests in the sand. Then, the adult turtles swim back to Brazil.

4 ....
Birds and other animals eat some of the eggs. Two months later, the remaining eggs hatch. The tiny turtles try to run down the beach to the ocean. They follow the light from the moon. Many of them get lost or crabs and birds eat them. Humans also catch turtles illegally to make turtle soup or jewelry from their shells.

5 ....
The survivors find food in the water and then they swim west to join the adult turtles back in Brazil. A few years later, these survivors are going to swim back to the island where they were born.

2 Match the headings to the paragraphs.

Nests in the Sand
Babies in Danger
~~The Journey Begins~~
Going Home
A Difficult Journey

3 Discuss.

Should we protect the turtles? Why? / Why not?

4 Find Out More!

Find out about another animal that migrates. Which direction do they travel and why?

Search Engine

When you search for factual information, use websites that are well known for that subject. For facts about animals, try a natural history museum website.

Chapter 4 57

Warmer: Play "The Shark Game"

Write the word *migration* on the board. Make the meaning clear by drawing a rough world map with an arrow from one continent to another. Play the game using animals that migrate (see Games Bank p. 19).

1 Read. Where do the turtles lay their eggs?

- Elicit which continent is shown on the map. (*South America*) Ask the children to locate Brazil on the map.
- The children read the text. Ask *Where do turtles lay their eggs?* (*Ascension Island, on the beach*)

2 Match the headings to the paragraphs.

- Have the children look at the first paragraph again and identify the topic. Elicit why the first heading is appropriate. (*It is the start of the description of how the turtles travel.*)
- The children read and match the paragraphs and headings. Elicit answers.

Answers

1 The Journey Begins **2** A Difficult Journey **3** Nests in the Sand **4** Babies in Danger **5** Going Home

3 Discuss. 

- Have the children think about protecting turtles. Ask *Should we do it or shouldn't we? How should we do it?*
- Divide the class into pairs to talk to each other about protecting turtles. Encourage them to justify why it is important.
- Choose pairs to report their opinions to the class.

4 Find Out More! 

- The children research another animal that migrates, finding out the direction they travel and why. The **Search Engine** feature gives support on where to look. The children will need to complete this research before doing the follow-up activity in the Activity Book. (It could be set as homework.)

Optional activity: Read for specific information

Have a quick questions session to encourage the children to find facts and information quickly. Ask *How far do the adult turtles travel? Which animals eat the baby turtles?* and have children raise their hands when they have found the answer.

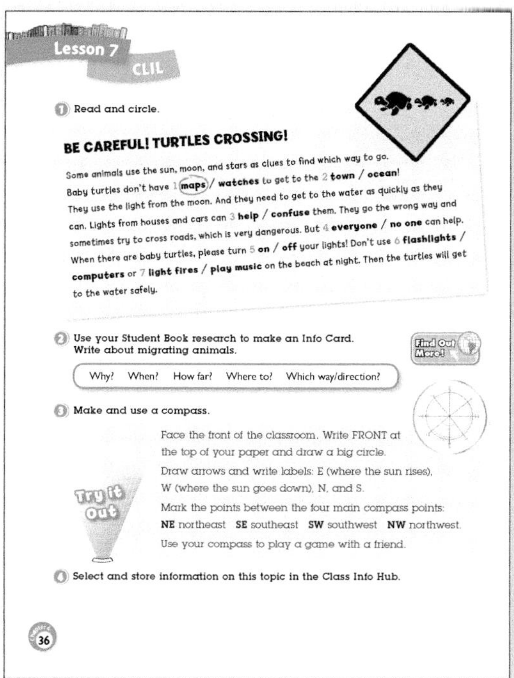

Lesson 7 CLIL

1 Read and circle.

BE CAREFUL! TURTLES CROSSING!

Some animals use the sun, moon, and stars as clues to find which way to go.
Baby turtles don't have 1 **maps** / **watches** to get to the 2 **town** / **ocean**!
They use the light from the moon. And they need to get to the water as quickly as they
can. Lights from houses and cars can 3 **help** / **confuse** them. They go the wrong way and
sometimes try to cross roads, which is very dangerous. But 4 **everyone** / **no one** can help.
When there are baby turtles, please turn 5 **on** / **off** your lights! Don't use 6 **flashlights** /
computers or 7 **light fires** / **play music** on the beach at night. Then the turtles will get
to the water safely.

2 Use your Student Book research to make an Info Card. Write about migrating animals.

Find Out More!

Why? When? How far? Where to? Which way/direction?

3 Make and use a compass.

Try it Out

Face the front of the classroom. Write FRONT at the top of your paper and draw a big circle.

Draw arrows and write labels: E (where the sun rises), W (where the sun goes down), N, and S.

Mark the points between the four main compass points:
NE northeast **SE** southeast **SW** southwest **NW** northwest.

Use your compass to play a game with a friend.

4 Select and store information on this topic in the Class Info Hub.

Chapter 4 36

1 Read and circle.

Ask *How do animals find their way?* to review what the children know about migration. The children read and complete the text by circling the correct option in each pair. Elicit answers.

Answers

1 maps **2** ocean **3** confuse **4** everyone **5** off **6** flashlights **7** light fires

2 Use your Student Book research to make an Info Card. Write about migrating animals.

Divide the class into groups. Have the children pool the information they learned from their research in the Student Book and the Activity Book. They write about and illustrate their ideas individually. Have the groups present their Info Cards to the class.

3 Make and use a compass.

Confirm which direction east is (where the sun rises). The children follow the **Try It Out** instructions to make a compass. They then play a game in pairs, taking turns prompting with an item in the classroom and using their compass to say which direction it is in.

4 Select and store information on this topic in the Class Info Hub.

Have the children vote for the most interesting Info Cards. Archive these in your Class Hub (see p. 41) in a folder called **Chapter 4 Migrating Animals**.

Cooler: Play "Odd One Out"

Play the game with the vocabulary from the lesson (see Games Bank p. 19).

Competency Focus

Act

The children carry out research to find out about other migrating animals and the reasons for migration.

Digital Resources

Student eBook • Use the SB for an alternative "heads-up" introduction to the topic (Activity 1 point 1).

Digital Activity Book • As support for less confident children, you could elicit findings orally before AB Activity 2. Use *Highlighter* on the word bank options (*Why?*, *When?*, etc.), one at a time, to elicit ideas from the class.

Teacher Resource Center • Print out CLIL Graphic Organizer 4 for the children to use in collating their Find Out More! research.

CLIL eBook • The children can use the CLIL eBook to expand their knowledge of the lesson topic.

Writing Project

Lesson objectives: review language from Chapter 4; write an itinerary for a trip and present it to the class
Materials: simple maps; Writing Template 4 [TRC printout] (optional)

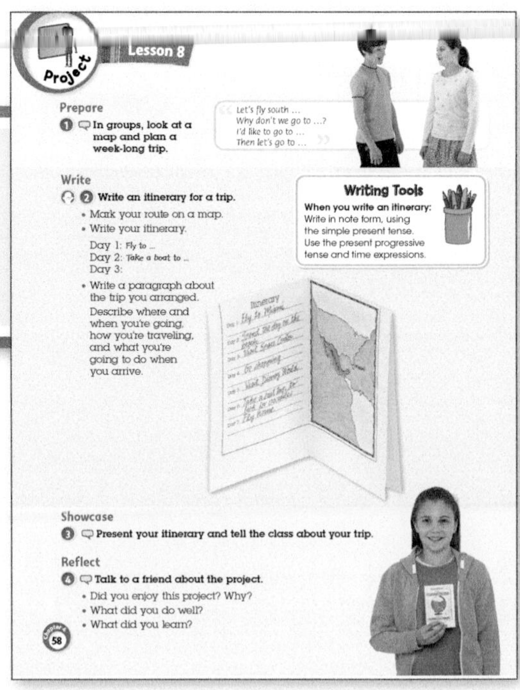
Project
Lesson 8
Prepare
1 In groups, look at a map and plan a week-long trip.

Write
2 Write an itinerary for a trip.
- Mark your route on a map.
- Write your itinerary.

Day 1: Fly to …
Day 2: Take a boat to …
Day 3:

- Write a paragraph about the trip you arranged. Describe where and when you're going, how you're traveling, and what you're going to do when you arrive.

Writing Tools
When you write an itinerary:
Write in note form, using the simple present tense.
Use the present progressive tense and time expressions.

Showcase
3 Present your itinerary and tell the class about your trip.

Reflect
4 Talk to a friend about the project.
- Did you enjoy this project? Why?
- What did you do well?
- What did you learn?

Chapter 4 58

Warmer: Get ready to go!

Draw a suitcase outline shape on the board and add a label for the destination. Say *You're going to Madagascar!* Have the children copy the suitcase, then draw and label five objects in it, e.g. *compass, map*. Elicit ideas.

Prepare

1 In groups, look at a map and plan a week-long trip.

- The children plan a week-long trip in groups, using the prompts supplied. Give each group a map. Groups report back to the class.

Write

2 Write an itinerary for a trip.

- Have the children read the itinerary as a model for their own writing.
- Read the **Writing Tools** box together. Elicit examples of simple present verbs, present progressive verbs, and time expressions.
- The children prepare an outline, using the instructions and the model itinerary. They write their itinerary and draw it on a map, then compare with a friend. Give support as necessary.

Showcase

3 Present your itinerary and tell the class about your trip.

- Choose children to present their itineraries to the class. Ask the class to listen for the places and identify activities they think are exciting.

Reflect

4 Vote for the best trip itinerary and talk to the class.

- Have children comment on which itinerary they liked best and why. Ask them to explain their reasons to the class. Have a class vote for which itinerary they liked the best.

Optional activity: Act out a trip

In groups, have the children choose one of their itineraries to act out. They could add sound effects, dialogues, etc. Have one child in each group act as the narrator while the others act out the trip for the class.

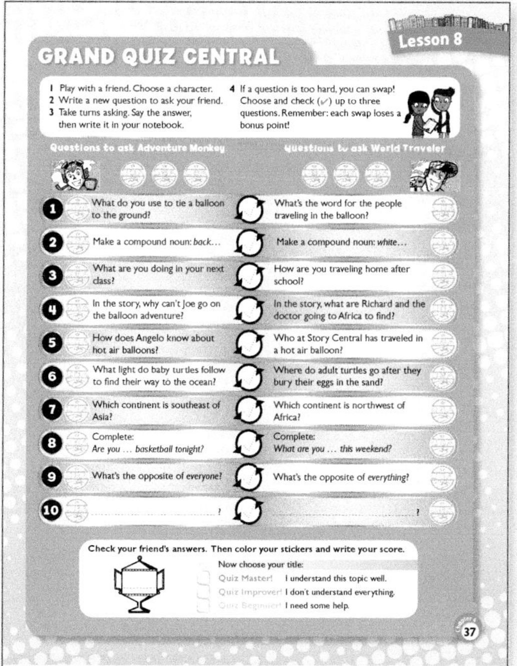
Lesson 8

GRAND QUIZ CENTRAL

1 Play with a friend. Choose a character.
2 Write a new question to ask your friend.
3 Take turns asking. Say the answer, then write it in your notebook.
4 If a question is too hard, you can swap! Choose and check (✓) up to three questions. Remember: each swap loses a bonus point!

	Questions to ask Adventure Monkey	Questions to ask World Traveler
1	What do you use to tie a balloon to the ground?	What's the word for the people traveling in the balloon?
2	Make a compound noun: *back*…	Make a compound noun: *white*…
3	What are you doing in your next class?	How are you traveling home after school?
4	In the story, why can't Joe go on the balloon adventure?	In the story, what are Richard and the doctor going to Africa to find?
5	How does Angelo know about hot air balloons?	Who at Story Central has traveled in a hot air balloon?
6	What light do baby turtles follow to find their way to the ocean?	Where do adult turtles go after they bury their eggs in the sand?
7	Which continent is southeast of Asia?	Which continent is northwest of Africa?
8	Complete: *Are you … basketball tonight?*	Complete: *What are you … this weekend?*
9	What's the opposite of *everyone*?	What's the opposite of *everything*?
10	……………………………………?	……………………………………?

Check your friend's answers. Then color your stickers and write your score.

Now choose your title:
Quiz Master! I understand this topic well.
Quiz Improver! I don't understand everything.
Quiz Beginner! I need some help.

37

Grand Quiz Central

See p. 43 for details of how to take the quiz.

Answers

1 ropes / passengers **2** backpack / whiteboard **3** I'm *verb*+ing **4** He's too young. / (the source of) the Nile **5** Someone gave him a book. / No one has traveled in a hot air balloon. **6** They follow the light from the moon. / They swim back home to Brazil. **7** Australia / North America **8** playing / doing **9** no one / nothing **10** Children's own answers.

Cooler: Mime time

Have the children think of an activity to do on a visit to Africa. Call out children to the front of the class to act out their mime while the others guess, e.g. *He's riding a camel.*

Competency Focus

Me

The children write their own itinerary for a trip, developing their sense of independence in the world.

Digital Resources

Student eBook • Use *Timer* to give the children one minute to study the SB Prepare box. Elicit the sentence openings. Ask different children to complete the sentence with a correct ending. Elicit class agreement.

- TIP Use *Add personal note* to log the results of the class vote. Involve the children in tallying the results and writing the scores.

Teacher Resource Center • Print out Writing Template 4 to use for the SB writing activity.

Language Review

Lesson objective: review language from Chapter 4
Materials: Tracks 4.8 and AB 4.1

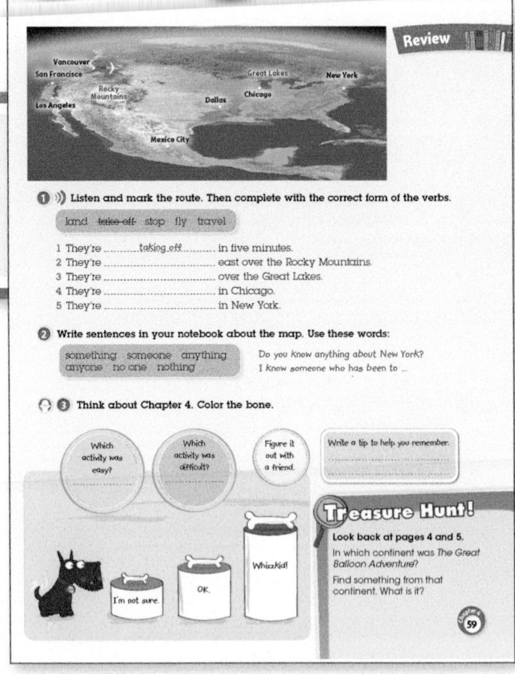
Review

1 Listen and mark the route. Then complete with the correct form of the verbs.

land ~~take off~~ stop fly travel

1 They're ....taking off.......... in five minutes.
2 They're .... east over the Rocky Mountains.
3 They're .... over the Great Lakes.
4 They're .... in Chicago.
5 They're .... in New York.

2 Write sentences in your notebook about the map. Use these words:

something someone anything anyone no one nothing

Do you know anything about New York?
I know someone who has been to ...

3 Think about Chapter 4. Color the bone.

Treasure Hunt!

Look back at pages 4 and 5.

In which continent was *The Great Balloon Adventure*?

Find something from that continent. What is it?

59

Warmer: The USA

Draw an outline map of the USA. Ask the children to say what country it is. Elicit what they know about the USA.

1 4.8 Listen and mark the route. Then complete with the correct form of the verbs.

- Have the children say the names of the places.
- Play Track 4.8. Children listen and mark the route.
- Play Track 4.8 again. They complete the sentences.

Audioscript

Ladies and gentlemen, this is your captain speaking. I'd like to welcome all passengers on flight AE 453. We're taking off from Vancouver in about five minutes. We're flying east over the Rocky Mountains. Enjoy the view! And then we're going across North America and we're traveling over the Great Lakes, north of Chicago.

We're not stopping in Chicago—we're flying straight through to the East Coast. We're landing in New York in about five hours and fifty minutes. Can everyone have their passports ready for landing? The weather is good, so now you can relax and have a safe flight.

Answers

1 taking off **2** flying **3** traveling **4** not stopping **5** landing

2 Write sentences in your notebook about the map. Use these words.

- Children look at the examples. Elicit other examples.
- They write sentences in their notebook.

Answers

Children's own answers.

3 Think about Chapter 4. Color the bone. 

- Have the children look back at Chapter 4 and color the bone to evaluate their progress (self-evaluation). The children choose and write a tip in their Student Book.

Treasure Hunt!

Ask *In which continent is Lake Chad?* (*Africa*) Have the children find an animal from that continent. (*a zebra*)

Cooler: I'm going to ...

Practice the present progressive for talking about the future by making a place/vacation activity chain around the class Start it off by saying *Next week I'm flying to France.* The first child responds with an appropriate activity, e.g. *I'm visiting my friends in Paris.* The next child gives the next prompt.

Competency Focus

Me: Self-evaluation

The children reflect on the chapter and express their opinions about their own progress.

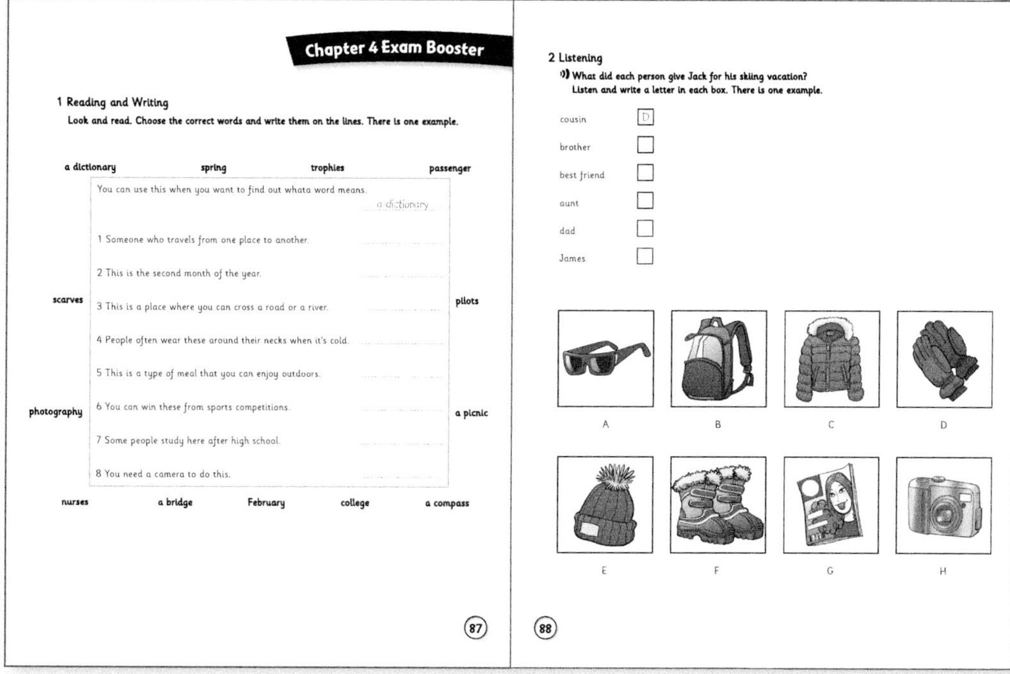

Chapter 4 Exam Booster

1 Reading and Writing

Look and read. Choose the correct words and write them on the lines. There is one example.

a dictionary | spring | trophies | passenger | scarves | pilots | photography | a picnic | nurses | a bridge | February | college | a compass

You can use this when you want to find out what a word means. a dictionary

1 Someone who travels from one place to another. ....

2 This is the second month of the year. ....

3 This is a place where you can cross a road or a river. ....

4 People often wear these around their necks when it's cold. ....

5 This is a type of meal that you can enjoy outdoors. ....

6 You can win these from sports competitions. ....

7 Some people study here after high school. ....

8 You need a camera to do this. ....

87

2 Listening

What did each person give Jack for his skiing vacation?
Listen and write a letter in each box. There is one example.

cousin D

brother

best friend

aunt

dad

James

A B C D

E F G H

88

3 Reading and Writing

Look and read. Choose the correct words and write them on the lines. There is one example.

hot-air balloon | pilot | passenger | take off | safe | land | view | passport | flight | train | ship | airplane | backpack

This is a type of transportation that runs on tracks. train

1 You can use this type of transportation to travel in the ocean. ....

2 This document has your name and picture. You use it to enter a different country. ....

3 This person controls a hot-air balloon or an airplane. ....

4 When airplanes leave the ground to begin a journey, they do this. ....

5 When airplanes return to the ground after a journey, they do this. ....

6 This person travels from one place to another place on an airplane, train, or ship. ....

7 This type of transportation floats in the air to travel and people stand in a basket. ....

8 People often enjoying looking at this when they travel to beautiful places. ....

Exam Tip

Read the definitions all the way through before choosing an answer.

89

1 Reading and Writing. Look and read. Choose the correct words and write them on the lines. There is one example.

The children complete the text using the words supplied. Check answers.

Answers

1 passenger **2** February **3** a bridge **4** scarves **5** a picnic **6** medal **7** college **8** photography

2))) AB 4.1 Listening. What did each person give Jack for his skiing vacation? Listen and write a letter in each box. There is one example.

Play AB Track 4.1 twice. The children write the letter of the correct object for each person. Check answers.

Answers (Audioscript on p. 222)

brother b, best friend f, aunt h, dad e, James c

3 Reading and Writing. Look and read. Choose the correct words and write them on the lines. There is one example.

The children complete the text using the words supplied. Check answers.

Answers

1 ship **2** passport **3** pilot **4** take off **5** land **6** passenger **7** hot-air balloon **8** view

Digital Resources

Teacher Resource Center • Print out Test Chapter 4 to use at the end of this lesson. The Test Generator also allows you to create customized tests.

Student's App • Encourage the children to play the games on their smartphone/tablet. Have a class vote on which of the three games they played is their favorite. (*The Inks* Apps are free and available on the App Store and Google Play.)

Chapter 5 Real or Imaginary?

Overview

The children will:

- use critical thinking skills to identify different materials.
- talk about things using *be made of* and *be used for.*
- read and understand a poem about a fantasy land.
- talk about different facts using the present passive.
- describe the chocolate-making process.
- find out about how tempera paint is made.
- write their own poem about a fantasy land.

Key Vocabulary

Materials: cotton, glass, leather, plastic, silk, silver, wood, wool
Verbs to describe processes: collect, deliver, dry, grind, mix, pick, remove, roast

Key Grammar

be made of / be used for

- What's the bag made of? It's made of cotton.
- It's used for carrying shopping.

Present passive

- Soccer is played at my school.
- Spanish and English are spoken in a lot of countries.

Reading Skills

Story: *This Strange Land*
Genre: fantasy poem

Literacy Development

- use reading skills to understand and predict content
- relate story theme to personal experience
- use adjectives for more descriptive writing

Functional Language

- I'm hungry. Those … look good.
- Help yourself!
- Thanks! Did you make them?
- No, I didn't. … made them.

Spelling

Different types of past participles

CLIL: Art—How tempera paint is made

The children find out about the process of making tempera paint.

Competency Focus

The children will:

use critical thinking skills to deduce the meaning of new vocabulary. (Lesson 1)

predict the content of a story. (Lesson 3)

activate new vocabulary and apply new grammar knowledge. (Lesson 2)

apply new grammar rules in a familiar context. (Lesson 5)

work in pairs to act out a dialogue. (Lesson 3)

work in pairs to describe a process. (Lesson 6)

relate the story theme to their personal experience. (Lesson 4)

invent and write a poem. (Lesson 8)

evaluate their own progress in the chapter. (Review)

research different products and how they are made. (Lesson 7)

Digital Overview

Teacher Presentation

Student eBook and Digital Activity Book

- Oral Storytelling Video 5.1: *The Gold Harvest*
- Interactive versions of AB activities
- Integrated audio and answer key for all activities

Teacher resources for planning, lesson delivery, and homework

Teacher Resource Center

- Class Planner Chapter 5
- Worksheets to print out (including notes and answers):
  - Grammar Worksheet 5A: *be made of / be used for*
  - Grammar Worksheet 5B: Present passive
  - Oral Storytelling Video Worksheet 5: *The Gold Harvest*
  - Phonics Worksheet 5
  - CLIL Graphic Organizer 5
  - Writing Template 5
  - Test Chapter 5 and Mid-year Test
- Test Generator
- Literacy Handbook

Watch the Oral Storytelling Video

Children's resources for consolidation and practice at home

Student eBook and Reader eBook

- Oral Storytelling Video 5.1: *The Gold Harvest*

The Inks Student's App

Vocabulary games: Materials and Verbs to describe processes

Chapter 5 Real or Imaginary?

Lesson 1

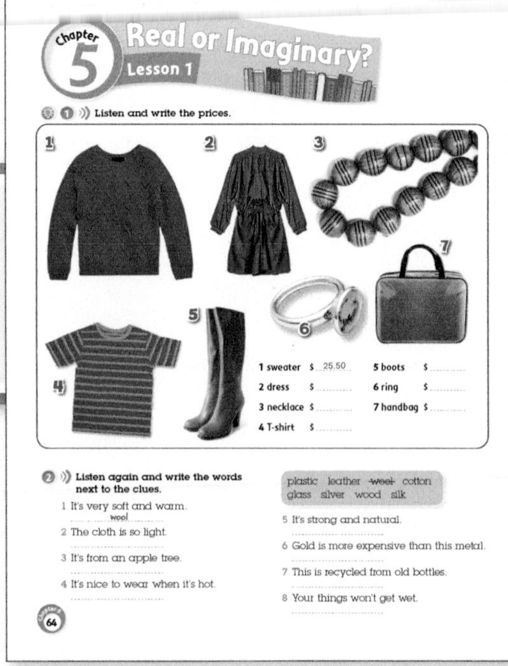
Chapter 5 Real or Imaginary?
Lesson 1

1 Listen and write the prices.

1 sweater $ 25.50
2 dress $ ......
3 necklace $ ......
4 T-shirt $ ......
5 boots $ ......
6 ring $ ......
7 handbag $ ......

2 Listen again and write the words next to the clues.

plastic leather ~~wool~~ cotton glass silver wood silk

1 It's very soft and warm. wool
2 The cloth is so light. ......
3 It's from an apple tree. ......
4 It's nice to wear when it's hot. ......
5 It's strong and natural. ......
6 Gold is more expensive than this metal. ......
7 This is recycled from old bottles. ......
8 Your things won't get wet. ......

64

Vocabulary

Lesson objectives: identify and use vocabulary for different materials
Key vocabulary: *cotton, glass, leather, plastic, silk, silver, wood, wool*
Materials: Track 5.1

Warmer: What's made from a tree?

Draw a picture of a tree on the board. Ask *What can be made from a tree?* (*a chair, a door, a table, a ruler,* etc.) Give the children two minutes to make a list of as many objects as possible. Elicit answers.

1 5.1 Listen and write the prices. 

- Write some prices on the board and have the class say them, e.g. *$3.50, $12.99, $75.00.*
- Divide the class into pairs to identify the objects pictured. Ask *What are they made of? Are they expensive?*
- Play Track 5.1. The children listen and complete the prices. Elicit answers.

Audioscript

Boy: *How much is that red sweater? It's great.*
Girl: *It's only $25.50. It's wool. Wool is very soft and warm. Ooh, that's a beautiful dress. The cloth is so light. It's silk.*
Boy: *How much is it?*
Girl: *Hm, $150. It's expensive. And this necklace is beautiful. It's wood from an apple tree. Wow, it's only $5. I'm going to buy it!*
Boy: *I like that T-shirt. $9.99. That's cheap! It's 100% cotton so it's nice to wear when it's hot. Do you like these boots?*
Girl: *Oh, yes! I like leather. It's strong and natural.*
Boy: *Hm.... $160. They're expensive.*
Girl: *I have a ring like this, but mine is gold.*
Boy: *Gold is more expensive than silver. This is silver and green glass. The glass is recycled from old bottles. This ring is $15.99.*
Girl: *I love this handbag. It's purple, plastic, and shiny.*
Boy: *Your things won't get wet in the rain. And it's only $12.99.*

Answers

1 sweater $25.50 **2** dress $150 **3** necklace $5 **4** T-shirt $9.99 **5** boots $160 **6** ring $15.99 **7** handbag $12.99

2 5.1 Listen again and write the words next to the clues.

- Ask the children to look at the first clue. Ask which picture it refers to and which material. (*picture 1, wool*)
- Play Track 5.1 again. They listen for familiar words they know to help them identify the materials, choosing from the words supplied.
- Elicit answers.

Answers

1 wool **2** silk **3** wood **4** cotton **5** leather **6** silver **7** glass **8** plastic

Optional activity: Design an advertising poster

Ask the children to draw a boy or a girl wearing an expensive outfit, including jewelry, and to label all the objects. Have them add advertising captions, e.g. *a light silk dress, an expensive gold necklace,* etc. They could also add prices.

Chapter 5 Real or Imaginary?
Lesson 1

1 Unscramble and write the words. Then look and number.

1 a cool onctot ......cotton...... T-shirt
2 some odow .... for the fire
3 a liks .... tie for Grandpa
4 some eterhal .... boots
5 some lowo .... for a new scarf
6 a isictap .... ruler for school
7 a vrlise .... clock for Mom's birthday
8 a slasg .... lamp for my bedroom

2 Write *true* or *false*.

1 You can see your face in a silver cup. ......true......
2 Wood isn't natural – people make it. ....
3 Plastic is always hard. ....
4 Glass usually breaks when it hits something. ....
5 Wool is warmer than cotton. ....

3 Look for things in your classroom. Tell a friend.

Your watch is silver. *There isn't any wood.*

4 Choose a way to categorize the new words in your notebook.

38

Cooler: Play "I Spy"

Adapt the traditional "I Spy" game to practice materials, e.g. *I spy with my little eye something made of glass.* (*window*) Have the children take turns making clues.

Competency Focus

Think! Critical Thinking

The children use critical thinking skills to understand the new vocabulary by using visual clues and processing the written and spoken forms.

1 Unscramble and write the words. Then look and number.

The children unscramble and write the materials. They then number the objects in the picture. Elicit answers.

Answers

1 cotton (t-shirt) **2** wood (wood) **3** silk (tie) **4** leather (boots) **5** wool (balls of wool) **6** plastic (ruler) **7** silver (clock) **8** glass (lamp)

2 Write *true* or *false*.

The children write true or false for the sentences. Elicit answers, including the correct version of the false sentences.

Answers

1 true **2** false **3** false **4** true **5** true

3 Look for things in your classroom. Tell a friend.

The children find items in the classroom and discuss what they are made of in pairs. Then have them say which materials are absent.

4 Choose a way to categorize the new words in your notebook.

Have the children brainstorm appropriate categories in pairs. Prompt as necessary, e.g. *soft/hard, alphabetical order, most to least useful.* The children choose the best categories for them and list the words in their notebook.

Answers

Children's own answers.

Digital Resources

Student eBook • Play "Kim's Game" with the new vocabulary. Display the SB page. Have the class read the words aloud. Use *Timer* to give the class one minute to memorize the pictures, then one minute to recall them. Repeat several times.

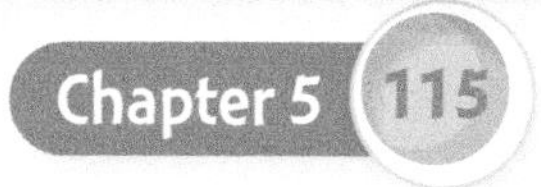

Grammar

Lesson objectives: talk about what things are made of and what they are used for
Key grammar: present passive—statements and questions with *made of / used for*
Secondary language: *condition, Moroccan, slippers, jewelry*
Materials: Grammar Worksheet 5A [TRC printout] (optional)

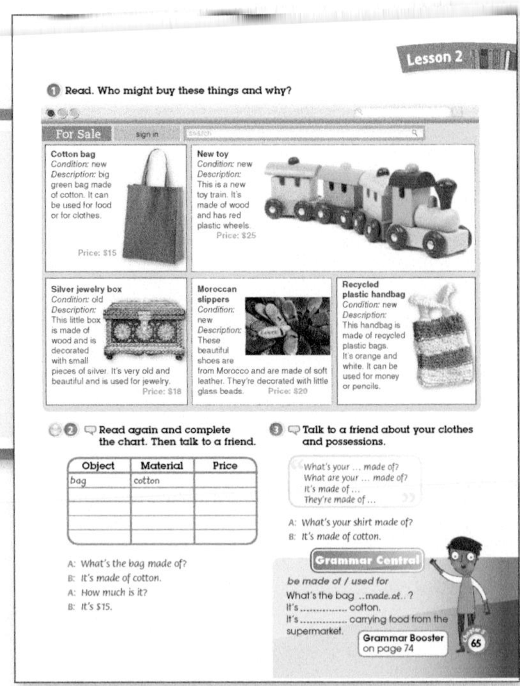
Lesson 2

1 Read. Who might buy these things and why?

For Sale | sign in | search

Cotton bag
Condition: new
Description: big green bag made of cotton. It can be used for food or for clothes.
Price: $15

New toy
Condition: new
Description: This is a new toy train. It's made of wood and has red plastic wheels.
Price: $25

Silver jewelry box
Condition: old
Description: This little box is made of wood and is decorated with small pieces of silver. It's very old and beautiful and is used for jewelry.
Price: $18

Moroccan slippers
Condition: new
Description: These beautiful shoes are from Morocco and are made of soft leather. They're decorated with little glass beads.
Price: $20

Recycled plastic handbag
Condition: new
Description: This handbag is made of recycled plastic bags. It's orange and white. It can be used for money or pencils.

2 Read again and complete the chart. Then talk to a friend.

Object	Material	Price
bag	cotton	

A: What's the bag made of?
B: It's made of cotton.
A: How much is it?
B: It's $15.

3 Talk to a friend about your clothes and possessions.

What's your … made of?
What are your … made of?
It's made of …
They're made of …

A: What's your shirt made of?
B: It's made of cotton.

Grammar Central
be made of / used for
What's the bag ..made of..?
It's .... cotton.
It's .... carrying food from the supermarket.

Grammar Booster on page 74

65

Warmer: Play "Word Ping-Pong"

Divide the class into two teams. You "serve" the first material, e.g. *plastic*. The first team names an object made of that material, e.g. *bag*. The teams continue taking turns with different materials/items. Each correct answer gets a point. The team with the most points wins.

1 Read. Who might buy these things and why?

- Have the children look at the objects for sale on the website and read the captions quickly. Ask *Who might buy these and why?* (e.g. *A friend might buy a jewelry box as a gift.*)
- Ask *Would you buy any of these objects? Why/Why not?*

Answers

Children's own answers.

2 Read again and complete the chart. Then talk to a friend.

- Have the children read the text again. They write each object, material, and price in the chart. Elicit answers.
- Choose two children to read the example dialogue to the class. Then divide the class into pairs to practice using information from the chart.

Answers

bag—cotton—$15; toy—wood, plastic—$25;
jewelry box—wood, silver—$18;
slippers—leather, glass—$20; handbag—plastic—$8

Grammar Central

be made of / used for

Have the children complete the grammar examples. Elicit answers. Elicit the structures for describing materials (*is made of*) and what an object is for (*is used for*). The children write further examples in their notebook. For extra practice, try the **Grammar Booster** section in the Student Book (p. 74).

Answers p. 74

Activity 1: **1** made of **2** are, used for **3** are made of **4** is used for **5** is made of **6** are used for

Activity 2: **1** made of, used for, d **2** made of, used for, a **3** used for, made of, c **4** made of, used for, e **5** used for, made of, b

3 Talk to a friend about your clothes and possessions.

- Choose two children to read the example dialogue.
- Divide the class into pairs to practice the dialogue using their own ideas on clothes/materials. Have pairs perform for the class

Optional activity: Definitions

Ask the children to choose an object and write a sentence in their notebook about what it is made of and used for, e.g. *It's made of wood and glass. It's used for telling the time.* (*a clock*) Have the children read out their clues for the class to guess.

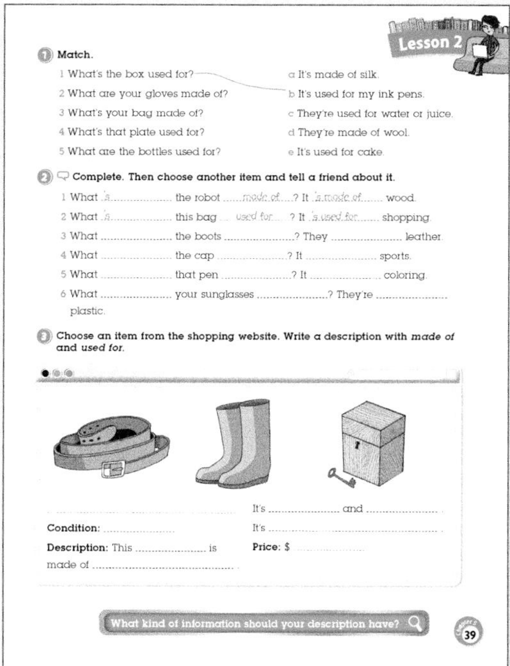

Lesson 2

1 Match.

1 What's the box used for? — a It's made of silk.
2 What are your gloves made of? — b It's used for my ink pens.
3 What's your bag made of? — c They're used for water or juice.
4 What's that plate used for? — d They're made of wool.
5 What are the bottles used for? — e It's used for cake.

2 Complete. Then choose another item and tell a friend about it.

1 What 's .... the robot made of ....? It 's made of .... wood.
2 What 's .... this bag used for ....? It 's used for .... shopping.
3 What .... the boots ....? They .... leather.
4 What .... the cap ....? It .... sports.
5 What .... that pen ....? It .... coloring.
6 What .... your sunglasses ....? They're .... plastic.

3 Choose an item from the shopping website. Write a description with *made of* and *used for*.

.... It's .... and ....
Condition: .... It's ....
Description: This .... is made of .... Price: $ ....

What kind of information should your description have?

Chapter 5 39

Cooler: Play "The Shark Game"

Play the game using vocabulary from the chapter so far (see Games Bank p. 19).

Competency Focus

Learn

By reading the text and completing the chart, the children demonstrate their understanding of the new grammatical structures.

1 Match.

The children match the questions and answers. Elicit answers, asking children to explain how they figured them out.

Answers

1 b **2** d **3** a **4** e **5** c

2 Complete. Then choose another item and tell a friend about it.

The children complete the questions and answers. Elicit answers.

Answers

1 's, made of, made of **2** 's, used for, used for
3 are, made of, 're made of **4** 's, used for, 's used for
5 's, used for, 's used for, **6** are, made of, made of

3 Choose an item from the shopping website. Write a description with *made of* and *used for*.

Elicit the items in the pictures and what they are made of / used for. The children choose one and write about it. Remind them to choose adjectives which will encourage people to buy their item! Ask *What kind of information should your description have?* (e.g. *adjectives, price, materials,* etc.)

Answers

Children's own answers.

Digital Resources

Digital Activity Book • Use the AB page to give feedback on activities, using the answer key or interactive digital activities, as appropriate.

Student eBook, Digital Activity Book • TIP With the answer key, you can show the answers all at once or one by one to customize feedback.

Teacher Resource Center • For extra grammar practice, print out Grammar Worksheet 5A.

Reading: Story Extract

Lesson objectives: talk about food; use the title and pictures to predict story content; read the extract from the fantasy poem *This Strange Land* (start)
Functional language: *I'm hungry. Those … look good. Help yourself! Thanks! Did you make them? No, I didn't. … made them.*
Secondary language: *ruled by, tower, free, sails*
Materials: Tracks 5.2 and 5.3

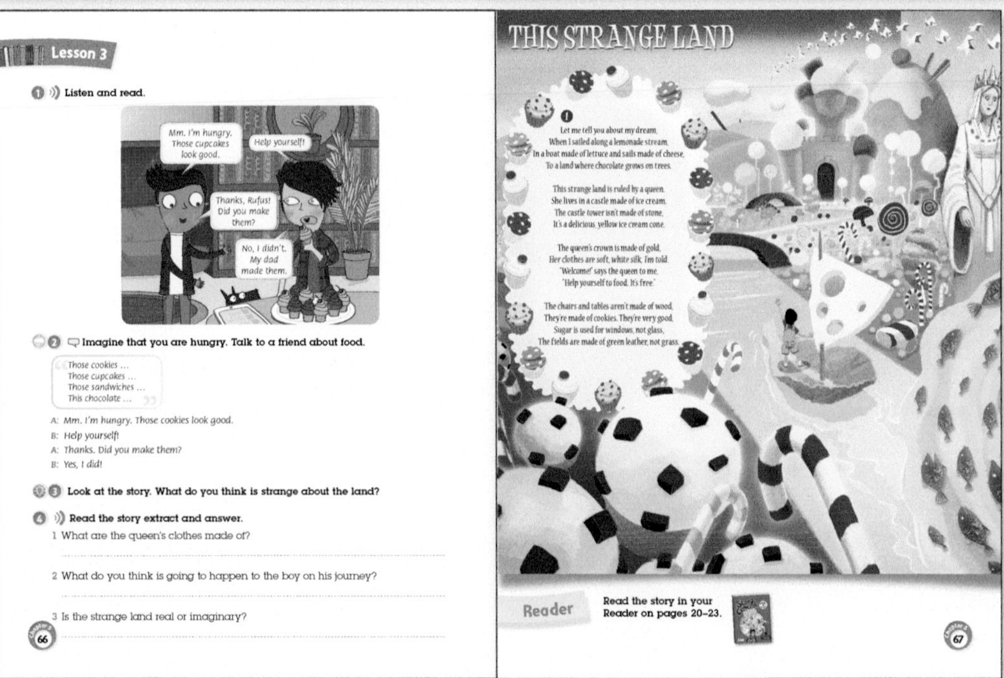
Lesson 3

1 Listen and read.

2 Imagine that you are hungry. Talk to a friend about food.

Those cookies …
Those cupcakes …
Those sandwiches …
This chocolate …

A: *Mm. I'm hungry. Those cookies look good.*
B: *Help yourself!*
A: *Thanks. Did you make them?*
B: *Yes, I did!*

3 Look at the story. What do you think is strange about the land?

4 Read the story extract and answer.
1 What are the queen's clothes made of?
2 What do you think is going to happen to the boy on his journey?
3 Is the strange land real or imaginary?

66

THIS STRANGE LAND

1
Let me tell you about my dream,
When I sailed along a lemonade stream,
In a boat made of lettuce and sails made of cheese,
To a land where chocolate grows on trees.

This strange land is ruled by a queen.
She lives in a castle made of ice cream.
The castle tower isn't made of stone,
It's a delicious, yellow ice cream cone.

The queen's crown is made of gold,
Her clothes are soft, white silk, I'm told.
"Welcome!" says the queen to me,
"Help yourself to food. It's free."

The chairs and tables aren't made of wood,
They're made of cookies. They're very good.
Sugar is used for windows, not glass,
The fields are made of green leather, not grass.

Reader
Read the story in your Reader on pages 20–23.

67

Warmer: Review *this/these* and *that/those*

Draw three circles (plates) on the board and invite three children to come to the board and draw food inside the circles, e.g. cookies, cakes, sandwiches. The children should explain, e.g. *This is a cupcake. These are sandwiches.*, etc. Point to one of the plates and ask *Are those cookies or cupcakes?* Invite children to comment.

Functional language

1 5.2 Listen and read.

- Play Track 5.2. The children listen and read along.
- Play Track 5.2 again for them to repeat.
- Divide the class into pairs to practice the dialogue.

2 Imagine you are hungry. Talk to a friend about food.

- Choose two children to read the example dialogue.
- The children practice in pairs using the prompts supplied and adding details. Have pairs do a dialogue for the class.

Note: The Reading Strategy activity for this chapter is best done before you read the extract. See p. 121 and the Literacy Handbook for details.

Before reading

3 Look at the story. What do you think is strange about the land?

- Have the children study the pictures. Ask *Is there anything different? What's the boat made of? What grows on the trees?*
- Ask the children to choose one strange thing to complete their answer.

4 5.3 Read the story extract and answer.

- Have the children read the extract and answer question 1.
- Play Track 5.3. They listen and complete their ideas for questions 2 and 3.
- Elicit answers, but do not confirm predictions: explain that they will have to read the story to find out.

Answers

1 Her clothes are made of soft, white silk. **2** Children's own answers. **3** The land is imaginary.

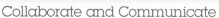

Lesson 3

1 Write another correct word. Then choose, write, and act out.

dress / cake / birthday card / necklace / ....

That .... *looks great!*

Thanks.

Did you make it?

No, I didn't. ....

2 Read the story in your Student Book. Write F (fantasy) or P (poem).

1 It tells you about what happened in a dream.
2 You can read it with rhythm.
3 There are rhyming words at the end of lines.
4 It has weird creatures like a giant fish made of jell-o.

3 Circle.

1 The boy is **awake** / **asleep** now.
2 His boat is made of **food** / **things you can't eat**.
3 The queen's castle is **very cold** / **really warm**.
4 The queen **is nice to** / **doesn't like** the boy.
5 In the strange land, **everything is** / **most things are** good to eat.

4 Who or what is the boy going to meet on his journey? Think and write.

Chapter 5 40

1 Write another correct word. Then choose, write, and act out.

The children choose another item to add. They then complete the dialogue about one of the items and act it out in pairs. Encourage the children to use what they know to adapt and extend the dialogue. Have pairs act out for the class.

2 Read the story in your Student Book. Write F (fantasy) or P (poem).

The children read the Student Book story extract again, then write whether each sentence describes a fantasy or a poem.

Answers

1 F **2** P **3** P **4** F

3 Circle.

The children complete the sentences by circling the correct word/phrase in each pair. Elicit answers.

Answers

1 awake **2** food **3** very cold **4** is nice to **5** most things are

4 Who or what is the boy going to meet on his journey? Think and write.

Elicit suggestions. The children write their own ideas, then compare with a friend. Elicit ideas.

Answers

Children's own answers.

Cooler: What's the next word?

The children close their Student Book. Read the poem aloud, pausing to elicit the rhyming words, e.g. *Let me tell you about my dream, When I sailed along a lemonade … (stream).*

Competency Focus

Collaborate and Communicate

The children work together, putting into practice new functional language by acting out a realistic dialogue.

Think! Critical Thinking

By analyzing visual clues and deducing from the context, the children use prediction skills to help them engage with the story.

Digital Resources

Student eBook • Use *Highlighter* on SB Activity 1 speech bubbles. Focus on *cupcakes* and *dad*, and elicit different things you could say in this context.

Digital Activity Book • Display the AB page for Activity 4 feedback. Have children use *Pen* to write their version of who or what the boy is going to meet on his journey. Elicit who in the class had the same response.

THIS STRANGE LAND

1
Let me tell you about my dream,
When I sailed along a lemonade stream,
In a boat made of lettuce and sails made of cheese,
To a land where chocolate grows on trees.

This strange land is ruled by a queen,
She lives in a castle made of ice cream,
The castle tower isn't made of stone,
It's a delicious, yellow ice cream cone.

The queen's crown is made of gold,
Her clothes are soft, white silk, I'm told.
"Welcome!" says the queen to me,
"Help yourself to food. It's free."

The chairs and tables aren't made of wood,
They're made of cookies. They're very good,
Sugar is used for windows, not glass,
The fields are made of green leather, not grass.

2
The queen never smiles. She just looks sad,
Is living here really so bad?
She says to me, "Make yourself at home,
But don't catch the fish when you're alone."

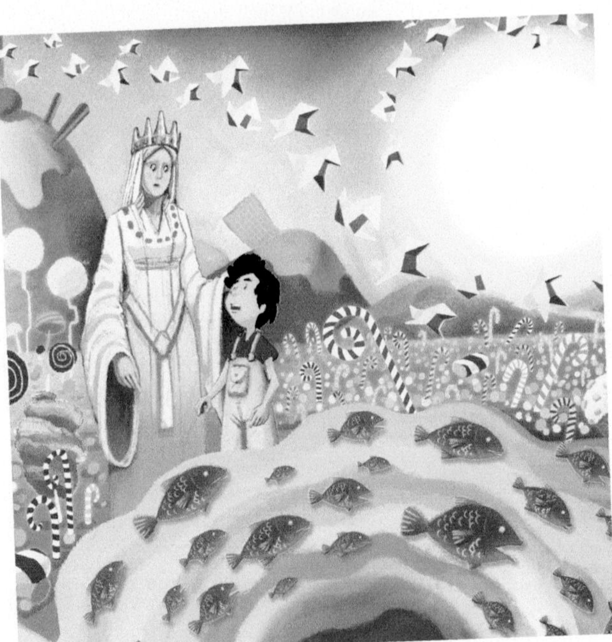

My boat sails slowly through
night and day,
Passing mountains and cotton fields
along the way,
There are clouds made of wool and trees
of bread,
And cute paper birds fly over my head.

3
In the water are small chocolate fish,
They swim around and splash and splish,
"Let's catch a chocolate fish," I think.
I need something now to eat and drink.

I sit in my boat and catch some fish,
They aren't easy to catch, but they're easy to miss,
"I've caught one!" I shout. "Don't let it go!"
But the boat starts to sway to and fro.

4
Where the stream meets the big gray sea,
There is nothing for miles, just the boat and me,
When the wind blows, the boat starts to shake,
When the rain falls, the monsters wake.

5
Then a giant fish made of lemon jell-o,
Jumps out of the water. He's big and yellow!
He opens his mouth to take a bite,
I can see his teeth in the moonlight.

6
He smashes the boat with his big yellow tail,
He eats the lettuce, and the cheese sail,
"Remember, he's made of jell-o," I think,
But then my little boat starts to sink.

7
I pick up a plastic spoon and I give him a poke,
The jell-o fish starts to cough and choke,
"Wake up!" I shout, "It's only a dream,"
Then I eat him for breakfast with strawberries and cream!

8
My poor little boat is now broken in pieces,
It floats in the water—tasty little lettuces,
Next time I go sailing, maybe I should,
Go in a boat that's made of wood.

Lesson objective: read and understand the fantasy poem *This Strange Land* in the Reader
Materials: Track 5.4; Reader; Oral Storytelling Video Worksheet 5 [TRC printout] (optional)

Warmer: Memory test

Ask the children (with Reader closed) to write down the seven food and drink items in the order they appear in the story extract. They check in their Reader. (*lemonade, lettuce, cheese, chocolate, ice cream, cookies, sugar*)

Story Summary

This story is a boy's dream of a land made of food. He travels in a boat made of lettuce, visits a queen in an ice cream castle, and sees chocolate fish in the water. He fights a big yellow jell-o fish with a spoon.

Theme: the importance of using your imagination

5.4 While reading

- Have the children look at the pictures in the Reader. Ask them to identify all the food in the pictures.
- Play Track 5.4. The children listen and read along. Ask *What happens to the boat?* (*It breaks.*)
- Ask questions to check comprehension, e.g. *What are the clouds and trees made of? (wool and bread) What happens when the boy catches a fish? (The boat sways to and fro.) What's the giant fish made of? (lemon jell-o)*
- Have the class read the story. Encourage them to enjoy using pronounced rhythm and cadence (see **Story Time**).

After reading: Reflect

- Ask questions to give the children the opportunity to think about the issues raised by the story, e.g. *How do the pictures change as the story becomes more dangerous? Does the boy know it might be dangerous? Is the boy scared?*

Optional activity: Create a story poem

Have the children write their own story poem in pairs. Elicit words which could be changed, e.g. *sail* → *swim, lemonade* → *cola, chocolate* → *candy*. Choose pairs to read out their story poems.

Story Time

Focus on rhythm

Read out the poem again, emphasizing the rhythm and cadence. Say lines for the children to repeat and tap out the rhythm with their hands, or you could use a musical instrument to set the rhythm. This is a fun way of focusing on stress and intonation patterns.

Reading Strategy

Visual Imagery

Visual Imagery is a very important strategy that good readers should apply while reading and listening to a story. It helps them personalize the story by building their own mental images as they read. It also offers good comprehension support.

For additional explanation and activities, see the Literacy Handbook on the Teacher Resource Center.

Cooler: Act out the end of the story

Agree on mimes for the poem, e.g. *take a bite*—use hand gesture, *smashes the boat*—have them bang on the desk. Divide the class into pairs—one child mimes the boy and the other the giant fish. Read the last four verses out slowly and have the children mime their actions.

Digital Resources

Student eBook • For the Warmer, have children use *Pen* to circle and link the food and drink items in order in the SB story extract.

Reader eBook • Show the Reader story one picture at a time as you play audio.

- Oral Storytelling Video 5.1 contains a different story on a related theme (*The Gold Harvest*). Watch and discuss it at the end of the lesson.

Teacher Resource Center • Print out Oral Storytelling Video Worksheet 5 to get the most out of the video.

Reading Comprehension and Critical Literacy

Lesson objectives: understand and evaluate the story; relate story theme to personal experience; write a description of an imaginary land
Materials: Track 5.4; Reader; Oral Storytelling Video Worksheet 5 [TRC printout] (optional)

Lesson 4 Time to Think

1 Read the story in your Reader on pages 20–23 again.
How many different things are there to eat and drink?

2 Comprehension
1 Why did the boy want to catch chocolate fish?
2 What happens to the boat?
3 How did the boy escape from the giant fish?
4 Did you know something bad was going to happen? What were the clues?

3 Critical Literacy
1 Why do you think the queen was sad?
2 Would you like to visit an imaginary place like the strange land?

Writing Workshop Using adjectives to make your writing more interesting.

4 Find adjectives in the story and write them in the chart. Write some more descriptions for an imaginary land.

opinion	size	shape	age	color	material	noun
delicious	small			yellow	chocolate	fish

A beautiful, small, round, red flower.

Writing Tools
Use adjectives to make your writing more interesting:
beautiful
big round
old green
silk

5 Text Connections
Do you know any other stories about imaginary lands?

68

Note: Please ensure that your class has read the Reader story before you do this lesson.

Warmer: Story recap

Write up fantasy objects/events from the story on the board in random order and have the children put them in order, e.g. *He sees chocolate on trees. He meets the Queen. He catches a fish.*, etc.

1 5.4 Read the story in your Reader.

- Have the children read the story. (Alternatively, play Track 5.4 and have them read along.) Elicit whether they were correct in their predictions in Lesson 3 Activity 4.
- Elicit how many items of food and drink they found. (*12*—counting chocolate on trees and chocolate fish separately)

2 Comprehension

- Ask the children to look at the first three questions in the activity. Have them look at the story and find their answers. Elicit answers. Then discuss question 4. Remind them of how the style of the pictures changes, then have them complete their answer.

Answers

1 He was hungry/he wanted something to eat. **2** The jell-o fish eats it/smashes it with his tail. **3** He woke up./He ate it. **4** Children's own answers.

3 Critical Literacy

- Ask *Why is the queen so sad?* Elicit what the children like/do not like about the strange land. Ask *Is there a problem there?* Elicit that it is full of tempting food but the big fish is dangerous.
- Ask *Would you like to visit an imaginary land? Why/Why not?* The children then complete their personalized answers. Imagining themselves in the story context helps them engage as readers.

Writing Workshop

Using adjectives to make your writing more interesting

4 Find examples of adjectives in the story and write them in the chart. Write some more descriptions for an imaginary land.

Read out the different types of adjectives. Explain that adjectives are used in the following order: *opinion + size + shape + age + color + material.* The children categorize the adjectives in the **Writing Tools** box, then find more examples of each category in the story. They write four sentences to describe their imaginary land in their notebook, using adjectives in the correct order. Elicit sentences.

Answers

Children's own answers.

5 Text Connections 

- Elicit other stories about imaginary lands. Write the titles on the board. Ask children to give brief descriptions.

Optional activity: Find the mistake

Focus on word order with adjectives. Write sentences on the board containing an error in word order, e.g. *I ate a chocolate, brown, delicious cake.* Choose a child to come to the board and correct the order. (*I ate a delicious, brown, chocolate cake.*) Repeat with other sentences.

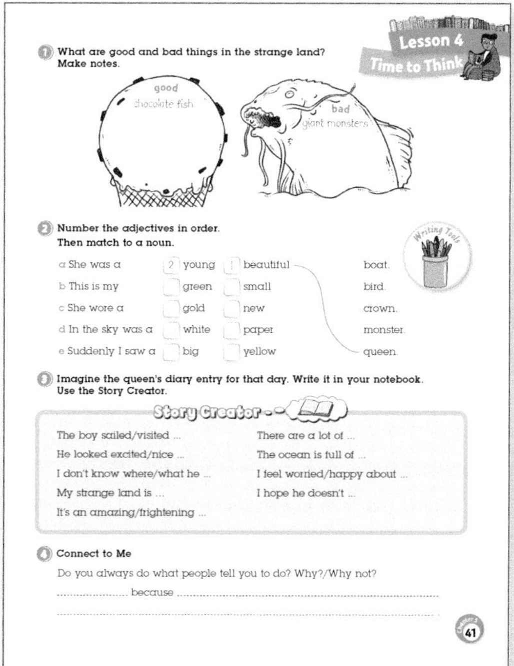

Lesson 4
Time to Think

1 What are good and bad things in the strange land? Make notes.

2 Number the adjectives in order. Then match to a noun.

Writing Tools

a She was a	2 young	1 beautiful	boat.
b This is my	green	small	bird.
c She wore a	gold	new	crown.
d In the sky was a	white	paper	monster.
e Suddenly I saw a	big	yellow	queen.

3 Imagine the queen's diary entry for that day. Write it in your notebook. Use the Story Creator.

Story Creator

The boy sailed/visited ...	There are a lot of ...
He looked excited/nice ...	The ocean is full of ...
I don't know where/what he ...	I feel worried/happy about ...
My strange land is ...	I hope he doesn't ...
It's an amazing/frightening ...	

4 Connect to Me

Do you always do what people tell you to do? Why?/Why not?

.... because ....

Chapter 5 41

1 What are good and bad things in the strange land? Make notes.

The children list good and bad things in the strange land. Elicit ideas and reasons.

Answers (suggested)

good: chocolate fish, chairs and tables made of cookies, chocolate grows on trees, free food, a nice queen
bad: giant monsters, a sad queen, you can't catch the chocolate fish, ice cream castle is cold

2 Number the adjectives in order. Then match to a noun.

Say *She was a young, beautiful queen.* Elicit the mistake. Look at the example together and how to number the adjectives. The children order the adjectives and match to the nouns. Elicit answers.

Answers

a 2 young, 1 beautiful queen; **b** 2 green, 1 small boat; **c** 2 gold, 1 new crown; **d** 1 white, 2 paper bird; **e** 1 big, 2 yellow monster

3 Imagine the queen's diary entry for that day. Write it in your notebook. Use the Story Creator.

Use the **Story Creator** to elicit ideas. The children write a diary entry in their notebook, then compare with a friend. Have children read out their diary entry for the class.

4 Connect to Me

Elicit whether the children always do what people tell them to or not. Encourage them to give reasons. They write their own response, then compare with a friend.

Cooler: Add an adjective

Write *I ate a cake* on the board. Children raise their hands to extend the sentence by adding an adjective and saying the new version. Write up the longer version each time if the child has inserted the adjective in the correct place, e.g. *I ate a delicious, big, round, fresh, brown, chocolate cake.* Repeat the activity with different sentences.

Competency Focus

Me: Critical Literacy

The children use critical literacy skills to reflect on the story and relate it to their own experiences.

Digital Resources

Student eBook • Have children use *Pen* to write the answers for SB Activity 2.

Student eBook, Reader eBook • The children can watch Oral Storytelling Video 5.1 at home with their family.

- If you haven't already, show Oral Storytelling Video 5.1 (a different story on a related theme).

Teacher Resource Center • If you haven't already, print out Oral Storytelling Video Worksheet 5 to do the support activities.

Grammar and Reading

Lesson objective: make positive sentences in the present passive
Key grammar: present passive—statements with *be* + past participle
Secondary language: *penguins, silly, strange*
Materials: Track 5.5; Grammar Worksheet 5B [TRC printout] (optional); animal pictures (Warmer)

Lesson 5

Book Club

1 Listen and read. Are there penguins in Africa?

Scarlett: The Strange Land sounds a bit scary, but amazing.
Rufus: Yes, imagine a land where chairs are made of cookies and chocolate grows on trees. Mm!
Yasmin: Hey, Angelo, true or false? 1) Chocolate grows on trees.
Angelo: It's true! Chocolate is made from cocoa, and cocoa trees are grown all over South America.
Yasmin: That's right. 2) Brazilian is spoken in Brazil.
Angelo: False. They don't speak Brazilian. They speak Portuguese.
Yasmin: Correct. 3) Kangaroos are eaten in Australia.
Angelo: True. They eat kangaroo meat in Australia.
Yasmin: That's right. 4) Penguins are found in Africa.
Angelo: No way! Penguins like cold countries.
Yasmin: No, it's true. They live in South Africa, too. 5) The moon is made of cheese.
Angelo: Now you're being silly!
Yasmin: Ha, ha, ha, ha!

2 Write passive sentences.

1 Farmers grow cocoa trees in South America.
Cocoa trees are grown in South America.
2 They speak Portuguese in Brazil.
3 People eat kangaroos in Australia.
4 You can find penguins in Africa.

3 Complete with the correct form of the verb. Then talk to a friend.

play grow ~~ride~~ make

1 Ostriches are (ride) ...ridden... in South Africa.
2 Basketball is (play) .... in India.
3 Glass is (make) .... of sand.
4 Cotton is (grow) .... on plants.

A: Ostriches are ridden in South Africa.
B: Yes, that's true!

Grammar Central
Present passive
Soccer ..is played.. at my school.
Spanish and English .... in a lot of countries.

Grammar Booster on page 75

Chapter 5 69

Warmer: Where do the animals live?

Show animal pictures or write animal names on the board, e.g. *elephant, camel, crocodile, polar bear.* Ask *Where do these animals live?* Write *Elephants live in India and Africa.* Elicit similar sentences following the pattern.

1 5.5 Listen and read. Are there penguins in Africa?

- Ask *Are there penguins in Africa?* Have a show of hands for yes/no. Play Track 5.5. The children listen and read along to confirm the answer. (*Yes, there are.*)
- Play Track 5.5 again. The children underline Yasmin's quiz questions. Elicit how the question is structured. (*the verb* to be + *a past participle*)
- Write on the board *The dogs eat sandwiches.* and *Sandwiches are eaten by dogs.* Explain the concept of active and passive. Elicit further examples.

2 Write passive sentences. 

- Have the children look at the example. Elicit how the passive is formed. (*the verb* to be + *a past participle*)
- They change the sentences from active to passive, then compare answers with a friend. Elicit answers.

Answers

1 Cocoa trees are grown in South America. **2** Portuguese is spoken in Brazil. **3** Kangaroos are eaten in Australia. **4** Penguins are found in Africa.

Grammar Central

Present passive

Have the children complete the grammar examples. Elicit answers. Elicit how the present passive is formed. (*the verb* to be + *a past participle*) The children write further examples with sports and languages in their notebook. For extra practice, try the **Grammar Booster** section in the Student Book (pp. 75–77).

Answers p. 75

Activity 1: **1** is grown **2** are spoken **3** is served

Activity 2: are decorated **2** is taught **3** are played **4** is used **5** are written **6** is made **7** is eaten **8** are given

p. 76

Activity 1: **1** is grown **2** is washed **3** are collected **4** is used for **5** is delivered **6** are cut **7** are made of **8** are sent

Activity 2: a made, **4** b separated, **2** c picked, **1** d sold, **6** e delivered, **3** f sewn, **5**

p. 77

Activity 1: **1** exciting **2** are visited **3** something **4** is located **5** are spoken **6** is called **7** have lived **8** are found **9** used for **10** are worn **11** made of **12** are produced **13** are sent

Activity 2: Children's own answers.

3 Complete with the correct form of the verb. Then talk to a friend.

- The children complete the sentences with the present passive, writing the past participle.
- Choose two children to read the example dialogue.
- Divide the class into pairs. They take turns asking and responding to true/false sentences using the information in the activity.

Answers

1 ridden **2** played **3** made **4** grown

Optional activity: Have a class quiz

Write *languages, sports, animals* on the board. Say *Tigers are found in the USA.* to elicit *true* or *false*. In groups, the children prepare a true/false quiz question for each category. Have groups take turns asking the class.

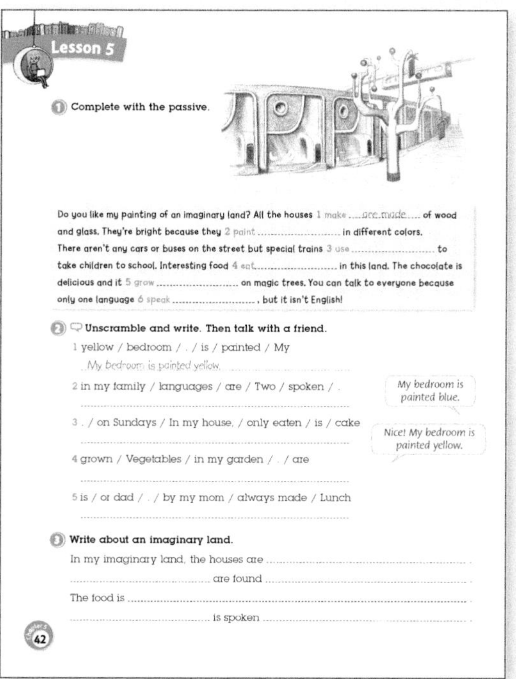

Lesson 5

1 Complete with the passive.

Do you like my painting of an imaginary land? All the houses 1 make ....are made.... of wood and glass. They're bright because they 2 paint .... in different colors. There aren't any cars or buses on the street but special trains 3 use .... to take children to school. Interesting food 4 eat.......................... in this land. The chocolate is delicious and it 5 grow .... on magic trees. You can talk to everyone because only one language 6 speak ...., but it isn't English!

2 Unscramble and write. Then talk with a friend.

1 yellow / bedroom / . / is / painted / My
My bedroom is painted yellow.
2 in my family / languages / are / Two / spoken / .
....
3 . / on Sundays / In my house, / only eaten / is / cake
....
4 grown / Vegetables / in my garden / . / are
....
5 is / or dad / . / by my mom / always made / Lunch
....

My bedroom is painted blue.

Nice! My bedroom is painted yellow.

3 Write about an imaginary land.

In my imaginary land, the houses are ....
.... are found ....
The food is ....
.... is spoken ....

Chapter 5 42

1 Complete with the passive.

The children complete the text with the passive form of the verbs supplied. Elicit answers.

Answers

1 are made **2** 're painted **3** are used **4** is eaten
5 is grown **6** is spoken

2 Unscramble and write. Then talk with a friend.

The children unscramble and write the sentences. Elicit answers. The children then comment on the sentences in pairs, using their own experience.

Answers

1 My bedroom is painted yellow. **2** Two languages are spoken in my family. **3** In my house, cake is only eaten on Sundays. **4** Vegetables are grown in my garden. **5** Lunch is always made by my mom or dad.

3 Write about an imaginary land.

Encourage the children to imagine their own land and write descriptions of it. Elicit descriptions.

Answers

Children's own answers.

Cooler: My country

Have the children give more examples of what is grown in their country, what animals are found there, and what sports are played. Write examples on the board. You could ask them to write a few sentences on the topic *My country* for homework.

Competency Focus

Learn

The children demonstrate their understanding of the new language by reading the text and completing the activity.

Digital Resources

Digital Activity Book • Put the class into groups of six. Have groups discuss their ideas for AB Activity 3. The children use *Pen* to write details of their imaginary land, each child writing one detail. Take a class vote on which land the children would most like to visit.

Student eBook • Have children use *Highlighter* to identify the present passive in SB Activity 1.

Teacher Resource Center • For extra grammar practice, print out Grammar Worksheet 5B.

Vocabulary, Listening, and Spelling

Lesson objectives: understand and talk about the chocolate-making process; practice spelling past participles
Key vocabulary: *collect, deliver, dry, grind, mix, pick, remove, roast*
Secondary language: *cocoa pods, beans*
Materials: Track 5.6; Phonics Worksheet 5 [TRC printout] (optional)

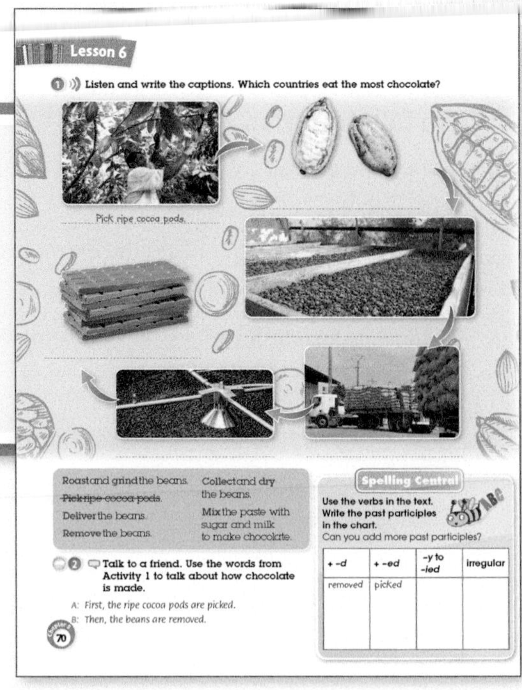
Lesson 6

1 Listen and write the captions. Which countries eat the most chocolate?

Pick ripe cocoa pods.

Roast and grind the beans.
~~Pick ripe cocoa pods.~~
Deliver the beans.
Remove the beans.
Collect and dry the beans.
Mix the paste with sugar and milk to make chocolate.

2 Talk to a friend. Use the words from Activity 1 to talk about how chocolate is made.

A: *First, the ripe cocoa pods are picked.*
B: *Then, the beans are removed.*

70

Spelling Central

Use the verbs in the text. Write the past participles in the chart.
Can you add more past participles?

+ -*d*	+ -*ed*	-*y* to -*ied*	irregular
removed	picked		

Warmer: Pre-teach vocabulary

Pre-teach the vocabulary by giving definitions or sentences showing them in context, e.g. *The mailman delivers letters and parcels. Roast means making something very hot.* Repeat the definitions/sentences, pausing to elicit the key word.

1 5.6 Listen and write the captions. Which countries eat the most chocolate?

- Have the children look at the process of making chocolate. Pre-teach *cocoa pod* and *beans* by pointing to the pictures in the Student Book.
- Ask the children to read the captions in the box.
- Play Track 5.6 twice. They listen and write the correct caption next to its picture. Elicit answers.
- Elicit which countries eat the most chocolate. (*Switzerland, Belgium, and the UK*)

Audioscript

1 Cocoa beans grow inside pods on cacao trees. When they are ripe, the pods are picked from the trees.
2 The cocoa beans are removed from the pods. They don't look like chocolate. They're white!
3 The beans are collected on banana leaves and dried in the sun.
4 Then the beans are delivered to chocolate factories in different countries.
5 In the factories, the beans are cleaned and roasted. Then they are ground into a paste.
6 The paste is mixed with sugar and milk to make chocolate. People in Switzerland, Belgium, and the UK eat the most chocolate!

Answers

1 Pick ripe cocoa pods. **2** Remove the beans. **3** Collect and dry the beans. **4** Deliver the beans. **5** Roast and grind the beans. **6** Mix the paste with sugar and milk to make chocolate.

2 Talk to a friend. Use the words from Activity 1 to talk about how chocolate is made.

- Tell the children to look at the examples. Elicit the rule again for making a passive and remind them about using past participles. Write irregular forms, e.g. *grind—ground*, on the board to help them.
- Divide the class into pairs to describe how chocolate is made. Monitor to check use of past participles.

Spelling Central

Past participles

Highlight the different spelling patterns in the chart. The children write the past participles of the verbs in Activity 1, writing them in the correct place. Elicit more examples. (e.g. *danced, walked, been*)

Answers

+ *–d:* removed; + *–ed:* picked, roasted, mixed, collected, delivered; *change –y to –ied:* dried; *irregular:* ground

Optional activity: Describe another process

Choose another simple process that the children might know, e.g. producing coffee, making pizza. Have the class explain the process using passive verbs. Draw diagrams on the board and list ingredients to help them.

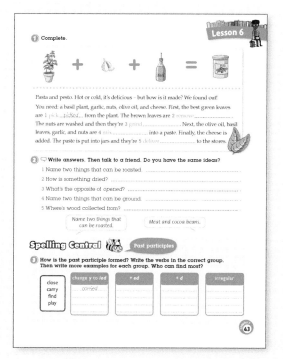

Lesson 6

1 Complete.

Pasta and pesto. Hot or cold, it's delicious – but how is it made? We found out!
You need: a basil plant, garlic, nuts, olive oil, and cheese. First, the best green leaves are 1 pick ...*picked*... from the plant. The brown leaves are 2 remove .... The nuts are washed and then they're 3 grind .... Next, the olive oil, basil leaves, garlic, and nuts are 4 mix .... into a paste. Finally, the cheese is added. The paste is put into jars and they're 5 deliver .... to the stores.

2 Write answers. Then talk to a friend. Do you have the same ideas?

1 Name two things that can be roasted. ....
2 How is something dried? ....
3 What's the opposite of *opened*? ....
4 Name two things that can be ground. ....
5 Where's wood collected from? ....

Name two things that can be roasted.
Meat and cocoa beans.

Spelling Central — Past participles

3 How is the past participle formed? Write the verbs in the correct group. Then write more examples for each group. Who can find most?

close / carry / find / play

change y to ied	+ ed	+ d	irregular
carried			

Chapter 5 43

1 Complete.

Using the pictures, elicit or pre-teach *basil, garlic, olive oil, pesto*. The children read the text and complete the present passive verbs by writing the past participles of the verbs supplied. Elicit answers.

Answers

1 picked **2** removed **3** ground **4** mixed **5** delivered

2 Write answers. Then talk to a friend. Do you have the same ideas?

The children write answers and then ask and answer in pairs. Elicit ideas.

Answers (suggested)

1 *any two of:* meat, vegetables, coffee beans, cocoa beans **2** with air or heat **3** closed **4** *any two of:* nuts/(wheat for) flour/coffee beans/cocoa beans/pepper/rice **5** the countryside/old trees/the beach

3 How is the past participle formed? Write the verbs in the correct group. Then write more examples for each group. Who can find the most?

To practice the **Spelling Central** feature, the children make the past participles of the verbs supplied and write them in the correct category (according to how they are formed). Elicit answers. Ask the class if they know the past participles of any other verbs.

Answers

change –y to –ied: carried, (dried)
+ *–ed:* played (mixed/delivered/roasted/collected/picked/washed)
+ *–d:* closed (removed)
irregular: found (put/made/ground)

Cooler: Play "The Pizza Game"

Have the children draw a pizza with eight slices, number the slices, and add a verb from Activity 1 on each slice. Have the children play in pairs. They take turns saying a number. Their friend gives the infinitive and they have to say the past participle correctly.

Competency Focus

Collaborate and communicate

The children work together and use their interpersonal skills to describe the process of making chocolate, incorporating the new vocabulary.

Digital Resources

Student eBook • TIP Use *Timer* to set a time limit for the SB Spelling Central activity.

Teacher Resource Center • For phonics practice, print out Phonics Worksheet 5.

Student's App • Encourage the children to play the games on their smartphone/tablet. They could do this with a friend as a fun way to review the chapter vocabulary together. (*The Inks* Apps are free and available on the App Store and Google Play.)

CLIL: Art—How tempera paint is made

Lesson objective: find out about the process of making tempera paint
Materials: paint box (Warmer); CLIL Graphic Organizer 5 [TRC printout] (optional)

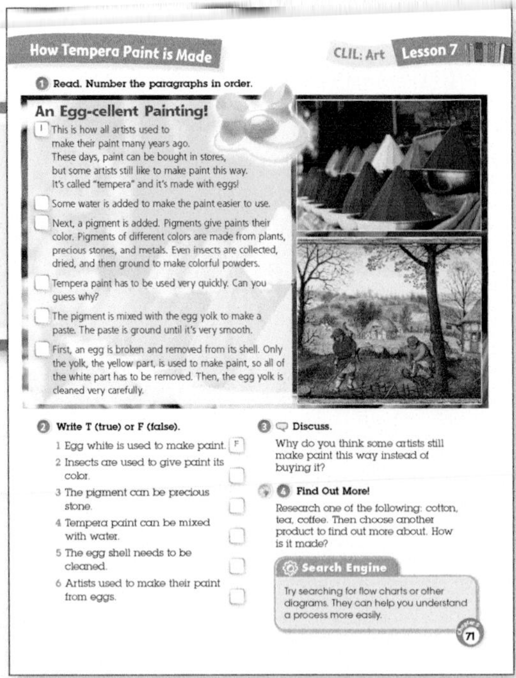

How Tempera Paint is Made — CLIL: Art — Lesson 7

1 Read. Number the paragraphs in order.

An Egg-cellent Painting!

[1] This is how all artists used to make their paint many years ago. These days, paint can be bought in stores, but some artists still like to make paint this way. It's called "tempera" and it's made with eggs!

[ ] Some water is added to make the paint easier to use.

[ ] Next, a pigment is added. Pigments give paints their color. Pigments of different colors are made from plants, precious stones, and metals. Even insects are collected, dried, and then ground to make colorful powders.

[ ] Tempera paint has to be used very quickly. Can you guess why?

[ ] The pigment is mixed with the egg yolk to make a paste. The paste is ground until it's very smooth.

[ ] First, an egg is broken and removed from its shell. Only the yolk, the yellow part, is used to make paint, so all of the white part has to be removed. Then, the egg yolk is cleaned very carefully.

2 Write T (true) or F (false).

1 Egg white is used to make paint. [F]
2 Insects are used to give paint its color. [ ]
3 The pigment can be precious stone. [ ]
4 Tempera paint can be mixed with water. [ ]
5 The egg shell needs to be cleaned. [ ]
6 Artists used to make their paint from eggs. [ ]

3 Discuss.

Why do you think some artists still make paint this way instead of buying it?

4 Find Out More!

Research one of the following: cotton, tea, coffee. Then choose another product to find out more about. How is it made?

Search Engine

Try searching for flow charts or other diagrams. They can help you understand a process more easily.

71

Warmer: Unscramble the colors

Show the children your paint box if you have one. Ask *What kind of paint do you usually paint with?* Prompt as necessary, e.g. *watercolors, poster paint.* Ask *What do you think the paint is made of?* Ask *How do you mix new colors?* Write up scrambled versions to elicit how colors are made, e.g. *theiw + lakcb = rayg*, etc.

1 Read. Number the paragraphs in order.

- Ask the children to look at the pictures and identify *egg shell* and *yolk*. Pre-teach *pigment*.
- The children read the text, then number the paragraphs in order.
- Ask *What are the ingredients for tempera paint?* (*egg yolk, pigment, and water*) *Why is the paint used quickly?* (*The egg gets rotten and smelly.*)

Answers

1, 5, 3, 6, 4, 2

2 Write (T) true or (F) false.

- Elicit why the example answer is false. (*Egg yolk is used, not egg white.*)
- The children read the text again and write T (true) or F (false) for each sentence. Elicit answers, including the correct version of the false sentences.

Answers

1 F **2** T **3** T **4** T **5** F **6** T

3 Discuss. 

- Ask the children to think about this kind of paint and why artists might use it. Elicit suggestions and write their reasons on the board.

4 Find Out More! 

- The children choose one of cotton, tea, or coffee, plus another product, and research how they are made. The **Search Engine** feature gives support on where to look. The children will need to complete this research before doing the follow-up activity in the Activity Book. (It could be set as homework.)

Optional activity: Make a concertina book

Distribute a piece of paper to each child. Show them how to fold it lengthwise, then into four sections (concertina-style) to make their mini-book. Ask them to choose one of the processes they researched and draw simple diagrams with captions to explain the process.

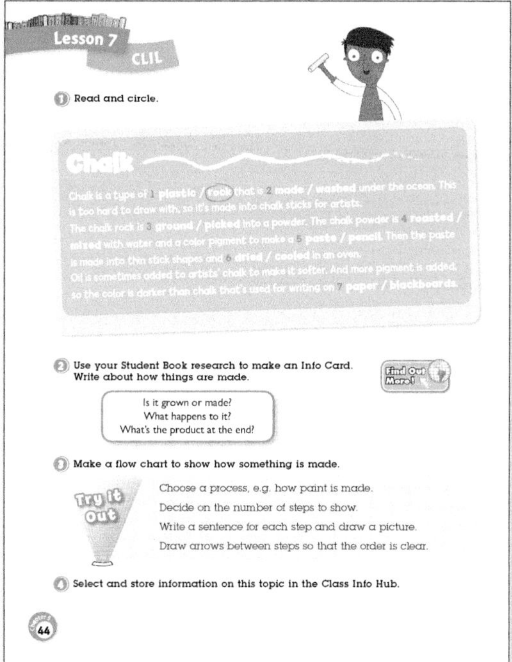

1 Read and circle.

The children read and complete the text by circling the correct option in each pair. Elicit answers.

Answers

1 rock **2** made **3** ground **4** mixed **5** paste **6** dried **7** blackboards

2 Use your Student Book research to make an Info Card. Write about how things are made.

Divide the class into groups. Have the children pool the information learned from their research in the Student Book and the Activity Book. They write about and illustrate their ideas individually. Have the groups present their Info Cards to the class.

3 Make a flow chart to show how something is made.

Draw an example of a simple flow chart on the board, e.g. to show how tea is made. Number the steps, write a simple sentence for each, and join them with arrows. Divide the class into groups to make a flow chart following the **Try It Out** instructions. They then present it to the class.

Answers

Children's own answers.

4 Select and store information on this topic in the Class Info Hub.

Have the children vote for the most interesting Info Cards and flow charts. Archive these in your Class Hub (see p. 41) in a folder called **Chapter 5 How Things are Made**.

Cooler: More past participles

Have the children underline all the past participles in the Student Book Activity 1 text. Then ask them to work in pairs and test each other, spelling the word, e.g. *buy* (*bought*).

Competency Focus

Act

The children carry out research to find out about other simple products and the processes by which they are made.

Digital Resources

Student eBook • To extend feedback on SB Activity 2, have children use *Highlighter* to identify the section of the text which gives the answer to each question.

• For the Cooler, have children use *Highlighter* to identify the past participles in SB Activity 1.

Teacher Resource Center • Print out CLIL Graphic Organizer 5 for the children to use in collating their Find Out More! research.

CLIL eBook • The children can use the CLIL eBook to expand their knowledge of the lesson topic.

Writing Project

Lesson objectives: review language from Chapter 5; write a fantasy poem and present it to the class
Materials: Writing Template 5 [TRC printout] (optional)

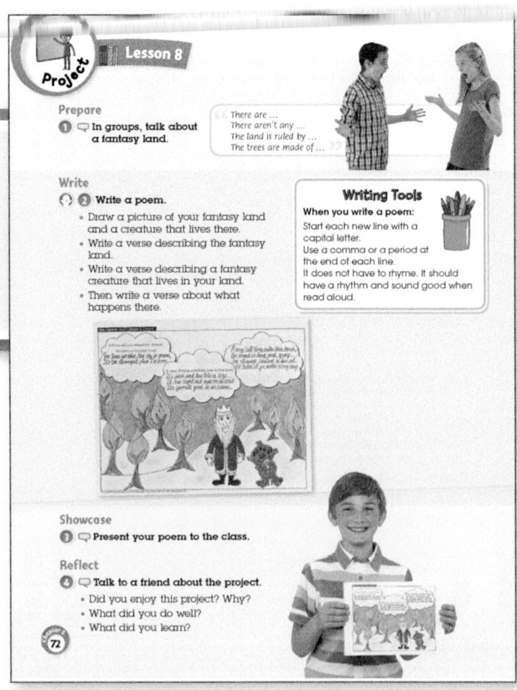
Project Lesson 8

Prepare

1 In groups, talk about a fantasy land.

There are …
There aren't any …
The land is ruled by …
The trees are made of …

Write

2 Write a poem.

- Draw a picture of your fantasy land and a creature that lives there.
- Write a verse describing the fantasy land.
- Write a verse describing a fantasy creature that lives in your land.
- Then write a verse about what happens there.

Writing Tools

When you write a poem:
Start each new line with a capital letter.
Use a comma or a period at the end of each line.
It does not have to rhyme. It should have a rhythm and sound good when read aloud.

Showcase

3 Present your poem to the class.

Reflect

4 Talk to a friend about the project.

- Did you enjoy this project? Why?
- What did you do well?
- What did you learn?

72

Warmer: Picture dictation

Dictate some sentences about your own fantasy land for the children to draw, e.g. *There are two tall trees—they are made of cheese. There are some flying fish.*, etc. Have children show their pictures to a friend.

Prepare

1 In groups, talk about a fantasy land. 

- The children discuss a fantasy land in groups, using the prompts supplied. Groups report back to the class.

Write

2 Write a poem.

- Have the children read the poem as a model for their own writing.
- Read the **Writing Tools** box together. Elicit examples in the model of poem features.
- The children prepare an outline, using the instructions and the model poem. They write and illustrate their poem, then compare with a friend. Give support as necessary.

Showcase

3 Present your poem to the class. 

- Choose children to read their poems to the class. Ask the rest of the class to listen for the strange creatures and what strange things happen there.

Reflect

4 Vote for the best poem and talk to the class. 

- Have children comment on which poem they liked best and why. Have a class vote for which one they liked the best.

Optional activity: Write an extra verse

Have the class imagine strange kinds of transportation which might exist in their fantasy land, e.g. flying cars, bicycles that go backwards, etc. Ask them to write an extra verse about transportation for their poem.

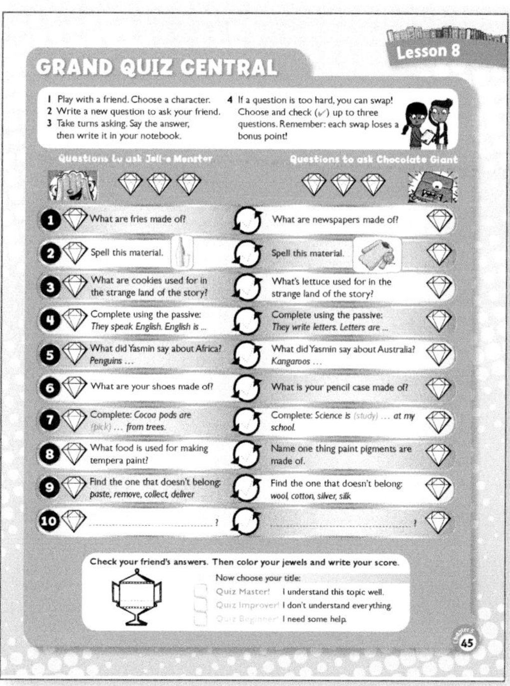

Grand Quiz Central

See p. 43 for details of how to take the quiz.

Answers

1 potatoes / paper **2** glass / wool **3** They're used for making chairs. / It's used for a boat. **4** spoken / written **5** are found in Africa. / are eaten in Australia. **6** They're made of … / It's made of … **7** picked / studied **8** eggs / *any one of:* plants, precious stones, metals, insects **9** paste / silver **10** Children's own answers.

Cooler: Make a tongue twister

Choose a letter and ask the class to make a tongue twister about their fantasy land. Model with *f*, e.g. *The flying fish flew far to find their favorite food.*

Competency Focus

Me

The children invent and write a poem, exploring their imagination and creativity.

Digital Resources

Student eBook • Pairs look at the picture and discuss what you could say in a poem about it. Elicit ideas. Then show the text and have the children compare their own ideas with the model poem.

Teacher Resource Center • Print out Writing Template 5 to use for the SB writing activity.

Language Review

Lesson objective: review language from Chapter 5
Materials: Tracks 5.7, AB 5.1 and AB 5.2

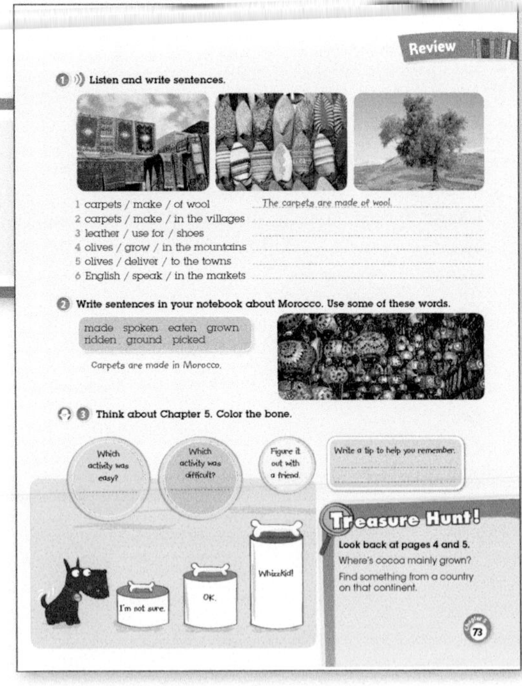
Review

1 Listen and write sentences.

1 carpets / make / of wool — The carpets are made of wool.
2 carpets / make / in the villages
3 leather / use for / shoes
4 olives / grow / in the mountains
5 olives / deliver / to the towns
6 English / speak / in the markets

2 Write sentences in your notebook about Morocco. Use some of these words.

made spoken eaten grown ridden ground picked

Carpets are made in Morocco.

3 Think about Chapter 5. Color the bone.

Which activity was easy? Which activity was difficult? Figure it out with a friend. Write a tip to help you remember.

I'm not sure. OK. Whizzkid!

Treasure Hunt!
Look back at pages 4 and 5.
Where's cocoa mainly grown?
Find something from a country on that continent.

73

Warmer: What's it made of?

Ask children to talk with their friend about their own clothes and possessions.

1 5.7 Listen and write sentences.

- Have the children identify the things in the pictures.
- Play Track 5.7 twice and ask them to listen for what the things are made of. Then they write their sentences.

Audioscript

When you visit Morocco, you should go to the market. You can buy beautiful carpets made of wool. They're made by hand by people in the villages and they aren't expensive. Morocco is famous for leather goods. The leather is used for shoes in all different colors. There's also a lot of jewelry made of silver.

There are a lot of olive trees and olives are grown in the mountains in Morocco. The olives are delivered by trucks to different towns and then sold in the markets. They're delicious.

English is spoken in most of the markets so it's easy to buy things. Pretty boxes made of wood are great gifts for your friends and family.

Answers

1 The carpets are made of wool.
2 The carpets are made in the villages.
3 Leather is used for making shoes.
4 The olives are grown in the mountains.
5 The olives are delivered to the towns.
6 English is spoken in the markets.

2 Write sentences in your notebook about Morocco. Use some of these words.

- The children write their sentences in their notebook.

Answers

Children's own answers.

3 Think about Chapter 5. Color the bone. 

- Have the children look back at Chapter 5 and color the bone to evaluate their progress (self-evaluation). Discuss ideas for using new grammar. The children choose and write a tip in their Student Book.

Treasure Hunt!

Ask *In which continent is cocoa mainly grown?* (*South America*) Have the children look at pp. 4–5 to find something from a country in that continent. (*a Brazilian soccer shirt*)

Cooler: Play "Bingo"

Play the game using material vocabulary from the chapter (see Games Bank p. 19).

Competency Focus

Me: Self-evaluation

The children reflect on the chapter and express their opinions about their own progress.

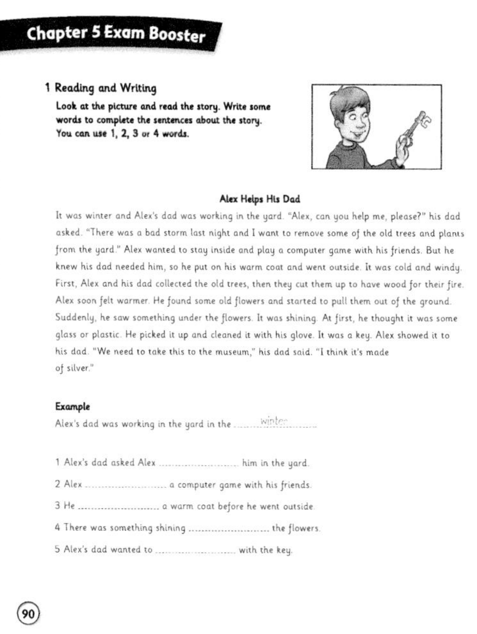

Chapter 5 Exam Booster

1 Reading and Writing

Look at the picture and read the story. Write some words to complete the sentences about the story. You can use 1, 2, 3 or 4 words.

Alex Helps His Dad

It was winter and Alex's dad was working in the yard. "Alex, can you help me, please?" his dad asked. "There was a bad storm last night and I want to remove some of the old trees and plants from the yard." Alex wanted to stay inside and play a computer game with his friends. But he knew his dad needed him, so he put on his warm coat and went outside. It was cold and windy. First, Alex and his dad collected the old trees, then they cut them up to have wood for their fire. Alex soon felt warmer. He found some old flowers and started to pull them out of the ground. Suddenly, he saw something under the flowers. It was shining. At first, he thought it was some glass or plastic. He picked it up and cleaned it with his glove. It was a key. Alex showed it to his dad. "We need to take this to the museum," his dad said. "I think it's made of silver."

Example

Alex's dad was working in the yard in the ......winter......

1 Alex's dad asked Alex .... him in the yard.

2 Alex .... a computer game with his friends.

3 He .... a warm coat before he went outside.

4 There was something shining .... the flowers.

5 Alex's dad wanted to .... with the key.

90

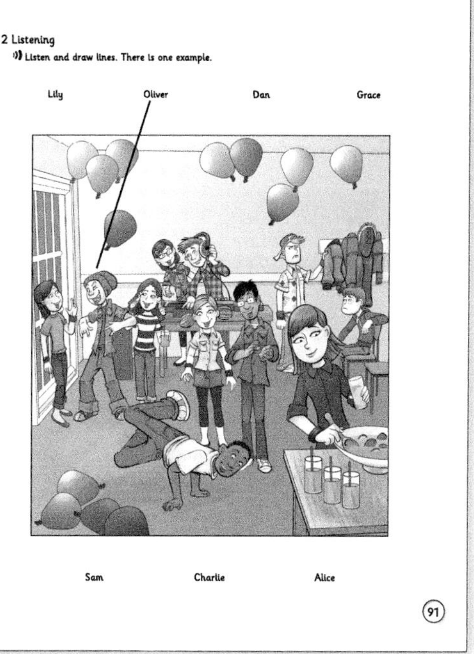

2 Listening

Listen and draw lines. There is one example.

91

3 Listening

Listen and draw lines. There is one example.

Exam Tip

Don't worry if you miss something on the first listening. Stay calm and listen for it the second time the audio is played.

92

1 Reading and Writing. Look at the picture and read the story. Write some words to complete the sentences about the story. You can use 1, 2, 3 or 4 words. There is one example.

The children read the text and complete the sentences.

Answers

1 to help **2** wanted to play **3** put on **4** under **5** go to the museum

2))) AB 5.1 Listening. Listen and draw lines. There is one example.

Play AB Track 5.1 twice. The children listen and match.

Answers (Audioscript on p. 223)

Lines between: Lily—girl with earrings; Charlie—boy dancing; Dan—boy getting his coat; Alice—girl mixing the fruit juice; Grace—girl talking to DJ

3))) AB 5.2 Listening. Listen and draw lines. There is one example.

Play AB Track 5.2 twice. The children listen and match.

Answers (Audioscript on p.223)

Lines between: Robert - man selling toy giraffe; Miss Jones - girl holding two dollars; Ben - boy selling clothes; Mr and Mrs Green - selling cups and plates; Karen - girl talking on her phone; Dad - man holding basket

Digital Resources

Teacher Resource Center • Print out Test Chapter 5 and Mid-year Test to use at the end of this lesson. The Test Generator also allows you to create customized tests.

On the Ocean Waves

Overview

The children will:

- use critical thinking skills to identify vocabulary about ocean rescue.
- talk about past events using the past progressive.
- read and understand a story about the Titanic.
- talk about past events using *when/while*.
- talk about events related to the ocean.
- find out about icebergs and global warming.
- write their own diary entry of a Titanic survivor.

Key Vocabulary

Ocean rescue: crew, drown, lifeboat, life jacket, rescue, rock, save, sinking, survivor

Ship and ocean: captain, destroy, flag, float, holes, mast, pirate, waves

Key Grammar

Past progressive

- I was doing my homework when you walked in.
- We were watching TV when the doorbell rang.

Past progressive: *when/while*

- While you were reading the story, I fell asleep.
- When I fell asleep, you were reading the story.
- What were you doing while the ship was sinking?

Reading Skills

Story: *The Journal*

Genre: historical fiction

Literacy Development

- use reading skills to understand and predict content
- relate story theme to personal experience
- use playscript writing conventions

Functional Language

- Oh, no! Are we going to be late for …?
- No. Don't worry. It's going to be OK.

Spelling

Irregular plurals

CLIL: Geography—Icebergs

The children find out about icebergs and global warming.

Competency Focus

The children will:

use critical thinking skills to deduce the meaning of new vocabulary. (Lesson 1) predict the content of a story. (Lesson 3)	activate new vocabulary and apply new grammar knowledge. (Lesson 2) apply new grammar rules in a familiar context. (Lesson 5)	work in pairs to act out a dialogue. (Lesson 3) work in pairs to retell events from a song. (Lesson 6)	relate the story theme to their personal experience. (Lesson 4) imagine a trip on the *Titanic* and write their own diary entry. (Lesson 8) evaluate their own progress in the chapter. (Review)	find out more about global warming. (Lesson 7)

Digital Overview

Teacher Presentation

Student eBook and Digital Activity Book

- Music Video 6.1: *The Golden Vanity*
- Interactive versions of AB activities
- Integrated audio and answer key for all activities

Teacher resources for planning, lesson delivery, and homework

Teacher Resource Center

- Class Planner Chapter 6
- Worksheets to print out (including notes and answers):
  - Grammar Worksheet 6A: Past progressive
  - Grammar Worksheet 6B: Past progressive: *when/while*
  - Phonics Worksheet 6
  - CLIL Graphic Organizer 6
  - Writing Template 6
  - Test Chapter 6
- Test Generator
- Speaking Assessment: Cambridge English Young Learners Exams
- Literacy Handbook

Watch the Music Video

Children's resources for consolidation and practice at home

Student eBook

- Music Video 6.1: *The Golden Vanity*

The Inks Student's App

Vocabulary games: Ocean rescue and Ship/ocean

Chapter 6

On the Ocean Waves

Lesson 1

Vocabulary

Lesson objectives: identify and use vocabulary to describe ocean rescue
Key vocabulary: *crew, drown, lifeboat, life jacket, rescue, rock, save, sinking, survivor*
Materials: Track 6.1

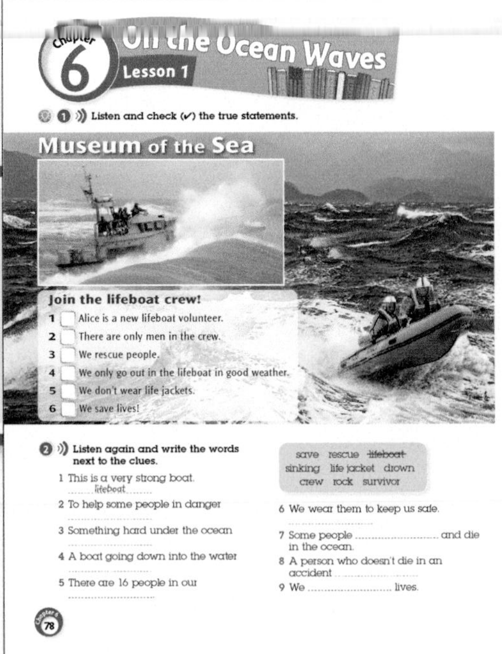
Chapter 6 On the Ocean Waves
Lesson 1

1 Listen and check (✔) the true statements.

Museum of the Sea

Join the lifeboat crew!
1 Alice is a new lifeboat volunteer.
2 There are only men in the crew.
3 We rescue people.
4 We only go out in the lifeboat in good weather.
5 We don't wear life jackets.
6 We save lives!

2 Listen again and write the words next to the clues.

save rescue ~~lifeboat~~ sinking life jacket drown crew rock survivor

1 This is a very strong boat. lifeboat
2 To help some people in danger ....
3 Something hard under the ocean ....
4 A boat going down into the water ....
5 There are 16 people in our ....
6 We wear them to keep us safe. ....
7 Some people .... and die in the ocean.
8 A person who doesn't die in an accident ....
9 We .... lives.

78

Warmer: Play "Running Board Race"

Play the game using vocabulary the children think of connected to the chapter title (see Games Bank p. 19).

1 6.1 Listen and check (✔) the true statements. 

- Have the children look at the pictures. Ask *Who are the people?*
- Tell the children to listen to Alice talking about her first time on the lifeboat. Ask them to study the sentences and say which ones they think are true.
- Then play Track 6.1. The children listen and check the true sentences. Elicit answers. Whenever you elicit answers, remember to check with the class to see if they agree.

Audioscript

Hi, I'm Alice, and I'm a new lifeboat volunteer. I went out to the ocean in the lifeboat last week. The lifeboat is a very strong boat. It was my first time and I was excited but worried, too. We had to help some people in danger. We had to rescue some people from a fishing boat. The fishing boat hit something hard. There was a big rock under the ocean close to their boat. The boat started going down into the water. It was sinking and the passengers were scared.

There are 16 people in our crew—men and women; we work together on the lifeboat. We go out in all weather—good or bad. We're all very good at swimming, but we have to wear life jackets. We wear them to keep us safe. There were five people on the fishing boat that we went to rescue. Sadly, one man almost died. He was drowning in the ocean and is now in the hospital. He was lucky he didn't drown. So every person was a survivor, and they thanked us because we saved their lives. But it's our job—we save lives.

Answers

✔ *by:* 1, 3, 6

2 6.1 Listen again and write the words next to the clues.

- Look at the sentence and elicit what clues there are in the sentence for the example answer. (*strong, boat*)
- Play Track 6.1 again. The children complete their answers. Elicit answers.

Answers

1 lifeboat **2** rescue **3** rock **4** sinking **5** crew **6** life jacket **7** drown **8** survivor **9** save

6.1

Optional activity: What comes next?

Play Track 6.1 again or read out the text slowly, pausing to elicit key words, e.g. *A lifeboat is a very …* (*strong boat*).

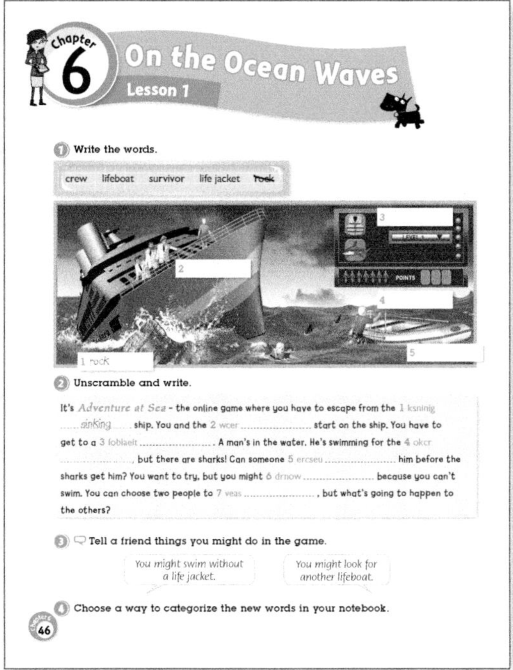
Chapter 6

On the Ocean Waves

Lesson 1

1 Write the words.

crew lifeboat survivor life jacket ~~rock~~

1 rock 2 3 4 5

2 Unscramble and write.

It's *Adventure at Sea* - the online game where you have to escape from the 1 ksninig ...... sinking ...... ship. You and the 2 wcer .... start on the ship. You have to get to a 3 foblaelt .... A man's in the water. He's swimming for the 4 okcr ...., but there are sharks! Can someone 5 ercseu .... him before the sharks get him? You want to try, but you might 6 drnow .... because you can't swim. You can choose two people to 7 veas ...., but what's going to happen to the others?

3 Tell a friend things you might do in the game.

You might swim without a life jacket.

You might look for another lifeboat.

4 Choose a way to categorize the new words in your notebook.

46

1 Write the words.

The children label the items pictured. Elicit answers.

Answers

1 rock **2** crew **3** life jacket **4** survivor **5** lifeboat

2 Unscramble and write.

The children unscramble and write the words. Elicit answers.

Answers

1 sinking **2** crew **3** lifeboat **4** rock **5** rescue **6** drown **7** save

3 Tell a friend things you might do in the game.

Ask the children to imagine they are playing the *Adventure at Sea* game and think of things they might do to survive or escape. They share ideas in pairs.

4 Choose a way to categorize the new words in your notebook.

Have the children brainstorm appropriate categories in pairs. Prompt as necessary, e.g. *verbs/nouns, words to do with danger/words to do with safety.* The children individually choose the best categories for them and list the words in their notebook.

Answers

Children's own answers.

Cooler: Mime time

Read out sentences containing key vocabulary items. Have the class work in pairs to figure out a mime to illustrate the meaning, e.g. *We put on life jackets.*

Competency Focus

Think! Critical Thinking

The children use critical thinking skills to understand the new vocabulary by using visual clues and processing the written and spoken forms.

Digital Resources

Digital Activity Book • Have the class do the AB interactive digital activities, or set them for homework.

Grammar

Lesson objective: talk about past events using the past progressive (interrupted)
Key grammar: past progressive—statements
Secondary language: *cruise ship, divers, deck, island*
Materials: Grammar Worksheet 6A [TRC printout] (optional)

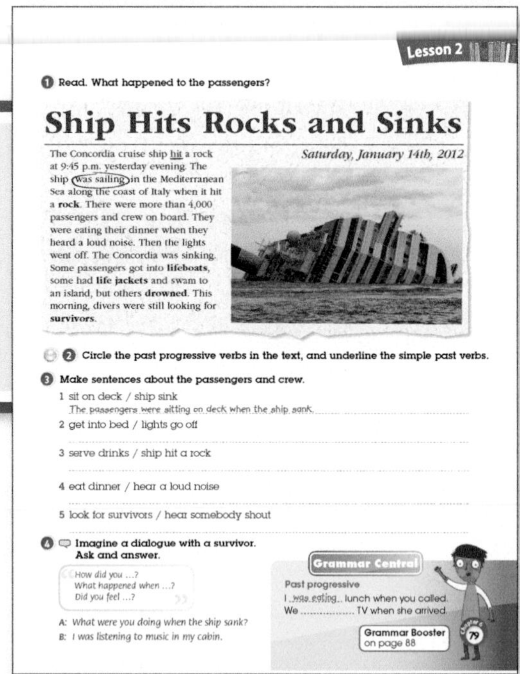

Lesson 2

1 Read. What happened to the passengers?

Ship Hits Rocks and Sinks

Saturday, January 14th, 2012

The Concordia cruise ship hit a rock at 9:45 p.m. yesterday evening. The ship was sailing in the Mediterranean Sea along the coast of Italy when it hit a **rock**. There were more than 4,000 passengers and crew on board. They were eating their dinner when they heard a loud noise. Then the lights went off. The Concordia was sinking. Some passengers got into **lifeboats**, some had **life jackets** and swam to an island, but others **drowned**. This morning, divers were still looking for **survivors**.

2 Circle the past progressive verbs in the text, and underline the simple past verbs.

3 Make sentences about the passengers and crew.

1 sit on deck / ship sink
The passengers were sitting on deck when the ship sank.
2 get into bed / lights go off
3 serve drinks / ship hit a rock
4 eat dinner / hear a loud noise
5 look for survivors / hear somebody shout

4 Imagine a dialogue with a survivor. Ask and answer.

How did you ...?
What happened when ...?
Did you feel ...?

A: What were you doing when the ship sank?
B: I was listening to music in my cabin.

Grammar Central
Past progressive
I was eating lunch when you called.
We .... TV when she arrived.

Grammar Booster on page 88

79

Warmer: Think about boats

Choose a child to come to the board and draw a large ship. Pre-teach *cruise ship* and ask *How many passengers do you think there are?* Pre-teach *deck* using the ship on the board.

1 Read. What happened to the passengers?

- Have the children look at the newspaper article and quickly find the number of passengers.
- Then have them look at the picture. Ask *What happened to the passengers? (Some got into lifeboats, some swam to an island, others drowned.)*

2 Circle the past progressive verbs in the text, and underline the simple past verbs.

- Have the children read and circle the past progressive verbs and underline the simple past verbs.
- Elicit answers.

Answers

Circled: was sailing, were eating, was sinking, were (still) looking; *Underlined:* hit, hit, were, heard, went (off), got, had, swam, drowned

Grammar Central

Past progressive

Have the children complete the grammar examples. Elicit answers. Elicit the rules for the singular and plural forms. (*was –ing, were –ing*) The children write further examples in their notebook. For extra practice, try the **Grammar Booster** section in the Student Book (p. 88).

Answers p. 88

Activity 1: **1** was, doing **2** were, doing **3** were eating **4** was playing

Activity 2: (answers will vary) **1** was washing the truck **2** were + verb-ing **3** was + verb-ing **4** were + verb-ing **5** was + verb-ing **6** was + verb-ing

3 Make sentences for the passengers and crew.

- The children complete the verbs in the activity, then compare with a friend. Elicit answers.

Answers

1 The passengers were sitting on deck when the ship sank. **2** Some people were getting into bed when the lights went off. **3** The crew was serving drinks when the ship hit a rock. **4** The passengers were eating dinner when they heard a loud noise. **5** They were looking for survivors when they heard somebody shout. **6** I was swimming to an island when a lifeboat rescued me.

4 Imagine a dialogue with a survivor. Ask and answer.

- Choose two children to read the example dialogue.

- Divide the class into pairs to practice the dialogue using the prompts supplied and their own ideas for actions and events. Have pairs perform for the class.

Optional activity: Play "Verb Ping-Pong"

Divide the class into two teams. Any child can call out a simple past verb as a prompt. The other team has to respond with the same verb in the past progressive. They then prompt with a different verb. If a team repeats a verb, gives an incorrect verb form, or takes longer than five seconds, the other team wins a point. The team with the most points wins.

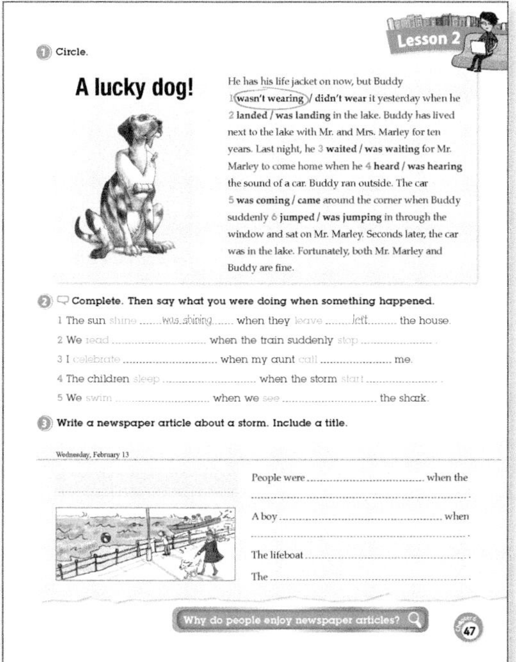

Lesson 2

1 Circle.

A lucky dog!

He has his life jacket on now, but Buddy 1 **wasn't wearing** / **didn't wear** it yesterday when he 2 **landed / was landing** in the lake. Buddy has lived next to the lake with Mr. and Mrs. Marley for ten years. Last night, he 3 **waited / was waiting** for Mr. Marley to come home when he 4 **heard / was hearing** the sound of a car. Buddy ran outside. The car 5 **was coming / came** around the corner when Buddy suddenly 6 **jumped / was jumping** in through the window and sat on Mr. Marley. Seconds later, the car was in the lake. Fortunately, both Mr. Marley and Buddy are fine.

2 Complete. Then say what you were doing when something happened.

1 The sun shine ......was shining...... when they leave ......left...... the house.
2 We read .... when the train suddenly stop ....
3 I celebrate .... when my aunt call .... me.
4 The children sleep .... when the storm start ....
5 We swim .... when we see .... the shark.

3 Write a newspaper article about a storm. Include a title.

Wednesday, February 13

People were .... when the ....
A boy .... when ....
The lifeboat ....
The ....

Why do people enjoy newspaper articles?

47

1 Circle.

The children complete the text by circling the correct option in each pair. Remind them of the difference between the simple past and past progressive. Elicit answers.

Answers

1 wasn't wearing **2** landed **3** was waiting **4** heard **5** was coming **6** jumped

2 Complete. Then say what you were doing when something happened.

The children look at the example and explain why the two different tenses are used. They complete the other sentences individually. They then discuss in pairs what they were doing when something happened. Elicit answers.

Answers

1 was shining, left **2** were reading, stopped **3** was celebrating, called **4** were sleeping, started **5** were swimming, saw

3 Write a newspaper article about a storm. Include a title.

Ask the children to talk about the picture and what happened in the storm. They write their own newspaper article, completing the sentences and writing a title. Fast finishers could add more sentences. Then they compare with a friend. Invite children to read their articles for the class. Discuss why people enjoy reading newspaper articles. (*They often tell exciting/interesting stories. / They tell us what is happening where we live/around the world.*)

Answers

Children's own answers.

Cooler: Play "Tic-Tac-Toe"

Play the game (see Games Bank p. 19). Give verb prompts. The children say a sentence using the past progressive to win a square.

Competency Focus

Learn

By reading the text and identifying the verbs, the children demonstrate their understanding of the new grammatical structures.

Digital Resources

Student eBook • Use *Highlighter* to identify the past progressive in the SB Activity 1 text.

Teacher Resource Center • For extra grammar practice, print out Grammar Worksheet 6A.

Reading: Story Extract

Lesson objectives: reassure someone; use title and pictures to predict story content; read the extract from the historical fiction *The Journal* (middle)

Functional language: *Oh, no! Are we going to be late for ...? No. Don't worry. It's going to be OK.*

Secondary language: *confusing, tightly, rowed*

Materials: Tracks 6.2 and 6.3

Lesson 3

1 Listen and read.

2 Imagine your friend is worried about something. Give them reassurance.

be late for ...
miss the bus
fail the exam
find the classroom

A: Oh, no! Are we going to miss the bus?
B: No. Don't worry. It's going to be OK.

3 Look at the story. Who do you think wrote the journal pages?

4 Read the story extract and answer.

1 Why are the characters getting into a lifeboat?

2 What do you think is going to happen to the journal?

3 How are the characters dressed?

80

The Journal

8 The passengers and crew were waiting for the captain to give orders. There were so many people, and it was very confusing.

9

10 No one wanted to go. I saw a lady in a green coat. She was crying and holding her baby tightly. Her husband kissed them both and said goodbye. Then, she got in the lifeboat and sat down, and they rowed away.

11

12 Then, it was our turn. We were waiting in line when a man pushed in front of us. He was very frightened and was shouting. But an officer pulled him away.

13

Reader Read the story in your Reader on pages 24–30.

81

Warmer: Play "The Shark Game"

Play the game using vocabulary from the chapter so far (see Games Bank p. 19).

Functional language

1 6.2 Listen and read.

- Play Track 6.2. The children listen and read along.
- Play Track 6.2 again for them to repeat.
- Divide the class into pairs to practice the dialogue.

2 Imagine you are worried about something. Give your friend reassurance.

- Choose two children to read the example dialogue.
- The children practice in pairs using the prompts supplied and adding details. Have pairs do a dialogue for the class.

Before reading

3 Look at the story. Who do you think wrote the journal pages?

- Have the children study the pictures. Ask *Who do you think wrote the journal pages? (Amy)* Elicit ideas.
- Ask *Who dropped something? What was it?*

4 6.3 Read the story extract and answer.

- Have the children read the story and answer question 1.
- Play Track 6.3. They listen and complete their ideas for questions 2 and 3.
- Elicit answers, but do not confirm predictions: explain that they will have to read the story to find out.

Answers

1 They're getting into a lifeboat because the ship is sinking. **2** Children's own answers. **3** They're wearing clothes from the past./The women are wearing long dresses.

Lesson 3

1 Write another phrase for each part. Then choose, write, and act out.

miss dinner / fail the test / find the movie theater / ....

try again / ask someone / call my dad / ....

Are we going to .... ?

Don't worry. We can ....

2 Read the story in your Student Book. Check (✓) *journal* or *dialogue*.

Which text ... journal dialogue

1 ... is written in the past?
2 ... tells you what happens more clearly?
3 ... is more exciting?
4 ... tells you more about how people are feeling?

3 Write *true* or *false*.

1 The passengers on the deck know what to do. *false*
2 Men have to get in the lifeboat last.
3 The lady in the green coat doesn't want to be saved.
4 The man who pushes in front of Amy is scared.
5 Amy is worried about her journal.

4 What was Amy doing that evening before the *Titanic* hit the iceberg? Think and write her journal.

April 14th, 1912

48

1 Write another phrase for each part. Then choose, write, and act out.

Elicit ideas for another phrase for each part. The children choose and complete the dialogue, then act it out in pairs. Encourage the children to use what they know to adapt and extend the dialogue. Have pairs act out their dialogue for the class.

2 Read the story in your Student Book. Check (✓) *journal* or *dialogue*.

The children read the Student Book story extract again. Elicit the differences between a journal and a dialogue. The children then identify whether each sentence describes a journal or a dialogue, checking the appropriate box. Elicit answers.

Answers

journal: 1, 2, 4 *dialogue:* 3

3 Write *true* or *false*.

The children write true or false for each sentence. Elicit answers, including the correct version of the false sentences.

Answers

1 false **2** true **3** false **4** true **5** true

4 What was Amy doing that evening before the *Titanic* hit the iceberg? Think and write her journal.

Elicit suggestions on what Amy was doing before the boat hit the iceberg. The children write their own ideas, then compare with a friend. Elicit ideas.

Answers

Children's own answers.

Cooler: Remember the dialogue

Use the dialogue in Picture 11. (*Please get in the boat, Madam. This is an emergency …*) Draw a line for each word giving just the underlined words as clues.

Have the children guess each word. When the dialogue is complete, have them practice reading it in pairs.

Competency Focus

Collaborate and Communicate

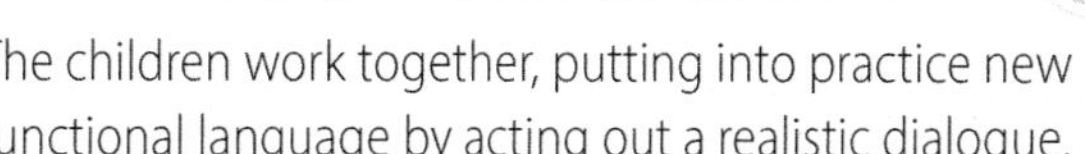

The children work together, putting into practice new functional language by acting out a realistic dialogue.

Think! Critical Thinking

By analyzing visual clues and deducing from the context, the children use prediction skills to help them engage with the story.

Digital Resources

Student eBook • Show the bubbles in the SB Activity 1 dialogue. Use *Highlighter* on *be late for the movie*. Elicit different things you could say in this context.

• Focus on the different people pictured in the story extract. Each time, elicit how they are feeling.

The Journal

1
Amy: What was that? … Aunt Edith! Auntie! Are you OK?

2
Monday, April 15th, 1912

I was sleeping in bed when a loud noise woke me up. Then a man knocked on my door. He said, "Come to the boat deck and bring your life jacket." I was frightened. While I was putting on my clothes and life jacket, I put this journal into my pocket.

3
Crew member: Everyone go to the deck now!

Amy: Aunt Edith, wake up!

4
There were a lot of people in the hallway. My aunt was wearing her nightclothes and a coat when she came out of her cabin. No one was running or shouting. Everyone was talking quietly.

5
Aunt Edith: It's OK, I'm here, Amy.

Amy: Where are we going? What's happening?

Crew member: We hit an iceberg.

Amy: Is the ship sinking? Are we going to drown?

Crew member: No. It's OK. Don't worry. The *Titanic* is unsinkable! It's the best ship ever built.

6
It was cold and dark outside. We were standing on the deck when an enormous iceberg passed us. It looked like a huge, white rock. Pieces of ice were falling off it onto the deck. Some children made snowballs from the ice and threw them into the water. It was warm and light inside the Titanic and the band was playing in the lounge. My aunt was cold so she went inside to listen to the band.

8
The passengers and crew were waiting for the captain to give orders. There were so many people, and it was very confusing.

9
Officer: Get in the lifeboats. Women and children first!

10
No one wanted to go. I saw a lady in a green coat. She was crying and holding her baby tightly. Her husband kissed them both and said goodbye. Then, she got in the lifeboat and sat down, and they rowed away.

11
Officer: Please get in the boat, Madam. This is an emergency and we're trying to save lives.

Woman: No, I can't leave my husband.

Officer: Take your baby and go. Your husband can get in the next boat.

12
Then, it was our turn. We were waiting in line when a man pushed in front of us. He was very frightened and was shouting. But an officer pulled him away.

13
Man: Let me go! I need to get in that lifeboat! I have three children. I need to go home!

Amy: Argh! My journal!

14
My heart was thumping and my hands were shaking as I climbed into the lifeboat. I looked for Aunt Edith. I didn't want to lose her. A man was helping her down to the boat.

16
As we sailed away, we watched the ship. The Titanic was sinking into the ocean. The band was still playing. It was dark. The sky was full of stars. Then, everything was silent.

17
Aunt Edith: It's alright, Amy. We're safe now. You're a survivor. The crew will rescue the others.

Amy: Look, my journal!

Lesson objective: read and understand the historical fiction *The Journal* in the Reader
Materials: Track 6.4; Reader

Warmer: True or false?

Make true/false sentences about the story extract, e.g. *A lady got into the lifeboat with her child and her husband.* (*false*) *Amy lost her journal.* (*true*)

Story Summary

Through her own journal extracts, Amy tells the exciting story of what happened to her and her Aunt Edith on the *Titanic*. The story also includes dialogue between Amy, Aunt Edith, the crew, and other passengers.

Theme: passing on memories to the future

6.4 While reading

- Have the children look at the pictures in the Reader. Ask *Who's Amy traveling with? (her aunt)*
- Play Track 6.4. The children listen and read along. Ask *Did Amy and Aunt Edith survive?* (*yes*)
- Ask questions to check comprehension, e.g. *What were the passengers doing? (talking quietly/waiting for the captain to give orders) What was it like outside? (cold and dark) Did Amy feel happy getting into the boat? (No—she was frightened.)*
- Read the story again with the class, allocating the roles of the passengers/officer/narrator, etc. Bring the story to life using sounds effects and music (see **Story Time**).

After reading: Reflect

- Ask questions to give the children the opportunity to think about the issues raised by the story, e.g. *Who was brave? Who was very scared? Who was helpful? What would you do if this happened to you?*

Optional activity: Write a captain's log

The children imagine they are the captain of the *Titanic*. They write the last few sentences in the ship's log.

Story Time

Using sound effects

Use sound effects and/or music to bring the story to life. Use musical instruments for basic sounds, e.g. cymbals for a crash/bang. For the band ask children to mime a violin, or drum on the desk with pencils. As well as keeping the children involved in the story, this caters for more kinesthetic learners.

Reading Strategy

Page Shrinking

Page Shrinking is a form of summarizing in which the children focus on the main events that take place on each page of the story. By dividing up the story, the children are given support in understanding the plot and identifying the key ideas, so that they can then go on to express them orally or in writing.

For additional explanation and activities, see the Literacy Handbook on the Teacher Resource Center.

Cooler: Who said it?

Read out a sentence from the story to elicit the speaker. Repeat with other sentences.

Digital Resources

Student eBook • For the Warmer, have children use *Highlighter* to identify in the story extract the text that shows whether each statement you make is true or false.

Reader eBook • Explain that sound effects can be used to make storytelling more dramatic (see SB Story Time). Have children use *Pen* to circle scenes or details in the story for the class to suggest a sound effect.

- For the Optional activity, have children first use *Pen* to identify details in the story to include in the captain's log.

Reading Comprehension and Critical Literacy

Lesson objectives: understand and evaluate the story; relate story theme to personal experience; write examples of story dialogue
Materials: Track 6.4; Reader

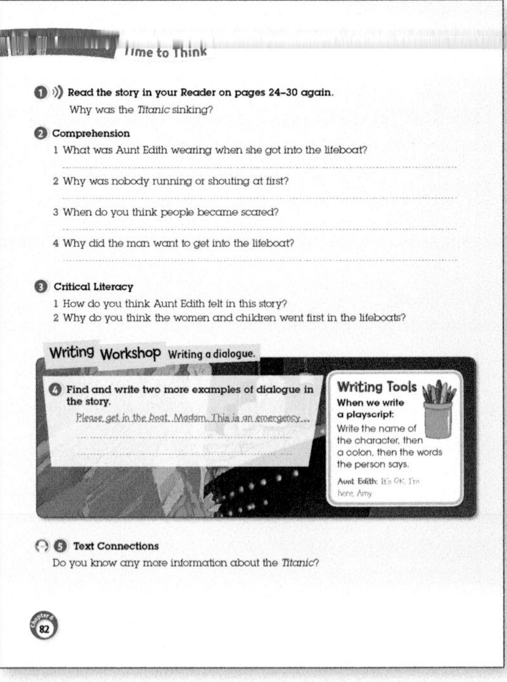
Time to Think

1 Read the story in your Reader on pages 24–30 again.
Why was the *Titanic* sinking?

2 Comprehension
1 What was Aunt Edith wearing when she got into the lifeboat?
2 Why was nobody running or shouting at first?
3 When do you think people became scared?
4 Why did the man want to get into the lifeboat?

3 Critical Literacy
1 How do you think Aunt Edith felt in this story?
2 Why do you think the women and children went first in the lifeboats?

Writing Workshop Writing a dialogue.

4 Find and write two more examples of dialogue in the story.
Please get in the boat, Madam. This is an emergency ...

Writing Tools
When we write a playscript:
Write the name of the character, then a colon, then the words the person says.
Aunt Edith: It's OK. I'm here, Amy.

5 Text Connections
Do you know any more information about the *Titanic*?

82

Note: Please ensure that your class has read the Reader story before you do this lesson.

Warmer: Matching and story recap

Choose key words from the story, e.g. *journal, iceberg, lifeboat, passengers, rescue*. Write word halves on the board randomly, e.g. *jour/nal, ice/berg*. The children match to form words, then re-tell the story using the words.

1 6.4 Read the story in your Reader.

- Have the children read the story. (Alternatively, play Track 6.4 and have them read along.) Elicit whether they were correct in their predictions in Lesson 3 Activity 4.
- Ask *Why was the* Titanic *sinking? (It was sinking because it hit an iceberg.)*

2 Comprehension

- Establish what time it was when the iceberg hit the *Titanic* (indicate clues, e.g. Aunt Edith's nightclothes). Ask the children to think about the voices in the story and when people started to panic. Have them consider how the tone in the dialogue changes.
- The children then answer the questions. Elicit answers.

Answers

1 She was wearing her nightclothes and a coat. **2** They weren't scared. **3** Children's own answers. **4** Children's own answers./He was scared./He wanted to go home.

3 Critical Literacy

- Say *Imagine you are Aunt Edith. How did you feel when you came out of the cabin? How did you feel at the end? What did you worry about?* Elicit answers with reasons.
- Ask *Why did the women and children go first? Do you agree?* Encourage the children to consider the reasoning behind the actions of the characters and to decide if they agree with the behavior. Engaging with broader issues like this helps children engage constructively with the story.

Writing Workshop

Writing a dialogue

4 Find and write two more examples of dialogue in the story.

Have a child read the example. Ask *Who said this in the story?* (*officer*) Look at the **Writing Tools** box together and explain the use of the colon. Ask them to add the speaker to the example. (Officer:) The children find and write two more examples from the story in their notebook, then compare answers in pairs.

Answers

Children's own answers.

5 Text Connections 

- Ask *Have you seen the movie* Titanic *or read another* Titanic *story?* Elicit any information the children know and write key facts on the board.

Optional activity: Stand up, sit down!

Divide the class into three groups: "people" words / "ocean-related" words / "past progressive." Read the story slowly. When they hear a word in their group, the children should stand up and sit down again very quickly.

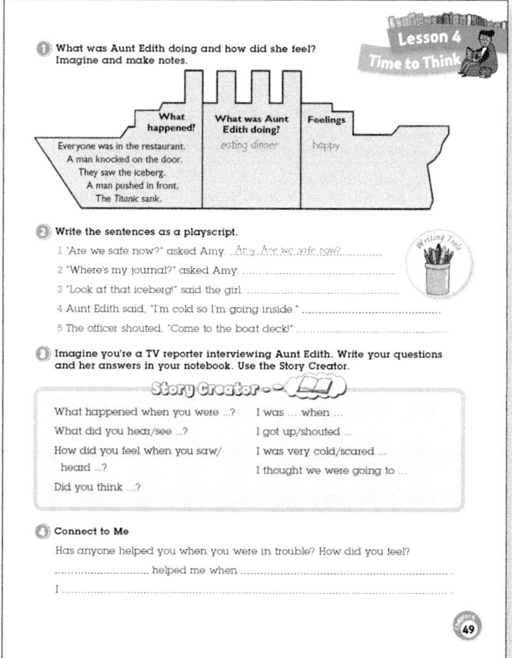

Lesson 4
Time to Think

1 What was Aunt Edith doing and how did she feel? Imagine and make notes.

What happened?	What was Aunt Edith doing?	Feelings
Everyone was in the restaurant. A man knocked on the door. They saw the iceberg. A man pushed in front. The *Titanic* sank.	eating dinner	happy

2 Write the sentences as a playscript.

Writing Tools

1 "Are we safe now?" asked Amy. Amy: Are we safe now?
2 "Where's my journal?" asked Amy. ....
3 "Look at that iceberg!" said the girl. ....
4 Aunt Edith said, "I'm cold so I'm going inside." ....
5 The officer shouted, "Come to the boat deck!" ....

3 Imagine you're a TV reporter interviewing Aunt Edith. Write your questions and her answers in your notebook. Use the Story Creator.

Story Creator

What happened when you were ...?	I was ... when ...
What did you hear/see ...?	I got up/shouted ...
How did you feel when you saw/heard ...?	I was very cold/scared ...
Did you think ...?	I thought we were going to ...

4 Connect to Me

Has anyone helped you when you were in trouble? How did you feel?

.... helped me when ....

I ....

Chapter 6 49

1 What was Aunt Edith doing and how did she feel? Imagine and make notes.

The children make notes on what Aunt Edith was doing at each stage and imagine how she felt. Elicit ideas.

Answers

Children's own answers.

2 Write the sentences as a playscript.

Elicit how text is set out for a play. (*name, colon, direct speech*) The children re-write the sentences in playscript form.

Answers

1 Amy: Are we safe now?
2 Amy: Where's my journal?
3 Girl: Look at that iceberg!
4 Aunt Edith: I'm cold so I'm going inside.
5 Officer: Come to the boat deck!

3 Imagine you're a TV reporter interviewing Aunt Edith. Write your questions and her answers in your notebook. Use the Story Creator.

Use the **Story Creator** to elicit ideas. The children write an interview in their notebook, then compare with a friend. Have children read out their interview for the class.

4 Connect to Me

Elicit examples from the children of a time when people have helped them in a difficult situation. They write their own response, then compare with a friend.

Cooler: Play "Spelling Bee"

Play the game with words from the chapter so far (see Games Bank p. 19).

Competency Focus

Me: Critical Literacy

The children use critical literacy skills to reflect on the story and relate it to their own experiences.

Digital Resources

Student eBook • Have children use *Highlighter* to identify examples of dialogue in the story for the SB Activity 4 task.

Student eBook, Digital Activity Book • TIP Use *Timer* to make activities more fun and challenging. For the Cooler, you could ask children in teams to see how many words they can spell correctly in one minute.

• TIP You can move the answer key pop-up window to show the answers by the activity.

Lesson 5

Book Club

1 Listen and read. Why didn't Angelo know about the *Titanic*?

Scarlett: Were you listening to that story?
Rufus: Yes, I was, but while I was listening, I was looking up the *Titanic* on the Internet. Listen. Another ship, called the *Carpathia*, tried to rescue them.
Yasmin: Was the *Carpathia* close to the *Titanic* while it was sinking?
Rufus: No, it didn't arrive for almost two hours, but it picked up more than 700 survivors. A lot of the passengers on the *Titanic* were leaving England.
Yasmin: Where were they going?
Rufus: They were going to live in America. They were sailing close to Newfoundland when they saw the iceberg.
Scarlett: And was the band really still playing music while the ship was sinking?
Rufus: Well, yes, some people say it was.
Angelo: Really? I didn't know that.
Yasmin: But we just read that in the story!
Angelo: Oh, sorry. While you were reading the story, I fell asleep.

2 Write *when* or *while*.

1 What was Rufus doing ....while.... he was listening to the story?
2 Where were the passengers going .... the ship sank?
3 Where was the ship sailing to .... they saw the iceberg?
4 What was the band doing .... the ship was sinking?
5 What was Yasmin doing .... Angelo fell asleep?

3 Ask and answer the questions in Activity 2.

A: *What was the band doing while the ship was sinking?*
B: *It was playing music.*

Grammar Central

Past progressive: *when / while*
...While... you were reading the story, I fell asleep.
When I fell asleep, you were .... the story.
What .... you doing while the ship was sinking?

Grammar Booster on page 89

Chapter 6 83

Grammar and Reading

Lesson objectives: ask and say what people were doing
Key grammar: past progressive—statements, questions with *when/while*
Secondary language: *almost, fell asleep, picked up, still*
Materials: Track 6.5; Grammar Worksheet 6B [TRC printout] (optional); past progressive prompts (Warmer)

Warmer: Mime time

Write some past progressive sentences, including two actions, for the children to mime, e.g. *I was walking when it started to rain.* Distribute a sentence to each pair of children. Have the children prepare, then call out pairs to the front to act out their sentence for the class to guess.

1 6.5 Listen and read. Why didn't Angelo know about the *Titanic*?

- Play Track 6.5. The children listen. Ask *Why didn't Angelo know about the* Titanic? (*He fell asleep.*)
- Write on the board *While Scarlett was reading the story, Angelo fell asleep.* Have a child circle the verbs. Elicit the tenses used.
- Play Track 6.5 again. The children raise their hand when they hear a *when* or *while* sentence.

2 Write *when* or *while*. 

- The children read the text again and complete each sentence with *when* or *while*.
- Elicit answers.

Answers

1 while **2** when **3** when **4** while **5** when

Grammar Central

Past progressive: *when / while*

Have the children complete the grammar examples. Elicit answers. Elicit how *when* and *while* are used with the past progressive/simple past. (when + *simple past;* while + *past progressive*) The children write further examples in their notebook. For extra practice, try the **Grammar Booster** section in the Student Book (pp. 89–91).

Answers p. 89

Activity 1: **1** while **2** when **3** while **4** when **5** While **6** When

Activity 2: **1** when **2** While **3** while **4** when **5** when **6** while

p. 90

Activity 1: **1** was **2** were watching **3** saw **4** were visiting **5** landed **6** made **7** stopped **8** were waiting

Activity 2: **1** while **2** when **3** while **4** when **5** while

p. 91

Activity 1: **1** were getting **2** was working **3** were packing **4** was cleaning **5** was moving **6** While **7** is/was made of **8** was looking **9** were laughing **10** was talking **11** while **12** when **13** were celebrating **14** were preparing

Activity 2: Children's own answers.

3 Ask and answer the questions in Activity 2. 

- Choose two children to read the example dialogue.
- Divide the class into pairs to ask and answer the questions in Activity 2.

Optional activity: Alibi

Say *A bank was robbed last night.* Select two "suspects." Have the class write "police" questions, e.g. *What were you doing last night?* Call in the first "suspect" to question, and then the second. The class questions their alibi, e.g. *What were you doing while (Pedro) was watching TV?*

Lesson 5

1 Circle.

I'm really interested in the *Titanic* story. No one knows how many passengers were traveling on the ship 1 **when / while** it sank. Why? Because some people didn't buy tickets. They were called "stowaways" and they got onto the ship 2 **while / when** it was preparing to leave. 3 **While / When** the crew on the ship weren't looking, they found places to hide. Some of the stowaways were probably hiding 4 **when / while** the ship hit the iceberg. It was scary for them. 5 **While / When** the accident happened, they were thinking about their new life.

2 Complete with *when* or *while*.

1 The teacher was talking ....while.......... you were looking out of the window.
2 What were they doing .... the door opened?
3 .... you were playing the piano, I left the room.
4 .... the bell rang, you were eating your lunch.
5 What were you doing .... I was looking for my bag?

3 Write about what happened at home last night. Then tell a friend.

Last night, I was watching TV when ....
While my mom/dad/brother .... , I was ....
I was ....
When I ....

Last night, I was watching TV when the dog broke a vase.

50

1 Circle.

The children complete the text by circling the option in each pair. Elicit answers.

Answers

1 when **2** while **3** While **4** when **5** When

2 Complete with *when* or *while*.

The children complete the sentences with *when* or *while*. Elicit answers.

Answers

1 while **2** when **3** While **4** When **5** while

3 Write about what happened at home last night. Then tell a friend.

Tell the children to imagine they were home last night when something exciting/dramatic happened. Elicit ideas. They complete their story individually, then tell a friend.

Answers

Children's own answers.

Cooler: Play "The Telephone Game"

Divide the class into teams, sitting in lines. Whisper a sentence with the past progressive to one child in each team (e.g. *While I was watching TV, I fell asleep.*). The message is passed down the line, with each child whispering it to the next. Have the last child say or write what they hear. Compare answers. A correct answer wins the team a point. Repeat with other sentences, asking different children to start the message at the back of the line.

Competency Focus

Learn

The children demonstrate their understanding of the new language by reading the text and completing the activity.

Digital Resources

Student eBook • Have children identify key language in SB Activity 1, using *Highlighter* to identify the past progressive and *Pen* to underline *when* and circle *while.*

Teacher Resource Center • For extra grammar practice, print out Grammar Worksheet 6B.

Vocabulary, Song, and Spelling

Lesson objectives: identify and use words related to the ocean; practice spelling irregular plurals

Key vocabulary: *captain, destroy, flag, float, holes, mast, pirate, waves*

Secondary language: *ship ahoy!, cabin boy, dived*

Materials: Track 6.6; Phonics Worksheet 6 [TRC printout] (optional)

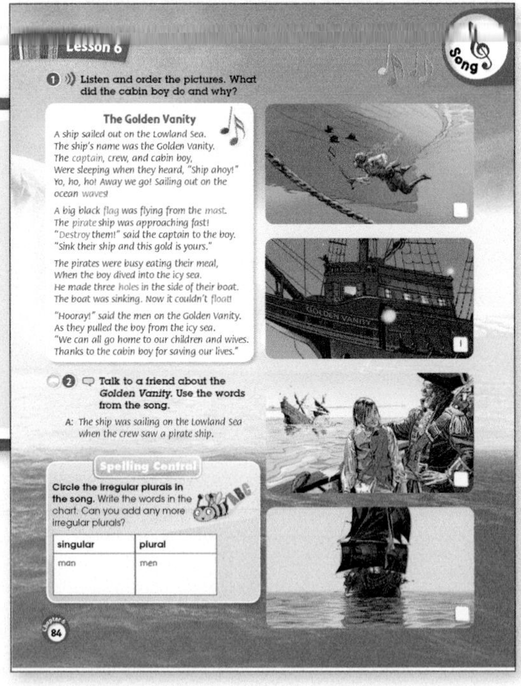

Lesson 6 Song

1 Listen and order the pictures. What did the cabin boy do and why?

The Golden Vanity

A ship sailed out on the Lowland Sea.
The ship's name was the Golden Vanity.
The captain, crew, and cabin boy,
Were sleeping when they heard, "Ship ahoy!"
Yo, ho, ho! Away we go! Sailing out on the ocean waves!

A big black flag was flying from the mast.
The pirate ship was approaching fast!
"Destroy them!" said the captain to the boy.
"Sink their ship and this gold is yours."

The pirates were busy eating their meal,
When the boy dived into the icy sea.
He made three holes in the side of their boat.
The boat was sinking. Now it couldn't float!

"Hooray!" said the men on the Golden Vanity.
As they pulled the boy from the icy sea.
"We can all go home to our children and wives.
Thanks to the cabin boy for saving our lives."

2 Talk to a friend about the *Golden Vanity*. Use the words from the song.

A: *The ship was sailing on the Lowland Sea when the crew saw a pirate ship.*

Spelling Central

Circle the irregular plurals in the song. Write the words in the chart. Can you add any more irregular plurals?

singular	plural
man	men

Chapter 6 84

Warmer: Pre-teach vocabulary

Pre-teach the vocabulary using mimes. Say the words to elicit the mimes.

1 6.6 Listen and order the pictures. What did the cabin boy do and why?

- Pre-teach *cabin boy* (*a young boy who works on a ship*). Ask *What's the name of the ship?*
- Play Track 6.6 twice. The children listen and put the pictures in the correct order. Elicit answers.
- Ask *What did the cabin boy do and why?* (*He made three holes in the pirates' boat. He wanted the boat to sink/to save the Golden Vanity.*)
- Play Track 6.6 again for the children to sing along.

Answers

Order of pictures: 3, 1, 4, 2

2 Talk to a friend about the *Golden Vanity*. Use the words from the song.

- Have the children look at the beginning of the song and the example sentence with past progressive + *when.*
- Divide them into pairs to talk about the song using more sentences with *when* or *while.*
- Elicit responses.

Spelling Central

Irregular plurals

Write *wife* on the board and ask the children to make it plural. Then ask them to find the irregular plurals for *man* and *child* in the song. Ask the class if they know any other irregular plurals. (e.g. *life/lives* in the song; *foot/feet, woman/women, mouse/mice, sheep/sheep,* etc.) Provide definitions as clues.

Answers

Circled: men, children, wives, lives

man—men, child—children, wife—wives, life—lives

Optional activity: Play "Odd One Out"

Play the game with the vocabulary from the chapter so far (see Games Bank p. 19).

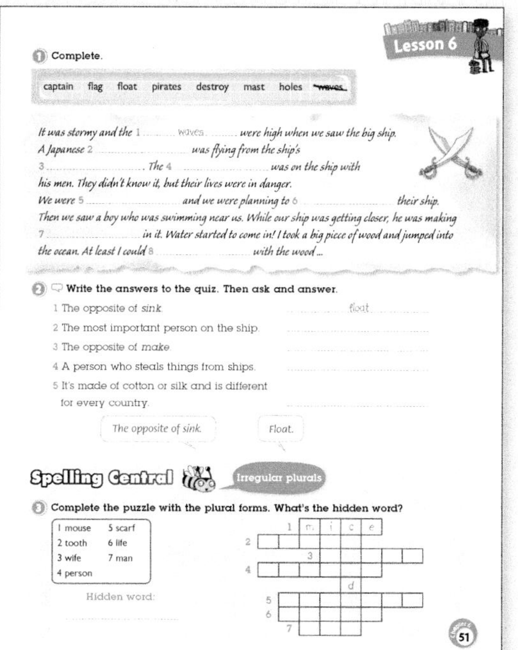

Lesson 6

1 Complete.

captain flag float pirates destroy mast holes ~~waves~~

It was stormy and the 1 ..... waves ..... were high when we saw the big ship. A Japanese 2 ..... was flying from the ship's 3 ..... . The 4 ..... was on the ship with his men. They didn't know it, but their lives were in danger. We were 5 ..... and we were planning to 6 ..... their ship. Then we saw a boy who was swimming near us. While our ship was getting closer, he was making 7 ..... in it. Water started to come in! I took a big piece of wood and jumped into the ocean. At least I could 8 ..... with the wood ...

2 Write the answers to the quiz. Then ask and answer.

1 The opposite of *sink*. ..... float .....
2 The most important person on the ship. .....
3 The opposite of *make*. .....
4 A person who steals things from ships. .....
5 It's made of cotton or silk and is different for every country. .....

The opposite of *sink*.

Float.

Spelling Central — Irregular plurals

3 Complete the puzzle with the plural forms. What's the hidden word?

1 mouse
2 tooth
3 wife
4 person
5 scarf
6 life
7 man

Hidden word: .....

1 m i c e
d

51

Cooler: Play "The Spelling Game"

Divide the class into two teams. Draw a line down the center of the board. Choose a child from each team to stand at the board. Call out a word and have the children write the plural form of the word. The first correct answer wins a point. Repeat with other words/children.

Competency Focus

Collaborate and communicate

The children work together and use their interpersonal skills to share their ideas on the topic, incorporating the new vocabulary.

1 Complete.

The children read and complete the text, using the words supplied. Elicit answers.

Answers

1 waves **2** flag **3** mast **4** captain **5** pirates **6** destroy **7** holes **8** float

2 Write the answers to the quiz. Then ask and answer.

The children answer the quiz questions individually. They then ask and answer in pairs.

Answers

1 float **2** captain **3** destroy **4** pirate **5** flag

3 Complete the puzzle with the plural forms. What's the hidden word?

To practice the **Spelling Central** feature, the children complete the puzzle using the plural forms of the prompts. Then they write the hidden word (on the blue squares). Elicit answers and spellings.

Answers

1 mice **2** teeth **3** wives **4** people **5** scarves **6** lives **7** men
Hidden word: children

Digital Resources

Student eBook • Play Music Video 6.1 and encourage the children to sing along, using the graphic lyrics on screen. Pause the video for the children to continue singing. Monitor to check the children are participating and identify any who are struggling.

Teacher Resource Center • For phonics practice, print out Phonics Worksheet 6.

Student eBook • Remind the children they can access Music Video 6.1 at home to practice the song.

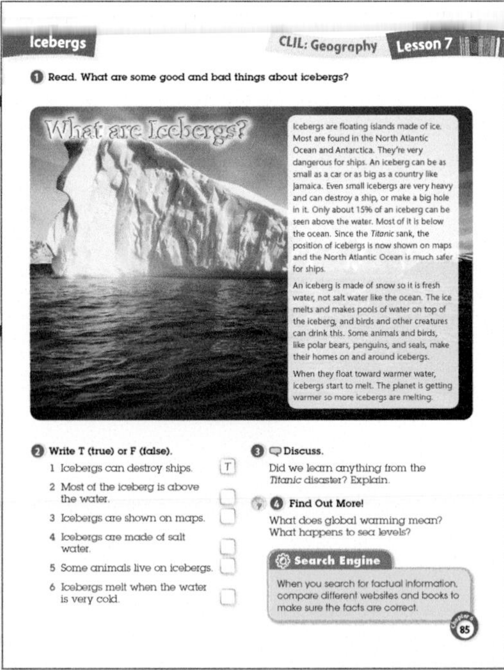
Icebergs CLIL: Geography Lesson 7

1 Read. What are some good and bad things about icebergs?

What are Icebergs?

Icebergs are floating islands made of ice. Most are found in the North Atlantic Ocean and Antarctica. They're very dangerous for ships. An iceberg can be as small as a car or as big as a country like Jamaica. Even small icebergs are very heavy and can destroy a ship, or make a big hole in it. Only about 15% of an iceberg can be seen above the water. Most of it is below the ocean. Since the *Titanic* sank, the position of icebergs is now shown on maps and the North Atlantic Ocean is much safer for ships.

An iceberg is made of snow so it is fresh water, not salt water like the ocean. The ice melts and makes pools of water on top of the iceberg, and birds and other creatures can drink this. Some animals and birds, like polar bears, penguins, and seals, make their homes on and around icebergs.

When they float toward warmer water, icebergs start to melt. The planet is getting warmer so more icebergs are melting.

2 Write T (true) or F (false).

1 Icebergs can destroy ships. T
2 Most of the iceberg is above the water.
3 Icebergs are shown on maps.
4 Icebergs are made of salt water.
5 Some animals live on icebergs.
6 Icebergs melt when the water is very cold.

3 Discuss.

Did we learn anything from the *Titanic* disaster? Explain.

4 Find Out More!

What does global warming mean? What happens to sea levels?

Search Engine

When you search for factual information, compare different websites and books to make sure the facts are correct.

Chapter 6 85

CLIL: Geography—Icebergs

Lesson objective: find out about icebergs and global warming
Materials: CLIL Graphic Organizer 6 [TRC printout] (optional); ice cubes, water, glass, marker pens; atlas/online map of Antarctica (optional)

Warmer: Arctic and Antarctic animals

Brainstorm on the board animals which live in the Arctic and Antarctic, e.g. *penguins, polar bears, seals,* etc. Ask the children to suggest where these animals get fresh water to drink. Explain that we cannot drink salt water.

1 Read. What is a good thing and what is a bad thing about icebergs?

- Have the children look at the picture of the iceberg and say what lives on/close to it.
- Have the children skim read the text to find a good and a bad thing about icebergs. (*good—animals and birds make their homes in and around icebergs; bad—icebergs can destroy a ship or make a big hole in it*)
- Ask *What are icebergs made of?* (*snow*) *How much of an iceberg can be seen above the water?* (*15%*)

2 Write T (true) or F (false).

- Elicit why the example answer is true. (*Icebergs are very heavy.*)
- The children read the text again and decide true or false for the other sentences. Elicit answers, including the correct version of the false sentences.

Answers

1 T **2** F **3** T **4** F **5** T **6** F

3 Discuss. 

- Have the children work in pairs to discuss whether we learned anything from the *Titanic* disaster. Guide them by referring them to the end of the first paragraph in the text.
- Have pairs report their ideas to the class.

4 Find Out More! 

- The children research global warming and its effect on sea levels. The **Search Engine** feature gives support on where to look. The children will need to complete this research before doing the follow-up activity in the Activity Book. (It could be set as homework.)

Optional activity: Where are the icebergs?

Use an atlas or online map to look at Antarctica and where the ice is. Have the children imagine what life would be like if global warming caused sea levels to rise.

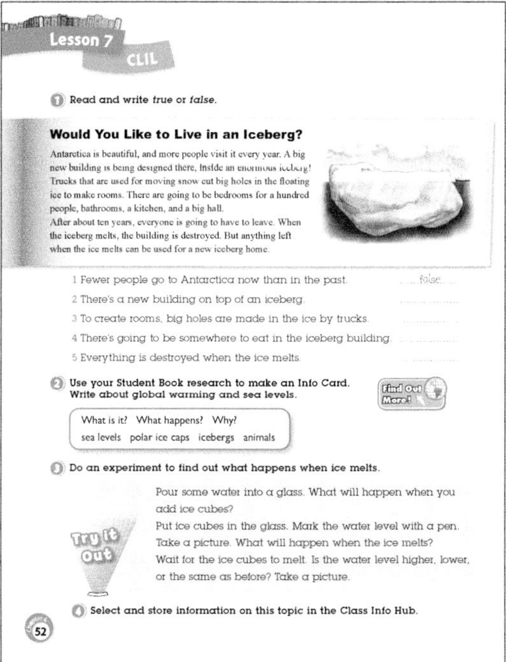
Lesson 7 CLIL

1 Read and write *true* or *false*.

Would You Like to Live in an Iceberg?

Antarctica is beautiful, and more people visit it every year. A big new building is being designed there, Inside an enormous iceberg! Trucks that are used for moving snow cut big holes in the floating ice to make rooms. There are going to be bedrooms for a hundred people, bathrooms, a kitchen, and a big hall.
After about ten years, everyone is going to have to leave. When the iceberg melts, the building is destroyed. But anything left when the ice melts can be used for a new iceberg home.

1 Fewer people go to Antarctica now than in the past. ....false....
2 There's a new building on top of an iceberg. ....
3 To create rooms, big holes are made in the ice by trucks. ....
4 There's going to be somewhere to eat in the iceberg building. ....
5 Everything is destroyed when the ice melts. ....

2 Use your Student Book research to make an Info Card. Write about global warming and sea levels.

Find Out More!

What is it? What happens? Why?
sea levels polar ice caps icebergs animals

3 Do an experiment to find out what happens when ice melts.

Try it Out

Pour some water into a glass. What will happen when you add ice cubes?
Put ice cubes in the glass. Mark the water level with a pen. Take a picture. What will happen when the ice melts?
Wait for the ice cubes to melt. Is the water level higher, lower, or the same as before? Take a picture.

4 Select and store information on this topic in the Class Info Hub.

52

1 Read and write *true* or *false*.

The children read the text and identify whether the statements are true or false. Elicit answers, including the correct version of the false sentences.

Answers

1 false **2** false **3** true **4** true **5** false

2 Use your Student Book research to make an Info Card. Write about global warming and sea levels.

Divide the class into groups. Have the children pool the information learned from their research in the Student Book and the Activity Book. They write about and illustrate their ideas individually. Have the groups present their Info Cards to the class.

3 Do an experiment to find out what happens when ice melts.

In their groups, the children follow the **Try It Out** instructions to carry out the experiment and note the results. Elicit findings. (*Add ice cubes: water level goes up. Ice cubes melt: water level remains the same.*)

4 Select and store information on this topic in the Class Info Hub.

Have the children vote for the most interesting Info Cards. Archive these in your Class Hub (see p. 41) in a folder called **Chapter 6 Global Warming and Sea Levels**.

Cooler: Brainstorm vocabulary

Draw an oval on the board and write *Water* and *Ice* inside. Call out children to add vocabulary items to the mind map to review vocabulary from the lesson/chapter.

Competency Focus

Act

The children carry out research to find out more about the topic of global warming. They consider a global problem and develop greater understanding of the importance of protecting our environment.

Digital Resources

Student eBook, Digital Activity Book, Reader eBook

- Remember—do not be afraid to turn off the screen! Children benefit from variety of pace and focus—sometimes you will want to work just with books or without prompts. Work the materials into your teaching in the way that suits you.

Teacher Resource Center • Print out CLIL Graphic Organizer 6 for the children to collate their Find Out More! research.

CLIL eBook • The children can use the CLIL eBook to expand their knowledge of the lesson topic.

Writing Project

Lesson objectives: review language from Chapter 6; write a diary entry and present it to the class

Materials: Writing Template 6 [TRC printout] (optional)

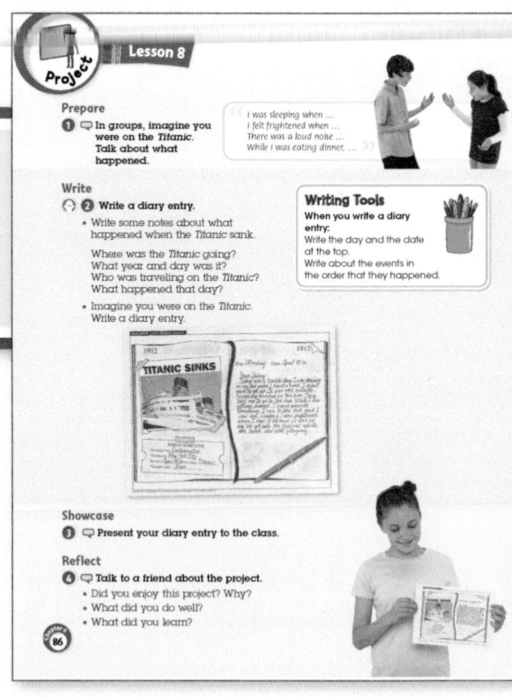
Lesson 8
Project

Prepare

1 In groups, imagine you were on the *Titanic*. Talk about what happened.

"I was sleeping when ...
I felt frightened when ...
There was a loud noise ...
While I was eating dinner, ..."

Write

2 Write a diary entry.

- Write some notes about what happened when the *Titanic* sank.

  Where was the *Titanic* going?
  What year and day was it?
  Who was traveling on the *Titanic*?
  What happened that day?

- Imagine you were on the *Titanic*. Write a diary entry.

Writing Tools
When you write a diary entry:
Write the day and the date at the top.
Write about the events in the order that they happened.

Showcase

3 Present your diary entry to the class.

Reflect

4 Talk to a friend about the project.

- Did you enjoy this project? Why?
- What did you do well?
- What did you learn?

86

Warmer: Play "The A–Z Game"

Play the game using vocabulary related to the ocean (see Games Bank p. 19).

Prepare

1 In groups, imagine you were on the *Titanic*. Talk about what happened.

- The children imagine they were on the *Titanic* and talk about it in groups, using the prompts supplied. Encourage them to be imaginative. Groups report back to the class.

Write

2 Write a diary entry.

- Have the children read the diary entry as a model for their own writing.
- Read the **Writing Tools** box together. Elicit examples in the model of diary features.
- The children prepare an outline, using the instructions and the model diary entry. They write their diary entry, then compare with a friend. Give support as necessary.

Showcase

3 Present your diary entry to the class. 

- Choose children to read their diary entries to the class. Ask the rest of the class to listen for the main events.

Reflect

4 Vote for the best diary entry and talk to the class.

- Have children comment on which diary entry they liked best and why. Have a class vote for the most popular.

Optional activity: Make a classroom display

After writing their diary entries, have children work in pairs or groups and read each other's work. They could comment orally and/or correct any errors they find. Have the children write up and illustrate their corrected versions. Create a classroom display with their work.

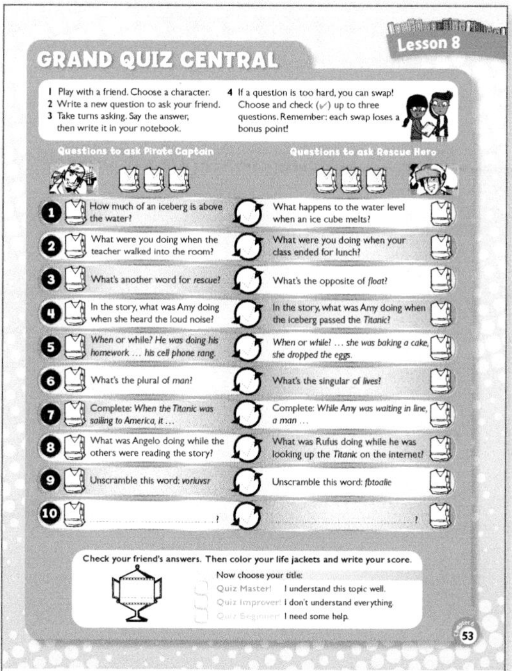

Lesson 8

GRAND QUIZ CENTRAL

1 Play with a friend. Choose a character.
2 Write a new question to ask your friend.
3 Take turns asking. Say the answer, then write it in your notebook.
4 If a question is too hard, you can swap! Choose and check (✓) up to three questions. Remember: each swap loses a bonus point!

	Questions to ask Pirate Captain	Questions to ask Rescue Hero
1	How much of an iceberg is above the water?	What happens to the water level when an ice cube melts?
2	What were you doing when the teacher walked into the room?	What were you doing when your class ended for lunch?
3	What's another word for *rescue*?	What's the opposite of *float*?
4	In the story, what was Amy doing when she heard the loud noise?	In the story, what was Amy doing when the iceberg passed the *Titanic*?
5	*When* or *while*? *He was doing his homework … his cell phone rang.*	*When* or *while*? *… she was baking a cake, she dropped the eggs.*
6	What's the plural of *man*?	What's the singular of *lives*?
7	Complete: *When the Titanic was sailing to America, it …*	Complete: *While Amy was waiting in line, a man …*
8	What was Angelo doing while the others were reading the story?	What was Rufus doing while he was looking up the *Titanic* on the internet?
9	Unscramble this word: *voriuvsr*	Unscramble this word: *fbtoalie*
10	………………………?	………………………?

Check your friend's answers. Then color your life jackets and write your score.

Now choose your title:
Quiz Master! I understand this topic well.
Quiz Improver! I don't understand everything.
Quiz Beginner! I need some help.

53

Grand Quiz Central

See p. 43 for details of how to take the quiz.

Answers

1 15% / It stays the same (as when the ice cube was solid). **2** I was … ing … **3** save / sink **4** She was sleeping in her cabin. / She was standing on the deck. **5** when / while **6** men / life **7** hit an iceberg / pushed in front (of her) **8** He was sleeping. / He was listening to the story. **9** survivor / lifeboat **10** Children's own answers.

Cooler: Play "Bingo"

Play the game using vocabulary from the chapter (see Games Bank p. 19).

Competency Focus

Me

The children imagine a trip on the *Titanic* and write their own diary entry, exploring their imagination and creativity.

Digital Resources

Student eBook • Have children use *Highlighter* to identify examples in the model text of the key features of the writing task: where, when, who, what happened.

Teacher Resource Center • Print out Writing Template 6 for the SB writing activity.

Language Review

Lesson objective: review language from Chapter 6

Materials: Tracks 6.7, AB 6.1, AB 6.2 and AB 6.3

Review

1 Listen and complete with the correct form of the verbs.

1 They (sail) ......were sailing...... around the world when the accident (happen) ......happened......

2 While they (sleep) .... the whales (hit) .... the boat.

3 Their sailing boat (sink) .... while they (watch) .... it.

4 They (have to) .... catch fish when they had no more food.

5 While they (fish) .... one day, their fishing pole (break) ....

6 They (see) .... sharks while they (float) .... across the ocean.

7 At last, the crew of a boat (see) .... them and (rescue) .... them.

2 Write sentences in your notebook about Bill and Simone. Imagine their recount of the story.

We were sailing ...
I was sleeping when ...
We jumped ...
After 20 days, we had to ...

3 Think about Chapter 6. Color the bone.

Which activity was easy?
Which activity was difficult?
Figure it out with a friend.
Write a tip to help you remember.

I'm not sure.
OK.
WhizzKid!

Treasure Hunt!

Look back at pages 4 and 5.
Where did the *Titanic* sink?
Find something from that ocean. What is it?

87

Warmer: Mini-story

Write random words from the chapter on the board, e.g. *lifeboat, whale, sank,* etc. Children work in pairs to tell a mini-story using all the words.

1 6.7 Listen and complete with the correct form of the verbs.

- Play Track 6.7. Children say how the people survived.
- Play Track 6.7. Children complete the sentences.

Audioscript

A man and woman floated at sea for 66 days in a lifeboat. Bill and Simone Butler were sailing around the world when an accident happened. While they were sleeping, some whales hit their boat and made a big hole. The water started to come in. Their boat was sinking so they jumped into a small lifeboat. While they were watching their sail boat, it sank to the bottom of the ocean. They had some food and water for the first 20 days in their small lifeboat. Then, they had to catch fish and make salt water into drinking water.

One day they were fishing when the fishing pole broke. So then, they had to catch fish with their hands. It wasn't easy. While they were floating across the ocean, there were storms and they saw sharks, but they were lucky. After 66 days, the crew of a boat saw them and rescued them.

Answers

1 were sailing, happened **2** were sleeping, hit **3** sank, were watching **4** had to **5** were fishing, broke **6** saw, were floating **7** saw, rescued

2 Write sentences in your notebook about Bill and Simone. Imagine their account of the story.

- The children write sentences.

Answers

Children's own answers.

3 Think about Chapter 6. Color the bone. 

- Have the children look back at Chapter 6 and color the bone to evaluate their progress (self-evaluation). Discuss ideas for more effective listening. The children choose and write a tip in their Student Book.

Treasure Hunt!

Ask *Where did the* Titanic *sink?* (*North Atlantic Ocean*) Have the children look at pp. 4–5 to find something from that ocean. (*a whale*)

Cooler: Play "Back to the Board"

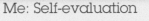

Play the game using vocabulary from the chapter (see Games Bank p. 19).

Competency Focus

Me: Self-evaluation

The children reflect on the chapter and express their opinions about their own progress.

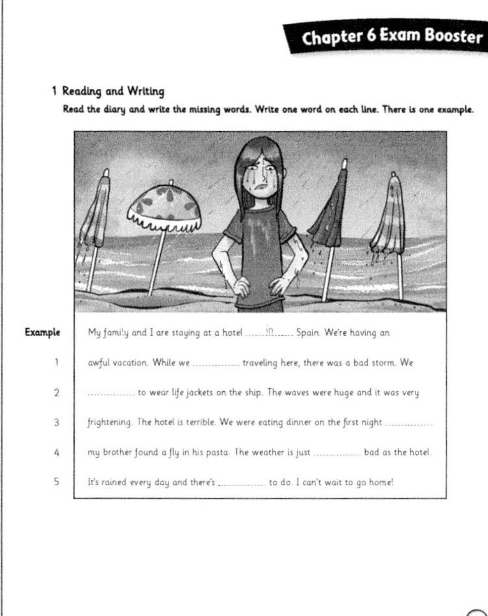

Chapter 6 Exam Booster

1 Reading and Writing

Read the diary and write the missing words. Write one word on each line. There is one example.

Example My family and I are staying at a hotel ......in...... Spain. We're having an
1 awful vacation. While we .... traveling here, there was a bad storm. We
2 .... to wear life jackets on the ship. The waves were huge and it was very
3 frightening. The hotel is terrible. We were eating dinner on the first night ....
4 my brother found a fly in his pasta. The weather is just .... bad as the hotel.
5 It's rained every day and there's .... to do. I can't wait to go home!

93

2 Listening

Listen and write. There is one example.

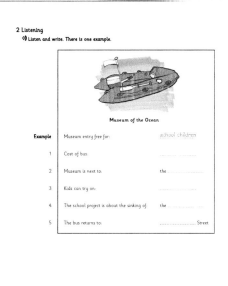

Museum of the Ocean

Example	Museum entry free for:	school children
1	Cost of bus:	....
2	Museum is next to:	the ....
3	Kids can try on:	....
4	The school project is about the sinking of:	the ....
5	The bus returns to:	.... Street

94

3 Speaking

1 Look at the pictures and listen to the beginning of the story. Then complete.

1 The family was relaxing at home ....

2 The kids .... while the parents were reading the newspaper.

2 Work with a partner. Look at the pictures and tell a story.

Where were they? What was happening outside? Who helped them?
What were they doing? How did they feel? Where did they go?

The Flood

3 Now listen and compare. Was your story the same?

Exam Tip
Find connections between the pictures to create a story.

95

3.1))) AB 6.2 Speaking. Look at the pictures and listen to the beginning of the story. Then complete.

Play AB Track 6.2. Children complete the sentences.

Answers (Audioscript on p. 223)

1 when it started to rain **2** were playing video games

3.2 Speaking. Work with a partner. Look at the pictures and tell a story.

The children write down their version of the story.

3.3))) AB 6.3 Speaking. Now listen and compare. Was your story the same?

Play AB Track 6.3 twice. The children listen to the order of events on the story and compare to their own.

(Audioscript on p. 223)

1 Reading and Writing. Read the diary and write the missing words. Write one word on each line. There is one example.

The children read and complete the text. Check answers.

Answers

1 were **2** had **3** when **4** as **5** nothing

2))) AB 6.1 Listening. Listen and write. There is one example.

AB Track 6.1 twice. Children listen and write the answers.

Answers (Audioscript on p. 223)

1 $2 **2** train station **3** life jackets **4** *Morning Star* **5** Morley street

Digital Resources

Teacher Resource Center • Print out Test Chapter 6 to use at the end of this lesson. The Test Generator also allows you to create customized tests.

Student's App • Encourage the children to play the games on their smartphone/tablet. Ask them to record their scores to compare in the next lesson. (*The Inks* Apps are free and available on the App Store and Google Play.)

Let's Cook!
Overview

The children will:

- use critical thinking skills to identify recipe ingredients and cooking verbs.
- give instructions using adverbs.
- read and understand a story about food.
- talk about quantity of foods using *too much / too many / enough.*
- talk about food and its different tastes.
- find out about food and the senses.
- write their own recipe.

Key Vocabulary

Ingredients and cooking verbs:
boil, chop, fry, oil, pan, pepper, pour, slice
Sense verbs and adjectives: bitter, crunchy, juicy, salty, smells, smelly, soft, sour, sweet, tastes, tasty

Key Grammar

Adverbs

- That's very noisy. Can you do that quietly, please?
- I did really badly on the exam. I couldn't answer anything.

Quantifiers: *too much / too many / enough*

- I eat too many cookies and I drink too much cola.
- I don't drink enough water and I don't eat enough fruit.

Reading Skills

Story: *The Best Food in the World*
Genre: modern family story

Literacy Development

- use reading skills to understand and predict content
- relate story theme to personal experience
- use adverbs to describe actions

Functional Language

- Look! I made this amazing …!
- Anyone can make a …. It's easy.

Spelling

Adjectives ending in *–y*

CLIL: Science—Food science

The children find out about food and the senses.

Competency Focus

The children will:

use critical thinking skills to deduce the meaning of new vocabulary. (Lesson 1) predict the content of a story. (Lesson 3)	activate new vocabulary and apply new grammar knowledge. (Lesson 2) apply new grammar rules in a familiar context. (Lesson 5)	work in pairs to act out a dialogue. (Lesson 3) work in pairs to talk about their own food tastes. (Lesson 6)	relate the story theme to their personal experience. (Lesson 4) develop their understanding of their own senses. (Lesson 7)	invent and write their own recipe. (Lesson 8) evaluate their own progress in the chapter. (Review)

Digital Overview

Teacher Presentation

Student eBook and Digital Activity Book

- Oral Storytelling Video 7.1: *The King's Party*
- Interactive versions of AB activities
- Integrated audio and answer key for all activities

Teacher resources for planning, lesson delivery, and homework

Teacher Resource Center

- Class Planner Chapter 7
- Worksheets to print out (including notes and answers):
  - Grammar Worksheet 7A: Adverbs
  - Grammar Worksheet 7B: Quantifiers: *too much/ too many/enough*
  - Oral Storytelling Video Worksheet 7: *The King's Party*
  - Phonics Worksheet 7
  - CLIL Graphic Organizer 7
  - Writing Template 7
  - Festival Worksheet: Earth Day
  - Test Chapter 7
- Test Generator
- Literacy Handbook

Watch the Oral Storytelling Video

Children's resources for consolidation and practice at home

Student eBook and Reader eBook

- Oral Storytelling Video 7.1: *The King's Party*

The Inks Student's App

Vocabulary games: Ingredients/cooking verbs and Sense verbs/adjectives

Chapter 7 Let's Cook!

Lesson 1

Vocabulary

Lesson objectives: identify and use vocabulary for recipe ingredients and cooking verbs
Key vocabulary: *boil, chop, fry, oil, pan, pepper, pour, slice*
Materials: Track 7.1

7 Let's Cook! Lesson 1

1 Listen and write the quantities.

Vegetable Soup Recipe

Ingredients
...2... onions
.... tomatoes
.... potato
.... cabbage
.... carrots
.... spoon of oil
a little salt and pepper

2 Listen again and write the missing words.

oil chop fry boil pan pepper pour ~~slice~~

1 ...Slice... the cabbage.
2 .... the other vegetables.
3 .... the onions in hot ....
4 Put the other vegetables in the ....
5 .... some water and .... it over the vegetables.
6 Add a little salt and ....

92

Warmer: Color food blitz!

Call out colors for children to write in their notebook, e.g. *red, yellow, orange, white, green.* Give the children three minutes to list fruits or vegetables by name in the correct category, e.g. *yellow: banana, pepper, lemon; red: apple, pepper, tomato, strawberry; white: potato, onion,* etc. Elicit answers for each category.

1 7.1 Listen and write the quantities. 

- Elicit the ingredients pictured.
- Play Track 7.1. The children listen and complete the vegetable quantities. Elicit answers. Whenever you elicit answers, remember to check with the class to see if they agree.
- Play Track 7.1 again and have the children copy your mimes for *slice, chop,* etc.

Audioscript

Boy: *What do you want for dinner?*
Girl: *I don't know. Look, here's a recipe. It tells you how to make vegetable soup.*
Boy: *OK, let's make that. What are the ingredients?*
Girl: *We need two onions and three tomatoes.*
Boy: *Yes, we've got those.*
Girl: *Do we have one potato and half a cabbage?*
Boy: *Yes, we do. And we've got three carrots.*
Girl: *We also need one spoon of oil and a little salt and pepper.*
Boy: *Great! It's really easy vegetable soup!*
Girl: *Um, first slice the cabbage. Then chop the onions, tomatoes, potato, and carrots. Put one spoon of oil into the pan. Fry the onions in hot oil until they start to turn brown. Put the other vegetables in the pan and fry them for five minutes. Boil some water and pour it over the vegetables in the pan, then cook it for 30 minutes. Try some of the soup, then add a little salt and pepper. You can put some cheese on top if you want, too. That's it! It's ready to eat.*
Boy: *Mm! Hot vegetable soup. It's delicious! Let's eat it.*

Answers

2 onions, 3 tomatoes, 1 potato, ½ (half) cabbage, 3 carrots, 1 spoon of oil

2 7.1 Listen again and write the missing words.

- Have the children look at the first clue and the verbs supplied. Then play Track 7.1. The children listen and complete the rest of the sentences using the words supplied. They compare with a friend. Elicit answers.
- Check children understand the different between *slice* and *chop.*

Answers

1 Slice **2** Chop **3** Fry, oil **4** pan **5** Boil, pour **6** pepper

Optional activity: What do you have for dinner?

Ask *Do you have soup for dinner?* Elicit answers. Then ask *What do you have for breakfast/lunch/dinner?* and elicit a few responses. Have the children mingle and find someone who eats the same thing as them for two of the meals.

Chapter 7 Let's Cook!
Lesson 1

1 Look and complete.

slice fry oil pan pour chop pepper ~~boil~~

Kids can Cook

1 ......Boil...... the water!
2 .... the lemon!
3 .... the milk!
4 .... the onions in the 5 ....!
6 .... the potatoes!
7 Wash the ....!
8 Grind the ....!

2 Write *true* or *false*.

1 You slice onions with a spoon. ......false......
2 You boil water and then you cook the pasta. ....
3 A pan is usually made of metal. ....
4 You can't chop peppers into small pieces. ....
5 You usually fry food in oil. ....

3 Tell a friend what you do in the kitchen.

I wash the pans, but I don't like it!

I slice the tomatoes for a salad.

4 Choose a way to categorize the new words in your notebook.

Chapter 7 54

Cooler: Play "Simon Says"

Play "Simon Says" with the new vocabulary, e.g. (*Simon says*) *chop the onions / put the water in the pan / fry the onions.*, etc. (see Games Bank p. 19).

1 Look and complete.

The children complete the instruction labels using the words supplied. Elicit answers.

Answers

1 Boil **2** Slice **3** Pour **4** Fry **5** oil **6** chop **7** pan **8** pepper

2 Write *true* or *false.*

Elicit why sentence 1 is false. (*You slice onions with a knife.*) The children decide if the other sentences are true or false. Elicit answers, including the correct version of false sentences.

Answers

1 false **2** true **3** true **4** false **5** true

3 Tell a friend what you do in the kitchen. 

The children tell their friend what they do (or don't do!) in the kitchen in pairs.

4 Choose a way to categorize the new words in your notebook.

Have the children brainstorm appropriate categories in pairs. Prompt as necessary, e.g. *verbs/food/utensils, I do/use at home/I don't do/use at home.* The children individually choose the best categories for them and list the words in their notebook.

Answers

Children's own answers.

Competency Focus

Think! Critical Thinking

The children use critical thinking skills to understand the new vocabulary and complete the activity by using visual clues and processing the written and spoken forms.

Digital Resources

Student eBook, Digital Activity Book • TIP Give children the opportunity to be your assistant! Choose a child to be responsible for choosing the relevant buttons (e.g. to go to the next activity or answer key).

Lesson 2

1 Read. Write a name for the recipe.

.... recipe

1 First, chop the chicken into pieces.
2 Then, pour some oil into a pan. When it's hot, add the chicken carefully.
3 Fry the chicken slowly until it is brown.
4 Meanwhile, wash the lettuce well. Slice the tomatoes and cucumber thinly and make a salad.
5 Put the chicken on top of the salad.
6 Mix some oil and lemon juice quickly. Add a little salt and pepper.
7 Pour it over the salad and eat immediately.

2 Find the adverbs in the text. Write the adverbs and adjectives in the chart.

Adverb	Adjective
carefully	careful

Grammar Central

Adverbs

That's very noisy. Can you do that ...more quietly... please?
I did really .... on the exam. I couldn't answer anything.

Grammar Booster on page 102

3 Choose a verb and an adverb. Give instructions to a friend.

slice pour fry chop

carefully quickly loudly angrily

A: Slice the bread carefully ...

93

Grammar

Lesson objective: give instructions on how to do something
Key grammar: adverbs
Secondary language: *mix, add*
Materials: Grammar Worksheet 7A [TRC printout] (optional); verb and adverb cards (Cooler)

Warmer: What's your favorite meal?

Ask *What's your favorite meal?* Elicit ideas. Write six on the board. Have the class vote on the most popular meal.

1 Read. Write a name for the recipe.

- Ask the children to look at the picture of the recipe. Ask *What are the ingredients?* (*chicken, oil, lettuce, tomatoes, cucumber, lemon juice, salt and pepper*)
- They read the recipe instructions and decide on a title. Elicit suggestions.

Answers

Children's own answers/Chicken salad.

Grammar Central

Adverbs

Elicit when adverbs are used (*with verbs*) and how they are formed (*generally, adjective* + ly). Have the children complete the grammar examples. Elicit answers. Elicit further sentences for practice. For extra practice, try the **Grammar Booster** section in the Student Book (p. 102).

Answers p. 102

Activity 1: **1** quickly **2** thinly **3** loudly **4** well

Activity 2: **1** carefully **2** well **3** gently **4** patiently **5** immediately **6** thinly

2 Find the adverbs in the text. Write the adverbs and adjectives in the chart.

- Ask the children to look at the chart and elicit the difference between an adjective and an adverb. (*Adjectives describe nouns; adverbs describe verbs.*) Ask them to underline more examples in the text, and complete the chart.
- Elicit answers.

Answers

adverb—adjective: carefully—careful, slowly—slow, well—good, thinly—thin, quickly—quick, immediately—immediate

3 Choose a verb and an adverb. Give instructions to a friend.

- Choose a child to read the example instruction.
- Divide the class into pairs to practice giving instructions, using the prompts supplied. Have pairs perform for the class.

Optional activity: TV cooks

Divide the class into pairs to prepare a simple recipe for a TV cooking show. Elicit ideas, e.g. *a pizza, a cake*. Have them present their recipe "on TV," i.e. for the class. One child mimes the actions and the other reads the recipe, e.g. *Chop the tomatoes carefully.*

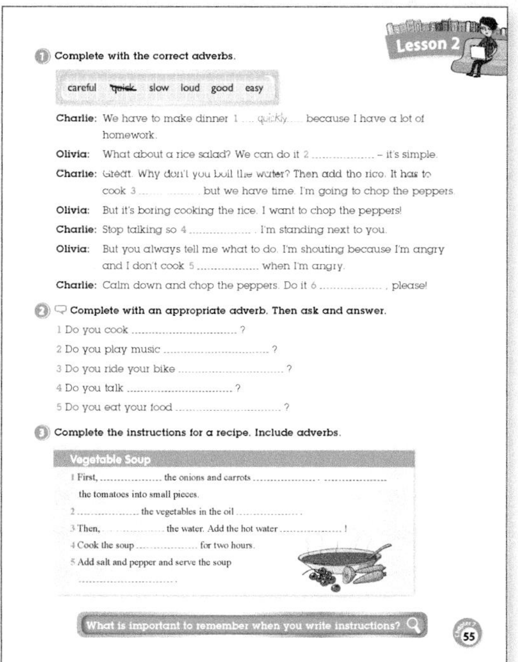

Lesson 2

1 Complete with the correct adverbs.

careful ~~quick~~ slow loud good easy

Charlie: We have to make dinner 1 ...quickly... because I have a lot of homework.
Olivia: What about a rice salad? We can do it 2 .... – it's simple.
Charlie: Great. Why don't you boil the water? Then add the rice. It has to cook 3 .... but we have time. I'm going to chop the peppers.
Olivia: But it's boring cooking the rice. I want to chop the peppers!
Charlie: Stop talking so 4 .... I'm standing next to you.
Olivia: But you always tell me what to do. I'm shouting because I'm angry and I don't cook 5 .... when I'm angry.
Charlie: Calm down and chop the peppers. Do it 6 .... , please!

2 Complete with an appropriate adverb. Then ask and answer.

1 Do you cook .... ?
2 Do you play music .... ?
3 Do you ride your bike .... ?
4 Do you talk .... ?
5 Do you eat your food .... ?

3 Complete the instructions for a recipe. Include adverbs.

Vegetable Soup

1 First, ... the onions and carrots .... the tomatoes into small pieces.
2 .... the vegetables in the oil ....
3 Then, ... the water. Add the hot water .... !
4 Cook the soup .... for two hours.
5 Add salt and pepper and serve the soup ....

What is important to remember when you write instructions?

55

1 Complete with the correct adverbs.

The children complete the sentences, making adverbs from the adjectives supplied. Elicit answers.

Answers

1 quickly **2** easily **3** slowly **4** loudly **5** well **6** carefully

2 Complete with an appropriate adverb. Then ask and answer. 

Elicit ideas for sentence 1. Make sure the children know there can be more than one appropriate answer. The children complete the sentences individually. They then ask and answer their questions in pairs.

3 Complete the instructions for a recipe. Include adverbs.

The children read and complete the instructions, then compare their work in pairs. Elicit answers. Ask *What is important to remember when you write instructions?* (*instructions in correct order and simple/easy to follow, timings and quantities included and accurate*)

Answers

Including suggestions for the adverbs: **1** First, slice the onions and carrots thinly. Chop the tomatoes into small pieces. **2** Fry the vegetables in the oil quickly. **3** Then, boil the water. Add the hot water carefully! **4** Cook the soup slowly/well for two hours. **5** Add salt and pepper and serve the soup quickly/immediately.

Cooler: Play "Verb to Adverb" 

Prepare some small cards for each group, using one color for verbs (*run, fry, eat, sing, dance, chop, swim, drink, pour, walk, climb, shout*) and another for adverbs (*quickly, carefully, slowly, sadly, happily, badly, quietly, loudly, angrily, strongly*). Divide the class into groups. Each group puts their cards face down. The children take turns choosing a verb card and an adverb card and reading them for the group to act out.

Competency Focus 

Learn

By reading the recipe and identifying the adverbs, the children demonstrate their understanding of new grammatical structures.

Digital Resources

Student eBook, Digital Activity Book • TIP As you monitor the children's progress, use *Add personal note* to keep a note of weaknesses in vocabulary, grammar, or pronunciation so you can review in later lessons.

Digital Activity Book • TIP The interactive activities in the AB can be done again and again, giving different children the chance to participate.

Teacher Resource Center • For extra grammar practice, print out Grammar Worksheet 7A.

Reading: Story Extract

Lesson objectives: boast about something to a friend; use the title and pictures to predict story content; read the extract from the modern family story *The Best Food in the World* (start)
Functional language: *Look! I made this amazing …! Anyone can make a …. It's easy.*
Secondary language: *village, bakery, luggage, greeting*
Materials: Tracks 7.2 and 7.3

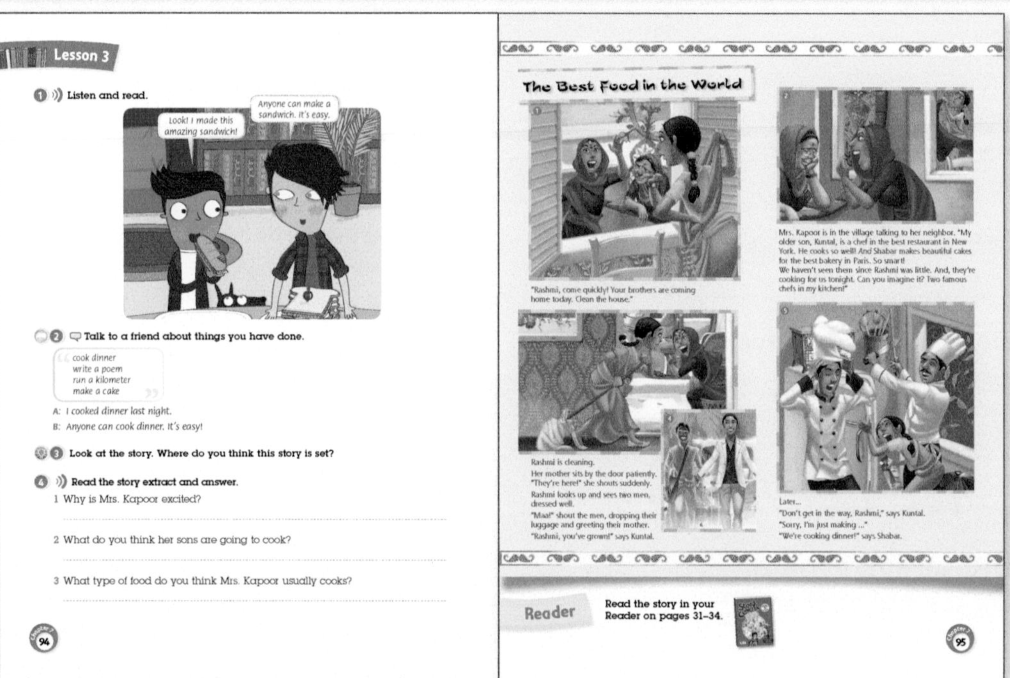

Lesson 3

1 Listen and read.

2 Talk to a friend about things you have done.

cook dinner
write a poem
run a kilometer
make a cake

A: I cooked dinner last night.
B: Anyone can cook dinner. It's easy!

3 Look at the story. Where do you think this story is set?

4 Read the story extract and answer.

1 Why is Mrs. Kapoor excited?

2 What do you think her sons are going to cook?

3 What type of food do you think Mrs. Kapoor usually cooks?

94

The Best Food in the World

"Rashmi, come quickly! Your brothers are coming home today. Clean the house."

Mrs. Kapoor is in the village talking to her neighbor. "My older son, Kuntal, is a chef in the best restaurant in New York. He cooks so well! *And* Shabar makes beautiful cakes for the best bakery in Paris. So smart!
We haven't seen them since Rashmi was little. And, they're cooking for us tonight. Can you imagine it? Two famous chefs in *my* kitchen!"

Rashmi is cleaning.
Her mother sits by the door patiently.
"They're here!" she shouts suddenly.
Rashmi looks up and sees two men, dressed well.
"Maa!" shout the men, dropping their luggage and greeting their mother.
"Rashmi, you've grown!" says Kuntal.

Later...
"Don't get in the way, Rashmi," says Kuntal.
"Sorry, I'm just making ..."
"We're cooking dinner!" says Shabar.

Reader
Read the story in your Reader on pages 31–34.

95

Warmer: Play "The A–Z Game"

Play the game using food words (see Games Bank p. 19).

Functional language

1 7.2 Listen and read.

- Play Track 7.2. The children listen and read along.
- Play Track 7.2 again for them to repeat.
- Divide the class into pairs to practice the dialogue.

2 Talk to a friend about things you have done.

- Choose two children to read the example dialogue.
- The children practice in pairs using the prompts supplied and adding details. Have pairs do a dialogue for the class.

Before reading

3 Look at the story. Where do you think this story is set?

- Have the children study the pictures. Ask *What is the house like? What are the clothes like?*
- Ask *Where do you think this story is set?* Elicit ideas. (*India*)
- Ask them to identify the main characters.

4 7.3 Read the story extract and answer.

- Have the children read the extract and answer question 1.
- Play Track 7.3. The children listen and answer questions 2 and 3.
- Elicit answers, but do not confirm predictions: explain that they will have to read the story to find out.

Answers

1 Her sons are coming home. **2** & **3** Children's own answers.

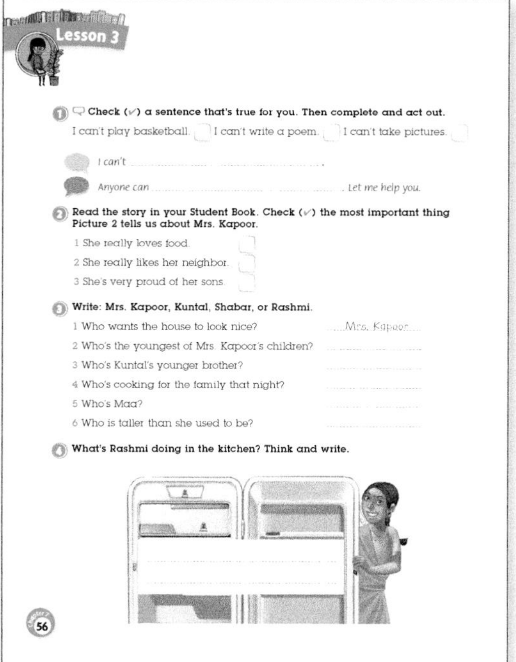
Lesson 3

1 Check (✓) a sentence that's true for you. Then complete and act out.

I can't play basketball. I can't write a poem. I can't take pictures.

I can't ...

Anyone can ... Let me help you.

2 Read the story in your Student Book. Check (✓) the most important thing Picture 2 tells us about Mrs. Kapoor.

1 She really loves food.
2 She really likes her neighbor.
3 She's very proud of her sons.

3 Write: Mrs. Kapoor, Kuntal, Shabar, or Rashmi.

1 Who wants the house to look nice? Mrs. Kapoor
2 Who's the youngest of Mrs. Kapoor's children?
3 Who's Kuntal's younger brother?
4 Who's cooking for the family that night?
5 Who's Maa?
6 Who is taller than she used to be?

4 What's Rashmi doing in the kitchen? Think and write.

56

1 Check (✓) a sentence that's true for you. Then complete and act out.

The children read the three sentences and choose one which is true for them. They complete and act out the dialogue in pairs. Encourage the children to use what they know to adapt and extend the dialogue. Have pairs act out their dialogue for the class.

2 Read the story in your Student Book. Check (✓) the most important thing Picture 2 tells us about Mrs. Kapoor.

The children read the Student Book story extract again, then look at picture 2 and identify the most important thing it tells them about Mrs. Kapoor. They check the appropriate sentence.

Answers

✓ *by:* 3

3 Write: Mrs. Kapoor, Kuntal, Shabar, or Rashmi.

The children read the sentences and write the character described each time. Point out that there may be more than one person. Elicit answers.

Answers

1 Mrs. Kapoor **2** Rashmi **3** Shabar **4** Kuntal and Shabar **5** Mrs. Kapoor **6** Rashmi

4 What's Rashmi doing in the kitchen? Think and write.

Elicit suggestions on what Rashmi is doing in the kitchen. The children write their own ideas, then compare with a friend. Elicit ideas.

Answers

Children's own answers.

Cooler: Who said it?

Read out lines of dialogue from the story extract and ask the children to identify the speaker, e.g. *Rashmi, clean the house!* (*Mrs. Kapoor*) Ask *What kind of person is Mrs. Kapoor? How does she treat Rashmi?* to talk more about the characters.

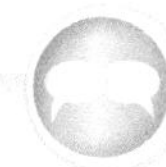

Competency Focus

Collaborate and Communicate

The children work together, putting into practice new functional language by acting out a realistic dialogue.

Think! Critical Thinking

By analyzing visual clues and deducing from the context, the children use prediction skills to help them engage with the story.

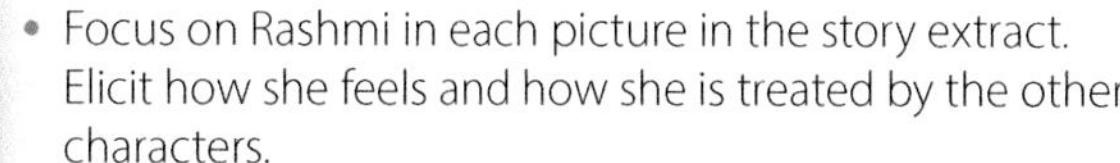

Digital Resources

Student eBook • Show the speech bubbles in the SB Activity 1 dialogue. Use *Highlighter* on *sandwich*, and elicit different things you could say in this context.

- Focus on Rashmi in each picture in the story extract. Elicit how she feels and how she is treated by the other characters.
- For the Cooler, have children identify the speaker in the Reader story each time, saying their name as they do so.

The Best Food in the World

1
"Rashmi, come quickly! Your brothers are coming home today. Clean the house."

2
Mrs. Kapoor is in the village talking to her neighbor.

"My older son, Kuntal, is a chef in the best restaurant in New York. He cooks so well! *And* Shabar makes beautiful cakes for the best bakery in Paris. So smart! We haven't seen them since Rashmi was little. And, they're cooking for us tonight. Can you imagine it? Two famous chefs in *my* kitchen!"

3
Rashmi is cleaning.

Her mother sits by the door patiently. "They're here!" she shouts suddenly.

Rashmi looks up and sees two men, dressed well.

"Maa!" shout the men, dropping their luggage and greeting their mother.

"Rashmi, you've grown!" says Kuntal.

5
Later . . .

"Don't get in the way, Rashmi," says Kuntal.

"Sorry, I'm just making ..."

"We're cooking dinner!" says Shabar.

6
"Look, Shabar! I use the best ingredients. This is the most expensive fish in the world."

"What are you making?" asks Shabar

"It's a delicious curry for Maa." answers Kuntal.

"Anyone can make curry! It's easy!" laughs Shabar.

"This is a special recipe," Kuntal says. "I chop some onions. Then I slice the fish thinly. I then fry them quickly in some oil. I mix pepper and spices with coconut milk and cook it very slowly. Finally, I carefully add some fish eggs . . . and a piece of real gold. Maa is going to love it."

7
"Well, I'm making a beautiful dessert for Maa," says Shabar.

"It's a tiny bird made from a delicious cookie, on a sugar nest. I boil some water and sugar in a pan. Then, I pour the mixture very carefully to make the nest. I have to do this quickly before the sugar cools. And look! I cut a tiny piece of mango to look like a fish in the bird's beak!"

"Fantastic!" says Kuntal.

"Dinner!" shouts Kuntal.

8
First, Kuntal proudly puts his food on the table. It doesn't look like the curry Maa makes.

"It has *gold* on it!" says Rashmi excitedly.

"It smells good. What is it?" asks Maa.

"It's curry, Maa. You like curry."

She smiles and eats her food. "It needs more pepper."

9
Then Shabar brings in his dessert.

"I can't eat it," says Maa. "It's too beautiful!"

They eat their meal silently.

Then, Rashmi says, "Maa, I'm still hungry."

"Me, too," says Shabar.

"Let's have the rice pudding that you made, Rashmi," says Maa.

Rashmi brings in a big bowl of hot rice pudding.

10
"Delicious!" says Shabar. "It's so sweet."

"I can smell the saffron," says Kuntal. "It makes me think of home."

"It's wonderful!" says Maa. "It makes me think of my family."

"But," says Kuntal, ... "it just needs a little piece of gold on top!"

Lesson objective: read and understand the modern family story *The Best Food in the World* in the Reader
Materials: Track 7.4; Reader; costumes for acting out; Oral Storytelling Video Worksheet 7 [TRC printout] (optional)

Warmer: Add the vowels

Write up food preparation verbs on the board, omitting the vowels, e.g. *slc* for *slice*. Use *slice, cut, chop, pour, boil, mix, add*. Have children work in pairs to figure out the verbs. Invite children to write the verbs in full on the board.

Story Summary

Two brothers, Kuntal the chef and Shabar the baker, return to their family village. They make a meal too beautiful to eat. Their younger sister makes a simple meal, which the family eats and thinks is delicious.

Theme: the importance of appreciating simple things in life

7.4 While reading

- Have the children look at the pictures in the Reader. Ask them to identify the main characters again.
- Play Track 7.4. The children listen and read along. Ask *Whose food do they like most?* (*Rashmi's*)
- Ask questions to check comprehension, e.g. *What does Kuntal add to his dish?* (*fish eggs and a piece of real gold*) *What does Shabar make from sugar?* (*a nest*) *Is it easy to do?* (*no*) *Does Maa like the food?* (*no*)
- Recall the story with the class. Bring the story to life by providing simple costumes (see **Story Time**).

After reading: Reflect

- Ask questions to give the children the opportunity to think about the issues raised by the story, e.g. *Did the brothers cook traditional food? Is it good to keep up traditions? Which food did everyone prefer?*

Optional activity: Change some details

There are four speaking parts in this story so it is ideal for group work. Divide the class into groups of four and allocate roles. Encourage the children to change the ingredients and cooking instructions. Ask groups to act out different scenes and make their adaptations.

Story Time

Using costumes

This story is set in India and provides a good opportunity for dressing up to motivate and bring a fun element to storytelling. Keep costumes very simple, so the children can easily swap them as they take turns as characters, e.g. headscarves, ties, jackets. Keep a dress-up box in the classroom for acting out.

Reading Strategy

Anticipation Guide

Anticipating what will happen helps the children engage with the story and the characters by using their own knowledge to predict the plot. It also prepares them to analyze the story and answer "after reading" or "while reading" comprehension questions.

For additional explanation and activities, see the Literacy Handbook on the Teacher Resource Center.

Cooler: Focus on food vocabulary

Have the children close their Reader. Give them a time limit (working in pairs) to remember all the food words from the story, including all the recipe verbs, e.g. *fry, chop, mix*. Then they check in their Reader.

Digital Resources

Reader eBook • For feedback on the Cooler, have children use *Highlighter* to identify the food words in the story text.
• Oral Storytelling Video 7.1 contains a different story on a related theme (*The King's Party*). Watch and discuss it together at the end of the lesson.

Teacher Resource Center • Print out Oral Storytelling Video Worksheet 7 to help you get the most out of the video.

Student eBook, Reader eBook • The children can watch Oral Storytelling Video 7.1 at home with their family.

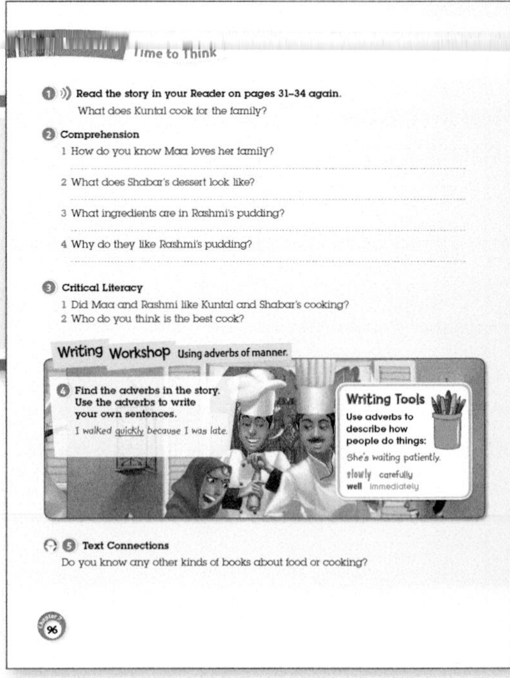

Time to Think

1 Read the story in your Reader on pages 31–34 again.
What does Kuntal cook for the family?

2 Comprehension
1 How do you know Maa loves her family?
2 What does Shabar's dessert look like?
3 What ingredients are in Rashmi's pudding?
4 Why do they like Rashmi's pudding?

3 Critical Literacy
1 Did Maa and Rashmi like Kuntal and Shabar's cooking?
2 Who do you think is the best cook?

Writing Workshop Using adverbs of manner.

4 Find the adverbs in the story. Use the adverbs to write your own sentences.
I walked quickly because I was late.

Writing Tools
Use adverbs to describe how people do things:
She's waiting patiently.
slowly carefully
well immediately

5 Text Connections
Do you know any other kinds of books about food or cooking?

96

Reading Comprehension and Critical Literacy

Lesson objectives: understand and evaluate the story; relate story theme to personal experience; write sentences with adverbs

Materials: Track 7.4; Reader; Oral Storytelling Video Worksheet 7 [TRC printout] (optional)

Note: Please ensure that your class has read the Reader story before you do this lesson.

Warmer: Story recap

Write the names of the four characters on the board. Elicit what they did/made in the story. Encourage the children to describe the characters and their feelings, too.

1 7.4 Read the story in your Reader.

- Have the children read the story. (Alternatively, play Track 7.4 and have them read along.) Elicit whether they were correct in their predictions in Lesson 3 Activity 4.
- Ask *What does Kuntal cook for the family?* (*fish curry*)

2 Comprehension

- Ask the children to look at the first question and find the scene with Mrs. Kapoor and her neighbor. Have them write their answer.
- Have the children consider the other questions. Then elicit suggestions for answers.

Answers

1 She is very proud of them when she tells her neighbor about them. **2** like a bird **3** rice, saffron (milk, sugar) **4** It makes them think of home/family.

3 Critical Literacy

- Have the children describe the dishes Kuntal and Shabar cooked. Prompt as necessary, e.g. *Were they simple? Were they traditional? Did they taste good?* Elicit who is the best cook, with reasons for their opinion. Discuss traditional versus new/experimental things and which are better. Analyzing the characters' behavior and attitudes in this way develops critical literacy.

Writing Workshop

Using adverbs of manner

4 Find the adverbs in the story. Use the adverbs to write your own sentences

Have a child read out the example. Read the **Writing Tools** box together: remind the children adverbs describe how people do things and highlight their position in a sentence. The children find more adverbs in the story and write four sentences of their own in their notebook, then compare in pairs. Elicit sentences.

Answers

Children's own answers.

5 Text Connections 

- Ask *Have you read any other books or stories about food or cooking?* Have the children compare these with the Reader story.

Optional activity: A traditional dish

Have the children name their favorite traditional dish and its ingredients. Ask if they know how to make it. Elicit instructions. Draw on the board for children to label, e.g. *chop, fry*.

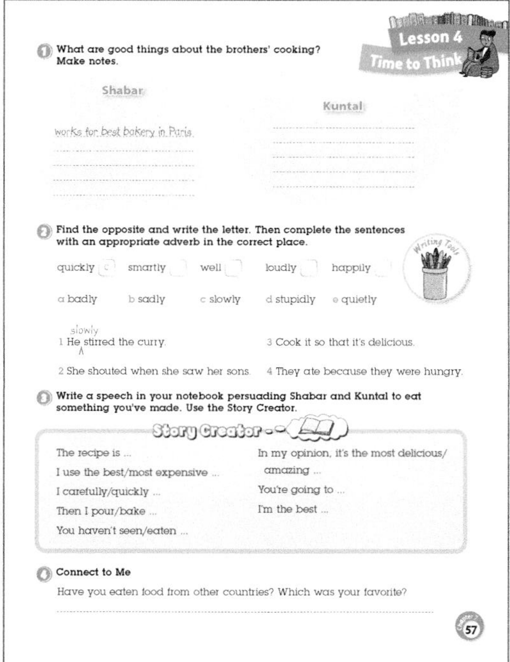

Lesson 4
Time to Think

1 What are good things about the brothers' cooking? Make notes.

Shabar

works for best bakery in Paris.

Kuntal

2 Find the opposite and write the letter. Then complete the sentences with an appropriate adverb in the correct place.

Writing Tools

quickly c smartly well loudly happily

a badly b sadly c slowly d stupidly e quietly

1 He slowly stirred the curry.
2 She shouted when she saw her sons.
3 Cook it so that it's delicious.
4 They ate because they were hungry.

3 Write a speech in your notebook persuading Shabar and Kuntal to eat something you've made. Use the Story Creator.

Story Creator

The recipe is ...
I use the best/most expensive ...
I carefully/quickly ...
Then I pour/bake ...
You haven't seen/eaten ...
In my opinion, it's the most delicious/amazing ...
You're going to ...
I'm the best ...

4 Connect to Me

Have you eaten food from other countries? Which was your favorite?

57

1 What are good things about the brothers' cooking? Make notes.

The children note appropriate information for each category, then compare in pairs. Elicit ideas.

Answers

Children's own answers.

2 Find the opposite and write the letter. Then complete the sentences with an appropriate adverb in the correct place.

The children match the adverb opposites. They then complete the sentences by writing an appropriate adverb in the right place. Elicit answers.

Answers

quickly c, smartly d, well a, loudly e, happily b

1 He slowly stirred the curry. **2** She shouted loudly/happily when she saw her sons. **3** Cook it well/slowly so that it's delicious. **4** They ate quickly/quietly/happily because they were hungry.

3 Write a speech in your notebook persuading Shabar and Kuntal to eat something you've made. Use the Story Creator.

Use the **Story Creator** to elicit ideas. The children write a speech in their notebook, then compare with a friend. Have children read out their speech for the class.

4 Connect to Me

Ask the class to give examples of international food they have eaten and say which was their favorite. The children write their own response, then compare with a friend.

Cooler: Play "Back to the Board"

Play the game using adverbs (see Games Bank p. 19).

Competency Focus

Me: Critical Literacy

The children use critical literacy skills to reflect on the theme of the story and relate it to their own experiences.

Digital Resources

Student eBook, Digital Activity Book • TIP Use the arrows to navigate to previous or later lessons.

Student eBook, Reader eBook • If you haven't already, show Oral Storytelling Video 7.1 (a different story on a related theme).

Teacher Resource Center • If you haven't already, print out Oral Storytelling Video Worksheet 7 to do the support activities.

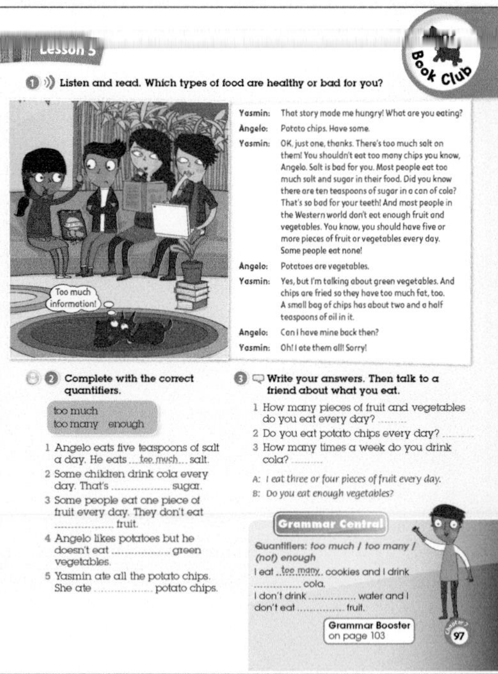

Lesson 5

Book Club

1 Listen and read. Which types of food are healthy or bad for you?

Yasmin: That story made me hungry! What are you eating?

Angelo: Potato chips. Have some.

Yasmin: OK, just one, thanks. There's too much salt on them! You shouldn't eat too many chips you know, Angelo. Salt is bad for you. Most people eat too much salt and sugar in their food. Did you know there are ten teaspoons of sugar in a can of cola? That's so bad for your teeth! And most people in the Western world don't eat enough fruit and vegetables. You know, you should have five or more pieces of fruit or vegetables every day. Some people eat none!

Angelo: Potatoes are vegetables.

Yasmin: Yes, but I'm talking about green vegetables. And chips are fried so they have too much fat, too. A small bag of chips has about two and a half teaspoons of oil in it.

Angelo: Can I have mine back then?

Yasmin: Oh! I ate them all! Sorry!

2 Complete with the correct quantifiers.

too much
too many enough

1 Angelo eats five teaspoons of salt a day. He eats ...too much... salt.
2 Some children drink cola every day. That's .... sugar.
3 Some people eat one piece of fruit every day. They don't eat .... fruit.
4 Angelo likes potatoes but he doesn't eat .... green vegetables.
5 Yasmin ate all the potato chips. She ate .... potato chips.

3 Write your answers. Then talk to a friend about what you eat.

1 How many pieces of fruit and vegetables do you eat every day? ....
2 Do you eat potato chips every day? ....
3 How many times a week do you drink cola? ....

A: *I eat three or four pieces of fruit every day.*
B: *Do you eat enough vegetables?*

Grammar Central

Quantifiers: *too much / too many / (not) enough*

I eat ..too many.. cookies and I drink .... cola.
I don't drink .... water and I don't eat .... fruit.

Grammar Booster on page 103

97

Grammar and Reading

Lesson objective: talk about quantities
Key grammar: quantifiers—statements with *too much / too many / enough*
Secondary language: *teaspoon, can (of cola), Western world*
Materials: Track 7.5; Grammar Worksheet 7B [TRC printout] (optional); food pictures from magazines (optional)

Warmer: What I eat

Ask *Do you eat potato chips/candy/chocolate? How many bags/bars do you eat in a week?* Then elicit the different fruit and vegetables they eat every day.

1 7.5 Listen and read. Which types of food are healthy or bad for you?

- Play Track 7.5. The children listen. Ask *Which types of food are healthy or bad for you?* (*Fruit and vegetables are healthy. Too much salt/sugar/fat is bad for you.*)
- Play Track 7.5 again. Check comprehension by having children explain why different foods are bad for you.

2 Complete with the correct quantifiers. 

- Have the children look at the quantifiers supplied and the example. Ask *Is salt uncountable or countable?* and elicit the rules for using *too much/too many.* (too much *with singular/uncountable;* too many *with countable*)
- The children find an example in the text with *enough* and underline. Make sure they understand that the negative form is *not … enough.*
- They read the text again and complete the sentences. Elicit answers.

Answers

1 too much **2** too much **3** enough **4** enough **5** too many

Grammar Central

Quantifiers: *too much / too many / enough*

Have the children complete the grammar examples. Elicit answers. Elicit which expressions are used with singular/uncountable nouns (*too much, enough*), and which are used with plural nouns (*too many, enough*). The children write a personalized example in their notebook. For extra practice, try the **Grammar Booster** section in the Student Book (pp. 103–105).

Answers p. 103

Activity 1: **2** too many **3** n't / not enough **4** too much

Activity 2: **1** n't/not enough **3** too many **4** too much **5** n't/not enough **6** too many **7** n't/not enough **8** too much, too many

p. 104

Activity 1: **1** quickly **2** too many **3** Carefully **4** too much **5** enough **6** smoothly **7** well

Activity 2: **1** Children's own answers.

p. 105

Activity 1: **1** patiently **2** immediately **3** too much **4** anything **5** firmly **6** is used **7** While **8** carefully **9** smoothly **10** when **11** was drying **12** too many **13** slowly **14** beautiful

Activity 2: Children's own answers.

3 Write your answers. Then talk to a friend about what you eat.

- Have the children read and complete their answers.
- Choose two children to read the example dialogue.

- Divide the class into pairs. They read each other's answers, then practice dialogues. Have pairs perform for the class.

Answers

Children's own answers.

Optional activity: Make a poster

Have the children make a poster, divided into two sections: healthy and unhealthy food. They can draw pictures or use pictures from magazines. They write a caption for each type of food, e.g. *Cookies have too much sugar.*

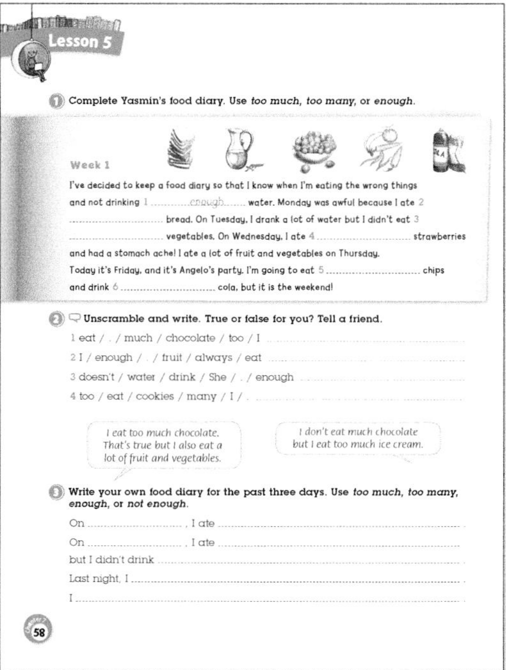

Lesson 5

1 Complete Yasmin's food diary. Use *too much, too many,* or *enough*.

Week 1

I've decided to keep a food diary so that I know when I'm eating the wrong things and not drinking 1 ....enough.... water. Monday was awful because I ate 2 .... bread. On Tuesday, I drank a lot of water but I didn't eat 3 .... vegetables. On Wednesday, I ate 4 .... strawberries and had a stomach ache! I ate a lot of fruit and vegetables on Thursday. Today it's Friday, and it's Angelo's party. I'm going to eat 5 .... chips and drink 6 .... cola, but it is the weekend!

2 Unscramble and write. True or false for you? Tell a friend.

1 eat / . / much / chocolate / too / I ....
2 I / enough / . / fruit / always / eat ....
3 doesn't / water / drink / She / . / enough ....
4 too / eat / cookies / many / I / . ...

I eat too much chocolate. *That's true but I also eat a lot of fruit and vegetables.*

I don't eat much chocolate but I eat too much ice cream.

3 Write your own food diary for the past three days. Use *too much, too many, enough,* or *not enough*.

On ...., I ate ....
On ...., I ate ....
but I didn't drink ....
Last night, I ....
I ....

58

1 Complete Yasmin's food diary. Use *too much, too many,* or *enough.*

The children complete the text using *too much, too many,* or *enough*. Elicit answers.

Answers

1 enough **2** too much **3** enough **4** too many **5** too many **6** too much

2 Unscramble and write. True or false for you? Tell a friend.

The children unscramble and write the sentences. They then decide if the sentences are true or false for them, and tell a friend.

Answers

1 I eat too much chocolate. **2** I always eat enough fruit. **3** She doesn't drink enough water. **4** I eat too many cookies.

3 Write your own food diary for the past three days. Use *too much, too many, enough,* or *not enough.*

The children complete their own food diary, using *too much, too many,* or *enough / not enough*. They then compare with a friend. Elicit answers.

Answers

Children's own answers.

Cooler: Let's complain!

Tell the children this is their big chance to complain about things they dislike at school. Ask them to make sentences with *too much / too many / not enough*, e.g. *There's too much homework. There are too many tests!*

Competency Focus

Learn

The children demonstrate their understanding of the new language by reading the text and completing the activity.

Digital Resources

Student eBook, Digital Activity Book • TIP Children love to be involved in using the digital resources. Give them as many opportunities as possible—completing interactive activities or showing answers, as well as writing and drawing on the board in more open-ended tasks. Make a point of encouraging less confident children to participate, because this will help them engage.

Teacher Resource Center • For extra grammar practice, print out Grammar Worksheet 7B.

Vocabulary, Listening, and Spelling

Lesson objectives: identify and talk about tastes; practice spelling adjectives ending in *–y*
Key vocabulary: *bitter, crunchy, juicy, salty, smells, smelly, soft, sour, sweet, tastes, tasty*
Secondary language: *scarf, flavor*
Materials: Track 7.6; Phonics Worksheet 7 [TRC printout] (optional)

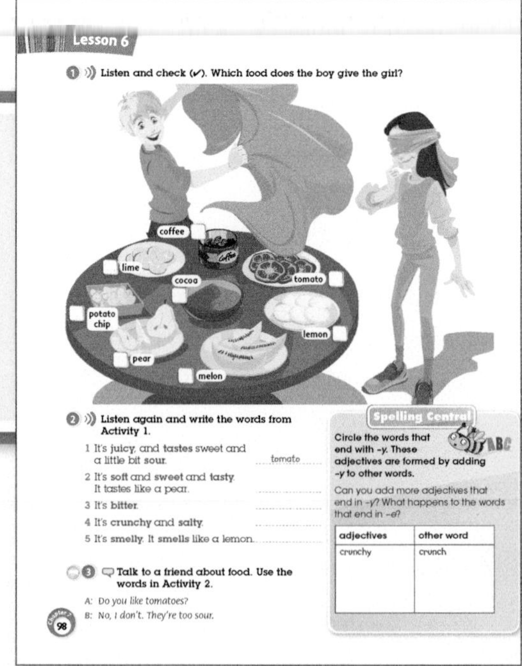
Lesson 6

1 Listen and check (✓). Which food does the boy give the girl?

2 Listen again and write the words from Activity 1.

1 It's juicy, and tastes sweet and a little bit sour. tomato
2 It's soft and sweet and tasty. It tastes like a pear. ....
3 It's bitter. ....
4 It's crunchy and salty. ....
5 It's smelly. It smells like a lemon. ....

3 Talk to a friend about food. Use the words in Activity 2.

A: *Do you like tomatoes?*
B: *No, I don't. They're too sour.*

Spelling Central

Circle the words that end with -y. These adjectives are formed by adding -y to other words.

Can you add more adjectives that end in -y? What happens to the words that end in -e?

adjectives	other word
crunchy	crunch

98

Warmer: Pre-teach vocabulary

Pre-teach the vocabulary using different foods, e.g. *Coffee tastes bitter. Oranges are juicy.* Then, prompt with sentences which are sometimes wrong, e.g. *Oranges are bitter.* The children clap if the sentence is correct and correct you if it is wrong.

1 7.6 Listen and check (✓). Which food does the boy give the girl?

- Have the children look at the pictures of the food and identify them.
- Explain the girl is trying to guess the food. Play Track 7.6. The children listen and check the correct items.
- Elicit answers.

Audioscript

Boy: *Let's cover your eyes with this scarf. Now guess the food and tell me what you think of it. OK, open your mouth.*
Girl: *It's juicy and it tastes sweet. Mm, I like it. It has a sour flavor, too. I think it's a tomato.*
Boy: *Yes, that's right. OK. Try this. It's chopped into little pieces.*
Girl: *Um, it's soft and very sweet. It's tasty. It tastes like a pear.*
Boy: *No, it's a melon. Now try this:*
Girl: *Yuk! It's bitter! It's horrible. Is it coffee?*
Boy: *No, it isn't. It's cocoa.*
Girl: *But I love chocolate!*
Boy: *I know, but this is cocoa with no sugar added … Now this one. It's easy!*
Girl: *Hm, it's crunchy and salty. There's too much salt! It isn't very healthy. It's a potato chip.*
Boy: *Yes, it is.*
Girl: *It's smelly! It smells like a lemon. Oh, that's really sour! I don't like it.*
Boy: *Ha, ha! Yes. That's a lime.*

Answers

lime, cocoa, tomato, potato chip, melon

2 7.6 Listen again and write the words from Activity 1.

- Have the children read the example sentences and study the new vocabulary. Then play Track 7.6 again. The children listen and write the correct food word. Elicit answers.
- Check comprehension of new vocabulary by asking the children to give you other examples, e.g. *What's sour?* (*a lemon*)

Answers

1 tomato **2** melon **3** coffee/cocoa **4** potato chip **5** lime

3 Talk to a friend about food. Use the words in Activity 2.

- Choose two children to read the example dialogue. Then divide the class into pairs and have them ask and answer about the food, describing their taste.
- Ask pairs to ask and answer for the class.

Spelling Central

Adjectives ending in –*y*

Have the children look back at the sentences in Activity 2 and circle the adjectives ending with –*y*. Then have them complete the chart. Elicit the rule for words ending in –*e* (*drop the* e). Have the children think of more examples. (e.g. *sunny, funny, snowy, rainy, healthy*.)

Answers

Circled: juicy, tasty, crunchy, salty, smelly
crunchy—crunch, juicy—juice, tasty—taste, salty—salt, smelly—smell

Optional activity: Play "Tic-Tac-Toe"

Play the game with foods, with the children saying a sentence describing the taste of the food to win the square (see Games Bank p. 19).

Lesson 6

1 Unscramble and write.

★ What's your favorite sandwich? Our winning recipe this week. ★

My favorite sandwich is a peanut butter and jelly banana dog. You need good, 1 ftos ....soft.... bread – don't use old, hard bread. Add your favorite jelly and some 2 unycrch .... peanut butter. The sandwich 3 sslime .... great because of the banana and the fruity jelly. When you 4 tseat .... it, you get a mix of flavors. First, there's the 5 twese .... jelly and banana and then the peanut butter which is 6 tylsa .... Sometimes I have mine with some 7 iuycj .... strawberries. Try it! It's a 8 ttyas .... and healthy sandwich!

2 Write the name of a food or drink for each group. Then compare ideas with a friend.

1 smelly ....blue cheese....
2 juicy ....
3 soft ....
4 not very tasty ....
5 sour ....
6 bitter ....

I think that blue cheese is very smelly.

Spelling Central — Adjectives ending in –y

3 Find and circle nouns with adjectives that end in *y*. Then write.

s	n	o	w	t	f
m	o	c	l	a	r
e	i			s	u
l	s	y		t	i
l	e	i	c	e	t
h	e	a	l	t	h

noun	adjective
ice	icy

59

1 Unscramble and write.

The children unscramble and write the words. Elicit answers.

Answers

1 soft **2** crunchy **3** smells **4** taste **5** sweet **6** salty **7** juicy **8** tasty

2 Write the name of a food or drink for each group. Then compare ideas with a friend.

The children write a food or drink for each category. They then compare in pairs. Elicit answers.

Answers

Children's own answers.

3 Find and circle nouns with adjectives that end in *y*. Then write.

To practice the **Spelling Central** feature, the children find and circle nouns in the wordsearch, then write the noun and corresponding adjective ending in –*y* in the grid. Elicit answers.

Answers

ice—icy, snow—snowy, smell—smelly, fruit—fruity, noise—noisy, taste—tasty, health—healthy

Cooler: Play "Guess the food!"

Divide the class into teams. Give each team in turn a food definition to guess, e.g. *They taste sweet and juicy and they're red.* (*strawberries*) Award points for correct guesses. You could ask the children to write their own definition clues.

Competency Focus

Collaborate and communicate

The children work together in pairs and use their interpersonal skills to share their ideas on the topic, incorporating the new vocabulary.

Digital Resources

Digital Activity Book • TIP Have children use *Pen* to complete the chart in AB Activity 3, before using the answer key to give feedback.

Teacher Resource Center • For phonics practice, print out Phonics Worksheet 7.

Student's App • Encourage the children to play the games on their smartphone/tablet. They could do this with a friend as a fun way to review the chapter vocabulary. (*The Inks* Apps are free and available on the App Store and Google Play.)

CLIL: Science—Food science

Lesson objective: find out about food and the senses
Materials: CLIL Graphic Organizer 7 [TRC printout] (optional); scarves and food items for tasting (Activity Book Activity 3)

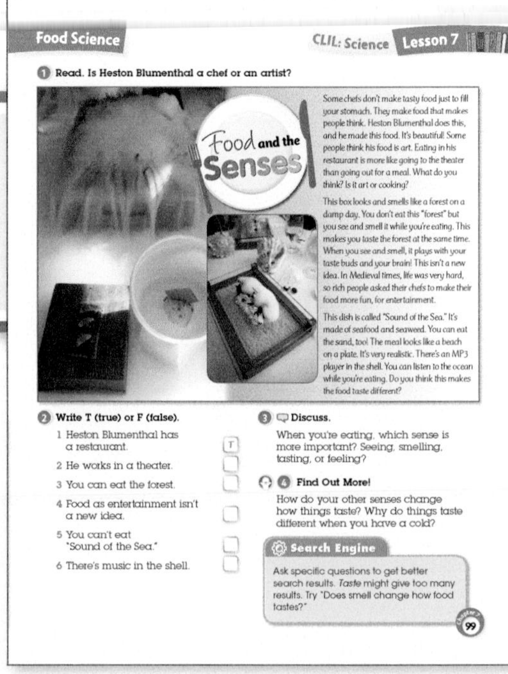

Food Science | CLIL: Science | Lesson 7

1 Read. Is Heston Blumenthal a chef or an artist?

Food and the Senses

Some chefs don't make tasty food just to fill your stomach. They make food that makes people think. Heston Blumenthal does this, and he made this food. It's beautiful! Some people think his food is art. Eating in his restaurant is more like going to the theater than going out for a meal. What do you think? Is it art or cooking?

This box looks and smells like a forest on a damp day. You don't eat this "forest" but you see and smell it while you're eating. This makes you taste the forest at the same time. When you see and smell, it plays with your taste buds and your brain! This isn't a new idea. In Medieval times, life was very hard, so rich people asked their chefs to make their food more fun, for entertainment.

This dish is called "Sound of the Sea." It's made of seafood and seaweed. You can eat the sand, too! The meal looks like a beach on a plate. It's very realistic. There's an MP3 player in the shell. You can listen to the ocean while you're eating. Do you think this makes the food taste different?

2 Write T (true) or F (false).

1 Heston Blumenthal has a restaurant. T
2 He works in a theater. ☐
3 You can eat the forest. ☐
4 Food as entertainment isn't a new idea. ☐
5 You can't eat "Sound of the Sea." ☐
6 There's music in the shell. ☐

3 Discuss.

When you're eating, which sense is more important? Seeing, smelling, tasting, or feeling?

4 Find Out More!

How do your other senses change how things taste? Why do things taste different when you have a cold?

Search Engine

Ask specific questions to get better search results. *Taste* might give too many results. Try "Does smell change how food tastes?"

Chapter 7 99

Warmer: How does it taste?

Review the food adjectives from the previous lesson. Call out food items and have the children say the adjective to describe them, e.g. *Lemon.* (*bitter*)

1 Read. Is Heston Blumenthal a chef or an artist?

- Have the children study the food pictures carefully. Ask *What are they?*
- The children then read the text. Ask *Is Heston Blumenthal a chef or an artist?* (*chef*)
- Ask *Is it a real forest?* (*no*) *What's unusual about the "Sound of the Sea" dish?* (*You can listen to the sound of the sea as you eat it.*) *Do you think this makes the food taste different?*

2 Write T (true) or F (false).

- Elicit why the example answer is true. (*His restaurant is mentioned in the first paragraph.*)
- The children then read the text again and write T (true) or F (false) for the other sentences. Elicit answers, including the correct version of the false sentences.

Answers

1 T **2** F **3** F **4** T **5** F **6** T

3 Discuss. 

- Review all the sense verbs with the class—*see, hear, feel, smell, touch*. Have the children imagine they are eating different foods, e.g. an ice cream, a pizza, a vegetable. Discuss with the class which senses they think are the most important for food.

4 Find Out More! 

- The children research how other senses affect our sense of taste. The **Search Engine** feature gives support on where to look. The children will need to complete this research before doing the follow-up activity in the Activity Book. (It could be set as homework.)

Optional activity: Invent a dish for Heston's restaurant

Have the children work in pairs to invent another elaborate and arty dish for Heston's restaurant. They draw a picture, list the ingredients, and then describe the taste to the class. Encourage them to be imaginative. You could research dishes on the Internet and show them pictures to inspire them.

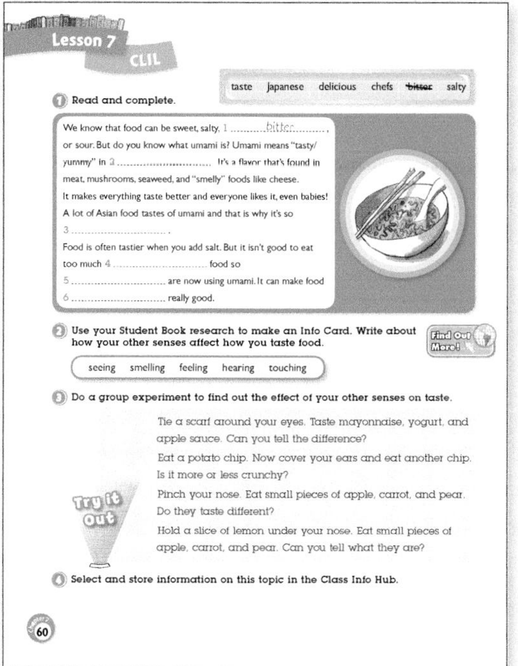
Lesson 7 CLIL

1 Read and complete.

taste Japanese delicious chefs ~~bitter~~ salty

We know that food can be sweet, salty, 1 ....bitter.........., or sour. But do you know what umami is? Umami means "tasty/yummy" in 2 .... It's a flavor that's found in meat, mushrooms, seaweed, and "smelly" foods like cheese. It makes everything taste better and everyone likes it, even babies! A lot of Asian food tastes of umami and that is why it's so 3 ....
Food is often tastier when you add salt. But it isn't good to eat too much 4 .... food so 5 .... are now using umami. It can make food 6 .... really good.

2 Use your Student Book research to make an Info Card. Write about how your other senses affect how you taste food. Find Out More!

seeing smelling feeling hearing touching

3 Do a group experiment to find out the effect of your other senses on taste.

Try it Out

Tie a scarf around your eyes. Taste mayonnaise, yogurt, and apple sauce. Can you tell the difference?

Eat a potato chip. Now cover your ears and eat another chip. Is it more or less crunchy?

Pinch your nose. Eat small pieces of apple, carrot, and pear. Do they taste different?

Hold a slice of lemon under your nose. Eat small pieces of apple, carrot, and pear. Can you tell what they are?

4 Select and store information on this topic in the Class Info Hub.

60

1 Read and complete.

The children read and complete the text using the words supplied. Elicit answers.

Answers

1 bitter **2** Japanese **3** delicious **4** salty **5** chefs **6** taste

2 Use your Student Book research to make an Info Card. Write about how your other senses affect how you taste food.

Divide the class into groups. Have the children pool the information learned from their research in the Student Book and the Activity Book. They write about and illustrate their ideas individually. Have the groups present their Info Cards to the class.

3 Do a group experiment to find out the effect of your other senses on taste.

Check for food allergies. Then divide the class into large groups. Give each group a scarf and small pieces of food to taste. The children follow the **Try It Out** instructions to carry out the experiment, taking turns and keeping a chart of their friends' answers. Groups present their findings to the class.

4 Select and store information on this topic in the Class Info Hub.

Have the children vote for the most interesting Info Cards. Archive these in your Class Hub (see p. 41) in a folder called **Chapter 7 How Does It Taste?**

Cooler: The Crazy Food Monster

Tell the children they are going to invent a meal for the monster. His brain is confused and he likes different tastes from normal people. Write prompt words on the board, e.g. *ice cream, pizza, potato chips, drink,* and have the children suggest new ideas/combinations for each one, e.g. *a smelly cheese ice cream, a strawberry pizza, chocolate potato chips,* etc.

Competency Focus

Me

The children reflect and find out more about the senses and the human body and relate it to their own senses and experiences.

Digital Resources

Student eBook, Digital Activity Book • TIP Store ideas in *Add personal note* for easy access during the lesson (here, other inventive food dishes).

- TIP When using the board for "heads-up" teaching, remember to give the children as much opportunity as possible to participate. Ask plenty of questions so they engage with the topic.

Teacher Resource Center • Print out CLIL Graphic Organizer 7 for the children to collate their Find Out More! research.

CLIL eBook • The children can use the CLIL eBook to expand their knowledge of the lesson topic.

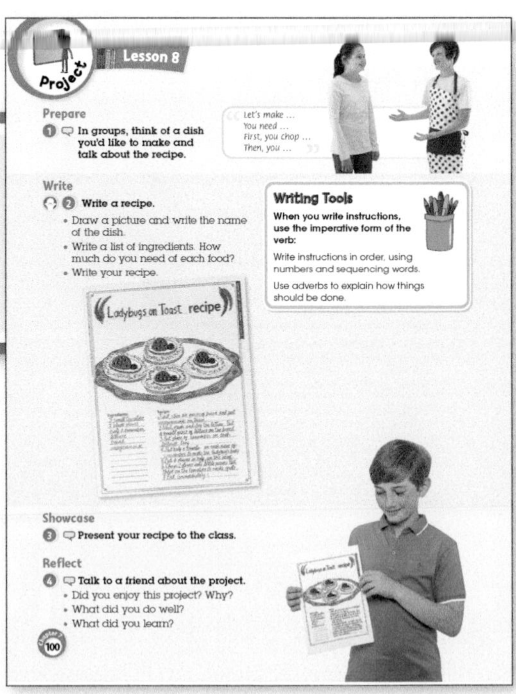
Project Lesson 8

Prepare

1 In groups, think of a dish you'd like to make and talk about the recipe.

Let's make ...
You need ...
First, you chop ...
Then, you ...

Write

2 Write a recipe.

- Draw a picture and write the name of the dish.
- Write a list of ingredients. How much do you need of each food?
- Write your recipe.

Ladybugs on Toast recipe

Writing Tools

When you write instructions, use the imperative form of the verb.

Write instructions in order, using numbers and sequencing words.

Use adverbs to explain how things should be done.

Showcase

3 Present your recipe to the class.

Reflect

4 Talk to a friend about the project.

- Did you enjoy this project? Why?
- What did you do well?
- What did you learn?

100

Writing Project

Lesson objectives: review language from Chapter 7; write a recipe and present it to the class

Materials: Writing Template 7 [TRC printout] (optional)

Warmer: Cooking categorization

Review cooking verbs as preparation for the lesson. Write on the board *cut, chop, slice, fry, pour, boil*. Have the children copy them into their notebook across the page. Call out food words and have them write the words under appropriate categories, e.g. *Onion.* (*slice/fry*) *Carrot.* (*chop/boil*) *Water.* (*pour/boil*)

Prepare

1 In groups, think of a dish you'd like to make and talk about the recipe.

- The children choose a recipe. They talk about the ingredients and how to make it in groups, using the prompts supplied. Groups present their recipe.

Write

2 Write a recipe.

- Have the children read the recipe as a model for their own writing.
- Read the **Writing Tools** box together. Elicit examples in the model of recipe features.
- The children prepare an outline, using the instructions and the model recipe. They write their recipe, then compare with a friend. Give support as necessary.

Showcase

3 Present your recipe to the class. 

- Choose children to read out their recipes to the class. Ask the rest of the class to listen and decide if they would like to eat it.

Reflect

4 Vote for the best recipe. 

- Have the children comment on which recipe they liked best and why. Write up the recipe titles on the board and have a class vote for their favorite.

Optional activity: Mime a recipe

Read out the following recipe slowly for the class to mime the actions:

Banana pancakes

Mix the flour and salt in a bowl. Add the milk, eggs, and sugar. Mix carefully. Chop the banana. Put it in the bowl. Pour a little mixture into a pan with oil—not too much. Cook for a minute, then flip your pancake.

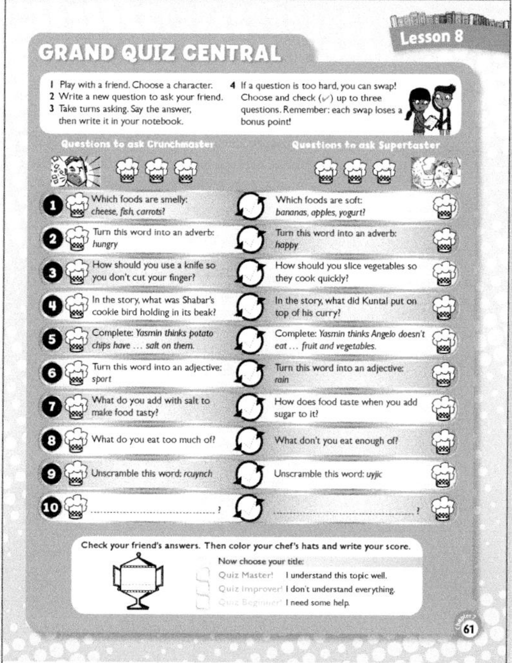

Lesson 8

GRAND QUIZ CENTRAL

1 Play with a friend. Choose a character.
2 Write a new question to ask your friend.
3 Take turns asking. Say the answer, then write it in your notebook.
4 If a question is too hard, you can swap! Choose and check (✓) up to three questions. Remember: each swap loses a bonus point!

	Questions to ask Crunchmaster	Questions to ask Supertaster
1	Which foods are smelly: *cheese, fish, carrots?*	Which foods are soft: *bananas, apples, yogurt?*
2	Turn this word into an adverb: *hungry*	Turn this word into an adverb: *happy*
3	How should you use a knife so you don't cut your finger?	How should you slice vegetables so they cook quickly?
4	In the story, what was Shabar's cookie bird holding in its beak?	In the story, what did Kuntal put on top of his curry?
5	Complete: *Yasmin thinks potato chips have … salt on them.*	Complete: *Yasmin thinks Angelo doesn't eat … fruit and vegetables.*
6	Turn this word into an adjective: *sport*	Turn this word into an adjective: *rain*
7	What do you add with salt to make food tasty?	How does food taste when you add sugar to it?
8	What do you eat too much of?	What don't you eat enough of?
9	Unscramble this word: *rcuynch*	Unscramble this word: *uyjic*
10	……………………………………?	……………………………………?

Check your friend's answers. Then color your chef's hats and write your score.

Now choose your title:
Quiz Master! I understand this topic well.
Quiz Improver! I don't understand everything.
Quiz Beginner! I need some help.

61

Grand Quiz Central

See p. 43 for details of how to take the quiz.

Answers

1 cheese and fish / bananas and yogurt **2** hungrily / happily **3** carefully / thinly **4** a little fish made of mango / fish eggs and a piece of gold **5** too much / enough **6** sporty / rainy **7** pepper / sweet **8** I eat too much / I don't eat enough … **9** crunchy / juicy **10** Children's own answers.

Cooler: Reviewing food vocabulary

Write the following category headings on the board: *Vegetables, Cooking verbs, Food adjectives.* Set a time limit of three minutes and have the children write down as many words as they can for each category.

Competency Focus

Me

The children invent and write their own recipe, developing their culinary skills.

Digital Resources

Student eBook • Have children use *Highlighter* to identify examples in the model text of the key features of the writing task: name of the dish, picture, ingredients, instructions.

- Have the children vote to select a topic from Chapters 4–7. Use *Timer* to give them one minute to recall all the words in the topic. Repeat with a different topic if you have time.

Teacher Resource Center • Print out Writing Template 7 to use for the SB writing activity.

Language Review

Lesson objective: review language from Chapter 7
Materials: Tracks 7.7 and AB 7.1

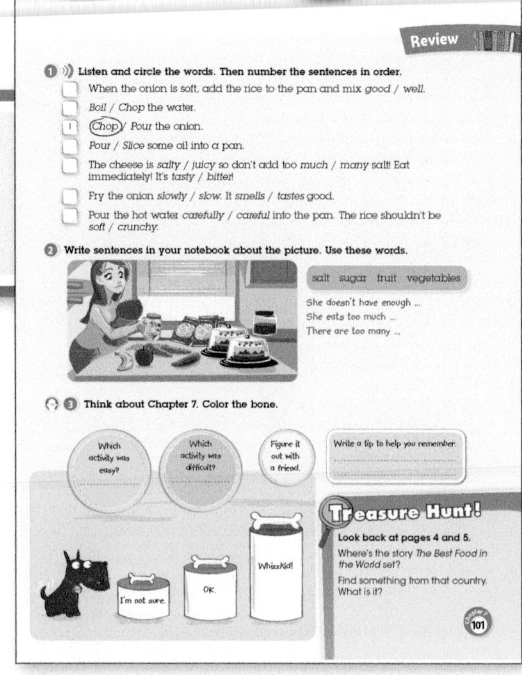
Review

1 Listen and circle the words. Then number the sentences in order.

- [ ] When the onion is soft, add the rice to the pan and mix *good* / *well*.
- [ ] *Boil* / *Chop* the water.
- [1] *Chop* / *Pour* the onion.
- [ ] *Pour* / *Slice* some oil into a pan.
- [ ] The cheese is *salty* / *juicy* so don't add too *much* / *many* salt! Eat immediately! It's *tasty* / *bitter*!
- [ ] Fry the onion *slowly* / *slow*. It *smells* / *tastes* good.
- [ ] Pour the hot water *carefully* / *careful* into the pan. The rice shouldn't be *soft* / *crunchy*.

2 Write sentences in your notebook about the picture. Use these words.

salt sugar fruit vegetables

She doesn't have enough ...
She eats too much ...
There are too many ...

3 Think about Chapter 7. Color the bone.

Which activity was easy?
Which activity was difficult?
Figure it out with a friend.
Write a tip to help you remember.

Treasure Hunt!
Look back at pages 4 and 5.
Where's the story *The Best Food in the World* set?
Find something from that country. What is it?

101

Warmer: Play "Chef Says"

Adapt the traditional "Simon Says" game. Call out commands for children to mime, e.g. *boil, fry, chop,* etc., and say *Yes, Chef!,* e.g. *Chef says "Chop the onions."* Children are out if they mime the action without *Chef says.*

1 7.7 Listen and circle the words. Then number the sentences in order.

- Play Track 7.7. The children circle the correct word in each instruction.
- Play Track 7.7 again. The children put the sentences in order, writing the numbers. Elicit answers.

Audioscript

This is a nice, easy recipe. First, chop the onion. Then, pour some oil into a pan. Fry the onion slowly. Mm … it smells good. OK, now the onion is soft. Add the rice and mix the onion and the rice together well. Now, let's boil some water. OK, I'm pouring the water carefully into the pan. Now, are you patient? You have to mix the rice for 15 minutes until it's cooked. It shouldn't be crunchy. OK, it's almost ready. Add some cheese, salt, and pepper, but be careful. Don't add too much salt because the cheese is salty. Great! It's ready. Eat it immediately while it's hot. Wow! That's tasty!

Answers

well; Boil; Chop; Pour; salty, much, tasty; slowly, smells; carefully, crunchy
4, 5, 1, 2, 7, 3, 6

2 Write sentences in your notebook about the picture. Use these words.

- Ask *Do you think she eats healthily?*
- The children write sentences in their notebook.

Answers

Children's own answers.

3 Think about Chapter 7. Color the bone. 

- Have the children look back at Chapter 7 and color the bone to evaluate their progress (self-evaluation). Discuss ideas for adapting model texts. The children choose and write a tip in their Student Book.

Treasure Hunt!

Ask *Where is the story* The Best Food in the World *set?* (*India*) Have the children look at pp. 4–5 to find something from that country. (*Indian elephant statue*)

Cooler: Read a proverb

Write this proverb on the board: *Too many cooks spoil the broth.* Explain the meaning to the class. Ask the children if they know any other proverbs.

Competency Focus

Me: Self-evaluation

The children reflect on the chapter and express their opinions about their own progress.

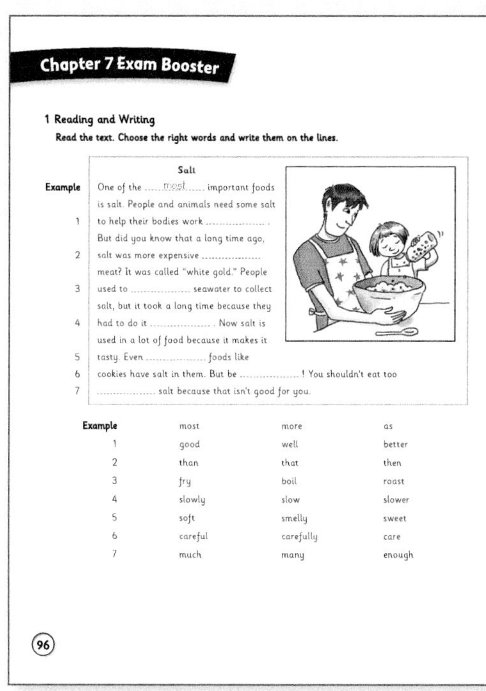

Chapter 7 Exam Booster

1 Reading and Writing

Read the text. Choose the right words and write them on the lines.

Salt

Example One of the ......most...... important foods is salt. People and animals need some salt
1 to help their bodies work ....
But did you know that a long time ago,
2 salt was more expensive ....
meat? It was called "white gold." People
3 used to .... seawater to collect
salt, but it took a long time because they
4 had to do it .... Now salt is
used in a lot of food because it makes it
5 tasty. Even .... foods like
6 cookies have salt in them. But be ....! You shouldn't eat too
7 .... salt because that isn't good for you.

Example	most	more	as
1	good	well	better
2	than	that	then
3	fry	boil	roast
4	slowly	slow	slower
5	soft	smelly	sweet
6	careful	carefully	care
7	much	many	enough

96

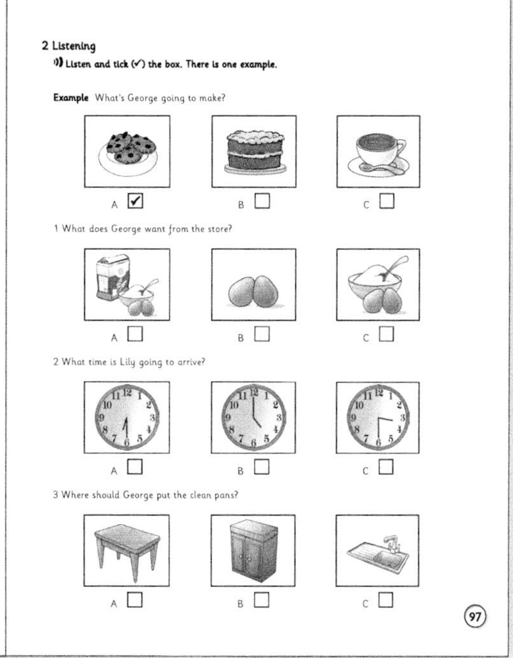

2 Listening

Listen and tick (✓) the box. There is one example.

Example What's George going to make?

A ☑ B ☐ C ☐

1 What does George want from the store?

A ☐ B ☐ C ☐

2 What time is Lily going to arrive?

A ☐ B ☐ C ☐

3 Where should George put the clean pans?

A ☐ B ☐ C ☐

97

Answers (Audioscript on p. 223)

1 c **2** a **3** b

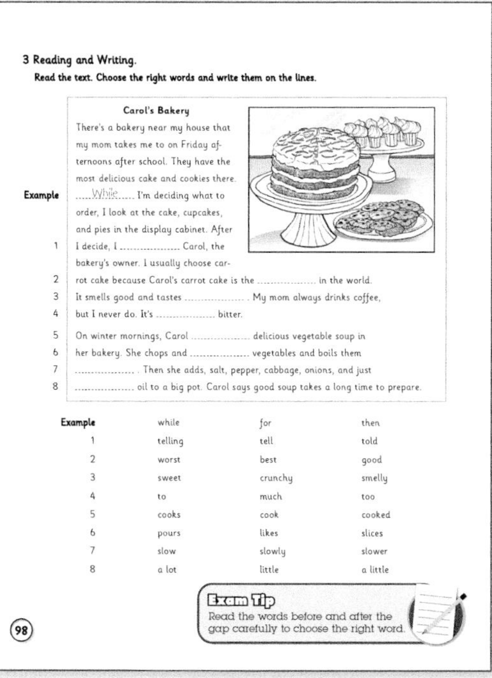

3 Reading and Writing.

Read the text. Choose the right words and write them on the lines.

Carol's Bakery

There's a bakery near my house that my mom takes me to on Friday afternoons after school. They have the most delicious cake and cookies there.
Example ......While...... I'm deciding what to order, I look at the cake, cupcakes, and pies in the display cabinet. After
1 I decide, I .... Carol, the bakery's owner. I usually choose car-
2 rot cake because Carol's carrot cake is the .... in the world.
3 It smells good and tastes .... My mom always drinks coffee,
4 but I never do. It's .... bitter.
5 On winter mornings, Carol .... delicious vegetable soup in
6 her bakery. She chops and .... vegetables and boils them
7 .... Then she adds, salt, pepper, cabbage, onions, and just
8 .... oil to a big pot. Carol says good soup takes a long time to prepare.

Example	while	for	then
1	telling	tell	told
2	worst	best	good
3	sweet	crunchy	smelly
4	to	much	too
5	cooks	cook	cooked
6	pours	likes	slices
7	slow	slowly	slower
8	a lot	little	a little

Exam Tip
Read the words before and after the gap carefully to choose the right word.

98

3 Reading and Writing. Read the text. Choose the right words and write them on the lines.

The children complete the text with one of the three words supplied for each blank. Check answers.

Answers

1 tell **2** best **3** good **4** too **5** cooks **6** slices **7** slowly **8** a little

1 Reading and Writing. Read the text. Choose the right words and write them on the lines. There is one example.

The children complete the text with one of the three words supplied for each blank. Check answers.

Answers

1 well **2** than **3** boil **4** slowly **5** sweet **6** careful **7** much

2 AB 7.1 Listening. Listen and tick (✓) the box. There is one example.

The children read the questions. Play AB Track 7.1 twice. They listen and check the correct picture in each section.

Digital Resources

Digital Activity Book • Have the class do the AB interactive digital activities, or set them for homework.

Teacher Resource Center • Print out Festival Worksheet: Earth Day to expand the children's knowledge of celebrations throughout the world.

• Print out Test Chapter 7 to use at the end of this lesson. The Test Generator also allows you to create customized tests.

Chapter 8 Speak Out! Overview

Reading Skills

Story: *Gulliver in Lilliput*
Genre: fantasy adventure

The children will:

- use critical thinking skills to identify reporting verbs.
- talk about what people say using reported speech.
- read and understand a fantasy adventure story.
- talk about language and communication.
- find out world language facts.
- write an interview report.

Literacy Development

- use reading skills to understand and predict content
- relate story theme to personal experience
- use reporting verbs in reported speech

Key Vocabulary

Reporting verbs: agree, argue, decide, disagree, joke, laugh, lie, offer, respect, share, tell
Spoken communication: accent, body language, mean, pronounce, repeat, signs, smile, translate, understand

Functional Language

- How do you say … in …?
- It's …
- Sorry! What did you say?
- I said it was …

Key Grammar

Reported speech

- "I'm very happy."—She said (that) she was very happy.
- "I don't like traveling."—She explained (that) she didn't like traveling.

Reported speech: questions

- "Where do you live?"—He asked where I lived.
- "Do you like reading?"—She asked if I liked reading.

CLIL: Math—World language statistics

The children find out world language facts.

Spelling

Words ending in silent *–e*

Competency Focus

The children will:

use critical thinking skills to deduce the meaning of new vocabulary. (Lesson 1)	activate new vocabulary and apply new grammar knowledge. (Lesson 2)	work in pairs to act out a dialogue. (Lesson 3)	relate the story theme to their personal experience. (Lesson 4)	find out more about their own language and its heritage. (Lesson 7)
predict the content of a story. (Lesson 3)	apply new grammar rules in a familiar context. (Lesson 5)	work in pairs to complete language-related speaking activities. (Lesson 6)	invent and write their own interview report. (Lesson 8)	
			evaluate their own progress in the chapter. (Review)	

Digital Overview

Teacher Presentation

Student eBook and Digital Activity Book

- Music Video 8.1: *I Don't Understand!*
- Interactive versions of AB activities
- Integrated audio and answer key for all activities

Teacher resources for planning, lesson delivery, and homework

Teacher Resource Center

- Class Planner Chapter 8
- Worksheets to print out (including notes and answers):
  - Grammar Worksheet 8A: Reported speech
  - Grammar Worksheet 8B: Reported speech: questions
  - Phonics Worksheet 8
  - CLIL Graphic Organizer 8
  - Writing Template 8
  - Test Chapter 8
- Test Generator
- Literacy Handbook

Children's resources for consolidation and practice at home

Student eBook

- Music Video 8.1: *I Don't Understand!*

The Inks Student's App

Vocabulary games: Reporting verbs and Spoken communication

Chapter 8

Speak Out!

Lesson 1

Lesson objectives: identify and use reporting verbs

Key vocabulary: *agree, argue, decide, disagree, joke, laugh, lie, offer, respect, share, tell*

Materials: Track 8.1; paper for posters (optional)

Warmer: Rules for a healthy life

Have the children work in pairs to write five rules for a healthy life. Write on the board *Always … Don't …* Give an example, e.g. *Don't eat a lot of candy.* Invite pairs to read out their examples.

1 8.1 Listen and check (✔) the rules that you hear on the poster.

- Have the children look at the poster of rules for a happy home. They read all the rules and try to figure out the meaning of the verbs.
- Play Track 8.1. The children check the rules they hear.
- Elicit answers. Whenever you elicit answers, remember to check with the class to see if they agree.

Audioscript

Mom: *What's that, Lisa?*
Lisa: *It's a poster. I've decided we need some rules for a happy home!*
Mom: *Why?*
Lisa: *Because Bobby argues with me all the time.*
Bobby: *I don't argue.*
Lisa: *Yes, you do.*
Bobby: *No, I don't.*
Lisa: *You see? You're arguing with me now! You shouldn't argue with me. And you should respect our parents.*
Bobby: *I do respect Mom and Dad.*
Lisa: *Are you sure?*
Bobby: *Yes! It's true!*
Lisa: *Good, because you should tell the truth. Look at the poster. It says, "Don't lie." Always tell the truth.*
Bobby: *I know.*
Mom: *What else is going to make our home happy, then?*
Lisa: *Well, we have to offer to help with the chores and always share our candy!*
Mom: *That sounds good.*
Bobby: *I'm going to eat all my candy now!*
Mom: *Bobby! No!*
Bobby: *I was joking, Mom. Look—it says you should laugh at my jokes.*
Lisa: *But that wasn't funny.*
Bobby: *Yes, it was!*
Mom: *OK, you two. Should we agree to disagree?*
Lisa: *Ha, ha. OK, yes, and I love you, Mom!*
Mom: *You too, kids! You should say "I love you," every day.*

Answers

✔ *by:* 1, 2, 3, 4, 5, 7, 9, 10

2 8.1 Listen again and write the correct form of the missing verbs.

- Ask the children to study the verbs supplied. Read the sample answer. Explain that they might need to change the verb form.
- Play Track 8.1 again. The children complete the sentences. Have them compare answers with a friend, then elicit answers.

- Talk to the children about which rules they think are the most important for a happy home.

Answers

1 decided **2** argue **3** respect **4** lie, tell **5** offer, share **6** joking, laugh **7** agree, disagree

Optional activity: Rules for a happy classroom

Have the children use the rules in Activity 1 as a model to write their own rules for a happy classroom, e.g. *Respect your teacher. Share your pens.* You could have the children make posters for the wall.

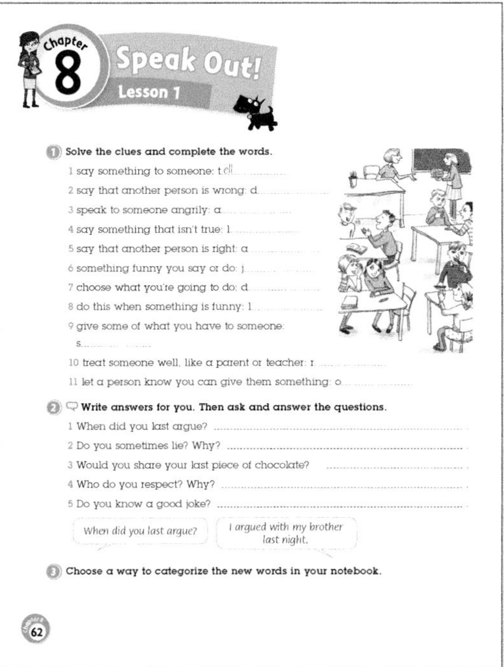

Chapter 8 Speak Out!
Lesson 1

1 Solve the clues and complete the words.

1 say something to someone: t ell
2 say that another person is wrong: d
3 speak to someone angrily: a
4 say something that isn't true: l
5 say that another person is right: a
6 something funny you say or do: j
7 choose what you're going to do: d
8 do this when something is funny: l
9 give some of what you have to someone: s
10 treat someone well, like a parent or teacher: r
11 let a person know you can give them something: o

2 Write answers for you. Then ask and answer the questions.

1 When did you last argue?
2 Do you sometimes lie? Why?
3 Would you share your last piece of chocolate?
4 Who do you respect? Why?
5 Do you know a good joke?

3 Choose a way to categorize the new words in your notebook.

62

1 Solve the clues and complete the words.

The children solve the clues and complete the words (the initial letters are given). Elicit answers.

Answers

1 tell **2** disagree **3** argue **4** lie **5** agree **6** joke **7** decide **8** laugh **9** share **10** respect **11** offer

2 Write answers for you. Then ask and answer the questions.

Elicit an example answer for each question. The children write answers for themselves, then ask and answer in pairs. Invite pairs to ask and answer for the class.

3 Choose a way to categorize the new words in your notebook.

Have the children brainstorm appropriate categories in pairs. Prompt as necessary, e.g. *positive/negative verbs, using sketches to illustrate the meaning of each word, alphabetical order.* The children choose the best categories for them and list the words in their notebook.

Answers

Children's own answers.

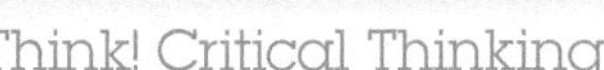

Cooler: Disappearing text

Write on the board, e.g. *Don't argue with your brothers or sisters.* Erase one word and have the children repeat the rule. Continue in this way, erasing another word each time until the children can say the whole rule from memory. Repeat with other rules.

Competency Focus

Think! Critical Thinking

The children use critical thinking skills to understand the new vocabulary by using visual clues and processing the written and spoken forms.

Digital Resources

Student eBook • Look at the sentence openings in SB Activity 1, showing just the first word or two. Elicit the rules in full.

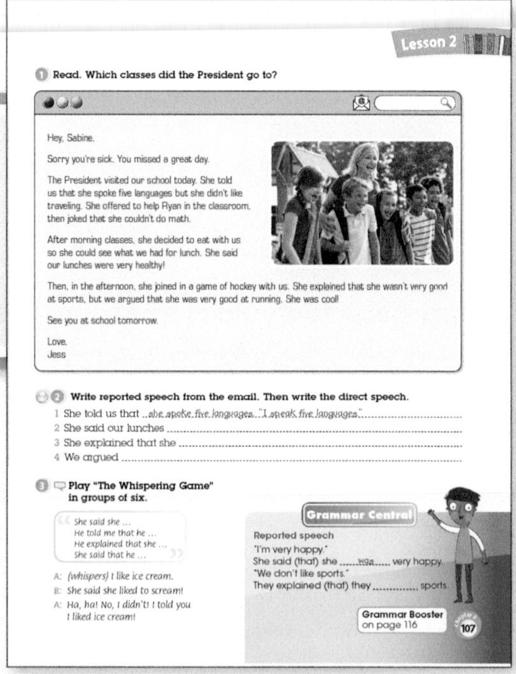

Lesson 2

1 Read. Which classes did the President go to?

Hey, Sabine,

Sorry you're sick. You missed a great day.

The President visited our school today. She told us that she spoke five languages but she didn't like traveling. She offered to help Ryan in the classroom, then joked that she couldn't do math.

After morning classes, she decided to eat with us so she could see what we had for lunch. She said our lunches were very healthy!

Then, in the afternoon, she joined in a game of hockey with us. She explained that she wasn't very good at sports, but we argued that she was very good at running. She was cool!

See you at school tomorrow.

Love,
Jess

2 Write reported speech from the email. Then write the direct speech.

1 She told us that she spoke five languages. "I speak five languages."
2 She said our lunches ...
3 She explained that she ...
4 We argued ...

3 Play "The Whispering Game" in groups of six.

She said she …
He told me that he …
He explained that she …
She said that he …

A: *(whispers) I like ice cream.*
B: *She said she liked to scream!*
A: *Ha, ha! No, I didn't! I told you I liked ice cream!*

Grammar Central

Reported speech
"I'm very happy."
She said (that) she was very happy.
"We don't like sports."
They explained (that) they ... sports.

Grammar Booster on page 116

107

Grammar

Lesson objective: report what people say
Key grammar: reported speech—statements
Secondary language: *President, joined in*
Materials: Grammar Worksheet 8A [TRC printout] (optional)

Warmer: Positive or negative?

Write the reporting verbs from Lesson 1 on the board. The children decide if each verb has a positive or negative meaning. (positive: *agree, share, laugh, offer, respect* / negative: *argue, disagree, lie*) Elicit sentences with them.

1 Read. Which lessons did the President go to?

- Ask *Who's visiting the school?* Then ask them to read the email fairly quickly and find which lessons the President went to. (*math, P.E.*)

Grammar Central

Reported speech

Have the children complete the grammar examples. Elicit answers. Elicit the rules for changing direct to reported speech (*reporting verb + main verb* → *past tense; I* → *she/ he*, etc.). They write further examples in their notebook with *to be* and *can*. For extra practice, try the **Grammar Booster** section in the Student Book (p. 116).

Answers p. 116

Activity 1: **1** loved **2** wasn't **3** liked **4** lived

Activity 2: **1** that he played on the basketball team at his school. **2** that his best friend's name is Sarah. **3** that strawberry was her favorite flavor of ice cream. **4** that she could speak English and Spanish. **5** that they lived with their grandparents. **6** that their birthday was in June.

2 Write examples of reported speech from the email. Then write the direct speech.

- The children underline the reporting verbs in the text and complete the reported speech sentences. They then write the direct speech versions. Elicit answers.

Answers

1 She told us that she spoke five languages. "I speak five languages." **2** She said our lunches were very healthy! "Your lunches are very healthy." **3** She explained that she wasn't very good at sports. "I'm not very good at sports." **4** We argued that she was very good at running. "You're very good at running."

3 Play "The Whispering Game" in groups of six.

- Choose two children to read the example dialogue.
- Divide the class into groups of six. The first child whispers a sentence to the second child. The second child passes it on in the same way. After the sixth child hears it, they report the sentence.
- Give the groups five minutes to transfer as many sentences as possible in this way. How many got through correctly?

Optional activity: Let's gossip!

Divide the class into pairs or groups. Tell them they are going to talk and gossip about a famous person they know. Tell them to say four pieces of information about the person, e.g. *He has ten cars. He doesn't like pizza.* Ask children to report their gossip to the class, e.g. *He/She said Ronaldo had ten cars.*

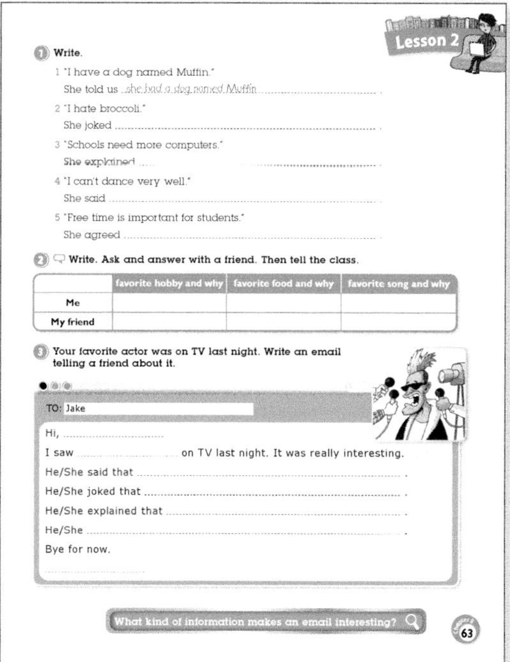

Lesson 2

1 Write.

1 "I have a dog named Muffin."
She told us she had a dog named Muffin.

2 "I hate broccoli."
She joked

3 "Schools need more computers."
She explained

4 "I can't dance very well."
She said

5 "Free time is important for students."
She agreed

2 Write. Ask and answer with a friend. Then tell the class.

	favorite hobby and why	favorite food and why	favorite song and why
Me			
My friend			

3 Your favorite actor was on TV last night. Write an email telling a friend about it.

TO: Jake

Hi,
I saw ... on TV last night. It was really interesting.
He/She said that
He/She joked that
He/She explained that
He/She
Bye for now.

What kind of information makes an email interesting?

63

1 Write.

The children re-write the direct speech as reported speech. They compare with a friend. Elicit answers.

Answers

1 (that) she had a dog named Muffin.
2 (that) she hated broccoli.
3 (that) schools needed more computers.
4 (that) she couldn't dance very well.
5 (that) free time was important for students.

2 Write. Ask and answer with a friend. Then tell the class.

The children note their own answers in the chart. They then ask a friend and complete their answers. Elicit responses.

3 Your favorite actor was on TV last night. Write an email telling a friend about it.

The children write an email about what a favourite actor said in an interview, then compare with a friend. Elicit responses. Ask *What kind of information makes an email interesting?* (*any unusual or personal information that tells us more about a person*)

Answers

Children's own answers.

Cooler: Presidential visit

Have the children imagine that the President or head of their country visited their school yesterday and spoke to them. Ask them to report what he/she said, e.g. *He told us our school was very good.*

Competency Focus

Learn

By reading the text and identifying examples of reported speech, the children demonstrate their understanding of the new grammatical structures.

Digital Resources

Student eBook • When you are focusing on the new structure in SB Grammar Central, have children use *Highlighter* to identify reported speech in SB Activity 1.

Student eBook, Digital Activity Book • TIP As you monitor the children's progress, use *Add personal note* to keep a note of weaknesses in vocabulary, grammar, or pronunciation so you can review in later lessons.

Teacher Resource Center • For extra grammar practice, print out Grammar Worksheet 8A.

Reading: Story Extract

Lesson objectives: ask about words in other languages; use the title and pictures to predict story content; read the extract from the fantasy adventure *Gulliver in Lilliput* (beginning)

Functional language: *How do you say … in …? It's … Sorry. What did you say? I said it was …*

Secondary language: *tied, appeared, arrows, chained, afraid*

Materials: Tracks 8.2 and 8.3

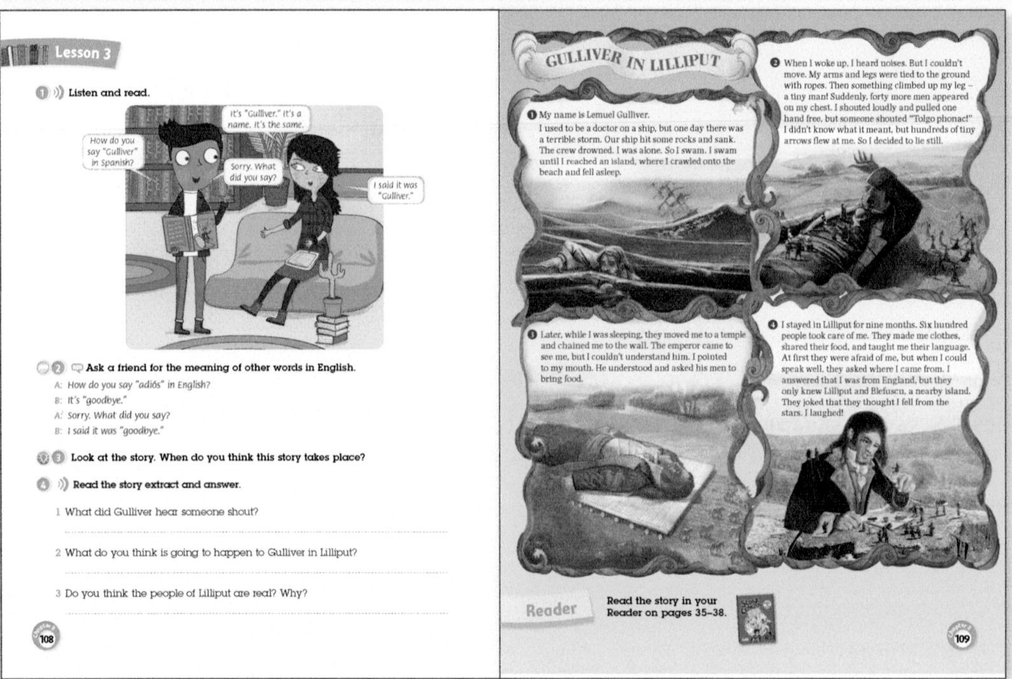

Lesson 3

1 Listen and read.

How do you say "Gulliver" in Spanish?
It's "Gulliver." It's a name. It's the same.
Sorry. What did you say?
I said it was "Gulliver."

2 Ask a friend for the meaning of other words in English.

A: *How do you say "adiós" in English?*
B: *It's "goodbye."*
A: *Sorry. What did you say?*
B: *I said it was "goodbye."*

3 Look at the story. When do you think this story takes place?

4 Read the story extract and answer.

1 What did Gulliver hear someone shout?

2 What do you think is going to happen to Gulliver in Lilliput?

3 Do you think the people of Lilliput are real? Why?

108

GULLIVER IN LILLIPUT

1 My name is Lemuel Gulliver.
I used to be a doctor on a ship, but one day there was a terrible storm. Our ship hit some rocks and sank. The crew drowned. I was alone. So I swam. I swam until I reached an island, where I crawled onto the beach and fell asleep.

2 When I woke up, I heard noises. But I couldn't move. My arms and legs were tied to the ground with ropes. Then something climbed up my leg – a tiny man! Suddenly, forty more men appeared on my chest. I shouted loudly and pulled one hand free, but someone shouted "Tolgo phonac!" I didn't know what it meant, but hundreds of tiny arrows flew at me. So I decided to lie still.

3 Later, while I was sleeping, they moved me to a temple and chained me to the wall. The emperor came to see me, but I couldn't understand him. I pointed to my mouth. He understood and asked his men to bring food.

4 I stayed in Lilliput for nine months. Six hundred people took care of me. They made me clothes, shared their food, and taught me their language. At first they were afraid of me, but when I could speak well, they asked where I came from. I answered that I was from England, but they only knew Lilliput and Blefuscu, a nearby island. They joked that they thought I fell from the stars. I laughed!

Reader

Read the story in your Reader on pages 35–38.

109

Warmer: Imagine a giant

Tell the children they are going to read a story about a giant. Ask if they know any stories/movies about giants. Ask *What problems would you have as a giant?*

Functional language

1 8.2 Listen and read.

- Play Track 8.2. The children listen and read along.
- Play Track 8.2 again for them to repeat.
- Divide the class into pairs to practice the dialogue.

2 Ask a friend for the meaning of other words in English.

- Choose two children to read the example dialogue.
- The children practice in pairs using the prompts supplied and adding details. Encourage them to replace *adiós* with a different word. Have pairs do a dialogue for the class.

Before reading

3 Look at the story. When do you think this story takes place?

- Have the children study the pictures. Ask *What are Gulliver's clothes like?* Then ask them to guess which time the story is set. (*18th century*) Provide some years as prompts if children are struggling, e.g. *1750, 1970, 1230.*

Answers

Children's own answers.

4 8.3 Read the story extract and answer.

- Have the children read the extract and answer question 1.
- Play Track 8.3. The children listen and complete their ideas for questions 2 and 3.
- Elicit answers, but do not confirm predictions: explain that they will have to read the story to find out.

Answers

1 "Tolgo phonac!" **2** & **3** Children's own answers.

Lesson 3

1 Write another correct word. Then choose, complete, and act out.

disagree / respect / argue / ....

How / you / say "..................." in ....?

It's ....

Sorry! What / you / say?

I said it was "...................."

2 Read the story in your Student Book. Circle the words that describe the story. Then check (✓) the story type.

travel funny strange creatures historical imaginary horror unusual place true

fantasy adventure ☐ factual biography ☐ comedy ☐

3 Write answers.

1 Why can't Gulliver move when he wakes up? ...He's tied with rope...

2 How does he feel? ....

3 What's Gulliver doing when they take him to the temple? ....

4 Where do the little people say Gulliver is from? ....

4 How did Gulliver travel to Lilliput? Check (✓) the correct options.

I, Lemuel Gulliver, ...

☐ *walked.* ☐ *fell from the stars.*

☐ *sailed in a ship.* ☐ *swam in the ocean.*

☐ *flew by helicopter.* ☐ *arrived by taxi.*

64

1 Write another correct word. Then choose, complete, and act out.

The children think of another reporting verb. They then complete and act out the dialogue in pairs. Encourage the children to use what they know to adapt and extend the dialogue. Have pairs act out their dialogue for the class.

2 Read the story in your Student Book. Circle the words that describe the story. Then check (✔) the story type.

The children read the Student Book story extract again, then circle any words which describe it. They check the story type. Elicit answers.

Answers

Circled: travel, strange creatures, historical, imaginary, unusual place

✔ *by* fantasy adventure

3 Write answers.

The children answer the comprehension questions. Elicit answers.

Answers

1 He's tied with rope. **2** He feels surprised/frightened. **3** He's sleeping. **4** They say he's from the stars.

4 How did Gulliver travel to Lilliput? Check (✔) the correct options.

Elicit answers for how Gulliver traveled to Lilliput. Remind the children that they can check more than one answer.

Answers

✓ *by* sailed in a ship. *and* swam in the ocean.

Cooler: Play "The Shark Game"

Play the game using sentences from the story, e.g. *Later, while I was sleeping, they moved me to a temple and chained me to the wall.* (see Games Bank p. 19).

Competency Focus

Collaborate and Communicate

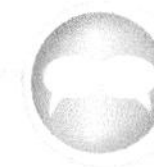

The children work together, putting into practice new functional language by acting out a realistic dialogue.

Think! Critical Thinking

By analyzing visual clues and deducing from the context, the children use prediction skills to help them engage with the story.

Digital Resources

Student eBook • For SB Activity 3, have children use *Pen* to circle clues to the answer in the story extract pictures. (*the style of the ship and Gulliver's clothes*) Ask *Is this a story about real life?* Elicit ideas, with reasons.

Student eBook, Digital Activity Book • TIP Give children the opportunity to be your assistant! Choose a child to be responsible for choosing the relevant buttons (e.g. to go to the next activity).

1
My name is Lemuel Gulliver.

I used to be a doctor on a ship, but one day there was a terrible storm. Our ship hit some rocks and sank. The crew drowned. I was alone. So I swam. I swam until I reached an island, where I crawled onto the beach and fell asleep.

2
When I woke up, I heard noises. But I couldn't move. My arms and legs were tied to the ground with ropes. Then something climbed up my leg—a tiny man! Suddenly, forty more men appeared on my chest. I shouted loudly and pulled one hand free, but someone shouted "Tolgo phonac!" I didn't know what it meant, but hundreds of tiny arrows flew at me. So I decided to lie still.

3
Later, while I was sleeping, they moved me to a temple and chained me to the wall. The emperor came to see me, but I couldn't understand him. I pointed to my mouth. He understood and asked his men to bring food.

4
I stayed in Lilliput for nine months. Six hundred people took care of me. They made me clothes, shared their food, and taught me their language. At first they were afraid of me, but when I could speak well, they asked where I came from. I answered that I was from England, but they only knew Lilliput and Blefuscu, a nearby island. They joked that they thought I fell from the stars. I laughed!

5
I asked the emperor to set me free. He told me to be patient. Then he asked me to agree to some rules. I respected him so I agreed, and he told his men to release me.

6
He explained that Lilliput was at war with Blefuscu. Lilliputians argued that eggs should be broken at the small end, but Blefuscudians disagreed. They broke theirs at the big end. They just couldn't agree. He wanted me to capture the Blefuscudian ships. I did this and pulled them back to Lilliput. It wasn't easy; I was attacked with arrows along the way.

7
Then the emperor wanted to capture the Blefuscudian people. I couldn't agree with this and didn't offer to help. He became angry. I knew I was in danger and needed to escape, so I swam to Blefuscu where I found an old boat. Thousands of Blefuscudians helped me drag it onto the beach and repair it. Finally, the boat was ready. They gave me animals for food, and I sailed away.

8
After two days, I saw your ship. You asked where I came from. I told you my story, but you didn't believe me. Here are some tiny animals from Blefuscu. Now do you believe me?

I am Lemuel Gulliver, and this is the truth.

Lesson objective: read and understand the fantasy adventure *Gulliver in Lilliput* in the Reader
Materials: Track 8.4; Reader

Warmer: Fantasy stories

Ask children to recap the story extract from the last lesson. Elicit similarities and differences between this story and *Down the Rabbit Hole*. Ask *How do you think Alice would feel in Lilliput?*

Story Summary

Gulliver, a doctor on a ship, washes up on a beach in Lilliput. The local people, who are very small, capture him, but then Gulliver makes friends with them. Lilliput is at war and he helps the emperor. Then Gulliver escapes and travels home.

Theme: appreciating that we are all different

Track 8.4 While reading

- Have the children look at the pictures in the Reader. Elicit the places (*Lilliput and Blefuscu*).
- Play Track 8.4. The children listen and read along. Ask *What did Gulliver bring from Blefuscu to prove he was there? (tiny animals)*
- Ask questions to check comprehension, e.g. *What did Gulliver ask the emperor? (to set him free) What rules did the emperor make for Gulliver? (Do not leave Lilliput. Do not squash people., etc.)*
- Have the class read the story aloud, with children taking turns reading. Alternatively, choose a scene to update and act out (see **Story Time**).

After reading: Reflect

- Ask questions to give the children the opportunity to think about the issues raised by the story, e.g. *What do the people of Lilliput and Blefuscu think of each other? Do you think the emperor was a kind person?*

Optional activity: Story summary

Summarize the story, pausing for the children to complete, e.g. *Gulliver was a … on a ship which …*, etc.

Story Time

Updating story contexts

Adapting the story to bring it up to date and more relevant to the children helps increase understanding. Have the children invent a new giant dressed in modern clothes and suggest a place for him to visit. Ask them to imagine a new scene and say what happens to him.

Reading Strategy

Story Map

Using a Story Map helps the children identify the characters of a story and the parts of the plot as well as the setting, problem, and solution. A basic story map focuses on the main parts of the story (beginning, middle, and end).

For additional explanation and activities, see the Literacy Handbook on the Teacher Resource Center.

Cooler: Act out a story scene

In groups, have the children choose a paragraph from the story (or allocate scenes to different groups). They prepare their mime/actions for the scene. Ask different groups to act out their scene for the class.

Digital Resources

Reader eBook • Show the Reader story one picture at a time as you play the audio. Before moving on each time, elicit what is going to happen next.

• For the Cooler, have the groups prepare their scene in secret, then act it out for the others to identify where it comes in the story. The first team to identify the scene chooses a team member to use *Pen* to circle the correct scene in the Reader.

Reading Comprehension and Critical Literacy

Lesson objectives: understand and evaluate the story; relate story theme to personal experience; write reported speech
Materials: Track 8.4; Reader

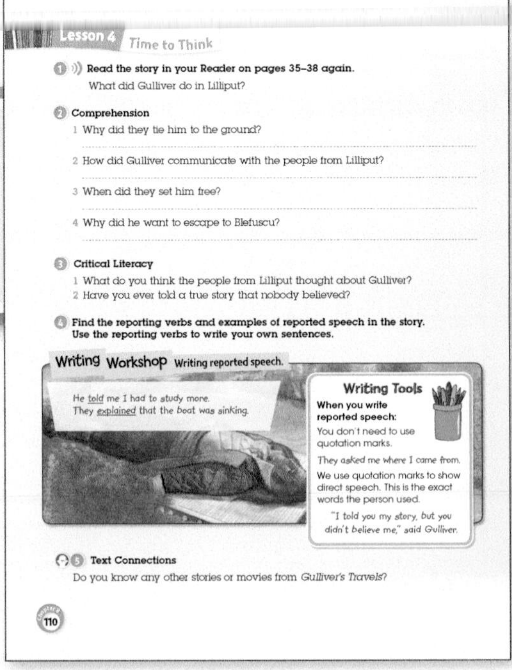
Lesson 4 Time to Think

1 Read the story in your Reader on pages 35–38 again.
What did Gulliver do in Lilliput?

2 Comprehension
1 Why did they tie him to the ground?
2 How did Gulliver communicate with the people from Lilliput?
3 When did they set him free?
4 Why did he want to escape to Blefuscu?

3 Critical Literacy
1 What do you think the people from Lilliput thought about Gulliver?
2 Have you ever told a true story that nobody believed?

4 Find the reporting verbs and examples of reported speech in the story. Use the reporting verbs to write your own sentences.

Writing Workshop Writing reported speech.

He told me I had to study more.
They explained that the boat was sinking.

Writing Tools
When you write reported speech:
You don't need to use quotation marks.
They asked me where I came from.
We use quotation marks to show direct speech. This is the exact words the person used.
"I told you my story, but you didn't believe me," said Gulliver.

5 Text Connections
Do you know any other stories or movies from *Gulliver's Travels*?

110

Note: Please ensure that your class has read the Reader story before you do this lesson.

Warmer: Story recap

Write key events from the story in random order and have the children re-order them, e.g. *Gulliver's ship sank. He swam to Lilliput. The people tied him up. The emperor wanted him to capture people.*

1 8.4 Read the story in your Reader.

- Have the children read the story. (Alternatively, play Track 8.4 and have them read along.) Elicit whether they were correct in their predictions in Lesson 3 Activity 4.
- Have them write the things Gulliver did in Lilliput. Elicit answers. (*He learned to speak Lilliputian/captured Blefuscudian ships.*)

2 Comprehension

- Ask the children to look at the first question and consider how the people in Lilliput felt when Gulliver arrived.
- The children then find answers to the other questions. Elicit answers. Ask *What kind of character is Gulliver?*

Answers

1 They were scared of him./They thought he was dangerous. **2** He used his hands/pointed to communicate. **3** They set him free when he agreed with the emperor's rules. **4** Gulliver knew he was in danger./The emperor was angry with him.

3 Critical Literacy

- Say *Imagine you lived in Lilliput. What did you think about Gulliver? How did your feelings about him change?* Empathizing with the characters is a very effective way to engage with the story.
- Ask *Have you ever told a true story that people didn't believe?* Elicit examples. Linking the story to their own experience helps the children appreciate its broader relevance.

Writing Workshop

Writing reported speech

4 Find the reporting verbs and examples of reported speech in the story. Use the reporting verbs to write your own sentences.

Have a child read the example. Read the **Writing Tools** box together. The children underline examples of reported speech. They write two new sentences using reporting verbs in their notebook, then compare in pairs. Elicit sentences.

Answers

Children's own answers.

5 Text Connections 

- Write *Books and Movies* on the board. Elicit versions of the Gulliver story (or movies/stories about a giant) that the children have read or seen. Elicit differences and similarities.

Optional activity: Interview Gulliver

Divide the class into pairs to ask and answer three questions as an interview with Gulliver back in England. Ask pairs to act out their interview for the class. Then have the children report back to the class using reported speech, e.g. *He told me … He explained that …*

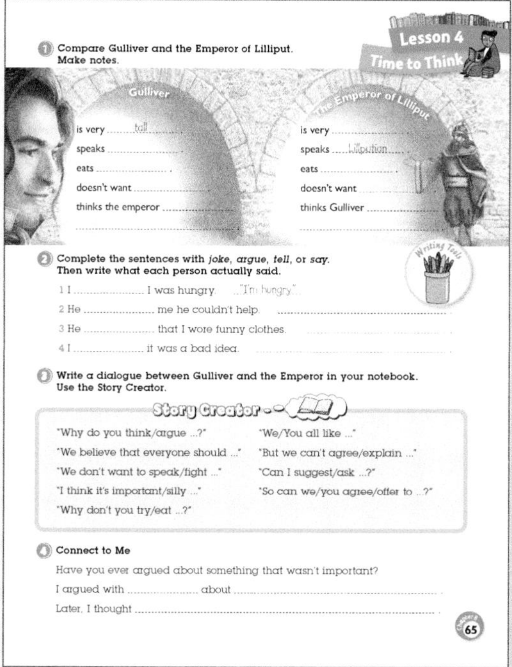

Lesson 4
Time to Think

1 Compare Gulliver and the Emperor of Lilliput. Make notes.

Gulliver
is very ......tall......
speaks ....
eats ....
doesn't want ....
thinks the emperor ....

The Emperor of Lilliput
is very ....
speaks ....Lilliputian....
eats ....
doesn't want ....
thinks Gulliver ....

2 Complete the sentences with *joke*, *argue*, *tell*, or *say*. Then write what each person actually said.

1 I .... I was hungry. ..."I'm hungry."...
2 He .... me he couldn't help. ....
3 He .... that I wore funny clothes. ....
4 I .... it was a bad idea. ....

3 Write a dialogue between Gulliver and the Emperor in your notebook. Use the Story Creator.

Story Creator

"Why do you think/argue ...?"
"We believe that everyone should ..."
"We don't want to speak/fight ..."
"I think it's important/silly ..."
"Why don't you try/eat ...?"
"We/You all like ..."
"But we can't agree/explain ..."
"Can I suggest/ask ...?"
"So can we/you agree/offer to ...?"

4 Connect to Me

Have you ever argued about something that wasn't important?
I argued with .... about ....
Later, I thought ....

65

1 Compare Gulliver and the Emperor of Lilliput. Make notes.

The children complete the notes describing Gulliver and the Emperor of Lilliput. Elicit ideas.

Answers

Children's own answers.

2 Complete the sentences with *joke, argue, tell,* or *say.* Then write what each person actually said.

The children complete the sentences, using the reporting verbs in the simple past. They then change the reported
sentence to direct speech. Remind them to use speech marks. Elicit answers.

Answers

1 said **2** told **3** joked **4** argued
1 "I'm hungry."
2 "I can't help (you)."
3 "You wear funny clothes."
4 "It's a bad idea."

3 Write a dialogue between Gulliver and the Emperor in your notebook. Use the Story Creator.

Use the **Story Creator** to elicit ideas. The children write a dialogue in their notebook, then compare with a friend. Have children act out their dialogue in pairs for the class.

4 Connect to Me

Elicit examples of times when the children have argued about something unimportant. They write their own response, then compare with a friend.

Cooler: A fantasy island

Have the children imagine a fantasy island. Prompt their imagination with questions, e.g. *Close your eyes. Imagine you are on an island. Who can you see? What are the people like? How do they greet you? How do you feel?* Ask the children to open their eyes and describe the people on the island.

Competency Focus

Me: Critical Literacy

The children use critical literacy skills to reflect on the theme of the story and relate it to their own experiences.

Digital Resources

Reader eBook • Have the children work in pairs to discuss the events of the story in the order they happened. Show the Reader. Elicit what happened in the story, and see if the children are correct.

Student eBook, Reader eBook • TIP With the answer key, you can show the answers all at once or one by one to customize feedback.

Grammar and Reading

Lesson objective: report *wh–* and *yes/no* questions
Key grammar: reported speech—questions
Secondary language: *author, spare time, get ideas*
Materials: Track 8.5; Grammar Worksheet 8B [TRC printout] (optional)

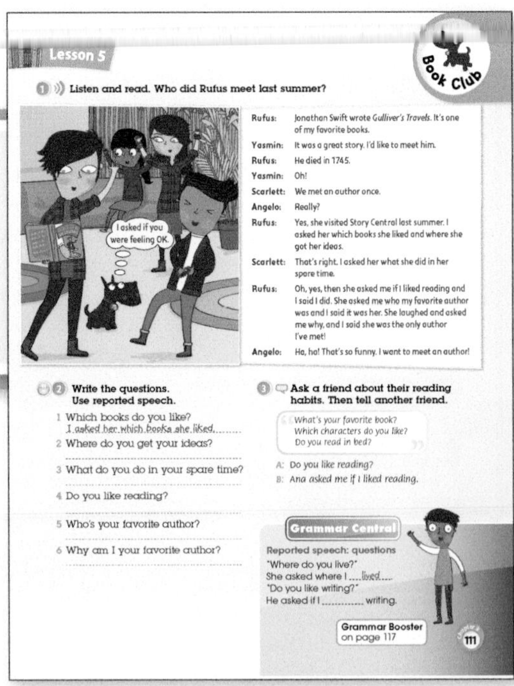
Lesson 5

Book Club

1 Listen and read. Who did Rufus meet last summer?

Rufus: Jonathan Swift wrote *Gulliver's Travels*. It's one of my favorite books.
Yasmin: It was a great story. I'd like to meet him.
Rufus: He died in 1745.
Yasmin: Oh!
Scarlett: We met an author once.
Angelo: Really?
Rufus: Yes, she visited Story Central last summer. I asked her which books she liked and where she got her ideas.
Scarlett: That's right. I asked her what she did in her spare time.
Rufus: Oh, yes, then she asked me if I liked reading and I said I did. She asked me who my favorite author was and I said it was her. She laughed and asked me why, and I said she was the only author I've met!
Angelo: Ha, ha! That's so funny. I want to meet an author!

2 Write the questions. Use reported speech.

1 Which books do you like?
I asked her which books she liked.
2 Where do you get your ideas?
3 What do you do in your spare time?
4 Do you like reading?
5 Who's your favorite author?
6 Why am I your favorite author?

3 Ask a friend about their reading habits. Then tell another friend.

"What's your favorite book?
Which characters do you like?
Do you read in bed?"

A: Do you like reading?
B: Ana asked me if I liked reading.

Grammar Central

Reported speech: questions
"Where do you live?"
She asked where I lived.
"Do you like writing?"
He asked if I ______ writing.

Grammar Booster on page 117

111

Warmer: Mini-survey

Write this question on the board: *What type of story books do you like?* Divide the class into pairs. Have the children ask and answer with a friend. Ask children to report back to the class, e.g. *He/She told me he/she liked …* Find out the most popular book type by a show of hands. Review reported speech tense shift with the class.

1 8.5 Listen and read. Who did Rufus meet last summer?

- Play Track 8.5. The children listen. Ask *Who did Rufus meet last summer? (an author)*
- Have the children look at the reported question in Hamish's thought bubble. Play Track 8.5 again and ask them to raise their hand when they hear a reported question.

2 Write the questions. 

- Have the children look at the text in Activity 1 again and underline the reported questions. Then ask them to write the reported questions. Elicit answers.
- Ask the class what the difference is reporting *wh–* questions and *yes/no* questions. Make sure they understand when to use *if*. (*when the answer is* yes *or* no)

Answers

1 I asked her which books she liked. **2** I asked her where she got her ideas. **3** I asked her what she did in her spare time. **4** She asked me if I liked reading. **5** She asked me who my favorite author was.

Grammar Central

Reported speech: questions

Have the children complete the grammar examples. Elicit answers. Elicit the rules for reporting questions. (*reporting verb + main verb → past tense; you → I/he/she*, etc.) They write further examples in their notebook. For extra practice, the **Grammar Booster** section in the Student Book (pp. 117–119).

Answers p. 117

Activity 1: **1** lived **2** liked **3** spoke **4** could

Activity 2: **1** She asked him why he wanted to learn Mandarin. **2** She asked him if he took Mandarin classes. **3** She asked him where his Mandarin classes were. **4** She asked him if he reads books in Mandarin. **5** She asked him who he spoke Mandarin with. **6** She asked him if Mandarin was difficult to learn.

p. 118

Activity 1: **1** told **2** sent **3** that **4** could **5** studied **6** wanted **7** if **8** were

Activity 2: **1** She said it was called the Teddy Bear Academy because it was a friendly place. **2** He said that he learned to introduce himself and order food. **3** She said that she wanted to visit both Portugal and Brazil. **4** They said that the teachers were great.

p. 119

Activity 1: **1** met **2** asked **3** if **4** loved **5** played **6** spoke **7** could **8** that **9** made **10** too many **11** was **12** said **13** well **14** if **15** kindly

Activity 2: Students' own answers.

3 Ask a friend about their reading habits. Then tell another friend.

- Choose two children to read the example dialogue.
- Divide the class into pairs to ask and answer about their reading habits. The children then get into different pairs and tell each other what they found out.

Optional activity: Interview an alien!

Have the class prepare questions to ask an alien, e.g. *Where do you live? Do you like . . . ? What do you eat?* Write the questions up on the board. Have the children ask and answer the questions in pairs, taking turns to act as the alien. Then have them report back to the class about their alien.

Lesson 5

1 Underline the reported questions. Then complete the direct speech.

I asked Rufus if he knew another good story about Gulliver and he told me to read one about Laputa. I asked why Laputa was a good story. He explained it was about a flying island. I asked what happened in the story. He said the Laputans knew many facts, but weren't clever. They loved to study math, but they weren't good at building houses. Then he asked me why I didn't just read the book. So I asked him why I should read it. I said that I knew the story already!

1 Do you know .... another good story about Gulliver?
2 .... Laputa a good story?
3 .... in the story?
4 .... you just read the book?
5 .... I read it?

2 Write the reported questions. Then tell a friend how the people responded.

1 I / my dad / if / likes cooking .... I asked my dad if he liked cooking.
2 I / my mom / who / her favorite actor ....
3 She / me / where / I want to go ....
4 My friend / me / what happens ....
5 He / me / which / soccer team / like ....

I asked my dad if he liked cooking. He explained that he didn't because he always burned the food!

3 Write about a conversation with a friend.

A: Are you going to .... ? B: ....
A: Can I .... ? B: ....

My friend asked me .... He/She asked if ....
I told him/her that .... I said that ....

66

1 Underline the reported questions. Then complete the direct speech.

The children underline the reported questions. They then complete the direct speech versions. Elicit answers.

Answers

Underlined—sentences beginning:
I asked Rufus . . ., I asked why . . ., I asked what . . ., Then he asked me . . ., So I asked him . . .
1 Do you know **2** Why is **3** What happens **4** Why don't **5** Why should

2 Write the reported questions. Then tell a friend how the people responded.

Write the first sentence frame on the board and have the class make the reported question. Then ask them to write the other questions individually. Elicit answers. The children ask and answer in pairs, imagining the answers from their family or friends.

Answers

1 I asked my dad if he liked cooking. **2** I asked my mom who her favorite actor was. **3** She asked me where I wanted to go. **4** My friend asked me what happened. **5** He asked me which soccer team I liked.

3 Write about a conversation with a friend.

Have the children complete the questions and answers, then complete the reported sentences. Elicit answers.

Answers

Children's own answers.

Cooler: Scrambled sentences

Write up one of the reported questions from the lesson on the board with the words randomly arranged. Give the class time to make a sentence. Then ask children to write the question one word at a time on the board. Repeat with other questions.

Competency Focus

Learn

The children demonstrate their understanding of the new language by reading the text and completing the activity.

Digital Resources

Student eBook • Have children use *Highlighter* to identify the reported speech in SB Activity 1 (e.g. *I asked her which books she liked.*). Each time elicit what the person actually said, i.e. the direct speech used (e.g. *Which books do you like?*).

Digital Activity Book • Have children use *Pen* to underline the reported speech in the AB Activity 1 text.

Teacher Resource Center • For extra grammar practice, print out Grammar Worksheet 8B.

Vocabulary, Song, and Spelling

Lesson objectives: identify and use words to do with language and communication; practice spelling words ending with silent *–e*

Key vocabulary: *accent, body language, mean, pronounce, repeat, signs, smile, translate, understand*

Secondary language: *clearly, sense*

Materials: Track 8.6; Phonics Worksheet 8 [TRC printout] (optional)

Lesson 6

Song

1 Listen and sing. Which language can everyone understand?

2 Talk to a friend. Do these speaking activities.

1 Repeat this five times:

"Red leather, yellow leather, red leather, yellow leather."

2 Translate "body language" into your language.
3 Say something in a funny accent.
4 Make a sign for "sunny".
5 Pronounce "communication" correctly.
6 Smile. Is your friend smiling, too?

Spelling Central

Circle the words in the song that end in -e. Can you hear this letter? How do you pronounce this?

Write the words in the chart. Can you add more words that end in silent -e?

words ending in silent -e
language

112

Warmer: Pre-teach vocabulary

Pre-teach the vocabulary by giving definitions or sentences showing the words in context, e.g. *He's from the US.—He speaks English with an American accent. "Repeat" means to do something again.* Repeat the definitions/sentences, pausing to elicit the key word.

1 8.6 Listen and sing. Which language can everyone understand?

- Play Track 8.6 and ask the children to focus on the highlighted words. Ask *Which language can everyone understand? (smiling)*
- Play Track 8.6 again for the children to sing along.
- Practice the new vocabulary by saying *Translate the word "dog" into your language. Show me a sign for "yes." Give me an example of body language.*

2 Talk to a friend. Do these speaking activities.

- Write the tongue twister supplied on the board and say it slowly. Have the children repeat. Then choose children to say it faster!
- Divide the class into pairs and have them follow the instructions for the other language-related activities.

Spelling Central

Silent –e

Write *language* on the board and underline the silent *–e*. Have the children circle other words in the song with silent *–e* at the end. Then ask them to complete the chart. Ask the children to suggest more words with silent *–e* (e.g. *online, Japanese, awake*, etc.). Provide definition clues as necessary.

Answers

Circled: language, translate, have, nice, take, time, pronounce, use, sense, smile, same

Optional activity: Tricky tongue twisters

Write other tongue twisters on the board and have fun pronouncing them, e.g.

She sells sea shells by the sea shore.

Three free throws.

A big black bug bit a big black dog on his big black nose.

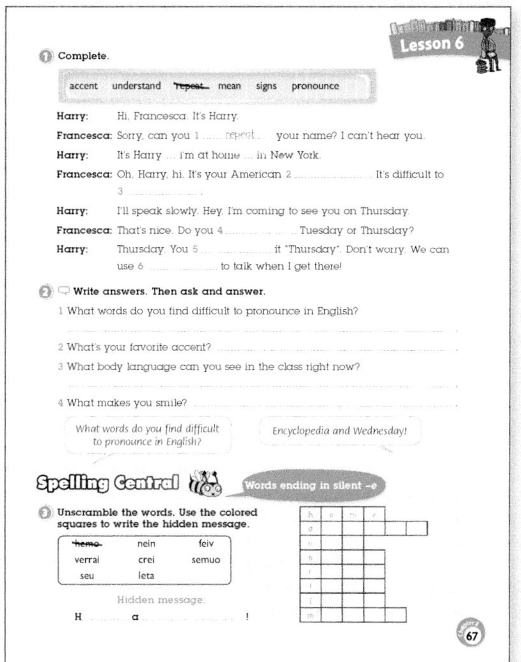

Lesson 6

1 Complete.

accent understand ~~repeat~~ mean signs pronounce

Harry: Hi, Francesca. It's Harry.
Francesca: Sorry, can you 1 ....repeat.... your name? I can't hear you.
Harry: It's Harry ... I'm at home ... in New York.
Francesca: Oh, Harry, hi. It's your American 2 .... It's difficult to 3 ....
Harry: I'll speak slowly. Hey, I'm coming to see you on Thursday.
Francesca: That's nice. Do you 4 .... Tuesday or Thursday?
Harry: Thursday. You 5 .... it "Thursday". Don't worry. We can use 6 .... to talk when I get there!

2 **Write answers. Then ask and answer.**

1 What words do you find difficult to pronounce in English?

2 What's your favorite accent?

3 What body language can you see in the class right now?

4 What makes you smile?

What words do you find difficult to pronounce in English?

Encyclopedia and Wednesday!

Spelling Central Words ending in silent *-e*

3 **Unscramble the words. Use the colored squares to write the hidden message.**

~~hemo~~ nein feiv
verrai crei semuo
seu leta

Hidden message:

H .... a .... !

h	o	m	e		
a					
u					
n					
r					
l					
f					
m					

67

Cooler: Play "Finger Spelling"

Divide your class into pairs. The children take turns writing simple words on their friend's back using one finger, letter by letter, for their friend to guess. Tell them to choose simple words, e.g. colors, nouns.

Competency Focus

Collaborate and communicate

The children work together in pairs and use their interpersonal skills to share their ideas on the topic, incorporating the new vocabulary.

1 Complete.

The children complete the dialogue, using the words supplied. Elicit answers.

Answers

1 repeat **2** accent **3** understand **4** mean **5** pronounce **6** signs

2 Write answers. Then ask and answer. 

Elicit answers to each of the questions. The children write their own answer. They then ask and answer in pairs. Have pairs ask and answer for the class.

Answers

Children's own answers.

3 Unscramble the words. Use the colored squares to write the hidden message.

To practice the **Spelling Central** feature, the children unscramble the words and write them in the correct place in the puzzle. Explain the letters in the message are in the order they appear in the puzzle. They use the letters in the blue squares to complete the hidden message. Give support as necessary: tell them to start by looking for words with the right number of letters and to fill in the message as they go. When they start to see what the message is, that will help them with the final words in the puzzle. Elicit answers.

Answers

home, arrive, use, nine, rice, late, five, mouse
Message: Have a nice time!

Digital Resources

Student eBook • After SB Activity 2, play Music Video 8.1 and encourage the children to sing along, using the graphic lyrics on screen. Pause the video for the children to continue singing.

- Remind the children they can access Music Video 8.1 at home to show their family and practice the song.

Teacher Resource Center • For phonics practice, print out Phonics Worksheet 8.

CLIL: Math—World language statistics

Lesson objective: find out about world language facts
Materials: CLIL Graphic Organizer 8 [TRC printout] (optional); set of quiz questions (optional); map of world for copying or photocopies of map of world (Activity Book A3)

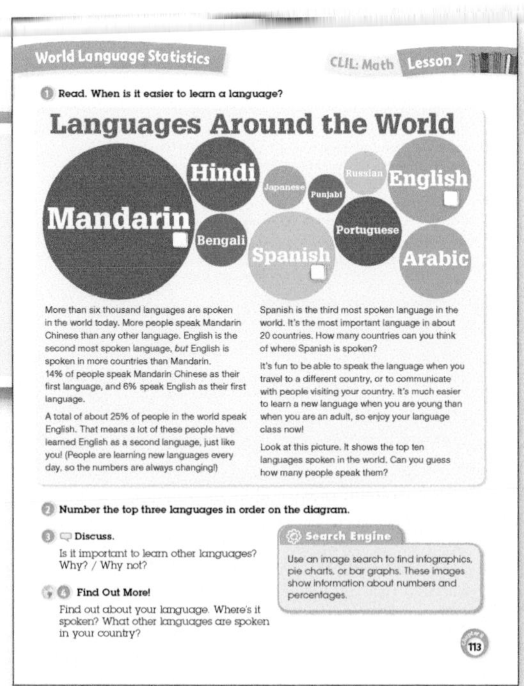

World Language Statistics

CLIL: Math Lesson 7

1 Read. When is it easier to learn a language?

Languages Around the World

More than six thousand languages are spoken in the world today. More people speak Mandarin Chinese than any other language. English is the second most spoken language, *but* English is spoken in more countries than Mandarin. 14% of people speak Mandarin Chinese as their first language, and 6% speak English as their first language.

A total of about 25% of people in the world speak English. That means a lot of these people have learned English as a second language, just like you! (People are learning new languages every day, so the numbers are always changing!)

Spanish is the third most spoken language in the world. It's the most important language in about 20 countries. How many countries can you think of where Spanish is spoken?

It's fun to be able to speak the language when you travel to a different country, or to communicate with people visiting your country. It's much easier to learn a new language when you are young than when you are an adult, so enjoy your language class now!

Look at this picture. It shows the top ten languages spoken in the world. Can you guess how many people speak them?

2 Number the top three languages in order on the diagram.

3 Discuss.

Is it important to learn other languages? Why? / Why not?

4 Find Out More!

Find out about your language. Where's it spoken? What other languages are spoken in your country?

Search Engine

Use an image search to find infographics, pie charts, or bar graphs. These images show information about numbers and percentages.

113

Warmer: Brainstorm languages

Have the children write down as many languages as they can in pairs. Give a time limit of two minutes. Then ask children to read their lists. Write up languages on the board and practice pronunciation/stress patterns, e.g. *Chinese*. Ask children to guess and put in order the three languages spoken by the most people. Do not confirm the answer.

1 Read. When is it easier to learn a language?

- Have the children read the text.
- Ask *How many people speak English as their first language?* (*6%*) Ask *When is it easier to learn a language?* (*when you are young*)

2 Number the top three languages in order on the diagram.

- Ask the children to look at the texts in Activity 1 and numbers of speakers again. Have the children number the top three languages in order. Elicit answers.

Answers

1 Mandarin Chinese **2** English **3** Spanish

3 Discuss. 

- Ask *Is it important to learn other languages?* Ask the children to give their opinions and reasons.
- Have the children imagine they are going to visit another country where they do not know the language. Ask *How will you communicate?*

4 Find Out More! 

- The children research where their own language is spoken and what other languages are spoken in their country. The **Search Engine** feature gives support on where to look. The children will need to complete this research before doing the follow-up activity in the Activity Book. (It could be set as homework.)

Optional activity: Have a languages quiz

Prepare some quiz questions about different countries/languages, e.g. *What languages are spoken in Canada?* (*English and French*) Divide the class into teams. Ask quiz questions to each team in turn. Award points for each correct answer.

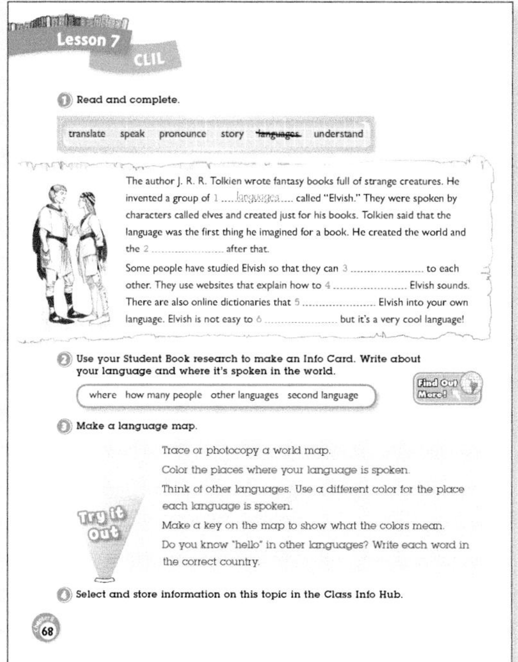

Lesson 7 CLIL

1 Read and complete.

translate speak pronounce story ~~languages~~ understand

The author J. R. R. Tolkien wrote fantasy books full of strange creatures. He invented a group of 1 ....languages.... called "Elvish." They were spoken by characters called elves and created just for his books. Tolkien said that the language was the first thing he imagined for a book. He created the world and the 2 .... after that.

Some people have studied Elvish so that they can 3 .... to each other. They use websites that explain how to 4 .... Elvish sounds. There are also online dictionaries that 5 .... Elvish into your own language. Elvish is not easy to 6 .... but it's a very cool language!

2 Use your Student Book research to make an Info Card. Write about your language and where it's spoken in the world.

where how many people other languages second language

Find Out More!

3 Make a language map.

Try it Out

Trace or photocopy a world map.

Color the places where your language is spoken.

Think of other languages. Use a different color for the place each language is spoken.

Make a key on the map to show what the colors mean.

Do you know "hello" in other languages? Write each word in the correct country.

4 Select and store information on this topic in the Class Info Hub.

68

1 Read and complete.

Write *Tolkien* on the board and elicit any stories he wrote. (*The Lord of the Rings, The Hobbit*) Explain that Tolkien invented languages for some characters. Pre-teach *elves* using the picture. The children read and complete the text using the words supplied. Elicit answers.

Answers

1 languages **2** story **3** speak **4** pronounce **5** translate **6** understand

2 Use your Student Book research to make an Info Card. Write about your language and where it's spoken in the world.

Divide the class into groups. Have the children pool the information they learned from their research in the Student Book and the Activity Book. They write about and illustrate their ideas individually. Have the groups present their Info Cards to the class.

Answers

Children's own answers.

3 Make a language map.

Provide a model map of the world for the children to copy or trace, or give each child a photocopy. They follow the **Try It Out** instructions, coloring it to show different language use, then write *hello* in different languages in the appropriate countries. Give help as necessary with spelling. Children present their maps to the class.

4 Select and store information on this topic in the Class Info Hub.

Have the children vote for the most interesting Info Cards and language maps. Archive these in your Class Hub (see p. 41) in a folder called **Chapter 8 Language Around the World**.

Cooler: Fun with languages

Elicit examples of *hello* in another language. Then challenge the children to count to ten in another language.

Competency Focus

Act

The children carry out research to find out more about the topic of their own language and their linguistic heritage. They become more conscious of their own culture and its role in the wider world.

Digital Resources

Student eBook • Ask true/false questions about the SB text. Elicit answers and have children use *Highlighter* to identify the phrase in the text which confirms the answer each time.

Student eBook, Digital Activity Book • TIP Store ideas in *Add personal note* for easy access during the lesson.

Teacher Resource Center • Print out CLIL Graphic Organizer 8 for the children to use in collating their Find Out More! research.

CLIL eBook • The children can use the CLIL eBook to expand their knowledge of the lesson topic.

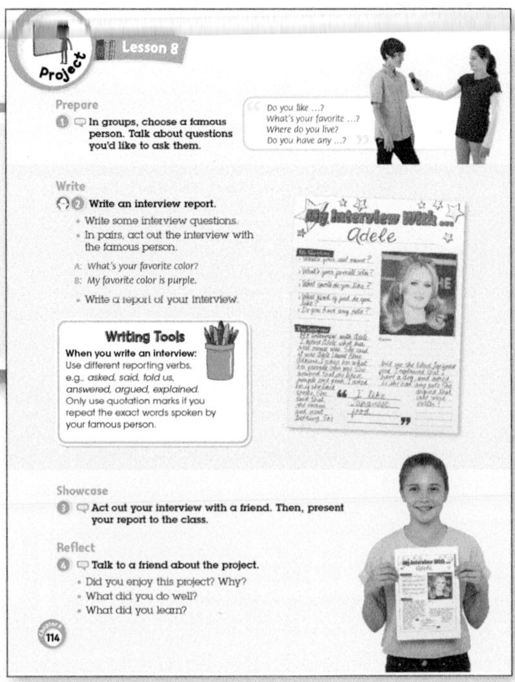
Project Lesson 8

Prepare

1 In groups, choose a famous person. Talk about questions you'd like to ask them.

Do you like ...?
What's your favorite ...?
Where do you live?
Do you have any ...?

Write

2 Write an interview report.

- Write some interview questions.
- In pairs, act out the interview with the famous person.

A: What's your favorite color?
B: My favorite color is purple.

- Write a report of your interview.

Writing Tools
When you write an interview:
Use different reporting verbs, e.g., asked, said, told us, answered, argued, explained.
Only use quotation marks if you repeat the exact words spoken by your famous person.

Showcase

3 Act out your interview with a friend. Then, present your report to the class.

Reflect

4 Talk to a friend about the project.

- Did you enjoy this project? Why?
- What did you do well?
- What did you learn?

114

Writing Project

Lesson objectives: review language from Chapter 8; write an interview report and present it to the class
Materials: Writing Template 8 [TRC printout] (optional); sunglasses, soccer ball, hat (optional)

Warmer: Think of famous people

Write these headings on the board: *Sports, Movies, Books, Other.* Have the children work in pairs or groups to think of famous people for each category. Elicit answers. Ask *Why are they famous?*

Prepare

1 In groups, choose a famous person. Talk about questions you'd like to ask them.

- The children choose one of the famous people they identified in the Warmer and prepare interview questions for them in groups, using the prompts supplied.

Write

2 Write an interview report.

- Have the children read the interview report as a model for their own writing.
- Read the **Writing Tools** box together. Elicit examples in the model of interview report features.
- The children prepare an outline, using the instructions and the model interview report. They write their interview report, then compare with a friend. Give support as necessary.

Showcase

3 Act out your interview with a friend. Then, present your report to the class. 

- Have the children practice their interview again. Then ask children to read out their interview reports. Have the class listen for interesting details.

Reflect

4 Vote for the best report and talk to the class.

- Have children comment on which report they liked best and why. Then, ask them to vote for their favorite.

Optional activity: TV interviews

Bring the interviews to life by using simple props to denote the famous person, e.g. a pair of sunglasses, a soccer ball, a hat. Draw a large square on the board to represent the TV screen. Have two children do their interview "on TV."

Lesson 8

GRAND QUIZ CENTRAL

1 Play with a friend. Choose a character.
2 Write a new question to ask your friend.
3 Take turns asking. Say the answer, then write it in your notebook.
4 If a question is too hard, you can swap! Choose and check (✓) up to three questions. Remember: each swap loses a bonus point!

	Questions to ask Chatterbox	Questions to ask Big Mouth
1	Say in your language *I don't understand.*	Say in your language *Please speak more slowly.*
2	What did the author ask Rufus about reading?	What did Rufus ask the author about ideas?
3	What's the opposite of *tell the truth*?	What's the opposite of *agree*?
4	Change to reported speech: *"What's your name?" she asked.*	Change to reported speech: *"Do you like adventure stories?" he asked.*
5	Which word has a silent -e? *pronounce, accent, speak*	Which word has a silent -e? *mean, understand, translate*
6	Change to direct speech: *He explained that he didn't want it.*	Change to direct speech: *She agreed that it was a beautiful dress.*
7	In the story, what did Lilliputians and Blefuscudians argue about?	In the story, what did Gulliver and the Emperor disagree about?
8	What's the most spoken language in the world?	What's the third most spoken language in the world?
9	Unscramble this word: *trsecep*	Unscramble this word: *apetre*
10	……………………………?	……………………………?

Check your friend's answers. Then color your speech bubbles and write your score.

Now choose your title:
Quiz Master! I understand this topic well.
Quiz Improver! I don't understand everything.
Quiz Beginner! I need some help.

69

Grand Quiz Central

See p. 43 for details of how to take the quiz.

Answers

1 It's ... (*teacher to provide answer*) **2** She asked if he liked reading. / He asked her where she got her ideas. **3** lie / disagree **4** She asked what my name was. / He asked if I liked adventure stories. **5** pronounce / translate **6** "I don't want it," he explained. / "It's a beautiful dress," she agreed. **7** They argued about which end eggs should be broken at. / They disagreed about capturing the Blefuscudian people. **8** Mandarin Chinese / Spanish **9** respect / repeat **10** Children's own answers.

Cooler: Play "Guess The Person"

Tell the class you have interviewed a lot of famous people. Make statements about famous people familiar to the class. e.g. *He told me that he scored a goal on Saturday.* (famous soccer player) *She told me she wrote a new book last year.* (famous writer) They guess who told you the information.

Competency Focus

Me

The children invent and write their own interview report, exploring their imagination and creativity.

Digital Resources

Student eBook • Give answers to the questions in the SB model interview in random order, e.g. *I have a cat and a dog.* Have children use *Highlighter* to identify the corresponding question each time. (e.g. *5 Do you have any pets?*)

Teacher Resource Center • Print out Writing Template 8 to use for the SB writing activity.

Language Review

Lesson objective: review language from Chapter 8
Materials: Tracks 8.7, AB 8.1 and AB 8.2

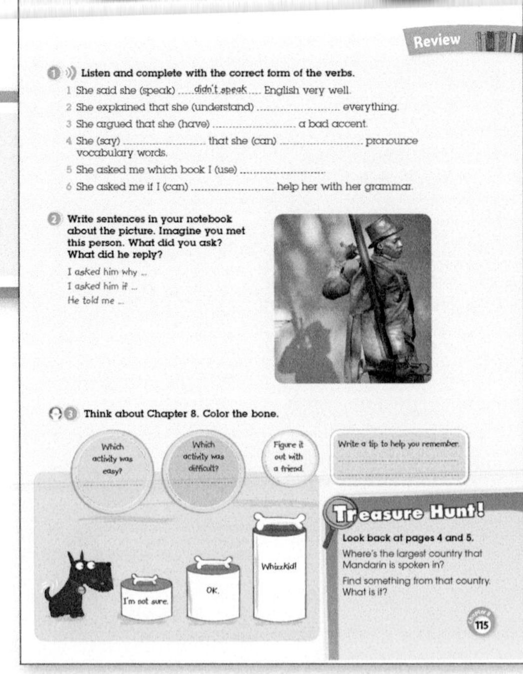

Review

1 Listen and complete with the correct form of the verbs.

1 She said she (speak) ......didn't speak..... English very well.
2 She explained that she (understand) .... everything.
3 She argued that she (have) .... a bad accent.
4 She (say) .... that she (can) .... pronounce vocabulary words.
5 She asked me which book I (use) ....
6 She asked me if I (can) .... help her with her grammar.

2 Write sentences in your notebook about the picture. Imagine you met this person. What did you ask? What did he reply?

I asked him why ...
I asked him if ...
He told me ...

3 Think about Chapter 8. Color the bone.

Which activity was easy?
Which activity was difficult?
Figure it out with a friend.
Write a tip to help you remember.

I'm not sure.
OK.
Whizzkid!

Treasure Hunt!
Look back at pages 4 and 5.
Where's the largest country that Mandarin is spoken in?
Find something from that country. What is it?

115

Warmer: Top tips

A boy/girl from the US is visiting their class, but he/she does not speak their language very well. Write on the board *speaking, listening, reading, writing, grammar.* Ask *What are the top three tips you would give them?*

1 8.7 Listen and complete with the correct form of the verbs.

- Play Track 8.7. Children say if the new friend is good at English.
- Play Track 8.7 again and have the children complete the reported questions. Elicit answers.

Audioscript

Boy: *Excuse me. Is this the English language class?*
Girl: *Sorry?*
Boy: *Do you speak English? Is this the English class?*
Girl: *Um, sorry! I don't speak English very well.*
Let me explain. I understand everything, but speaking is more difficult.
Boy: *But your accent is good.*
Girl: *No, it isn't. I have a very bad accent and I can't pronounce vocabulary words very well. I … can't pronounce vocabulary. Which book do you use? Can you help me with my grammar?*

Answers

1 didn't speak **2** understood **3** had **4** said, couldn't **5** used **6** could

2 Write sentences in your notebook about the picture. Imagine you met this person. What did you ask? What did he reply?

- Have the children write the questions they asked him in their notebook. Then have them swap notebooks with a friend and write the reported replies.

Answers

Children's own answers.

3 Think about Chapter 8. Color the bone. 

- Have the children look back at Chapter 8 and color the bone to evaluate their progress (self-evaluation). Children choose and write a tip in their Student Book.

Treasure Hunt!

Ask *Which is the largest country where Mandarin is spoken?* (*China*) Have the children look at pp. 4–5 to find something from that country. (*Chinese lantern*)

Cooler: Vocabulary review

Have the children make a mind map of the language-related vocabulary they have learned in the chapter, e.g. Language - reporting verbs, world languages, ways of speaking, etc.

Competency Focus

Me: Self-evaluation

The children reflect on the chapter and express their opinions about their own progress.

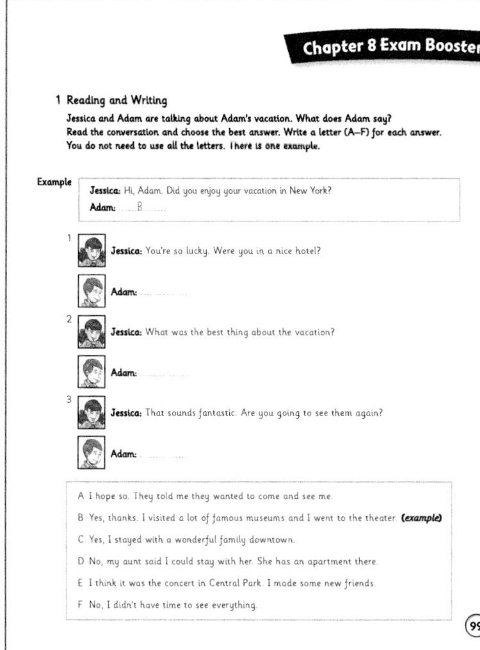
Chapter 8 Exam Booster

1 Reading and Writing

Jessica and Adam are talking about Adam's vacation. What does Adam say?
Read the conversation and choose the best answer. Write a letter (A–F) for each answer.
You do not need to use all the letters. There is one example.

Example
Jessica: Hi, Adam. Did you enjoy your vacation in New York?
Adam: ......B......

1 Jessica: You're so lucky. Were you in a nice hotel?
Adam: ....

2 Jessica: What was the best thing about the vacation?
Adam: ....

3 Jessica: That sounds fantastic. Are you going to see them again?
Adam: ....

A I hope so. They told me they wanted to come and see me.
B Yes, thanks. I visited a lot of famous museums and I went to the theater. *(example)*
C Yes, I stayed with a wonderful family downtown.
D No, my aunt said I could stay with her. She has an apartment there.
E I think it was the concert in Central Park. I made some new friends.
F No, I didn't have time to see everything.

99

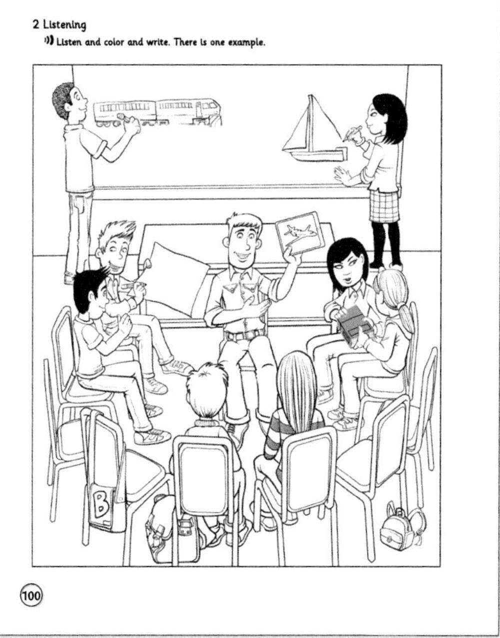

1 Reading and Writing. Jessica and Adam are talking about Adam's vacation. What does Adam say? Read the conversation and choose the best answer. Write a letter (A–F) for each answer. You do not need to use all the letters.

The children read the questions and write the letters.

Answers

1 d **2** e **3** a

2))) AB 8.1 Listening. Listen and color and write. There is one example.

Play AB Track 8.1 twice. Children listen color or write.

Answers (Audioscript on p. 224)

train: colored green, car: drawn on paper, Thursday: written on whiteboard, plain sweater: yellow, bag without B: colored orange

3))) AB 8.2 Listening. Listen and Color and write. There is one example.

Play AB Track 8.2 twice. The children listen and color or write the objects according to the recording. Check answers.

Answers (Audioscript on p. 224)

1 sweater colored green **2** book colored yellow **3** write teen room on wall sign **4** umbrella colored red **5** write 'quiet' on table sign

Digital Resources

- Teacher Resource Center • Print out Test Chapter 8 to use at the end of this lesson. The Test Generator also allows you to create customized tests.
- For the Cambridge English Young Learners Exams preparation activities on the AB page, choose the audio buttons to access the recordings.

Student's App • Encourage the children to play the games on their smartphone/tablet. Ask them to record their scores to compare in the next lesson. (*The Inks* Apps are free and available on the App Store and Google Play.)

Chapter 9 Into the Future

Overview

The children will:

- use critical thinking skills to identify city and environment vocabulary.
- talk about life in the future using *will/won't*.
- read and understand a story about memory and computers.
- ask about the future.
- find out about houses of the future.
- write their own description of a future school.

Key Vocabulary

Cities: area, bike path, building, downtown, pollution, sidewalk, traffic, tram, village, wildlife

Technology: driverless, gadgets, rechargeable batteries, recyclable, solar panels, touch screen controls, wind turbines, wireless

Key Grammar

Future: *will/won't*

- In the future, everyone will travel by bike or tram / you won't need a car.

Future: *will* questions

- Will we drive cars?
- Yes, we will. / No, we won't.
- What will people wear?

Reading Skills

Story: *The Memory Bank*

Genre: science fiction story

Literacy Development

- use reading skills to understand and predict content
- relate story theme to personal experience
- use relative clauses with *who/where/that*

Functional Language

- What's the matter?
- I'm worried about … tomorrow.
- Good luck! I'm sure you'll …

Spelling

Suffixes *–able* and *–less*

CLIL: Science—Future living

The children find out about houses of the future.

Competency Focus

The children will:

use critical thinking skills to deduce the meaning of new vocabulary. (Lesson 1) predict the content of a story. (Lesson 3)	activate new vocabulary and apply new grammar knowledge. (Lesson 2) apply new grammar rules in a familiar context. (Lesson 5)	work in pairs to act out a dialogue. (Lesson 3) work in pairs to talk about their predictions. (Lesson 6)	relate the story theme to their personal experience. (Lesson 4) invent and write their own description of a school in the future. (Lesson 8) evaluate their own progress in the chapter. (Review)	research technology for the home in the future. (Lesson 7)

Digital Overview

Teacher Presentation

Student eBook and Digital Activity Book

- Oral Storytelling Video 9.1: *The Strawberry—a Modern Myth*
- Interactive versions of AB activities
- Integrated audio and answer key for all activities

Teacher resources for planning, lesson delivery, and homework

Teacher Resource Center

- Class Planner Chapter 9
- Worksheets to print out (including notes and answers):
  - Grammar Worksheet 9A: Future: *will/won't*
  - Grammar Worksheet 9B: Future: *will* questions
  - Oral Storytelling Video Worksheet 9: *The Strawberry—a Modern Myth*
  - Phonics Worksheet 9
  - CLIL Graphic Organizer 9
  - Test Chapter 9 and End-of-year Test
- Test Generator
- Speaking Assessment: Cambridge English Young Learners Exams
- Literacy Handbook

Watch the Oral Storytelling Video

Children's resources for consolidation and practice at home

Student eBook and Reader eBook

- Oral Storytelling Video 9.1: *The Strawberry—a Modern Myth*

The Inks Student's App

Vocabulary games: Cities and Technology

Chapter 9

Into the Future

Lesson 1

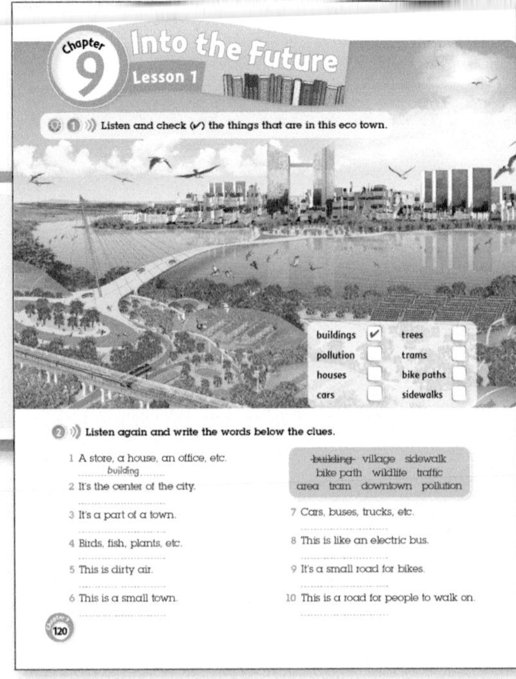
Chapter 9 Into the Future Lesson 1

1 Listen and check (✔) the things that are in this eco town.

buildings ✔ trees
pollution trams
houses bike paths
cars sidewalks

2 Listen again and write the words below the clues.

~~building~~ village sidewalk bike path wildlife traffic area tram downtown pollution

1 A store, a house, an office, etc. building
2 It's the center of the city.
3 It's a part of a town.
4 Birds, fish, plants, etc.
5 This is dirty air.
6 This is a small town.
7 Cars, buses, trucks, etc.
8 This is like an electric bus.
9 It's a small road for bikes.
10 This is a road for people to walk on.

120

Vocabulary

Lesson objectives: identify and use city/environment vocabulary
Key vocabulary: *area, bike path, building, downtown, pollution, sidewalk, traffic, tram, village, wildlife*
Materials: Track 9.1

Warmer: Brainstorm town vocabulary

Have the children think of ten places in their own town or where they live, e.g. *shopping mall, school, park*, etc. Have them raise their hand when they have a list of ten places. Choose a child to read out their list. Remind the children that *green* means *eco-friendly*. Ask *Is your town green? What makes it green?*

1 9.1 Listen and check (✔) the things that are in this eco town.

- Ask the children to look carefully at the places in the picture and read the words supplied.
- Play Track 9.1. They check the places in the eco town. Elicit answers. Whenever you elicit answers, remember to check with the class to see if they agree.
- Play Track 9.1 again and ask them to say where the city is and if it exists already. (*The city is being built now in China.*)

Audioscript

Boy: *Wow! Look at this place. This city looks great. Look at the buildings downtown. This city has a lot of different areas. That's the business area. The buildings are very tall and have offices in them. And there are a lot of green areas for wildlife where you can see plants and birds. Everywhere looks beautiful and the air isn't dirty. It's clean because there are so many trees. There isn't any pollution.*
Girl: *Are there any houses?*
Boy: *No, there aren't. Look—people live in these apartments in villages around the city.*
Girl: *Where are all the cars?*
Boy: *There aren't any cars. There isn't much traffic, only buses and trams that carry a lot of people. Trams are like electric buses. And there are a lot of bike paths so you don't have to ride your bike on the road. Look at these amazing sidewalks. They're high up in the sky above your head. It's really safe to walk around this city.*
Girl: *So, is this the city of the future?*
Boy: *No. This city is being built now, in China!*

Answers

✔ *by:* buildings, trams, bike paths, sidewalks, trees

2 9.1 Listen again and write the words below the clues.

- Ask the children to look at the first clue and study the words supplied.
- Play Track 9.1 again. The children listen and write the word for each definition. Elicit answers.

Answers

1 building **2** downtown **3** area **4** wildlife **5** pollution **6** village **7** traffic **8** tram **9** bike path **10** sidewalk

Optional activity: Play "Back to the Board"

Play the game using new vocabulary introduced in this lesson (see Games Bank p. 19).

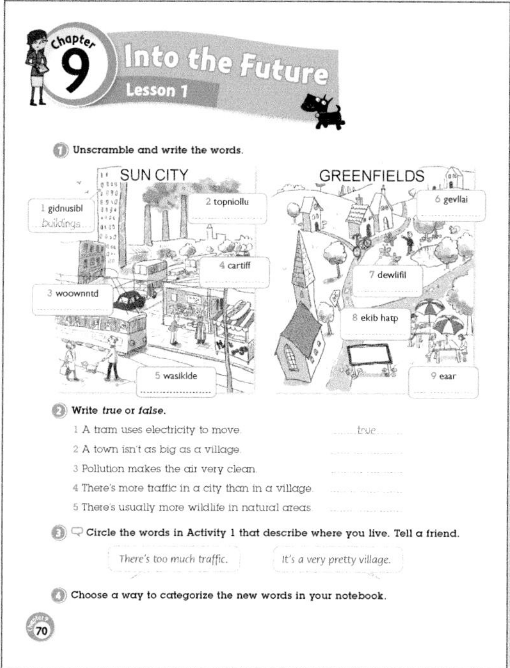
Chapter 9 Into the Future
Lesson 1

1 Unscramble and write the words.

SUN CITY
GREENFIELDS

1 gidnusibl buildings
2 topniollu
3 woownntd
4 cartiff
5 wasiklde
6 gevllai
7 dewlifil
8 ekib hatp
9 eaar

2 Write *true* or *false*.

1 A tram uses electricity to move. true
2 A town isn't as big as a village.
3 Pollution makes the air very clean.
4 There's more traffic in a city than in a village.
5 There's usually more wildlife in natural areas.

3 Circle the words in Activity 1 that describe where you live. Tell a friend.

There's too much traffic.
It's a very pretty village.

4 Choose a way to categorize the new words in your notebook.

70

1 Unscramble and write the words.

The children unscramble and write the labels. Elicit answers.

Answers

1 buildings **2** pollution **3** downtown **4** traffic **5** sidewalk **6** village **7** wildlife **8** bike path **9** area

2 Write *true* or *false*.

Read out the first sentence and elicit why it is true. (*Trams are electric.*) The children write *true* or *false* for the other sentences. Elicit answers, including the correct version of the false sentences.

Answers

1 true **2** false **3** false **4** true **5** true

3 Circle the words in Activity 1 that describe where you live. Tell a friend.

The children think about their own town or village and circle the appropriate words in Activity 1. They then discuss where they live with a friend.

4 Choose a way to categorize the new words in your notebook.

Have the children brainstorm appropriate categories in pairs. Prompt as necessary, e.g. *country/city/both, transportation/places/other, alphabetical order.* The children choose the best categories for them and list the words in their notebook.

Answers

Children's own answers.

Cooler: Play "Ready, Set, Draw"

Play the game using vocabulary from the lesson (see Games Bank p. 19).

Competency Focus

Think! Critical Thinking

The children use critical thinking skills to understand the new vocabulary by using visual clues and processing the written and spoken forms.

Digital Resources

Student eBook • Play "Kim's Game." Show each key item pictured in SB Activity 1 to elicit the word. Divide the class into teams. Use *Timer* to give them one minute to memorize the items, then one minute to recall them. Repeat several times.

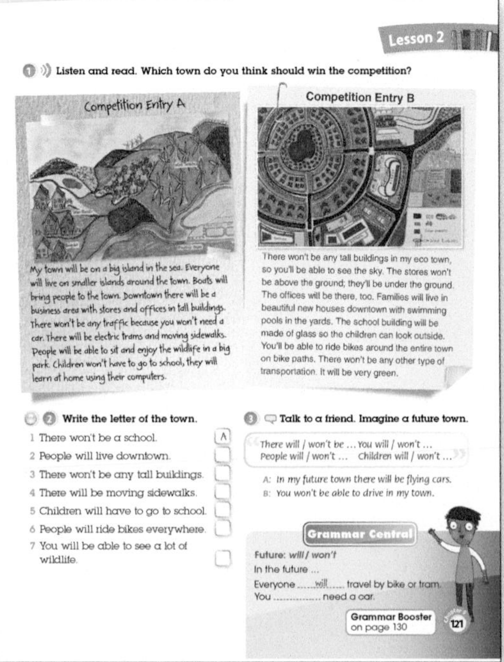
Lesson 2

1 Listen and read. Which town do you think should win the competition?

Competition Entry A

My town will be on a big island in the sea. Everyone will live on smaller islands around the town. Boats will bring people to the town. Downtown there will be a business area with stores and offices in tall buildings. There won't be any traffic because you won't need a car. There will be electric trams and moving sidewalks. People will be able to sit and enjoy the wildlife in a big park. Children won't have to go to school, they will learn at home using their computers.

Competition Entry B

There won't be any tall buildings in my eco town, so you'll be able to see the sky. The stores won't be above the ground; they'll be under the ground. The offices will be there, too. Families will live in beautiful new houses downtown with swimming pools in the yards. The school building will be made of glass so the children can look outside. You'll be able to ride bikes around the entire town on bike paths. There won't be any other type of transportation. It will be very green.

2 Write the letter of the town.

1 There won't be a school. A
2 People will live downtown.
3 There won't be any tall buildings.
4 There will be moving sidewalks.
5 Children will have to go to school.
6 People will ride bikes everywhere.
7 You will be able to see a lot of wildlife.

3 Talk to a friend. Imagine a future town.

There will / won't be … You will / won't …
People will / won't … Children will / won't …

A: In my future town there will be flying cars.
B: You won't be able to drive in my town.

Grammar Central

Future: *will / won't*

In the future …

Everyone ...will... travel by bike or tram.
You .... need a car.

Grammar Booster on page 130

121

Grammar

Lesson objective: talk about the town of the future
Key grammar: future—statements
Secondary language: *business, transportation, entire*
Materials: Track 9.2; Grammar Worksheet 9A [TRC printout] (optional)

Warmer: Play "Bingo"

Play the game using vocabulary from Lesson 1 (see Games Bank p. 19).

1 9.2 Listen and read. Which town do you think should win the competition?

- Tell the children they are going to judge a competition. Ask them to look at the two pictures and describe the towns.
- Play Track 9.2 twice. The children listen and read along. Ask *Who should win? Why?*

Answers

Children's own answers.

2 Write the letter of the town. 

- Have the children read the texts again and underline the verbs *will* and *won't*. Then ask them to read the sentences and identify the town described each time, writing A or B. Elicit answers.

Answers

1 A **2** B **3** B **4** A **5** B **6** B **7** A

Grammar Central

Future: *will / won't*

Have the children complete the grammar examples. Elicit answers. Elicit rules for using the future forms (*will/won't* + verb). They write a positive and a negative example in their notebook. For extra practice, try the **Grammar Booster** section in the Student Book (p. 130).

Answers p. 130

Activity 1: **1** will travel **2** won't need **3** will be **4** won't be

Activity 2: **1** will drink **2** will grow **3** won't need **4** will create **5** won't use **6** won't be **7** Children's own answers.

3 Talk to a friend. Imagine a future town. 

- Choose two children to read the example dialogue.
- Divide the class into pairs to practice the dialogue using the sentence openings supplied and ideas of their own. Have pairs perform for the class.

Optional activity: Make a poster—My future town

Have the children imagine a town in the future. It could be their own town/city or an imaginary one. Ask them to draw a picture, label the places and write a paragraph about it using *will* and *won't*.

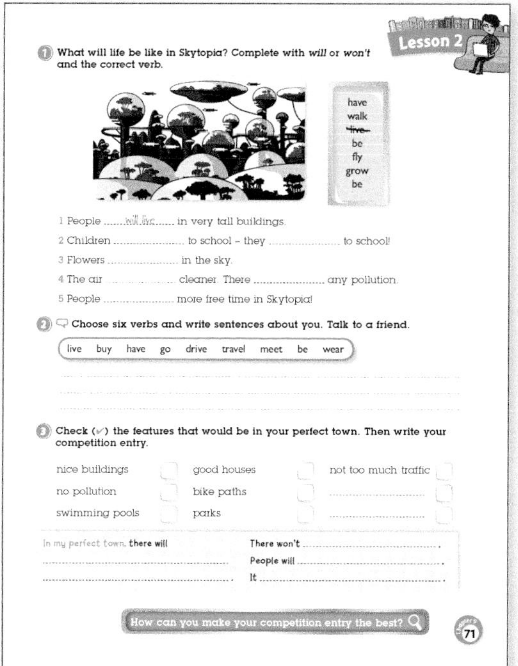

Lesson 2

1 What will life be like in Skytopia? Complete with *will* or *won't* and the correct verb.

have
walk
~~live~~
be
fly
grow
be

1 People ......will live...... in very tall buildings.
2 Children .... to school – they .... to school!
3 Flowers .... in the sky.
4 The air .... cleaner. There .... any pollution.
5 People .... more free time in Skytopia!

2 Choose six verbs and write sentences about you. Talk to a friend.

live buy have go drive travel meet be wear

3 Check (✓) the features that would be in your perfect town. Then write your competition entry.

nice buildings ☐ good houses ☐ not too much traffic ☐
no pollution ☐ bike paths ☐ .... ☐
swimming pools ☐ parks ☐ .... ☐

In my perfect town, there will .... There won't ....
.... People will ....
.... It ....

How can you make your competition entry the best?

Chapter 9 71

Cooler: Palm reading

Walk around the class asking children to show you their palm, and pretend to read it. Make some fun predictions, e.g. *You will be very rich and have six children.* Have the children make their own fun predictions in pairs.

Competency Focus

Learn

By reading the text and completing the activity, the children demonstrate their understanding of the new grammatical structures.

1 What will life be like in Skytopia? Complete with *will* or *won't* and the correct verb.

The children complete the sentences using *will/won't* + the correct verb from those supplied. Elicit answers.

Answers

1 will live **2** won't walk, 'll fly **3** will grow **4** will be, won't be **5** will have

2 Choose six verbs and write sentences about you. Talk to a friend.

The children choose six verbs to make sentences about their future, e.g. *I will travel around the world.* They then share their ideas in pairs.

Answers

Children's own answers.

3 Check (✓) the features that would be in your perfect town. Then write your competition entry.

The children check the features that they would have in their perfect town and add two of their own. They then write their competition entry. Have children read their entries for the class. Discuss with the children how they can make their entry the best. (*Use exciting language, e.g. lots of interesting adjectives, unusual ideas.*)

Answers

Children's own answers.

Digital Resources

Digital Activity Book • To give feedback on AB Activity 2, have a child write a personalized sentence about the future. Elicit who wrote the same thing by a show of hands. Repeat with children who have different ideas.

Student eBook, Digital Activity Book • TIP Use *Add personal note* to note weaknesses in the children's vocabulary, grammar, or pronunciation so you can revisit in later lessons.

Teacher Resource Center • For extra grammar practice, print out Grammar Worksheet 9A.

Reading: Story Extract

Lesson objectives: talk about important events; use the title and pictures to predict story content; read the extract from the science fiction story *The Memory Bank* (start)
Functional language: *What's the matter? I'm worried about … tomorrow. Good luck! I'm sure you'll …*
Secondary language: *store, full, the rest of*
Materials: Tracks 9.3 and 9.4; picture of a town (Warmer); memory game cards (Cooler)

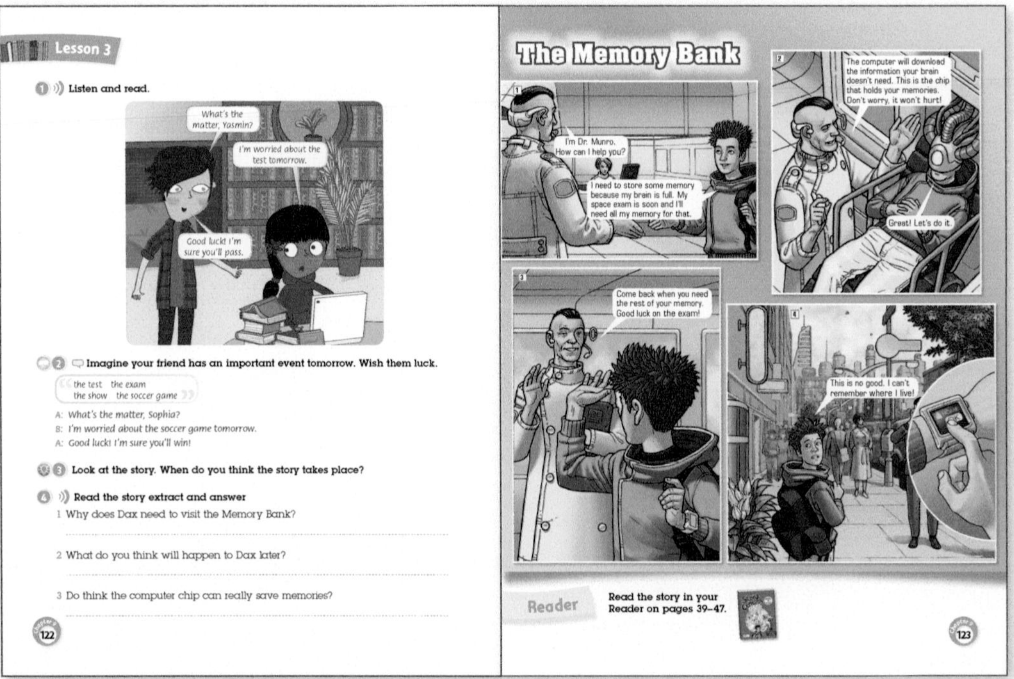

Lesson 3

1 Listen and read.

2 Imagine your friend has an important event tomorrow. Wish them luck.

the test the exam
the show the soccer game

A: What's the matter, Sophia?
B: I'm worried about the soccer game tomorrow.
A: Good luck! I'm sure you'll win!

3 Look at the story. When do you think the story takes place?

4 Read the story extract and answer
1 Why does Dax need to visit the Memory Bank?
2 What do you think will happen to Dax later?
3 Do think the computer chip can really save memories?

122

The Memory Bank

Reader Read the story in your Reader on pages 39–47.

123

Warmer: Memory test

Show the children a picture of a town for one minute. Then remove the picture. Have the children write a list of all the items they can remember. See who got the most. Ask *Do you think you have a good memory?*

Functional language

1 9.3 Listen and read.

- Play Track 9.3. The children listen and read along.
- Play Track 9.3 again for them to repeat.
- Divide the class into pairs to practice the dialogue.

2 Imagine your friend has an important event tomorrow. Wish them luck.

- Choose two children to read the example dialogue.
- The children practice in pairs using the prompts supplied and adding details. Have pairs do a dialogue for the class.

Before reading

3 Look at the story. When do you think the story takes place?

- Have the children study the story pictures. Ask *Where are they? What are their clothes like?*
- Ask *When do you think the story takes place?* Elicit ideas. (*in the future*)

4 9.4 Read the story extract and answer.

- Have the children read the story and answer question 1.
- Play Track 9.4. They listen and complete their ideas for questions 2 and 3.
- Elicit answers, but do not confirm predictions: explain that they will have to read the story to find out.

Answers

1 He needs to store some memories because his brain is full.
2 & **3** Children's own answers.

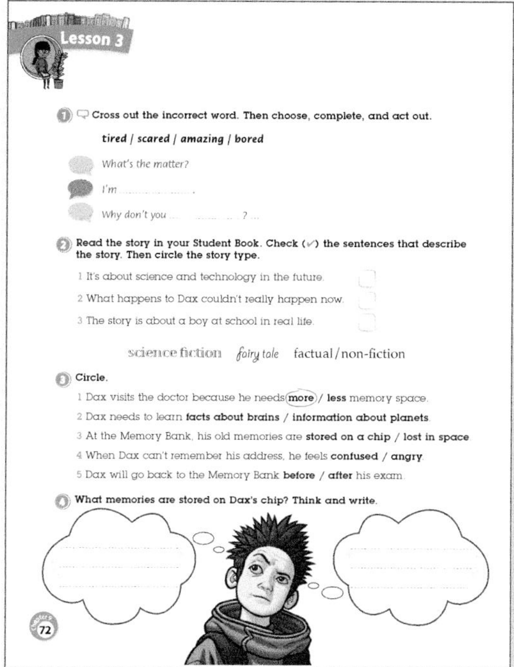
Lesson 3

1 Cross out the incorrect word. Then choose, complete, and act out.

tired / scared / amazing / bored

What's the matter?

I'm ....

Why don't you .... ?

2 Read the story in your Student Book. Check (✓) the sentences that describe the story. Then circle the story type.

1 It's about science and technology in the future.
2 What happens to Dax couldn't really happen now.
3 The story is about a boy at school in real life.

science fiction   fairy tale   factual/non-fiction

3 Circle.

1 Dax visits the doctor because he needs **more** / **less** memory space.
2 Dax needs to learn **facts about brains** / **information about planets**.
3 At the Memory Bank, his old memories are **stored on a chip** / **lost in space**.
4 When Dax can't remember his address, he feels **confused** / **angry**.
5 Dax will go back to the Memory Bank **before** / **after** his exam.

4 What memories are stored on Dax's chip? Think and write.

72

1 Cross out the incorrect word. Then choose, complete, and act out.

The children identify which phrase is incorrect. (*amazing*) They then choose one of the others and act out the dialogue with a friend. Encourage the children to use what they know to adapt and extend the dialogue. Have pairs act out their dialogue for the class.

2 Read the story in your Student Book. Check (✓) the sentences that describe the story. Then circle the story type.

The children read the Student Book story extract again, then check the sentences that describe it. They then circle the story type.

Answers

✓ *by* **1** *and* **2**
circle: science fiction

3 Circle.

The children read and complete the sentences by choosing the correct option in each pair. Elicit answers.

Answers

1 more **2** information about planets **3** stored on a chip **4** confused **5** after

4 What memories are stored on Dax's chip? Think and write.

Elicit suggestions on what memories are stored on Dax's chip. The children write their own ideas, then compare with a friend. Elicit ideas.

Answers

Children's own answers.

Cooler: More memory fun

Make two sets of flashcards (pictures and words) with town/city vocabulary from Lessons 1 and 2. Have the children study the cards. Give them one minute to remember the details. Remove the cards and ask them to remember words or details from the pictures. Ask *Is it easier to remember pictures or words?*

Competency Focus

Collaborate and Communicate

The children work together, putting into practice new functional language by acting out a realistic dialogue.

Think! Critical Thinking

By analyzing visual clues and deducing from the context, the children use prediction skills to help them engage with the story.

Digital Resources

Digital Activity Book • Display the AB page for Activity 4 review. Have children use *Pen* to write one of Dax's stored memories. Repeat with children who have different ideas. Have a class vote on the most interesting memory.

Student eBook, Digital Activity Book • TIP Give children the opportunity to be your assistant! Ask a child to be responsible for choosing the relevant buttons (e.g. answer key).

- TIP With the answer key, you can show the answers all at once or one by one to customize feedback.

The Memory Bank

1
Dr. M: I'm Dr. Munro. How can I help you?

Dax: I need to store some memory because my brain is full. My space exam is soon and I'll need all my memory for that.

2
Dr. M: The computer will download the information your brain doesn't need. This is the chip that holds your memories. Don't worry, it won't hurt!

Dax: Great! Let's do it.

3
Dr. M: Come back when you need the rest of your memory. Good luck on the exam!

4
Dax: This is no good. I can't remember where I live!

6
Mom: Hi, Dax, what's the matter?

Dax: Where do we live?

Mom: Take the K2 – that's the sky tram that goes to Kepler Village. We live in Building 17, downtown.

7
Later …

Mom: But Dax, you love pancakes, remember?

Dax: No, I don't remember. I know how long it takes to travel to different solar systems, though!

8
That Thursday …

Dax: Mom, I'm on the bike path. Where am I taking the exam?

Mom: The building is called the Meteor Space Academy. Good luck! You won't need it! You're a great student, remember?

Dax: *Um …*

9
A few weeks later …

Dax: An A+!

Mia: Aaargh!

10
Tutor: Mia, are you OK?

Dax: I'm so sorry.

Mia: My head.

Tutor: I think you're OK, but you need to rest at home.

Dax: *She's taking her exam next week. She'll fail, and it's all my fault.*

11
Dax: I'd like my old memories back now. You can download some of my exam information to the chip. I don't need it ... but can I share that information with a friend?

12
The next day …

Dax: Come with me to see Dr. Munro.

Mia: Who's he?

Dax: He's the doctor who works at the memory bank.

13
Mia: Will I get an A+, too?

Dr. M: You'll have all the information, but you might remember it differently.

14
Students: But that's cheating!

Mia: I feel bad.

Dax: Don't worry. Let's get a drink.

15
Dax: Seaweed shake, please.

Mia: That's my favorite, too!

16
Dax: I like to sit here. There's no pollution here so there's a lot of wildlife.

Mia: So do I. Cool! We like the same things.

17
Mia: When I was young, I used to walk my dog, Apollo, here because there was no traffic. What a great dog!

18
Dax: Oh, no, Apollo was *my* dog! I think we should go see Dr. Munro.

19
Dr. M: Um, it's bad news. There was a problem with the computer. Some of your old memories were saved on the chip we gave Mia. Dax, your memory is growing on her brain! We need to erase it completely or she will lose all of her own memory, forever.

20
Mia: It's OK. I'll just learn everything again and take the exam next year.

21
Dax: Will she remember me, Doctor?

Dr. M: I don't know. She might forget *everything.*

22
Dax: How are you feeling?

Mia: I'm OK, Dax.

Dax: You remember me!

Mia: Of course. You're the boy who knocked me over!

Come on! Let's get a seaweed shake.

23
Dr. M: We won't use this again.

Lesson objective: read and understand the science fiction story *The Memory Bank* in the Reader
Materials: Track 9.4; Reader; Oral Storytelling Video Worksheet 9 [TRC printout] (optional)

Warmer: Yes or no?

Recap the story extract using yes/no sentences. Make statements about the story and have the class answer *yes* or *no*, e.g. *Dax loses all his memories.* (*no*)

Story Summary

Dax and Mia are students living in the future who are studying space at school. They ask a doctor to store some of their memory to help with an upcoming exam. By accident, the doctor saves Dax's memory in Mia's brain. Mia decides to erase her memory and take the exam the following year.

Theme: the importance of being honest

9.4 While reading

- Have the children look at the pictures in the Reader and identify the main characters.
- Play Track 9.4. The children listen and read along. Ask *Does Mia remember Dax?* (*yes*)
- Ask questions to check comprehension, e.g. *What happens to Mia? (She trips over Dax's bag and hurts her head.) Why is Dax taking Mia to see Doctor Munro? (to download Dax's exam information into her brain)*
- Have the class read the story again in groups of five. Allocate the roles of Dax, Dr. Munro, Mia, Mom, and Tutor. Encourage them to practice correct pronunciation and intonation (see **Story Time**).

After reading: Reflect

- Ask questions to give the children the opportunity to think about the issues raised by the story, e.g. *Is Dr. Munro a good character? Do you think Dax and Mia were cheating? What would you do?*

Optional activity: Extend the story

Tell the class to introduce a new character into the story, e.g. another person who visited Dr. Munro's memory lab. Ask them to make up their own dialogue for an extra scene. Choose children to perform their dialogues for the class.

Story Time

Practicing authentic intonation

This dialogue story is really a play and lends itself to acting out and creating a class performance using costumes, props, etc. It provides an opportunity to improve pronunciation and authentic intonation, and stress patterns through repetition. You could take it a step further and prepare your performance for the end of the semester or to perform for another class.

Reading Strategy

Think-Pair-Share

Think–Pair–Share can be used before, while, and after reading. The children work individually, then in pairs or in groups of three, and then as a class. Ask questions related to the story which the children think about on their own, then discuss in pairs before sharing their ideas with the class.

For additional explanation and activities, see the Literacy Handbook on the Teacher Resource Center.

Cooler: Make predictions about the future

Have the children make predictions about the future using *will/won't*. Agree categories, e.g. *Transportation*, *School*, *Clothes*, etc. Elicit answers.

Digital Resources

Reader eBook • Oral Storytelling Video 9.1 contains a different story on a related theme (*The Strawberry—a Modern Myth*). Watch and discuss it together at the end of the lesson.

Teacher Resource Center • Print out Oral Storytelling Video Worksheet 9 to help you get the most out of the video.

Student eBook, Reader eBook • The children can watch Oral Storytelling Video 9.1 at home.

Reading Comprehension and Critical Literacy

Lesson objectives: understand and evaluate the story; relate story theme to personal experience; give extra information using relative clauses
Materials: Track 9.4; Reader; Oral Storytelling Video Worksheet 9 [TRC printout] (optional)

Lesson 4 Time to Think

1 Read the story in your Reader on pages 39–47 again.
Why is the place called the Memory Bank?

2 Comprehension
1 What is Dr. Munro's job?
2 What grade did Dax get on his exam?
3 How did Mia get some of Dax's memories?
4 Does the story have a happy ending?

3 Critical Literacy
1 Is Mia cheating if she uses Dax's memories to do her space exam?
2 Is Dax the same kind of person throughout the story or does he change?

Writing Workshop Using relative clauses to give more information.

4 Find information about these people, places, and things. Write your own relative clauses.
Mia – the girl who hurt her head
The memory bank – the place where ...
The computer chip – the chip that ...
your friend –
your playground –
your Story Central Plus book –

Writing Tools
Use relative clauses to add more information to a sentence:
who where that

5 Text Connections
Does this story remind you of another time when technology went wrong?

124

Note: Please ensure that your class has read the Reader story before you do this lesson.

Warmer: Story recap

Write key events from the story on the board in random order, e.g. *Dax went to the memory bank. Dr. Munro stored some memories. Dax forgot many basic things.* Have the children put them in the correct order to tell the story.

1 94 Read the story in your Reader.

- Have the children read the story. (Alternatively, play Track 9.4 and have them read along.) Elicit whether they were correct in their predictions in Lesson 3 Activity 4.
- Ask *Why is the place called the Memory Bank?* Elicit answers. (*It's a place where you can store memories.*)

2 Comprehension

- Have the children find the information in the story. Check answers with the class, asking for their opinions about the ending.

Answers

1 He works at the Memory Bank./He's a scientist. **2** A+
3 Some of Dax's memories were on the chip that Dr. Munro gave to Mia. **4** Children's own answers./Yes!

3 Critical Literacy

- Ask *Do you think Mia is cheating?* Analyzing characters' motivations is a good way for the children to engage with the story. Have a class vote.
- Discuss the character of Dax, eliciting adjectives to describe him at different stages of the story, e.g. *intelligent, forgetful, helpful, worried.* Ask *What does Dax learn?* Making comparisons and considering how the character changes as the story progresses helps readers understand the underlying message of the story.

Writing Workshop

Using relative clauses to give more information

4 Find information about these people, places, and things. Write your own relative clauses.

Have a child read the example. Read the **Writing Tools** box together. Elicit one more example for each word (*who, where, that*). The children write relative clauses using the prompts supplied in their notebook. Elicit answers.

Answers

Children's own answers.

5 Text Connections 

- Ask the children if their own computer has ever gone wrong and what happened. Elicit other examples of technology going wrong in real life or a story.

Optional activity: Definitions quiz

Have the children prepare three quiz questions in pairs, defining a person, a place, and an object, e.g. *It's a place where we borrow books.* (*the library*) Choose pairs to read out their quiz questions for the class to guess.

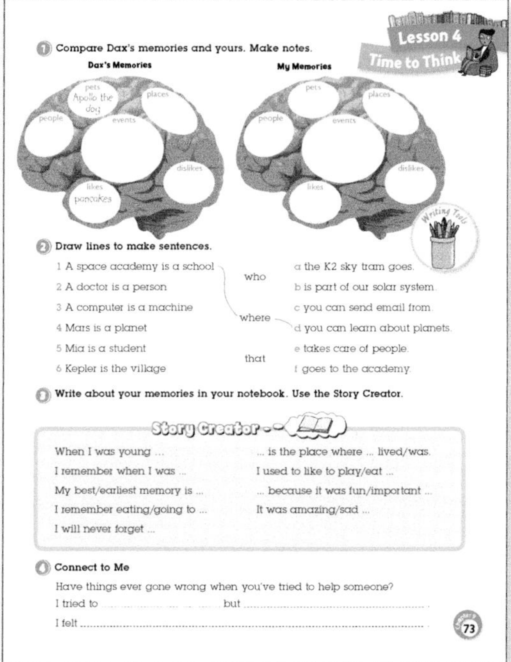
Lesson 4
Time to Think

1 Compare Dax's memories and yours. Make notes.

2 Draw lines to make sentences.

1 A space academy is a school
2 A doctor is a person
3 A computer is a machine
4 Mars is a planet
5 Mia is a student
6 Kepler is the village

who
where
that

a the K2 sky tram goes.
b is part of our solar system.
c you can send email from.
d you can learn about planets.
e takes care of people.
f goes to the academy.

3 Write about your memories in your notebook. Use the Story Creator.

Story Creator

When I was young ... | ... is the place where ... lived/was.
I remember when I was ... | I used to like to play/eat ...
My best/earliest memory is ... | ... because it was fun/important ...
I remember eating/going to ... | It was amazing/sad ...
I will never forget ...

4 Connect to Me

Have things ever gone wrong when you've tried to help someone?
I tried to .... but ....
I felt ....

73

1 Compare Dax's memories and yours. Make notes.

The children note a memory for Dax for each topic, then note memories of their own. Elicit responses.

Answers

Children's own answers.

2 Draw lines to make sentences.

Elicit when *who*, *where*, and *that* are used. (*for a person/a place/a thing*, respectively) The children then draw lines to complete the sentences. Elicit answers.

Answers

1 where d, **2** who e, **3** that c, **4** that b, **5** who f, **6** where a

3 Write about your memories in your notebook. Use the Story Creator.

Use the **Story Creator** to elicit ideas. The children write about their memories in their notebook, then compare with a friend. Have children read out their memories for the class.

4 Connect to Me

Elicit examples of a time when the children tried to help but it went wrong. They write their own response, then compare with a friend.

Cooler: Our memory bank

Tell the children that they are going to make a class memory bank. Ask them to choose a treasured memory to store in it. Ask children to talk about memories they want to keep forever.

Competency Focus

Me: Critical Literacy

The children use critical literacy skills to reflect on the theme of the story and relate it to their own experiences.

Digital Resources

Reader eBook • Show the Reader story picture by picture without the audio. Minimize the screen. Use *Timer* to give the children two minutes to recall the main events of the story in pairs.

• Children use *Highlighter* to identify the relative clauses in the Reader story.

Student eBook, Reader eBook • If you haven't already, show Oral Storytelling Video 9.1 (a different story on a related theme).

Teacher Resource Center • If you haven't already, print out Oral Storytelling Video Worksheet 9.

Grammar and Reading

Lesson objectives: ask and answer questions about the future
Key grammar: future—questions with *will*
Secondary language: *gas, energy, memory stick*
Materials: Track 9.5; Grammar Worksheet 9B [TRC printout] (optional)

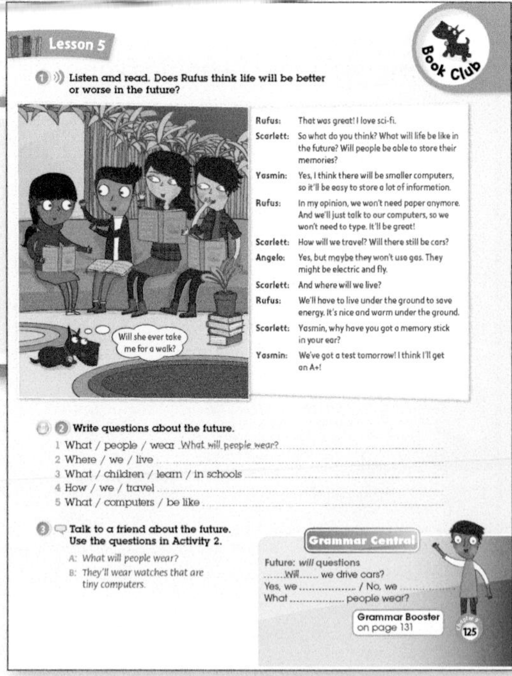

Lesson 5

Book Club

1 Listen and read. Does Rufus think life will be better or worse in the future?

Rufus: That was great! I love sci-fi.
Scarlett: So what do you think? What will life be like in the future? Will people be able to store their memories?
Yasmin: Yes, I think there will be smaller computers, so it'll be easy to store a lot of information.
Rufus: In my opinion, we won't need paper anymore. And we'll just talk to our computers, so we won't need to type. It'll be great!
Scarlett: How will we travel? Will there still be cars?
Angelo: Yes, but maybe they won't use gas. They might be electric and fly.
Scarlett: And where will we live?
Rufus: We'll have to live under the ground to save energy. It's nice and warm under the ground.
Scarlett: Yasmin, why have you got a memory stick in your ear?
Yasmin: We've got a test tomorrow! I think I'll get an A+!

2 Write questions about the future.

1 What / people / wear *What will people wear?*
2 Where / we / live
3 What / children / learn / in schools
4 How / we / travel
5 What / computers / be like

3 Talk to a friend about the future. Use the questions in Activity 2.

A: *What will people wear?*
B: *They'll wear watches that are tiny computers.*

Grammar Central

Future: *will* questions
......Will...... we drive cars?
Yes, we .... / No, we ....
What .... people wear?

Grammar Booster on page 131

125

Warmer: Review *will* and *won't*

Write *computers, travel, houses* on the board. Have the children make predictions about the future for each topic. Encourage them to make positive and negative statements.

1 9.5 Listen and read. Does Rufus think life will be better or worse in the future?

- Ask *Do you think life will be better or worse in the future?* Then play Track 9.5. The children listen and say Rufus's opinion. (*He thinks life will be better.*) Ask *Do you agree with him?* Elicit responses.
- Play Track 9.5 again and ask the children to listen for what each child says about the future. Elicit answers.

2 Write questions about the future. 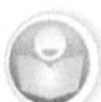

- Have the children look at the first question about the future. Explain that they need to reorder the words and use *will* to form the questions.
- The children write the rest of the questions, then compare with a friend. Elicit answers.

Answers

1 What will people wear?
2 Where will we live?
3 What will children learn in schools?
4 How will we travel?
5 What will computers be like?

Grammar Central

Future: *will* questions

Have the children complete the grammar examples. Elicit answers. Elicit the rules for making future questions. (*will + subject + verb*) They write further examples in their notebook. For extra practice, try the **Grammar Booster** section in the Student Book (pp. 131–133).

Answers p. 131

Activity 1: **1** will, drive **2** will, wear **3** Will, use **4** will, buy

Activity 2: **1** Where will **2** Will **3** Will, be **4** How will **5** What will, study **6** Children's own answers.

p. 132

Activity 1: **1** will wear **2** will have **3** won't need **4** will wear **5** will clean **6** won't use **7** WIll **8** won't

Activity 2: **1** No, they won't. **2** They will help people stay warm or cool. **3** We won't need heating or cooling in homes, offices, or schools. **4** They'll clean themselves in the sun. **5** We won't need washers or dryers. **6.** Children's own answers

p. 133

Activity 1: **1** will like **2** will, study **3** will be **4** will, wear **5** sold **6** Will, be **7** will **8** could **9** will, talk **10** will speak **11** will learn **12** Will, be **13** won't **14** was

Activity 2: Children's own answers.

3 Talk to a friend about the future. Use the questions in Activity 2.

- Choose two children to read the example dialogue.
- Divide the class into pairs to practice asking and answering the questions in Activity 2. Elicit ideas.

Optional activity: A visit from the future

Have the class prepare two or three questions to interview someone from 100 years in the future, e.g. *What will people eat?* Have children come to the front of the class and act as the time traveler and answer questions from the class.

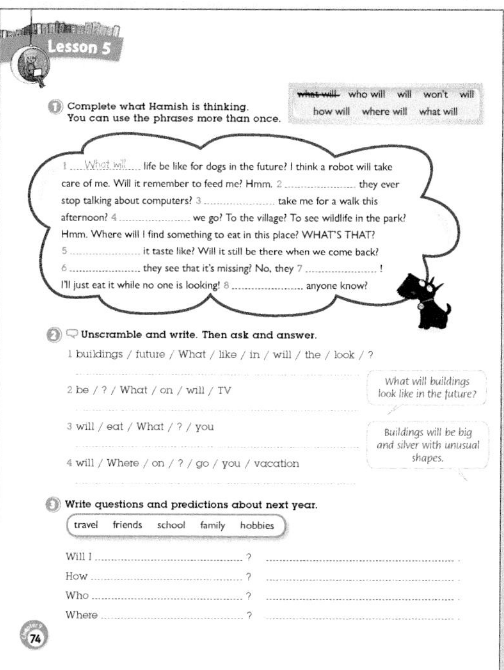

Lesson 5

1 Complete what Hamish is thinking. You can use the phrases more than once.

~~what will~~ who will will won't will how will where will what will

1 What will life be like for dogs in the future? I think a robot will take care of me. Will it remember to feed me? Hmm. 2 .... they ever stop talking about computers? 3 .... take me for a walk this afternoon? 4 .... we go? To the village? To see wildlife in the park? Hmm. Where will I find something to eat in this place? WHAT'S THAT? 5 .... it taste like? Will it still be there when we come back? 6 .... they see that it's missing? No, they 7 .... ! I'll just eat it while no one is looking! 8 .... anyone know?

2 Unscramble and write. Then ask and answer.

1 buildings / future / What / like / in / will / the / look / ?

2 be / ? / What / on / will / TV

3 will / eat / What / ? / you

4 will / Where / on / ? / go / you / vacation

What will buildings look like in the future?

Buildings will be big and silver with unusual shapes.

3 Write questions and predictions about next year.

travel friends school family hobbies

Will I .... ? ....

How .... ? ....

Who .... ? ....

Where .... ? ....

74

1 Complete what Hamish is thinking. You can use the phrases more than once.

The children complete the text using the words supplied. Elicit answers.

Answers

1 What will **2** Will **3** Who will **4** Where will **5** What will **6** Will **7** won't **8** How will

2 Unscramble and write. Then ask and answer.

The children unscramble and write the questions. Elicit answers. They then ask and answer in pairs. Fast finishers can make other questions. Have pairs ask and answer for the class.

Answers

1 What will buildings look like in the future? **2** What will be on TV? **3** What will you eat? **4** Where will you go on vacation?

3 Write questions and predictions about next year.

The children write their own questions and answers, choosing from the prompts supplied. Elicit their predictions.

Answers

Children's own answers.

Cooler: Class vote

Have the children recap what things they think will be better/worse in the future. Then have a class vote on whether they think life will be better or worse.

Competency Focus

Learn

The children demonstrate their understanding of the new language by reading the text and completing the activity.

Digital Resources

Student eBook, Digital Activity Book • TIP Give the children as many opportunities as possible to use the digital resources—completing AB interactive activities, showing answers, writing and drawing on the board, etc. Encourage less confident children to participate, because this will help them engage.

Teacher Resource Center • For extra grammar practice, print out Grammar Worksheet 9B.

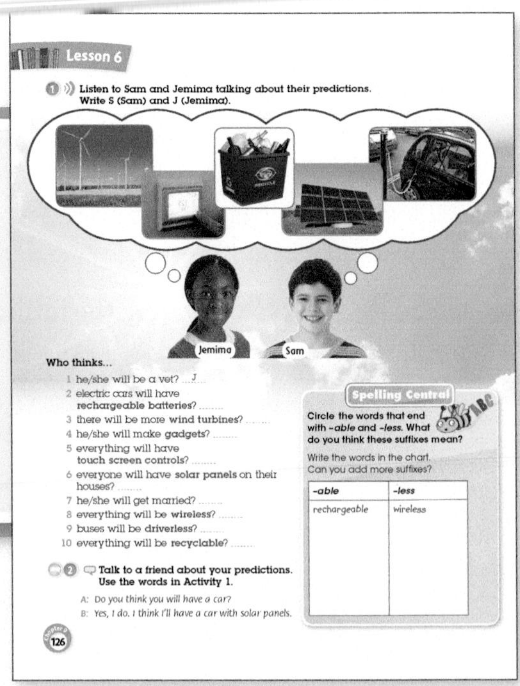
Lesson 6

1 Listen to Sam and Jemima talking about their predictions. Write S (Sam) and J (Jemima).

Jemima

Sam

Who thinks...

1 he/she will be a vet? J
2 electric cars will have **rechargeable batteries**? ....
3 there will be more **wind turbines**? ....
4 he/she will make **gadgets**? ....
5 everything will have **touch screen controls**? ....
6 everyone will have **solar panels** on their houses? ....
7 he/she will get married? ....
8 everything will be **wireless**? ....
9 buses will be **driverless**? ....
10 everything will be **recyclable**? ....

2 Talk to a friend about your predictions. Use the words in Activity 1.

A: *Do you think you will have a car?*
B: *Yes, I do. I think I'll have a car with solar panels.*

Spelling Central

Circle the words that end with *-able* and *-less*. What do you think these suffixes mean?

Write the words in the chart. Can you add more suffixes?

-able	*-less*
rechargeable	wireless

Chapter 9 126

Vocabulary, Listening, and Spelling

Lesson objectives: identify and talk about technology; practice spelling words with suffixes *–able* and *–less*

Key vocabulary: *driverless, gadgets, rechargeable batteries, recyclable, solar panels, touch screen controls, wind turbines, wireless*

Secondary language: *biometric, interactive, controls*

Materials: Track 9.6; picture of a futuristic car (optional); Phonics Worksheet [TRC printout] (optional)

Warmer: Pre-teach vocabulary

Pre-teach the vocabulary by giving definitions or sentences showing the words in context, e.g. *Driverless means there's no driver. My cell phone has touch screen controls—you touch the screen to make it do different things.* Repeat the definitions/sentences, pausing to elicit the key word.

1 9.6 Listen to Sam and Jemima talking about their predictions. Write S (Sam) and J (Jemima).

- Ask the children to study the list of predictions. Have them focus on the highlighted words and match them where possible with the correct pictures.
- Play Track 9.6. Have them listen and identify each prediction as Sam's (writing S) or Jemima's (J). Elicit answers.
- Play Track 9.6 again. Ask *Do you think your own life will be more like Sam's or Jemima's?* Elicit responses.

Audioscript

Woman: *What do you think life will be like for you in the future? Sam, where will you be in 15 years?*
Sam: *Hm, in 15 years I'll be 26, so I think I will have a job. I really like math and science so I'll work in a company that makes gadgets. I'll live in the countryside in a house with a big yard. It'll be a really modern house. Everything will be wireless. It will have touch screen controls for everything. Everything will be interactive! I'm sure I'll get married and I'll have children. There will be electric cars that have rechargeable batteries. I really want one of those!*

Woman: *What about you, Jemima?*
Jemima: *When I'm 26, I won't be married. I will live in another country, where there are mountains, because I want to travel and I love walking. I think I will have an apartment in a city somewhere. It will be really clean because everything will be recyclable. I love animals so I will work as a vet. I will go to college to study before that, of course. I don't think I'll have a car because I like to bike everywhere. I think roads will be much safer in 15 years and buses will be driverless—they will be controlled by computers. I expect to see a lot of technology that's used to save energy in the future. So there'll be more wind turbines and everyone will have solar panels on their houses.*

Answers

1 J **2** S **3** J **4** S **5** S **6** J **7** S **8** S **9** J **10** J

2 Talk to a friend about your predictions. Use the words in Activity 1.

- Choose two children to read the example dialogue. Then divide the class into pairs to make predictions about future technology. Elicit ideas.

Spelling Central

Words that end in *-able/-less*

Write *rechargeable* and *wireless* on the board. Ask the children to identify the endings and explain the word *suffix*. Have the children read the predictions in Activity 1 and circle more suffixes. Then have them complete the chart. Give more examples of other words with similar suffixes, e.g. *fashionable, valuable, countable, careless, useless.*

Answers

Circled and in chart:
–able: rechargeable, recyclable
–less: wireless, driverless

Optional activity: Design a car of the future

Show the children a picture of a futuristic car. If you do not have a picture, elicit ideas of what a futuristic car might look like. Have the children draw a picture of their car of the future. Ask them to label any gadgets it has and write two or three sentences about how it works.

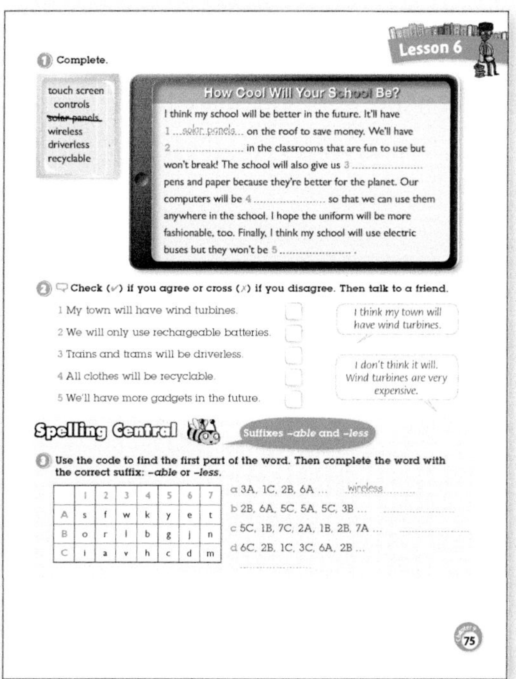
Lesson 6

1 Complete.

touch screen controls
~~solar panels~~
wireless
driverless
recyclable

How Cool Will Your School Be?

I think my school will be better in the future. It'll have 1 ...solar panels... on the roof to save money. We'll have 2 .... in the classrooms that are fun to use but won't break! The school will also give us 3 .... pens and paper because they're better for the planet. Our computers will be 4 .... so that we can use them anywhere in the school. I hope the uniform will be more fashionable, too. Finally, I think my school will use electric buses but they won't be 5 ....

2 Check (✓) if you agree or cross (✗) if you disagree. Then talk to a friend.

1 My town will have wind turbines.
2 We will only use rechargeable batteries.
3 Trains and trams will be driverless.
4 All clothes will be recyclable.
5 We'll have more gadgets in the future.

I think my town will have wind turbines.

I don't think it will. Wind turbines are very expensive.

Spelling Central — Suffixes *–able* and *–less*

3 Use the code to find the first part of the word. Then complete the word with the correct suffix: *–able* or *–less*.

	1	2	3	4	5	6	7
A	s	f	w	k	y	e	t
B	o	r	l	b	g	j	n
C	i	a	v	h	c	d	m

a 3A, 1C, 2B, 6A ... wireless
b 2B, 6A, 5C, 5A, 5C, 3B ...
c 5C, 1B, 7C, 2A, 1B, 2B, 7A ...
d 6C, 2B, 1C, 3C, 6A, 2B ...

75

1 Complete.

The children complete the text using the words supplied. Elicit answers.

Answers

1 solar panels **2** touch screen controls **3** recyclable **4** wireless **5** driverless

2 Check (✓) if you agree or cross (✗) if you disagree. Then talk to a friend.

A child reads out the example. Have the class raise their hand if they agree. Ask them to check or cross next to the sentence. They then read the other sentences and mark a check or cross. In pairs, they say if they agree or disagree, and give reasons why.

3 Use the code to find the first part of the word. Then complete the word with the correct suffix: *-able* or *-less.*

Ask the children to find what letter corresponds to 3A. (*w*) Work through the example with them, showing how you add a suffix to make the answer. (*wireless*) To practice the **Spelling Central** feature, the children figure out the other words, using the code and adding the appropriate suffix. Elicit answers.

Answers

1 wireless **2** recyclable **3** comfortable **4** driverless

Cooler: Play "Spelling Bee"

Play the game with technology words from the lesson (see Games Bank p. 19).

Competency Focus

Collaborate and communicate

The children work together and use their interpersonal skills to make predictions about technology in the future, incorporating the new vocabulary.

Digital Resources

Student eBook • TIP Use *Add personal note* for easy access to a link to the futuristic car picture for the Optional activity.

• TIP Use *Timer* to set a time limit for the SB Spelling Central activity. Have children use *Highlighter* to identify words that end in *–able/–less*, and *Pen* to complete the chart.

Teacher Resource Center • For phonics practice, print out Phonics Worksheet 9.

Student's App • Encourage the children to play the games on their smartphone/tablet. (*The Inks* Apps are free and available on the App Store and Google Play.)

CLIL: Science—Future living

Lesson objective: find out about houses of the future

Materials: CLIL Graphic Organizer 9 [TRC printout] (optional)

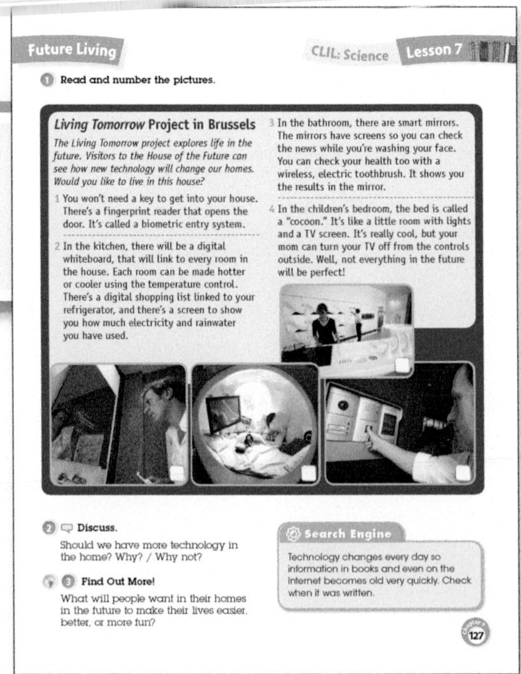

Future Living — CLIL: Science — Lesson 7

1 Read and number the pictures.

Living Tomorrow **Project in Brussels**

The Living Tomorrow project explores life in the future. Visitors to the House of the Future can see how new technology will change our homes. Would you like to live in this house?

1 You won't need a key to get into your house. There's a fingerprint reader that opens the door. It's called a biometric entry system.

2 In the kitchen, there will be a digital whiteboard, that will link to every room in the house. Each room can be made hotter or cooler using the temperature control. There's a digital shopping list linked to your refrigerator, and there's a screen to show you how much electricity and rainwater you have used.

3 In the bathroom, there are smart mirrors. The mirrors have screens so you can check the news while you're washing your face. You can check your health too with a wireless, electric toothbrush. It shows you the results in the mirror.

4 In the children's bedroom, the bed is called a "cocoon." It's like a little room with lights and a TV screen. It's really cool, but your mom can turn your TV off from the controls outside. Well, not everything in the future will be perfect!

2 Discuss.

Should we have more technology in the home? Why? / Why not?

3 Find Out More!

What will people want in their homes in the future to make their lives easier, better, or more fun?

Search Engine

Technology changes every day so information in books and even on the Internet becomes old very quickly. Check when it was written.

127

Warmer: A future house

Draw a large square on the board to represent a house and divide it into four smaller squares for the kitchen, living room, bathroom, and bedroom. Ask the children for their ideas of what houses of the future might have in each room.

1 Read and number the pictures.

- Ask *What are the pictures of?*
- The children read the text and match the pictures and paragraphs by numbering the pictures. Elicit answers.
- Have the children read the text again. Ask *How will you get into the house? (a fingerprint reader/biometric entry system)*

Answers

kitchen 2, bathroom 3, bedroom 4, entrance 1

2 Discuss. 

- Discuss with the class if having so much technology in our homes is a good or bad thing. Divide the class into pairs to discuss and share their opinions with reasons.

3 Find Out More! 

- The children research what people will want in their homes in the future to improve their lives. The **Search Engine** feature gives support on where to look. The children will need to complete this research before doing the follow-up activity in the Activity Book. (It could be set as homework.)

Optional activity: Play "Running Board Race" 

Play the game using long sentences from the text (see Games Bank p. 19).

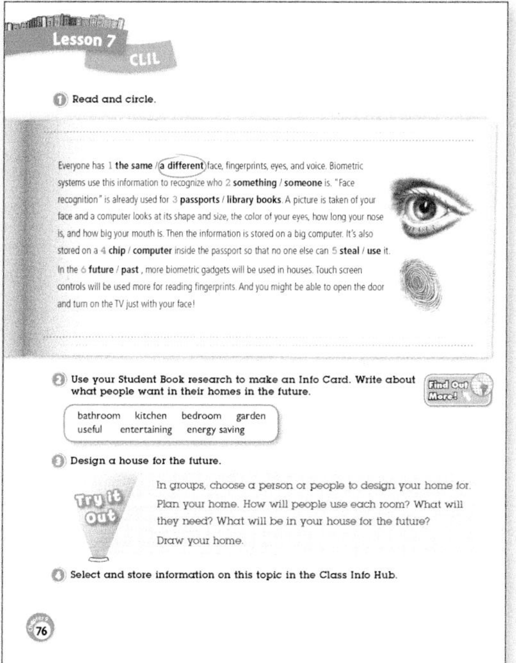
Lesson 7
CLIL

1 Read and circle.

Everyone has 1 **the same** / **a different** face, fingerprints, eyes, and voice. Biometric systems use this information to recognize who 2 **something** / **someone** is. "Face recognition" is already used for 3 **passports** / **library books**. A picture is taken of your face and a computer looks at its shape and size, the color of your eyes, how long your nose is, and how big your mouth is. Then the information is stored on a big computer. It's also stored on a 4 **chip** / **computer** inside the passport so that no one else can 5 **steal** / **use** it. In the 6 **future** / **past**, more biometric gadgets will be used in houses. Touch screen controls will be used more for reading fingerprints. And you might be able to open the door and turn on the TV just with your face!

2 Use your Student Book research to make an Info Card. Write about what people want in their homes in the future. Find Out More!

bathroom kitchen bedroom garden useful entertaining energy saving

3 Design a house for the future.

Try it Out

In groups, choose a person or people to design your home for. Plan your home. How will people use each room? What will they need? What will be in your house for the future? Draw your home.

4 Select and store information on this topic in the Class Info Hub.

76

1 Read and circle.

Ask *How can we recognize people's identity?* The children read and complete the text by circling the correct option in each pair. Elicit answers.

Answers

1 a different **2** someone **3** passports **4** chip **5** use **6** future

2 Use your Student Book research to make an Info Card. Write about what people want in their homes in the future.

Divide the class into groups. Have the children pool the information they learned from their research in the Student Book and the Activity Book. They write about and illustrate their ideas individually. Have the groups present their Info Cards to the class.

3 Design a house for the future.

Divide the class into groups. They follow the **Try It Out** instructions to discuss and plan their house. Ask groups to present their future homes to the class.

4 Select and store information on this topic in the Class Info Hub.

Have the children vote for the most interesting Info Cards and house designs. Archive these in your Class Hub (see p. 41) in a folder called **Chapter 9 Future Homes**.

Cooler: What's missing?

Write key vocabulary items from the chapter on the board, e.g. *digital, wireless, screen, gadget,* etc. Have the children close their eyes while you erase one word. The children look and say which word is missing. Continue until all the words are erased.

Competency Focus

Act

The children carry out research to find out more about the uses of technology in the future. They consider a global trend and relate to the wider world.

Digital Resources

Student eBook • TIP When using the board for "heads-up" teaching, give the children as much opportunity as possible to participate. Make sure you ask plenty of questions to give them the chance to engage with the text.

Teacher Resource Center • Print out CLIL Graphic Organizer 9 for the children to use in collating their Find Out More! research.

CLIL eBook • The children can use the CLIL eBook to expand their knowledge of the lesson topic.

Lesson 8

Project

Prepare

1 In groups, talk about what school will be like in the future.

I think that children will travel ...
We might wear / eat / play ...
I don't think children will ...
We will be able to ...

Write

2 Write about a school in the future.
- Draw a picture of your school in the future.
- Write a paragraph about it.
- What will or won't be there?

Writing Tools
When you write about your predictions for the future:
Use *will* and *won't*.
Give opinions using *I think ...*
In my opinion ... I believe ...

Showcase

3 Present your school to the class.

Reflect

4 Talk to a friend about the project.
- Did you enjoy this project? Why?
- What did you do well?
- What did you learn?

128

Writing Project

Lesson objectives: review language from Chapter 9; write a description of a future school and present it to the class

Warmer: Vocabulary review

Ask the children to think about all the new words they have learned in the chapter. Ask them to choose their top three most useful ones. Elicit suggestions. Have children spell them aloud. Write the words on the board.

Prepare

1 In groups, talk about what school will be like in the future.

- The children discuss their ideas about future schools in groups, using the prompts supplied. Groups report back to the class.

Write

2 Write about a school in the future.

- Have the children read the article as a model for their own writing.
- Read the **Writing Tools** box together. Elicit examples in the model of the future tense and expressions used to introduce an opinion.
- The children prepare an outline, using the instructions and the model article. They write and illustrate their article, then compare with a friend. Give support as necessary.

Showcase

3 Present your school to the class. 

- Choose children to read their descriptions to the class. Encourage the children to give their story atmosphere. They could use sound effects if they want.

Reflect

4 Vote for the best description of a future school.

- Have children comment on which description they liked best and why. Have a class vote for their favorite.

Optional activity: Find someone who …

Ask *Do you think everyone will have a flying car?* Have the children mingle and ask their own similar question about the future. Have them write down the name of children who answer *Yes.* Have children say their question and who agreed with it.

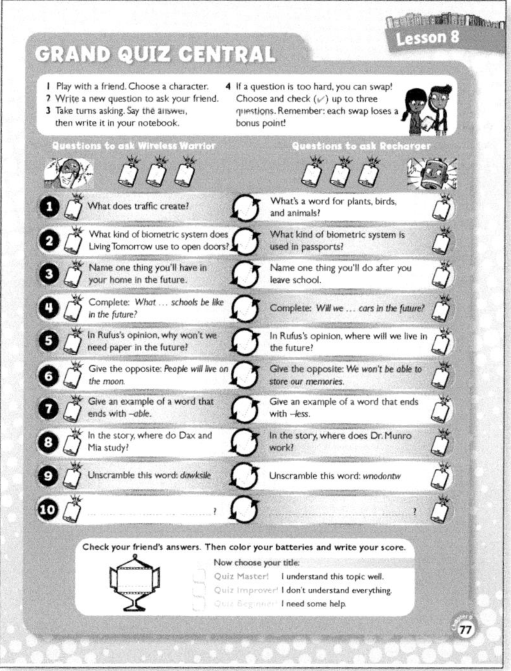
Lesson 8

GRAND QUIZ CENTRAL

1 Play with a friend. Choose a character.
2 Write a new question to ask your friend.
3 Take turns asking. Say the answer, then write it in your notebook.
4 If a question is too hard, you can swap! Choose and check (✓) up to three questions. Remember: each swap loses a bonus point!

	Questions to ask Wireless Warrior	Questions to ask Recharger
1	What does traffic create?	What's a word for plants, birds, and animals?
2	What kind of biometric system does Living Tomorrow use to open doors?	What kind of biometric system is used in passports?
3	Name one thing you'll have in your home in the future.	Name one thing you'll do after you leave school.
4	Complete: *What … schools be like in the future?*	Complete: *Will we … cars in the future?*
5	In Rufus's opinion, why won't we need paper in the future?	In Rufus's opinion, where will we live in the future?
6	Give the opposite: *People will live on the moon.*	Give the opposite: *We won't be able to store our memories.*
7	Give an example of a word that ends with *–able*.	Give an example of a word that ends with *–less*.
8	In the story, where do Dax and Mia study?	In the story, where does Dr. Munro work?
9	Unscramble this word: *dawksile*	Unscramble this word: *wnodontw*
10	……………………………?	……………………………?

Check your friend's answers. Then color your batteries and write your score.

Now choose your title:
Quiz Master! I understand this topic well.
Quiz Improver! I don't understand everything.
Quiz Beginner! I need some help.

77

Competency Focus

Me

The children invent and write their own description of a school in the future, exploring their imagination and creativity.

Grand Quiz Central

See p. 43 for details of how to take the quiz.

Answers

1 pollution / wildlife **2** a fingerprint reader / face recognition **3** I will *or* I'll … **4** will / drive **5** We'll talk to computers and won't need to type. / We'll live under the ground. **6** People won't live on the moon./ We will be able to store our memories. **7** *any one of:* recyclable, comfortable, fashionable, rechargeable/driverless, wireless **8** at the Meteor Space Academy / at the Memory Bank **9** sidewalk / downtown **10** Children's own answers.

Cooler: Play "Odd One Out"

Play the game with the vocabulary from the chapter (see Games Bank p. 19).

Digital Resources

Student eBook • Have children use *Highlighter* to identify expressions to give opinions in the SB model text.

- TIP Remember—you can use *Add personal note* to log the results of the class vote. Involve the children in tallying the results and writing the scores on the board.
- The class chooses one topic from Chapters 1–9. The children review the vocabulary from that topic at home in preparation for a quiz that you can have in your next class.

Language Review

Lesson objective: review language from Chapter 9
Materials: Tracks 9.7, AB 9.1, AB 9.2 and AB 9.3

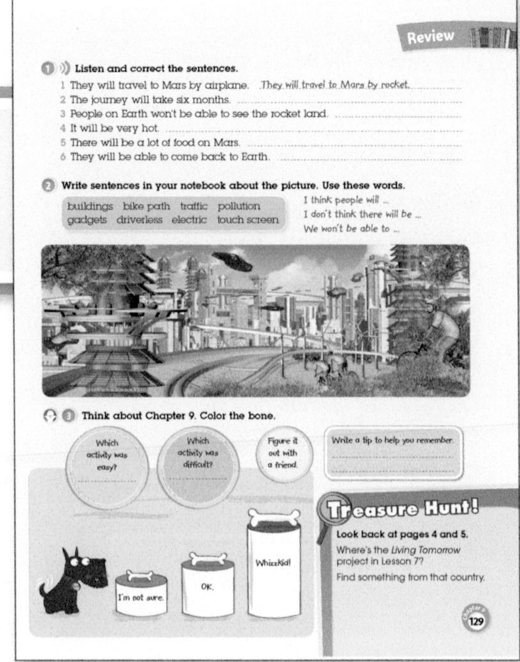
Review

1 Listen and correct the sentences.

1 They will travel to Mars by airplane. *They will travel to Mars by rocket.*
2 The journey will take six months.
3 People on Earth won't be able to see the rocket land.
4 It will be very hot.
5 There will be a lot of food on Mars.
6 They will be able to come back to Earth.

2 Write sentences in your notebook about the picture. Use these words.

buildings bike path traffic pollution gadgets driverless electric touch screen

I think people will ...
I don't think there will be ...
We won't be able to ...

3 Think about Chapter 9. Color the bone.

Treasure Hunt!

Look back at pages 4 and 5.
Where's the *Living Tomorrow* project in Lesson 7?
Find something from that country.

129

Warmer: Unscramble the sentence

Write on the board *In the future, people will live in space.*, scrambling the order of the words. Have the children write the sentence and discuss it.

1 9.7 Listen and correct the sentences.

- Play Track 9.7 and ask *Do you think life will be the same? Why?*
- Play Track 9.7 again. Children correct the sentences.

Audioscript

Thousands of people are interested in going to live on the planet Mars in 2023. Passengers will travel to the planet by rocket. The journey will take about seven months. People on Earth will watch the rocket land on TV. It will be very cold and there won't be any food on the planet. They might not survive. The first travelers will take a lot of food with them. There won't be any buildings on the planet. The people who travel to Mars will build houses and grow plants. More people will travel to the planet after two years. They won't be able to come back to Earth.

Answers

1 They will travel to Mars by rocket. **2** The journey will take seven months. **3** People on Earth will be able to see the rocket land on TV. **4** It will be very cold. **5** There won't be any food on Mars. **6** They won't be able to come back to Earth.

2 Write sentences in your notebook about the picture. Use these words.

- Have the children make sentences orally about the picture. Then they write sentences in their notebook.

Answers

Children's own answers.

3 Think about Chapter 9. Color the bone. 

- Have the children look back at Chapter 9 and color the bone to evaluate their progress (self-evaluation). Discuss ideas for improving your grammar. The children choose and write a tip in their Student Book.

Treasure Hunt!

Ask *In which city and country is the* Living Tomorrow *Project?* (*Brussels, Belgium*). Have the children find something from that country. (*Belgian flag on a box of candies*)

Cooler: Play "Tic Tac Toe"

Play the game using vocabulary from the chapter (see Games Bank p. 19).

Competency Focus

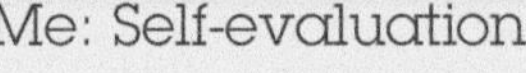
Me: Self-evaluation

The children reflect on the chapter and express their opinions about their own progress.

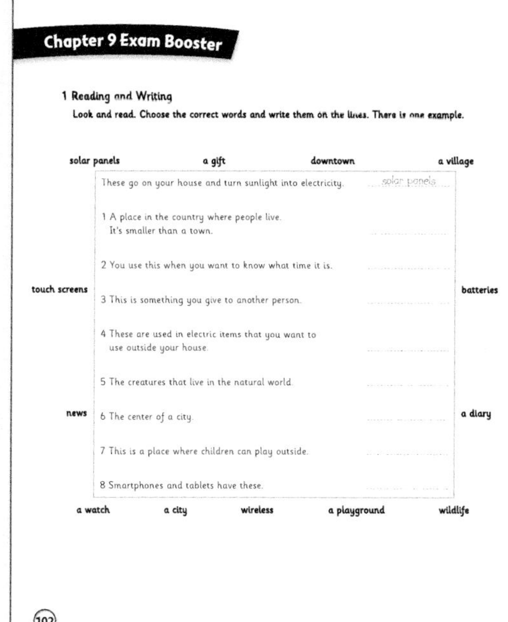
Chapter 9 Exam Booster

1 Reading and Writing
Look and read. Choose the correct words and write them on the lines. There is one example.

solar panels | a gift | downtown | a village | touch screens | batteries | news | a diary | a watch | a city | wireless | a playground | wildlife

These go on your house and turn sunlight into electricity. ... solar panels

1 A place in the country where people live. It's smaller than a town. ...

2 You use this when you want to know what time it is. ...

3 This is something you give to another person. ...

4 These are used in electric items that you want to use outside your house. ...

5 The creatures that live in the natural world. ...

6 The center of a city. ...

7 This is a place where children can play outside. ...

8 Smartphones and tablets have these. ...

102

2 Listening
Where did Sam's friends stay on vacation?
Listen and write a letter in each box. There is one example.

Charlie C
George
Daisy
Anna
Tom
Lucy

A B C D

E F G H

103

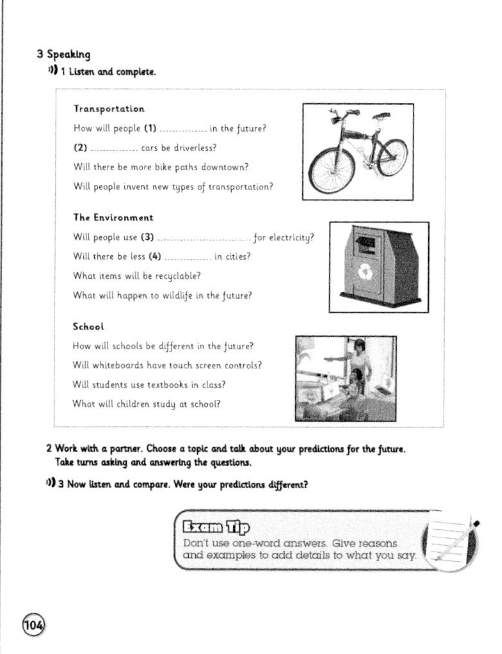
3 Speaking
1 Listen and complete.

Transportation
How will people (1) .... in the future?
(2) .... cars be driverless?
Will there be more bike paths downtown?
Will people invent new types of transportation?

The Environment
Will people use (3) .... for electricity?
Will there be less (4) .... in cities?
What items will be recyclable?
What will happen to wildlife in the future?

School
How will schools be different in the future?
Will whiteboards have touch screen controls?
Will students use textbooks in class?
What will children study at school?

2 Work with a partner. Choose a topic and talk about your predictions for the future. Take turns asking and answering the questions.

3 Now listen and compare. Were your predictions different?

Exam Tip
Don't use one-word answers. Give reasons and examples to add details to what you say.

104

1 Reading and Writing. Look and read. Choose the correct words and write them on the lines.

Children write the words defined by the sentences.

Answers

1 a village **2** a watch **3** a gift **4** batteries **5** wildlife **6** downtown **7** a playground **8** touch screens

2 AB 9.1 Listening. Where did Sam's friends stay on vacation? Listen and write a letter in each box.

Play AB Track 9.1 twice. Children write the letters.

Answers (Audioscript on p. 224)

George b, Daisy f, Anna g, Tom h, Lucy d

3.1 AB 9.2 Speaking. Listen and complete.

Play AB Track 9.2 twice. Children listen and write.

Answers (Audioscript on p. 224)

1 travel **2** Will **3** solar panels **4** pollution **5**

3.2 Speaking. Work with a partner. Choose a topic and talk about your predictions for the future.Take turns asking and answering the questions about the future.

Children work in pairs to ask and answer questions.

Answers

Students' own answers.

3.3 AB 9.3 Speaking.Now listen and compare. Were your predictions different?

Play AB Track 9.3 twice. Children listen and compare.

(Audioscript on p. 224)

Digital Resources

Digital Activity Book • Use the answer key to give feedback on AB Exam Booster activities. You can show the answers all at once or one by one to customize feedback.

Teacher Resource Center • Print out Test Chapter 9 and End-of-year Test to use at the end of this lesson. The Test Generator also allows you to create customized tests.

• For the Cambridge English Young Learners Exams preparation activities, there are speaking prompts available for this chapter.

AB 1.1

N: *What time did Jake arrive at school?*
G: *Hi, Jake. You're late for school today. It's one o'clock.*
B: *Hi, Kate. I'm not late. I went to the old school museum with my history class this morning. We got back at twelve thirty.*
G: *You're lucky. We had a math test at nine thirty this morning. It was really hard.*
N: *One. What does Jake have in his bag?*
G: *Jake, can I have your earphones for a minute? I want to listen to something.*
B: *Yes, of course, Kate. They're in my bag. Just a minute.*
G: *You have a lot in your bag. That's a huge dictionary.*
B: *I know, I know, and I have a lot of pens ... but I always lose them. No earphones! I'm sorry – I left them at home!*
N: *Two. What's Kate doing after school today?*
B: *Do you have basketball today, Kate?*
G: *No, that was yesterday.*
B: *Oh, good. Do you want to come to my house later?*
G: *OK, but I have a dance class until 6 o'clock.*
B: *That's fine. Should I cook a pizza for us?*
G: *No, it's OK, Jake. I can eat at home.*
N: *Three. What does Jake want to buy?*
G: *We could watch a movie on your computer tonight.*
B: *No, we can't. It's broken. I'd like to get a new laptop soon.*
G: *I got one for my birthday. I never watch TV now.*
B: *That's great. Why don't you bring it tonight?*
G: *OK.*

AB 2.1

G: *Dan, I just heard about the cooking competition. Who's it for?*
B: *It's for all the school children in this town.*
B: *Are you going to do it?*
G: *Hmm, I might ... but I'm going on vacation with Mom and Dad on Wednesday.*
B: *Well, it starts on Sunday and the final part of the competition is on Tuesday.*
G: *Is it at our school?*
B: *No, it's going to be at a hotel downtown. It's the big, white hotel close to the Beach – the Dalmeny. That's D-A-L-M-E-N-Y.*
G: *What time does it start?*
B: *You have to be at the hotel at eight thirty because the competition starts at 9 o'clock. If you arrive later than a quarter after nine, then you can't do it.*
G: *OK. What should I cook?*
B: *Hmm ... You have to cook something with a red pepper, an onion, and tomatoes.*
G: *That's easy. I might do a sauce or my specialty pizza. Is there anything else I need to know?*
B: *Yes, you have to pay for the competition, but it's cheap. Normally, it costs about \$50 but it's only \$35 because it's for school children. If you pay before Friday, it's even cheaper – it's \$30.*
G: *Oh – today's Friday! Quick, I have to pay now, and then I can think about what to cook!*

AB 2.2

B: *Hi, Samantha. Have you seen the school newsletter? – It has a list of the school clubs – Japanese, karate, cooking lessons, photography, chess, and creative writing.*
G: *Hi, Ron. I'm reading the list now!*
B: *Cooking looks interesting. It's on Wednesday at 3 p.m. in the school cafeteria.*
G: *Oh, look! The photography club is at the same time, Wednesday at 3. I prefer photography.*
B: *Where's the photography club?*
G: *It's in Room 7.*
B: *How about the creative writing class? You've written great stories! It's on Thursday at lunchtime in Room 11.*
G: *That sounds good. How about you?*
B: *I've done karate and chess before, but I want to try something new.*
G: *How about Japanese club? You can learn to speak a new language!*

AB 3.1

W: *Hi, Anna. Would you like to color this picture?*
G: *Yes. Is that the movie theater?*
W: *That's right. Can you see the man selling tickets?*
G: *Yes, I can.*
W: *The man is wearing a jacket. Can you color it?*
G: *OK, I'll color it blue.*
N: *One.*
G: *I love coloring.*
W: *Good. You can do some more! Look at the posters for the movies. Can you see Island Adventure?*
G: *Yes.*
W: *Can you see the boat? Color it red.*
G: *The one in the ocean?*
W: *No, the one on the beach.*
G: *OK. Done.*
N: *Two.*
W: *Now above the poster for the movie, write "New Movie' on the wall.*
G: *OK ... "New Movie".*
N: *Three.*
W: *Good job! OK. Can you see the children at the back?*
G: *The ones near the door?*
W: *That's right. The smaller boy has a backpack.*
G: *Yes, I'll color it green.*
W: *That's a nice idea.*
N: *Four.*
G: *What's next?*
W: *OK. Can you see the woman in the front?*
G: *Oh, yes, she's on her phone.*
W: *Color the woman's skirt yellow.*
N: *Five.*
W: *OK. This is the last thing. A man is selling food and drinks. Behind him, there's a sign.*
G: *Oh, yes, it says the price – but it doesn't say what it is.*
W: *That's right. Write the word "Drinks".*
G: *"Drinks". OK. I'm finished.*
N: *Now listen again.*

AB 3.2

G: *The girl in Picture A looks happier than the girl in Picture B.*
B: *Look at Picture B. This cake isn't as big as that one.*
G: *Yes, but there are cupcakes in Picture B. They look delicious.*

AB 3.3

G: *The girl in Picture A looks happier than the girl in Picture B.*
B: *Look at Picture B. This cake isn't as big as that one.*
G: *Yes, but there are cupcakes in Picture B. They look delicious.*
B: *The cakes are different, too. This cake says "10" and that cake says "11."*
G: *That's right. The girl in Picture A is younger than the girl in Picture B.*
B: *The girls look different, too. This girl has long, straight hair and that girl has short, curly hair.*
G: *Look, this girl is wearing pajamas with flowers. That girl is wearing pajamas with stars.*
B: *Both girls have movie posters in their rooms. The poster in Picture A says "The Monster on Fourth Street," but the poster in Picture B says "The Monster on Tenth Street."*
G: *The poster in this picture is scarier than the poster in that picture.*
B: *That's right! The monster in this poster is friendlier than that one.*

AB 4.1

N: *What did each person give Jack for his skiing vacation?*
G: *Do you have everything you need for your skiing vacation, Jack?*
B: *Not yet, but friends and family have given me a lot of things. I was staying with my cousin Alex*

last weekend and he gave me some gloves. He went skiing last year.

G: What about snow boots? They're expensive, but they're really important.

B: Yes, I know ... My best friend helped me. His boots are too small for him now, so I have them. They're really comfortable.

G: I know someone with a good ski jacket, but it's pink!

B: Oh, don't worry. When I was talking about a jacket at school yesterday, James offered me his. It's black and kind of old, but that's OK.

G: Fantastic. What about sunglasses?

B: Hmm, I don't have them yet. Mom and I looked for some yesterday in town but we couldn't find any.

G: Have you packed your bag yet?

B: No. I'm using my brother's. He offered it to me before he went on his school trip to New York. He came back a week ago but it's still full of his dirty clothes and weird hats.

G: Ugh, horrible. You should give him his clothes back, but you might need a good hat.

B: I know. Dad found one on a website that was selling ski hats. It was expensive, but I'm going to wear it all winter.

G: I think you have everything! Don't forget to take a lot of nice pictures.

B: Of course! My aunt loves photography and is giving me her camera for the week.

G: That's great.

AB 5.1

G: Oh, no! I'm feeling really nervous! I don't know anyone at this party.

B: Look, don't worry. I'm going to tell you who everyone is. They're all really nice and you're going to have a good time. The funniest person is Oliver. There he is, next to the window. He's wearing a weird hat. It's made of wool and he's making a funny face.

G: Yes, that's really funny.

G: Who's the girl next to Oliver?

B: There are two girls next to him. They're from our school. Which one do you mean?

G: The one with the big plastic earrings. I think they're fish. I love them.

B: Oh, that's Lily. She's a really good dancer.

G: Oh, look, someone started dancing.

B: Yes, that's Charlie. He loves showing everyone how he can dance. He won a prize in a competition for his breakdancing. He's good, but he isn't as good as Dan.

B: Can you see Dan in the corner?

G: Is he sitting down? He doesn't look happy.

B: No, he's getting his coat. That's strange. I think he's going home.

G: The only person I know who's coming is Alice. I talked to her today, but I can't see her.

B: There she is, at the table. She's mixing some fruit into the apple juice. Mm, that looks good.

G: Where's Grace? It's her birthday and I'd like to give her my present.

B: There she is. She's talking to the DJ. I think he's choosing some music. Come on – let's dance!

AB 5.2

G: Is this a photo from your yard sale?

B: Yes, Mom and Dad have one every year. They sell everything they don't want, and they invite neighbors to sell their things, too. That's my mom coming out of the house with a jug of water.

G: Who is the man wearing shorts? He's selling a toy giraffe made of wool.

B: That's our neighbor, Robert.

G: Who is the woman he's talking to?

B: Miss Jones. He's selling her the giraffe and Miss Jones is giving him two dollars.

G: Is that Ben? He's wearing our school sweatshirt.

B: The boy selling clothes? Yes, he lives on my street. He always comes to our yard sales.

B: That's Mr. and Mrs. Green. They're sitting there at the back, selling cups and plates. He is wearing a cap and she is wearing a striped dress.

G: Look, they have a customer. Someone is looking at the box made of wood while she's talking on the phone.

B: That's Karen. She's always talking on her phone!

G: Look at the man with curly hair and a beard. He's holding a basket.

B: That's my dad. The basket is used for toys.

G: Cool! Did you have fun at the yard sale?

B: Yes! It was great!

AB 6.1

G: Hi, Andy. Are you going on the school trip this afternoon?

B: To the Museum of the Ocean? Yes. I love learning about ships. What about you? Are you going?

G: Yes, I am, but I can't find the paper the teacher gave us with all the information.

B: I'll help you. What do you want to know?

G: How much does it cost?

B: Nothing! School children don't have to pay for it.

G: So I don't need any money?

B: Well, you need to bring $2 for the bus.

G: Oh—is it far?

B: Yes, it's next to the train station so we can't walk there.

G: Is there much to see?

B: Yes, there's a pirate ship and a lot of old photos. We can try on life jackets, too.

G: Cool. Do I need to take anything with me?

B: Yes, you need a notebook and a pencil.

G: Oh, yes. We need to take notes for our school project. What do we need to find out about?

B: The Morning Star.

G: Is that the ship that hit the rock and sank?

B: Yes. There are a lot of good stories about how the captain and crew rescued the people.

G: OK. What time do we get back?

B: We arrive at 5 o'clock but there's a school soccer game and the parking lot will be full. The bus is going to park on Morley Street – that's M.O.R.L.E.Y Street.

G: Thanks for that, Andy. I can't wait!

AB 6.2

N: These pictures tell a story. It's called "The Flood." Look at the pictures and listen to the example.

W: This is Mom, Dad, Amy, and Brandon. The family was relaxing at home when it started to rain. The kids were playing video games while the parents were reading the newspaper.

AB 6.3

W: This is Mom, Dad, Amy, and Brandon. The family was relaxing at home when it started to rain. The kids were playing video games while the parents were reading the newspaper. The weather got worse and worse. The wind was blowing, and the rain was coming down hard. Suddenly, water started coming in the house. Mom, Dad, Amy, and Brandon got ready to leave their house. They had to go outside to wave as the rescue boat came toward the house to pick them up. Amy held the cat while they were waiting. Then they climbed into the rescue boat. When they climbed in, the rescuers put blankets on them. And then, when they were climbing into the rescue boat, their house floated away! Finally, they arrived at the shelter; a kind lady gave them a cup of hot chocolate. They were safe!

AB 7.1

N: What's George going to make?

W: Hi, George. That smells good.

B: Thanks, Mom. It's chocolate!

W: Are you making a cake?

B: No, I made hot chocolate, but I'm going to bake some cookies later.

N: One. What does George want from the store?

W: I'm going shopping. Do you want anything?

B: Let me see. I have flour, but I need eggs.

W: What about sugar?

B: Oh, yes, please. There isn't much in this bag.

W: OK.

N: Two. What time is Lily going to arrive?

W: Lily is going to love these cookies!

B: Is she coming home soon? It's five o'clock.

W: Well, she usually finishes school at three thirty, but she had a school trip today and isn't going to be home until six thirty.

B: Oh, no! I want to eat the cookies now!

N: Three. Where should George put the clean pans?

W: Can you help me clean the kitchen before Lily arrives?

B: *OK. The pans on the table are dirty.*
W: *You need to wash them in the sink and then put them back in the cupboard.*
B: *OK.*

AB 8.1

M: *Let's see. What do you think it's a picture of?*
B: *I think it's a picture of students in a language class. I think they're all having fun.*
M: *Hmm, I'm not sure. Can you see the two girls on the right? They're arguing because they want the same dictionary. Color the dictionary.*
B: *OK. I'll make it blue.*
N: *One.*
B: *Can I do something else now?*
M: *Yes, of course. Can you see the whiteboard on the wall at the back?*
B: *Yes.*
M: *Color the picture on the left.*
B: *The train? OK. I'll make it green.*
M: *Yes, that would be great.*
N: *Two.*
B: *What should I do now?*
M: *Look at the boy on the left.*
B: *Which one? There are two.*
M: *Well, one of the boys has a pen in his hand and there's some paper in front of him. Write the word "car" on the paper.*
B: *"Car"? OK. I'll write that now.*
N: *Three.*
B: *I'd like to color something again.*
M: *OK. There is a girl near the whiteboard.*
B: *The one drawing a sailboat?*
M: *Yes, color her shirt yellow.*
B: *OK. Done.*
N: *Four.*
B: *Now what should I do?*
M: *Write the word "travel" on the whiteboard.*
B: *OK. I'll write "travel" under the drawing of the train.*
M: *Great!*
N: *Five.*
M: *OK, we're almost finished. Can you see the different bags?*
B: *Yes, I like the one with the B on it. That's cool.*
M: *Yes, look at the bag next to it. Can you color it orange?*
B: *Yes, I can. There you go. It's finished!*

AB 8.2

W: *Would you like to color this picture?*
G: *Is this the new afterschool club?*
W: *That's right. Do you see the big backpack?*
G: *Yes. It's next to the table where the boys are doing their homework.*
W: *Color the backpack blue.*
G: *OK. Done.*
N: *One.*
G: *What else should I color?*
W: *You can color the girl's sweater.*
G: *Which girl?*
W: *The girl playing video games.*
G: *I see her. She's lying on the rug looking at the TV. I'll color her sweater green.*
N: *Two.*
W: *Now color the book that the boy is holding.*
G: *Which boy?*
W: *The boy standing in front of the bookcase.*
G: *OK. I'll color the book yellow.*
N: *Three.*
W: *Would you like to write now?*
G: *Sure! I'll get my pencil.*
W: *Do you see the large sign on the wall?*
G: *Yes. It's near the door.*
W: *Write "teen room" on the sign.*
G: *OK, "teen room." Done.*
N: *Four.*
W: *Now you can choose what you'd like to color. You can color either the board game or the poster.*
G: *OK then … I want to color the umbrella on the poster. I'll color it red.*
W: *Good idea!*
N: *Five.*
W: *Do you see the two boys doing their homework at the table?*
G: *Yes. There is a sign on the table.*
W: *Write "quiet" on the sign.*
G: *Quiet?*
W: *Yes, that's right.*
G: *OK. I'm finished!*

AB 9.1

N: *Where did Sam's friends stay on vacation?*
W: *How was your first day back at school, Sam? Did everyone have a good vacation?*
B: *Yes, Charlie said that he swam every day. He was staying with his cousins. They live close to a big lake. He said the water was really clean.*
W: *What about Anna? Did she go camping this year?*
B: *No, she didn't. Her dad broke his leg just before the summer vacation. Her family had a relaxing vacation in a hotel. Her dad couldn't do anything, but Anna and her sister enjoyed swimming in the pool.*
W: *And Lucy? She loves swimming, too.*
B: *Yes, she usually goes to the beach. But this year her mom and dad took her to London. She said she loved staying downtown because there were a lot of interesting stores. She'll show us the pictures when she comes.*
W: *Oh, great. What about George?*
B: *Oh, George showed us a lot of pictures of his vacation. He doesn't like towns or cities so he went to stay with his grandpa. He has a house in the mountains. They went mountain biking every day.*
B: *Daisy went mountain biking, too, but she and her family were camping.*
W: *Daisy? Camping? She won't want to do that again.*
B: *Hmm, I don't know. She said that it was very cold at night but she'll take warmer clothes next time.*
W: *Oh, good. I thought Tom looked good when I saw him. Did he go somewhere hot?*
B: *Not this year. His uncle has a boat on a river. They spent two weeks on it, but it rained every day.*

AB 9.2

M: *Let's talk about transportation in the future. How will people travel in the future?*
G: *I think most people will ride bikes. Sometimes, we'll use cars.*
M: *Will cars be driverless?*
G: *No, they won't. People will still need to control cars.*
M: *Now let's talk about the environment. Will people use solar panels for electricity?*
G: *I think people will use solar panels and wind turbines.*
M: *Will there be less pollution in cities?*
G: *Yes, there will!*

AB 9.3

N: *Now listen again.*
M: *Let's talk about transportation in the future. How will people travel in the future?*
G: *I think most people will ride bikes. Sometimes, we'll use cars.*
M: *Will cars be driverless?*
G: *No, they won't. People will still need to control cars.*
M: *Now let's talk about the environment. Will people use solar panels for electricity?*
G: *I think people will use solar panels and wind turbines.*
M: *Will there be less pollution in cities?*
G: *Yes, there will!*
M: *Now let's talk about schools. How will schools be different in the future?*
G: *We'll use more technology in class. We'll learn in school and online!*
M: *Will whiteboards have touch screen controls?*
G: *Yes, they will. The teacher will use the touch screen controls to show us pictures and videos.*
M: *Will students use textbooks in class?*
G: *No, they won't. They'll use computers to save paper.*
M: *What will children study at schools?*
G: *They'll study the same things we do now — math, science, history, and languages. They'll also learn about technology.*